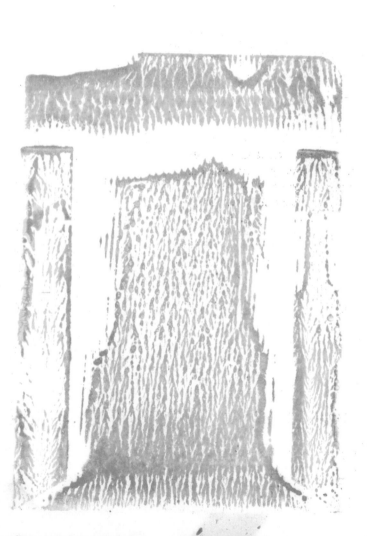

SHEPHERD'S GLOSSARY OF
GRAPHIC SIGNS AND SYMBOLS

Shepherd's Glossary of GRAPHIC SIGNS and SYMBOLS

COMPILED AND CLASSIFIED
FOR READY REFERENCE BY

Walter Shepherd

DOVER PUBLICATIONS, INC., NEW YORK

First published in 1971
© Walter Shepherd, 1971

Made in Great Britain
at the
Aldine Press · Letchworth · Herts
for
DOVER PUBLICATIONS, INC.,
NEW YORK

Library of Congress Catalog Card Number: 74-153895
International Standard Book Number: 0-486-20700-5

PREFACE

WHILE this is probably not the first attempt which has been made at a formal classification of the written marks by which mankind records ideas, it is believed to be the first extensive treatment of the subject to be published. It should, therefore, be no matter for surprise, still less for disappointment, if it fails to attain to the completeness and simplicity that are found in long-established works of reference. The work of an originator in any subject is not expected to be perfect. The results of the present essay will, it is hoped, be of some service, but they are issued with the expectation that future experience will improve their accuracy, polish their workmanship and increase their utility.

It should be clearly stated that the Key and the Tables contained in this *Glossary* require to be used strictly according to the rules laid down, and that this demands a small amount of patience and application until familiarity with the system has been acquired. How small this amount is the reader can best discover for himself by hunting up such simple signs as $\triangle$, and the block capital letters. He may start to do this straight away at the KEY to the Tables, on page 48.

It is intended that the *Glossary* should have uses in a number of different directions. Its prime object is to assist the self-educator who indulges in much technical reading, but all who consult obscure works, inscriptions, manuscripts, maps and charts will be liable to come across strange signs, or the letters of strange alphabets, to which some such work as this *Glossary* could alone afford a clue. It might, however, be objected that a student should at least know what subject he is reading, and that a simple list of the signs employed in that subject would

v

be much more serviceable to him than a miscellaneous classification of the signs employed in many subjects. Well, he has
such lists in his textbooks, and here we have added the convenience of separate indexes to the chief signs in seventeen
common subjects.

Further, it is hoped that the results of this classification will
interest those studying signs and symbols as subjects in themselves, as showing at a glance the multifarious meanings
attached to the same sign by different peoples or in different
circumstances. Those requiring to invent new signs for special
purposes will find a ready means of avoiding forms with
established meanings. The *Index of Signs with Names* should
also prove useful on occasion. Such words as ankh, büchse, del,
enneagram, hamza, pomega, schwa, trigram, triseme, *etc.*, are
not given in ordinary dictionaries, and it is generally difficult to
find illustrated references to such sets as the Signs of the
Soleras, tramps' 'smogger', national variants of the punctuation marks, and so on.

All things considered, it is felt that it is time something in
the nature of the present classification were in existence in
our libraries, and that the need will increase as internation-
alism in all its phases becomes a normal feature of civilization.
The author is very conscious of the imperfections of his scheme,
and if more able classifiers now produce better systems, he will
at least feel satisfied to have set the ball rolling.

The researches entailed in the compilation of this *Glossary*
were begun in 1948, and pursued intermittently through
twenty-two years. As opportunity arose, suggestions and
information were gathered from many people whose names
were not always noted at the time and cannot now be recalled.
For this lapse the Author craves pardon, and wishes here to
make a general expression of gratitude to all who have in any
way assisted him. He is happy to be able to name the following,

from whom he received correspondence: Mr C. R. Cosens, Mr Henry Emberson (for the Signs of the Soleras), the Rev. Frank Jennings (the 'tramps' parson' and an authority on 'smogger'), the late Professor Daniel Jones, Professor Randolph Quirk, the late Mr F. W. Thomas, and Miss M. J. Trubshawe. The Author would also like to express his appreciation of the patience and practical help extended to him by the long-suffering Publisher, and particularly of the continued encouragement he received from the late Mr E. F. Bozman and from Mr Martin Dent. Finally, the Author wishes it to be understood that he alone must be held responsible for any errors arising from his use of the information supplied, which had sometimes to be condensed or reformulated.

W. S.

1971

CONTENTS

CONTENTS

EXPLANATION

THE diversity of forms found in the graphic signs used by mankind makes a comprehensive classification difficult and complex. The multifarious origins of the signs themselves forbid an organic classification altogether, and the utmost that can be done is to devise a scheme based on an arbitrary selection of easily distinguishable forms, and to provide a set of rules for its use.

Several alternative selections have been tried, and that finally adopted is developed from the cardinal principle that any single mark able to be written on a plane surface must fall into one of three categories, according to the number of dimensions it occupies. These categories embrace marks occupying two dimensions, one dimension and (by geometric licence) no dimension, respectively, and are designated by the common terms, *Curve*, *Straight Line* and *Dot*. For reasons of convenience these basic forms are treated invariably in that order throughout the *Glossary*.

The method of treatment is to proceed from this simple classification of unit forms by a graded system of elaboration, until a sign of any complexity is built up and identified—or at least until it can be readily picked out from a display of closely similar signs. The treatment of *Curves* may be taken as an example of the general system.

All curves are first divided into two groups—*Closed Curves*, in which the extremities are joined so as to enclose a space, and *Open Curves*, in which the ends are separated. *Closed Curves* may be 're-entrant', as is a circle, and there are no extremities to such curves, but they may also have definite ends, as in a loop, $\wp$, where two of the limbs meet in a point and thus make

1

an angle. In an 'almond-shaped' figure, $\Longleftrightarrow$, there are two angles, and so on, but *so long as all the bounding lines of the figure are curved* it ranks as a closed curved figure. Such closures are always picked out first, no matter what other curves or straight lines may be present. Straight lines are not, in fact, to be considered at all until all the curves have been dealt with.

There is, however, a small degree of latitude allowed here, for the reader is not expected to examine such a figure as $\bigcirc$ with a microscope, to see if the extremities of the limbs are actually straight. They are either clearly straight, as in $\bigtimes\bigtimes$, or the natural assumption is that they are curved—and this must be allowed. By the same token, the loop φ is assumed to *be* a loop unless it is very distinctly intended to be a straight line *plus* a curve, so: P. Again, $\varnothing$ is assumed to be a loop because the limbs cross each other, though on a small scale the enclosure may appear circular owing to defects in writing or printing.

An *Open Curve* always has two extremities, though these may be joined by a straight line or attached to other straight lines or curves. Thus, $\bigtriangleup$ consists of a semicircle, $\frown$, and a straight line, ___ , and its *curve* clearly belongs to the group of *Open Curves.* The fact that the figure itself is closed is irrelevant at the first stage of the classification. It is referred to later as a 'blocked' curve, that is, one which has its extremities joined by a straight line (or lines) so as to shut off a space.

Since it is necessary when dealing with the curved parts of a sign to take care to consider the curved parts only, it will often be found useful to abstract these and draw them roughly with a pencil. Thus, the curve in $\bigcirc\!\!\!|$, when picked out, is clearly a circle, and the method safeguards against treating the sign as two semicircles. *The rule is always to abstract the first possible figure mentioned in the Key, irrespective of any other lines.*

2

When a curve has been abstracted from a sign, its parts must be considered in strict order according to the Key. Thus, ♉ looks like a complex curve, but the Key requires that any *Closed Curves* are to be taken first, and this separates the figure into a loop, ◊ , and two arcs, ⌒ and ⌒. Similarly, 8 becomes two loops, while ⊙ is separated into two circles (the circles taking precedence over the almond-shape in the centre) and is described as 'two circles with other figures'. The reader need not anticipate difficulty in deciding what is meant by a 'loop' or an 'almond-shape'. Not only are all the connotations used the most obvious ones, but all the terms employed are precisely defined in the *Definitions* on page 13.

It should be further pointed out here that *very nearly* closed curves are treated as if they were completely closed. The question sometimes arises in cursive scripts as to whether or not a nearly closed circle or ellipse is intended to represent these figures, as in the capital letter *O*. This is treated as an ellipse, for the nearest *open* curve to it recognized in the Tables is the gibbous figure *∪*, and it is quite plainly remote from this. Such questions do not arise with technical signs and symbols, nor with the majority of alphabetical signs, and it is seldom that the reader will be troubled with them.

In the case of *Open Curves*, each curve must always be taken as running without a break from one end of the continuously curved line to the other, and must be considered as a whole. Thus, ∿ (or S) is not two semicircles but a single 'wave', and this is not altered by the coincidence of, say, a straight line *S*. Similarly, ϵ is not a semicircle blocked by a straight line, with an arc below, but the gibbous figure C *plus* the straight line —, the said gibbous figure being by no means blocked thereby. No open curve, however, can contain an angle, so that a figure like ⌒⌣ consists of two *Open Curves—* a semicircle and an arc.

3

In describing such details here we are anticipating difficulties which may seldom arise. Most of the problems of this
kind which may have already occurred to the reader will be
found to solve themselves. To take an example from the
rectilinear signs, it might appear that some ruling should be
given as to whether the sign $+$ should be taken as two inter-
secting straight lines or four lines meeting in a point. But the
question never arises, because the four right-angles have
priority consideration in the Key and suffice to determine the
sign. The order in which the various characteristics are to be
taken will be automatically observed if the Key is duly
followed, though the curious will find the correct sequence
listed separately on page 37, under *Orders of Precedence.*

A word of warning regarding triangles, squares and rectangles might not, however, be out of place here. For example,
though the triangles in the figure ⊠ take precedence over the
enclosing square, the enumeration of four triangles involves
counting some of the same lines twice. The answer to the
question whether this is allowed is—yes. But lines must not
be counted needlessly and the figure ⊞ consists of four
squares—not five (though the perimeter of the figure actually
forms a fifth square).

A general rule should clearly be given, and it is that when a
group of closed rectilinear figures itself makes a closed figure,
the group figure is not considered. Thus, ⊡ consists of two
squares, ⟁ of four triangles, and △ of one triangle (the small
one) *plus* a trapezium. In extreme cases, however, it is necessary
to allow common sense to override the rule, for a sign like ▲
would be classified as a triangle containing other closed figures.
It must be assumed that the difficulty of treating it otherwise
is sufficiently evident.

A further warning regarding figures containing curves may
not be superfluous. Since the very first thing to do is to decide

4

whether or not a sign contains a curve, it is not sufficient to
look for large and distinct curves only. An apparently insignificant curve, occupying but a very small part of the sign, is
sufficient to place it in the category of signs containing curves.
Thus, although the reader knows that T is a straight-line sign,
he must expect to find *t* among the signs containing curves.
However, provision is made in the *Principles of Approximation*
set forth on page 30 for ignoring certain obviously trivial
features, especially some of those occurring in cursive writing.

We may illustrate the method of procedure by showing how
a familiar sign, such as the letter B, should be traced in the
Key. We begin at paragraph 1 on page 48, where the three
main classes of signs are listed, and since the letter B contains
curves it plainly belongs to the first of these—the *Signs with
curves*. The instruction opposite to this is (in full) 'turn to
paragraph 2', and in paragraph 2 we find a list of the three
chief groups of the signs containing curves. The letter B contains a straight line as well as curves, so that it belongs to the
second group, where we are referred to paragraph 6. Paragraph
6 gives us further points for consideration, and if we follow
on in this way, taking the instructions quite literally and as
precisely as possible, and never attempting to jump ahead, we
shall eventually be referred to the page number where the letter
B is illustrated and defined.

There is never any ambiguity in the *meaning* of the instructions, for the terms used refer simply to the figures to be looked
for. They must be either present or not, and that is all the
reader has to decide. By the law of excluded middle the answer
must always be 'yes' or 'no'. He may have difficulty, however,
if he try to skip any link in the chain, for success depends upon
selecting or eliminating the figures *in the right order*.

Or we may consider a more complex sign, like $\mathcal{E}$, which also
belongs clearly to the curved signs, and since it consists solely

of curves it is to be sought *via* paragraph 5. Here, we ask ourselves if the sign contains *any* closed curves, and since it does display a single small loop we turn at once to paragraph 12. Here, the presence of the angle in the loop refers us to paragraph 31, whence—the sign containing only one loop—we pass straight on to paragraph 62. Here we are required to sort out the remaining parts of the sign, namely the three S-shapes and the arc [∫ ≈ ‿]. Since the arc is accompanied by complex curves we now turn to paragraph 125, where the S-shapes are specified opposite a reference to Table 21, page 96. If we now turn to this page we shall find our sign and its definition.

. Again, the sign ·—··, which consists of a straight line and dots, will be found by turning successively to the paragraphs numbered, 3, 9, 23 and 56, where we are finally referred to Table 409, which gives the sign and its definition. And yet again, the sign 𝟫 may be traced through paragraphs 2, 7, 17, 42, 89 and Table 255. .

Some signs, and particularly punctuation marks, depend for their meaning partly upon their position with regard to the level of the writing, which is shown in the Tables by the level of the number of the sign. A 'dagger' indicates where the level is significant. Where the thickness of a line is important the words 'Thick' or 'Thin' are given in brackets.

Although the *Glossary* may be used without further instructions for tracing diagrammatic signs, it has been found necessary to broaden the meanings of such terms as *Circle, Right angle* and *Dot*, to include the less stable forms used in alphabetical signs, and particularly in cursive letters. These special meanings are given in the *Definitions* (page 13), and the system of extension on which they are based is explained in the *Principles of Approximation* to which we have already referred.

While we have set precise limits to the degree of approximation allowed, the difficulty of making accurate measurements

on the very small scales involved compels us to recommend the
reader to employ his own judgment rather than the more exact
methods of estimation used (to the best of our ability) in compiling the *Glossary*. This expedient happily carries very little
risk of error, and none at all of failure after two attempts.
Necessity herself provides the answer to criticism of this
admission of latitude, and the following two observations may
be further offered in its defence.

The first is that since no two things can possibly be identical,
all classification into groups involves a glossing over of minor
differences.* The work of science, in classification, is largely
to decide which differences are to be called 'minor' in this sense.
The scientific ideal is a system of classification in which the
glossed-over differences are completely negligible, but it is
important (not only philosophically) to recognize that they
must always be there. In our present classification of signs and
symbols we have openly admitted and provided for this
inherent weakness of all classifications. And we have deliber-
ately catered for that which science struggles to eliminate and
often simply ignores—the 'human element'.

Science does rightly in ignoring irrational elements, for its
classification must conform to a logical system—a theory of
organization. But behind our classification of signs there is no
such theory, and we are therefore not merely at liberty, but
are compelled, to take cognizance of every influence likely to
affect the practicability of our scheme. We cannot attach any
notion of *importance* to factors selected purely arbitrarily,
and must therefore widen our field to embrace as great a variety
of factors as possible under the minimum number of heads,
and so reduce the element of randomness.

The second observation is that, in point of fact, a principle

* Every *glossary* which attempts a classification is thus, by an ety-
mological coincidence—for the words are not cognate—also a 'glossary'.

of approximation actively governs the classifications employed in many sciences, and perhaps particularly in meteorology, geology, botany and psychology (in so far as psychology is a science). The definitions of cloud-forms in current use in meteorology, for instance, cover an infinitude of visible variations, as do those of faults and folds in geology, while in botany it has sometimes been found necessary to gloss over even statistical data.

The innumerable leaf-shapes described by botanists as 'oval' commonly include the presence of a sharp point at one end, leaves officially called 'oblong' are generally innocent of either straight lines or right angles, and so on. It is not that these words have special meanings in botany, but that they have no precise meanings in botany at all. This *Glossary* makes use of similar generalities but sets them within defined limits so that as little as possible is left to the judgment of the reader. With regard to statistical information we are able to be very much more precise than the botanist, for whereas it is seldom difficult to number the distinct parts of a sign, the number of leaflets or petals characteristic of a species of plant is liable to vary enormously.*

The widening of the definitions by the *Principles of Approximation* has one particular drawback. It occasions a small number of ambiguous cases which are not resolvable even by careful analysis and detailed application of the *Orders of Precedence*, and can be dealt with only by the facile device of listing them under all the possible categories. Obviously, if such a practice were extensively indulged in the whole system

---

* Thus we read in Edward Step's *Trees and Flowers of the Countryside* that the leaves of the cat's valerian 'are divided into four to ten pairs of lance-shaped leaflets', and that the lesser celandine 'varies a good deal in its make-up, its sepals being sometimes three, sometimes five, and its petals anything between seven and twelve. At times, it does without stamens or even without petals'. None of our graphic signs is anything like as variable as this.

8

of classification would be reduced to absurdity, but it is, perhaps, a point in favour of the present system that the ambiguous cases turn out to be remarkably rare. Their effect on the size of the volume is quite negligible, for out of a total of some 6,000 signs they number perhaps half a dozen.

If it is still considered a serious defect that the use of this *Glossary* should call for common sense and elementary knowledge on the part of the consultant, we can only point to the fact that a completely foolproof scheme, requiring no co-operation on the part of the reader (beyond the ability to read —that at least must be granted!), might supply his shelves with a monument of exasperating ingenuity but it would hardly provide him with the useful reference book he has been led to expect. Indeed, we fear we may have already been guilty of excessive particularity, yet this is surely better than over-simplification. Even in the present scheme as many as twenty signs appear in some of the Tables (or their sub-sections), though most contain about ten and the shortest only one.

So multitudinous and multifarious are the signs and symbols that have been used conventionally by man that a glossary of this size cannot be expected to contain more than a selection of signs from a selection of subjects. We have included as many as possible from subjects of wide interest or use, and especially those which have been settled by international agreement. There are also a number of signs with curious historical associations and a liberal complement of alphabetical signs, though many common scripts have only been sampled. Of Japanese, only the basic forms used in one of the modern syllabaries are given, and there are no complete alphabets of Eastern scripts except Hebrew and Arabic. The shorthands are represented by simple alphabetical signs from two of the most popular systems.

We have excluded from the Tables such signs as are purely

9

pictorial, it being assumed that a marked degree of convention-alization is necessary before a picture becomes a graphic sign. On the other hand, we include the special uses of letters for signs when they are not simply the initial letters of the words they stand for. Thus, the special uses of e and i in mathematics are not parallel with the use of $L.$ (for Linnaeus) in botany, but are strictly parallel with π, $+$ and $\triangle$, the letters having been chosen principally to avoid multiplication of new forms. The $L.$ in botany is the letter L, and we do not list it otherwise, but the e in mathematics is *not* the letter e, but another sign of the same shape (and name), and therefore we list both meanings of its form.* A sign is not, however, precluded from the Tables because it *contains* an initial letter. Thus, John Dalton's sign for lead, Ⓛ, is given because it is not complete without its circle, which is certainly not part of the letter L. An exception is made of the modern conventions used in the physical sciences, for if we include the use of Q for electric charge it would be a disservice to omit (for example) M for mutual inductance. Further, the same letters may be used with different meanings in different subjects, and there is sometimes a distinction to be made between capital and small letters; a significance may also be attached to special styles of type. Thus, M also stands for absolute magnitude, molecular weight and moment of resistance, **M** for intensity of magnetization, m for molar concentration and m. for metre. Of these, only the last is a simple initial covering the whole meaning.

The use of A, B, C, etc., for the names of (say) vitamins is yet again in different case. We regard these as signifying no more than alphabetical order. In the case of vitamins the order is presumably that of their discovery and is irrelevant to their chemical constitution. We do not therefore list these

---

* In origin, the letter e in mathematics is the initial of Euler, but this is not of significance in the *use* of the letter, as in the case with $L.$ for Linnaeus.

letters as the names of chemical substances. We also ignore purely local code usages of letters, such as the Metropolitan Police use of letters to indicate administrative divisions, and the use of letters on motor-vehicle number-plates. But we do list x as standing for an unknown quantity, for this use of it is general. It is true that the use of other letters for quantities in algebra is similar, but except where definite meanings are conventionally assigned to them we do not list them.

In technology the more complex symbols used are often built up of simple signs, just as words are built up of letters— or rather, as sentences are built up of words. Thus, in electricity the symbol for one type of thermionic valve is ⬡ , which is a combination of ⊥ for anode, ----- for grid and ∩ for hot-wire cathode. Again in meteorology ✲̇ , meaning sleet, is a combination of • for rain and ✕ for snow. In this glossary the component signs are always given separately, but we also include the simpler of the combinations in common use, especially when these are not readily analysable into their components.

Included among the symbols are the various conventions of 'shading' used in plans and diagrams in engineering, geology, soil-mechanics, heraldry, etc., for it is held that a type of shading universally adopted to indicate, say, 'brass' is exactly equivalent to the repeated use of any other symbol for brass. The identification of such shading will be found to present no difficulties whatever, the various types used falling among the simplest groups of classified items. The abbreviated description, Rep., signifies *indefinitely repeated or continued*, and covers all types of shading as well as the various symbolic lines of indeterminate length used for boundaries and roads in maps, charts, etc.

The signs classified cover a large number of subjects, and these are indicated in brackets before each definition according to the *Abbreviations* given on page 46. A few subjects overlap, and we may illustrate the method of dealing with this by its most important example—mathematics. The references to *Alg.*, *Cal.*, *Geom.*, *Trig.*, etc., apply to signs confined to these branches, while the broad reference, *Math.*, applies to signs which, like $+$ and $-$, are used indiscriminately in more than one branch of the subject. However, so complex are the ramifications and overlappings in this subject that the reader is warned not to take the limited meanings too strictly, but to allow for the possibility of extensions and exceptions.

By a similar rule the name of a language is given where a sign in punctuation or an accent is peculiar to it, but marks of punctuation or accents commonly used for the same purpose in more than one language are not so distinguished.

Finally, it is hoped that the methods adopted for circumventing incidental difficulties will be found to conform with the dictates of common sense, and not to rest upon reasons which seem obscure or purely academic. On this matter the reader himself must be the judge.

DEFINITIONS

The following definitions are those adopted in the
compilation of the Glossary. Most of the terms
employed are familiar words in common use, and
carry their common connotations (with small modi-
.fications of no importance to the ordinary inquirer).
Even apparently precise terms like 'circle' are
given common-sense interpretations rather than
strict geometrical ones. The reader will therefore
need to consult these definitions only in cases of
special difficulty.

Almond. An almond-shaped figure is the closed curve produced
by the double intersection of two arcs whose centres of curvature lie on opposite sides of the centre of the figure. The
typical example is ⌒⌄, of which an extreme form might be ◯.
Such figures always contain two curved angles.

Angle. The figure produced by the junction of any two lines
whose directions differ. Thus, ∠, ∨, ∨ and ∨ are angles,
but there is no angle in the figure ⌐, for the direction of the
curved line does not differ from that of the straight line at the
point where they join. No angle of 180° or more is considered
as an angle, so that the figure ＼＿ consists of one angle only,
while ♡ contains the *exterior* angle ⌒ and the *interior* angle ∨.
It should be noted that where one line meets another except at
its extremity it makes *two* angles, thus: ⊥ . Similarly, the
figure ⊔ contains three angles, and ⊥⊥ four. Lines which do
not actually meet do not form an angle. Thus, | ＿ is not an
angle but two free lines (unless there is no doubt they are

intended to meet). Again, two lines which *apparently* meet in the centre of a large dot do not constitute an angle, for in such a case they do not *in fact* meet. Thus, ⟨ consists of a dot and two lines, whereas ⟨ consists of a dot plus an angle. *See also* **Arm.**

ACUTE. Any angle less than a right angle.

CURVED. An angle in which either or both of the arms are curved.

EQUAL. Angles are said to be equal if they contain the same number of degrees, i.e. if their arms are equally inclined to one another. The length of the arms is immaterial. The following pairs of angles are equal: ⋀, ⋁ and ⟩, ⟋ and ⋀.

EXTERIOR. An angle forming part of a closed figure, but outside the enclosed area. Example: ⌐⋀ (the exterior angle being indicated by the dot).

INTERIOR. An angle forming part of a closed figure, but inside the enclosed area. Examples are afforded by the angles of a triangle, an almond or a crescent.

OBTUSE. Any angle greater than a right angle.

RIGHT. An angle of 90°. *See* **Right angle.**

Apex. *See* **Triangle.**

Arc. A portion of the circumference of a circle which is distinctly less than a semicircle. This term includes the separate parts of an ellipse bisected along the major axis. Thus, either half of ⊂⊃ constitutes an arc: ⌒ or ⌣. The precise limits of an arc are given in the *Principles of Approximation*. These will seldom be required, but it is useful to remember that a curve subtending an angle of 90° [⌐⌐] falls within the limits of an arc. All arcs are symmetrical, which serves to distinguish them from the **Hook** (q.v.)

14

Arm. Either of the lines forming an angle.

COMMON. A line which does double duty as an arm for each of two angles. Thus, in $\rightarrow$ or $\frown$ the middle line is a common arm, in $\perp$ or $\lrcorner$ the vertical line is a common arm, and in $\angle$ or $\sim$ the middle line is a common arm. In a figure like $\succ$ or $\times$ all the arms are said to be common.

Asymmetrical. Not yielding precisely the same form when viewed in a mirror. Thus, the letter A is held to be symmetrical, but N is asymmetrical, for viewed in a mirror it would become И. Similarly, U and V are symmetrical, but $\cup$ and $>$ are asymmetrical; $\therefore$ and $\cdot$—$\cdot$ are symmetrical, but % and $\cdots$—$\cdot$ are asymmetrical. For cases involving converging free lines, *see* **Symmetrical.**

Axis. *See* **Wave.**

Base. *See* **Triangle.**

Blocked. *See under* **Curve.**

Chord. An imaginary line joining the two horns of a crescent or the extremities of a simple, open-curved figure. Thus: $\mathcal{D}$, $\mathcal{C}$.

Circle. This is a closed or nearly closed figure corresponding with a geometrical circle within the limits defined in the *Principles of Approximation*. It need not, within these limits, be perfectly circular.

CIRCUMSCRIBED. A circle which completely encloses all other parts of a sign.

Column. In a column of figures (e.g. dots), the components are arranged in a vertical straight line. Cf. **Row.**

15

Concave. *See under* **Figure.**

Conic Section. This term is used in the explanatory matter only, and is a convenient general term embracing circles, ellipses, parabolae and hyperbolae, the last two being covered indiscriminately in this book by the term **Hoop** (q.v.).

Convex. *See under* **Figure.**

Crescent. The closed figure produced by two doubly inter-secting arcs, or an arc and a semicircle or gibbous figure, whose centres of curvature lie on the same side of the figure, thus: ⟩⟩ , of which an extreme form might be ⟩. Such figures always contain two curved angles.

Curve. Any line which continuously (not suddenly) changes its direction. A curve which meets itself, such as δ , thereby divides itself into two curves by the present classification, for the closed portion [the loop ○] takes precedence over the rest of the figure [the hoop ⌒]. *See also* **Arc, Circle, Hook, Spiral,** etc.

CLOSED. A closed curve consists of one or more curved lines completely enclosing a space (*all the lines involved being curved*). *See also* BLOCKED (curve) *and* NEARLY CLOSED (curve).

BLOCKED. A blocked curve is an open curve whose extrem-ities are joined by one or more straight lines, or with straight lines and curves, so as to enclose a space. Where more than one curve is involved, the first type of curve in the *Orders of Precedence* (i.e. the orders followed in the Key) is the one which is said to be blocked by all the other lines. For example, a figure like ⟍___⟍ would be treated as a blocked semicircle. Curves may be blocked *internally*, thus: ◠, ⟩⟨ , *externally*,

16

thus: ⌐, ⊓, or *collectively*, thus: ⊃. It should be noted that the blocking line (or lines), or part of them, must connect the *extremities of the curve*, so that the letter ℰ, for example, does not contain a blocked curve, though ⊃ does. The reason for this is that curves are always considered as wholes (in the order in which they turn up in the Key), and the gibbous curve in ℰ takes priority over the semicircular part of it which one might be tempted to consider 'blocked'. Thus, there is no opportunity provided for dealing with the semicircular part by itself.

COMPLEX. This term is used to distinguish curves in which the direction or degree of curvature alters from point to point, but excludes the conic sections. Except for the terms **Wave** (*S-shape*) and **Spiral,** there are no common names for complex curves. All other complex curves are therefore classed as IRREGULAR.

GIBBOUS. This term is commonly applied to the moon when it is three-quarters full, and it is here used for an arc of a circle or an ellipse which is distinctly greater than a semicircle or semi-ellipse, but falls short of the nearly closed figures. Thus, ⌣ and ⊂ are gibbous figures. A horseshoe with curved limbs very wide apart, ⊃, would also be classed as a gibbous figure, though the closing of the limbs would approach an *oval* (egg-shape) rather than an ellipse.

IRREGULAR. An irregular curve is one which plainly fails to conform to any general rule. ⌇ would be an irregular re-entrant closed curve, and ℰʃ would be an irregular open curve. The botanical symbol ♡ is an irregular closed curve containing one exterior angle.

NEARLY CLOSED. A curve of which the *extremities* are so nearly in contact that it would be taken normally for a completely closed figure is treated as a *closed* curve. The term *nearly closed* is therefore equivalent to *closed* in the classification. Thus

17

the nearly closed curves in ⃝ and ⊂⊃ are treated as closed figures. There is, however, no nearly closed element in ⌒◯, for here the extremities of the curve are by no means nearly in contact: *See* the *Principles of Approximation.*

OPEN. All open curves have two separated ends, though these may be attached to other curves provided they do not completely enclose a space. (Note, however, that two curves cannot, in this classification, be joined *continuously*, for such a conjunction would make a single—but more complex—curve.) They may also be attached to straight lines or dots, but the closing of a space *by means of a straight line* does not convert an open curve into a closed one, but into a *blocked* open curve. Thus the curves in ⟋ and ⟋⟍ are open curves blocked by straight lines. *See* BLOCKED (curve). In the first classification of curves all straight lines must be ignored. The hollow side of an open curve is referred to as the *concave* side; the other is the *convex* side.

RE-ENTRANT. A re-entrant curve is one which possesses no ends. When the figure is drawn, the pencil re-enters the curve without making an angle the moment the figure is completed. Examples: ⃝, ⌒◯.

SIMPLE. In contradistinction to *complex*, this term implies any well-known form of curve of no greater complexity than the conic sections. Names have been allocated to all the simple curves.

Detached. *See under* **Parts.**

Diagonal. Running diagonally with respect to the page or its equivalent. In scripts, running diagonally with respect to the line of writing or print.

Dot. Commonly a point, but the term point is not used in a

18

general sense because the significance of some dots depends upon their sizes and shapes. *See* **Point.** In any large dot the length must not be more than three times the breadth; otherwise it is classed as a thick line. If a line runs through a dot or is otherwise in contact with it, the dot is not held to divide the line, for the consideration of lines takes precedence over the consideration of dots. Thus,━■━ and ▬ are straight lines *plus* rectangular dots, ◖ is a circle *plus* a 'quarter' dot, ◗ is a circle *plus* a 'semicircular' dot, but ● is a circular dot, and ⊕ is a circular dot with *enclosed figures*. In the case of any doubt about enclosed figures the whole is considered as a dot if the area of the solid parts is greater than the area occupied by the figure. Thus ⊜ and ⊕ are dots with enclosed figures, but ⊖ is a circle containing one horizontal line (the top and bottom limbs of the circumference being thickened). Since a dot has, by definition, no admitted dimensions, the side of a dot is never recognized as making an angle. Thus, ▬ and ◀ are cases of a dot *plus* two straight lines, and ▮ and ⟶ are cases of a dot *plus* one straight line. However, ▙ and ◗ would be classified as a dot *plus* an angle, and ─+─ as a dot *plus* four angles, for the common-sense view is that both arms of the angles are intended to be present; similarly ▪▪▪▪ should be looked for under rectangular figures *plus* dots. The decision between two equally possible alternatives is decided by the *Orders of Precedence* (page 37), and both closed figures and angles take precedence over free straight lines. When the boundary of a dot forms a continuation of a curve, as in ◗, the dot is said to be *coincident* with the curve.

COMPLEX. A large dot of irregular or not otherwise classified shape, or with enclosed figures.

QUARTER. A dot with the shape of a quadrant or approximate quarter-circle, the curved side being subject to the same degree of approximation as an *arc*.

SEMICIRCULAR. A dot with a curved margin in the shape of a semicircle as defined in the *Principles of Approximation,* the other margin being straight.

THREE-QUARTER. A dot with the shape of three-quarters of a circle (the circle not being completed by a line), the curved side being subjected to the same degree of approximation as the *gibbous* figure.

Drop. More or less the shape of a drop of water, except that one or both of the limbs meeting to form the angle reverse the direction of the curve, so that both limbs spring continuously from a common line or 'stalk'. Examples: $\bigcirc$, $\bigcirc$. The limbs of a drop do not (or would not, if produced) cross each other as in a **Loop** (q.v.).

Ellipse. This is a closed or nearly closed figure corresponding with a geometrical ellipse within the limits defined in the *Principles of Approximation.*

Enclosed Figure. *See under* **Dot.**

Extremity. *See under* **Free End.**

Figure. A single component part of a *sign* or *symbol.* The term is never used for **Numeral** (q. v.).

BLOCKED. *See under* **Curve.**

CLOSED. A closed figure is one which completely encloses a space with *either* a curve (or curves) *or* straight lines, but not with both. (When both are present it is always a *blocked curve.*) *See also* NEARLY CLOSED (figure) and rule on page 4.

CONCAVE. Used of closed rectilinear figures in which at least one angle is exterior.

CONVEX. Used of closed rectilinear figures in which all the angles are interior.

ENCLOSED. A figure (usually in white) on the background of a dot.

EXTERNAL. Outside a closed or blocked figure. An external figure may or may not be in contact with the closed or blocked figure, but it must not intrude on the enclosed area.

GIBBOUS. *See under* **Curve.**

INTERNAL. Wholly within a closed or blocked figure, with the bounding lines of which it may or may not be in contact.

IRREGULAR. *See under* **Curve.**

NEARLY CLOSED. A figure which is so nearly closed as to be taken normally to represent a completely closed figure; it is treated as a *closed* figure. *See* the *Principles of Approximation* (page 30).

OPEN. Any figure which does not completely enclose a space (*nearly closed* figures excepted). A *curved* figure may be open even if it joins with a *straight line* to enclose a space, for straight lines are ignored while curves are being considered. *See under* **Curve** (BLOCKED).

SUBSIDIARY. Coming later in the *Orders of Precedence* than the type of figure mainly under consideration.

Form. The entire shape of a *sign* or *symbol*.

Free End. The end of a line which does not terminate by abutting on to another, on to part of itself, or in a dot. Thus, ℮ and ⊖ have two free ends, ◔ has one, ⊖ has none. Again, ⟩ has two free ends, but ≻ has three. *Nearly closed* figures are presumed to have no free ends. An enclosing or circumscribing figure does not make loose ends within it any the less free, so that ∾ contains two free ends. A dot at the end of a line robs it of its freedom, but the 'finishing marks' (such as serifs)

21

common to well-known scripts are ignored. See the *Principles of Approximation*.

Gibbous. *See under* **Curve.**

Heart. A closed curved figure with two angles, one interior and one exterior, typified by the conventional 'heart', ♡, but covering extreme forms such as ß.

Hexagon. A closed rectilinear figure with six sides and six angles.

Hook. Either half of the figure produced by bisecting an ellipse diagonally. Thus, ⬭ yields the two hooks ⌐ and ⌐. It may be regarded as an incipient spiral, but all such forms are called *hooks* unless the shorter limb, if produced in a straight line, would cut the longer. *See* **Spiral.** All hooks are asymmetrical, which serves to distinguish them readily from arcs.

DOUBLE. A *double hook* is a curve with a hook at each end, the hooks being both on the concave side of the curve, thus: ⊂⊃.

Hoop. Any parabola or hyperbola whose limbs are long enough to preclude its classification as a semicircle or arc. The term includes a semi-ellipse produced by bisection along the minor axis. Thus, ⬭ yields the hoops ⊂ and ⊃. A *hoop* is distinguished from a *hook* by the fact that its limbs are of equal length. (There is no *double hoop*; two hoops of equal size form an ellipse, and if one is smaller than the other the figure is a spiral.)

Horizontal. Running horizontally with respect to the page or

22

its equivalent. In scripts, running horizontally with respect to the line of writing or print. Boundary lines and other such marks which may be used in any position or orientation are illustrated as straight and horizontal.

Irregular. Not definable by the terms used in this *Glossary*. Of polygons, not having all sides and all angles equal. Also *see under* **Curve.**

Large. Of signs, never used less than ten times the size reproduced in the *Glossary*. Of parts of signs, comparable in size with two or more capital M's as used in the text of this book, but the term is subject to common-sense interpretation in any given context.

Letter. Any complete alphabetical sign. Printed letters with ornamental flourishes are described as '*swash*', those tilted at an angle as '*tumbling*', those lying on their sides as '*lazy*', and those completely inverted as '*turned*'. A letter may also be '*reversed*' from left to right, or be '*crossed*' by a short stroke as in the Polish L.

Limb. Any portion of a line clearly distinguishable from the remainder. When not precisely described the term *limb* refers to either of the extremities of a line.

    MIDDLE. The whole of a line *except* the extremities.

Line. Any single mark which is not a *dot*. All lines, whether curved or straight, are considered to be without width for the purposes of classification. When a particular line is noticeably thick, or of varying thickness, its form is taken to be that of an imaginary longitudinal bisector. Thus, the forms used for classifying $\mathbf{I}$ and $\boldsymbol{O}$ are taken to be $|$ and $\bigcirc$, respectively. *See also* **Straight Line.**

Termination of lines: Any line which is lacking in free ends is considered to terminate at any point where its direction is inescapably broken by an angle, or where a curve becomes a straight line. Thus, ∨ consists of three lines, but ⌒ of two lines. Similarly, D consists of two lines (one of which is curved) and U of three—one curved and two straight. As far as intersecting lines are concerned this definition is not necessary except for the sake of completeness, for it will be found that consideration of both curves and angles precedes the consideration of lines *as lines*, so that all intersecting lines are disposed of before any question of their terminations can arise. The occurrence of a dot on a line does not divide the line (*see* **Dot**). For the treatment of 'finishing-marks', such as serifs, see the *Principles of Approximation* (page 30). *See also* **Free End.**

Linear. Composed of lines as distinct from dots.

Loop. More or less the shape of a drop of water or a loop of string, but both the limbs making the angle must maintain the convexity of the general curve and would cross if produced. One or both of the limbs may, however, be virtually straight. These characteristics distinguish the *loop* from the **Drop** (q.v.). Examples of loops: ℓ, ◯, ⌒.

Medium-sized. This generally means comparable in size with a small or lower-case m as used in the text of this book, but the term is subject to common-sense interpretation in any given context.

Numeral. The written or printed sign for a number. The term *Figure* (q.v.) has a special connotation and is never used for a numeral.

Oval. Literally egg-shaped, i.e. a closed re-entrant curve with a sharper degree of curvature at one end than at the other. Very few cases arise, and these are classed initially as ellipses unless the difference in the ends is so great as to make reference to an ellipse absurd, in which case the figure would be classified first as **Irregular** (q.v.).

Parallelogram. A closed rectilinear figure with four sides in which the opposite sides are parallel but the angles other than right angles.

Parts. The parts of a sign are the figures or groups of figures of which it is composed.

DETACHED. Parts which are not contiguous with other parts and therefore require separate analysis.

Pentagon. A closed rectilinear figure with five sides and five angles. It need not be geometrically regular.

Point. A very small dot, i.e. with a diameter of, say, one sixty-fourth of an inch or less.

Polygon. Any closed rectilinear figure bounded by more than four straight lines and with an equal number of angles. Pentagons and hexagons are thus treated as varieties of polygon.

Prolongation. The limb of a figure is said to be *prolonged* when it is continued in a straight line beyond the boundaries of that figure. For example, one limb of a semicircle may be prolonged thus, ⌐, or both limbs thus, ⊏. The prolonged line is called a *prolongation*, and it may form only part of a straight line, as in __⊂__ , where the part of the line to the left of the curve is not part of the prolongation.

Quadrilateral. Any closed figure bounded by four straight lines.

25

Rectangle. A quadrilateral whose angles are all right angles but whose adjacent sides are unequal.

Rectilinear. Consisting solely of straight lines.

Right angle. An angle of 90°, or any variation from this allowed in the *Principles of Approximation*. A right angle may be set in any position; its arms are not necessarily vertical or horizontal.

Row. In a row of figures (e.g. dots) the components are arranged in a horizontal or diagonal straight line. Cf. **Column.**

Semicircle. An open curved figure corresponding with half the circumference of a geometrical circle, within the limits defined in the *Principles of Approximation*.

Sign. Any written, printed or carved mark which is used conventionally to convey an idea. The mathematical signs provide a ready example. The letters of modern alphabets are signs conveying auditory ideas. *See also* **Symbol.**

Small. Small in relation to accompanying signs. It generally means comparable in size with a lower-case n as used in the text of this book, or smaller, but the term is subject to common-sense interpretation in any given context.

Spiral. A line curved continuously in the same direction, but with a constant alteration in the degree of curvature. The simplest form of spiral is similar to a **Hook** (q.v.), except that the shorter limb, if produced as a straight line, would cut the longer. Thus, while ⌣ ranks as a *hook*, ⌒ ranks as a *spiral*. A watch-spring provides a ready example of a fully developed spiral. A spiral consisting of a single turn only is so called provided its extremities are wide apart or overlap for a notable distance. Otherwise it will be found that the figure is classed as a *nearly closed circle* or *ellipse* as defined in the *Principles of Approximation*. Thus, ◖ and ◗ are spirals, but ◯ is a nearly closed figure. These forms are not common but are among the few demanding the exercise of judgment by the inquirer. Note also that the graphic representation of a coil or helical spiral is not treated as a spiral in the present classification, for it disappears under analysis in the early stages of classification, being separated into loops and arcs. Thus, ՈՈՈ becomes a set of ၀ ၀ ၀ ၀ *plus* a set of ∼∼∼.

DOUBLE. The form ℮◗ is termed a *double spiral*, there being no other provision made for its classification, but ↄ↗ is already covered by the definition of a *wave*, though it may be further qualified as 'with limbs forming spirals'.

LEFT-HAND. Winding inwards in a clockwise direction: ℮.

RIGHT-HAND. Winding inwards in an anti-clockwise direction: ☉.

Square. A quadrilateral in which all the angles are right angles, and all the sides equal.

S-Shape. *See* Wave.

Straight Line. Any line which makes no change in its direction throughout its length.

CONTINUOUS. Continuous straight lines are continuous in *direction*, e.g. a 'broken' line consists of continuous straight lines.

CONVERGING. Two or more straight lines, not in contact, which are neither parallel nor continuous in direction. It should be noted that this definition includes cases of convergence at right angles, such as |— and ∖╱.

FREE. A straight line which is not attached in any way to any other line. It is not affected as a free line by contact with a dot.

NON-CONVERGING. Two or more straight lines which are either parallel or continuous in direction.

PARALLEL. Parallel straight lines are equidistant throughout equal lengths, though they need not be of equal length.

Symbol. A sign whose idea is itself intended to convey some other idea, such as 〰, which as a pictograph is a sign meaning water, but to astronomers is a symbol of the constellation *Aquarius.*

Symmetrical. Yielding precisely the same form when viewed in a mirror. *See* **Asymmetrical.** *Note:* The position of the mirror is not prescribed; it is sufficient if a position *can be found* for the mirror to yield a reflection which is identical in form with the original. This may apply to the lengths and arrangement of free lines (e.g. converging straight lines) as well as to connected figures.

Trapezium. A quadrilateral two only of whose sides are parallel. Examples: ▱, ◺.

Triangle. Any closed figure bounded by three straight lines. The side nearest to a horizontal position is termed the *base* of the triangle; the angle opposite the base is termed the *apex.*

EQUILATERAL. A triangle in which all three angles are equal and, therefore, in which all three sides are equal. This is a special case of *isosceles* triangle.

ISOSCELES. A triangle in which two of the angles, and two of the sides, are equal (within the limits allowed by the *Principles of Approximation*). Examples: △ and ◿.

RIGHT-ANGLED. A triangle in which one of the angles is a right angle; it may—or may. not—also be isosceles. *Note :* When it forms the apex of the triangle the right angle is easily overlooked. Examples: ◿ and △.

SCALENE. A triangle with all three sides of different lengths, and all three angles different.

Vertical. Running vertically with respect to the page (within the plane of the page) or its equivalent. In scripts, running vertically with respect to the line of writing or print.

Wave. An open curve in which the direction of curvature is reversed one or more times. When there is only one reversal it is often preferable to call this form an *S-shape*, which is so familiar as to leave the reader in no doubt as to its meaning. The sections of the figure characterized by different directions of curvature need not be equal in size or degree of curvature. Thus, ∿ ranks as a wave no less than ∿. But if one part of such a curve is enclosed in another part, as in ∫∅∫, the form is classified as an *irregular* open figure. In the case of a figure like ⊚⊚, which, while it clearly contains two spirals, yet obeys our definition of a wave, the *Orders of Precedence* must be strictly followed. These demand that the wave-like properties be considered first, and the figure is, in fact, no more than an S-shape with curly ends. The position of a wave is sometimes defined by the direction of its *axis*. This is the mid longitudinal line of the wave, and in a physical wave would indicate the direction of its motion. The broken lines show the axes in the following examples: ⌇ (axis vertical), ∿∿∿ (axis horizontal), ∿∫ (axis diagonal).

29

PRINCIPLES OF APPROXIMATION

In GENERAL it may be said that the names of geometrical forms used in this *Glossary* are intended to cover all reasonable approximations to the ideal forms, and while in practice this does not give rise to serious uncertainty, it has been felt necessary to establish definite rules governing the degree of approximation allowed, and to follow these (within reason) in the actual compiling of the *Glossary*.

These rules are invoked chiefly in dealing with cursive letters, to some extent with printed letters, but scarcely at all with special and technical signs. They fall under two general heads or *Principles,* covering the provision of latitude in the shapes of figures, and the elimination of minute and insignificant elements, respectively.

The small size of most graphic signs makes it advisable for the reader to judge by eye rather than measurement, which should be resorted to only in cases of real difficulty, and the rules for applying the *First Principle* have therefore been framed to give a maximum of reliability to such a method, and to provide for contingencies of misjudgment.

The reader is, however, warned to *scrutinize* the signs, especially in their smaller parts. For example, $\langle$ is a right angle no less than $\lfloor$, but the rectilinear angles in $\langle\rangle$ are greater than right angles. Again, the curves in $\curlyvee$ are not spirals or arcs, but semicircles. Such facts are not always apparent at a casual glance, yet they are plain enough to a critical eye without the use of instruments. The errors due to too hasty an examination of a sign are most often to be attributed to optical illusion or a false association of forms. They are seldom due to intellectual misjudgment.

30

The conditions under which certain minute elements, such as the serifs of letters, may be totally disregarded are set forth in the *Second Principle*, and here again a small demand is made of the reader—this time of elementary knowledge as well as of judgment. Among the few assumptions it has seemed expedient to make, familiarity with such devices as serifs is, perhaps, the chief. A logically perfect classification should, of course, assume nothing in the nature of a serif, but to provide for all such incidental marks would make the *Glossary* so complex that it would lose a great deal of the usefulness it ventures to claim in its present form. The reader must at least be allowed to have sufficient knowledge of letters to read the book, and the too meticulous critic is asked to allow him also a modest degree of intelligence and judgment.

The *Principles of Approximation* are as follows:

FIRST PRINCIPLE. *The permitted degree of departure from ideal forms is 5 per cent in rectilinear figures, 2½ per cent in curves and ten degrees in angles, according to the following rules:*

1. *Variations in Line.* Suppose the ideal form to be drawn in a thick line which is one-twentieth as wide as it is long. Then any variant from the ideal which will lie within the thick line is allowed to bear the name of the ideal. The variant of the ideal may itself be thick, but it will be remembered that its form is to be regarded as that displayed by a thin line along its centre. For example, the form of the line ◢ is ╱. It has a very slight curve, but this may be ignored because the line is easily contained within the limit of approximation, ╱, the width of which is 5 per cent of its length.

Again, *a*, in the cut, is a perfect circle measuring, say, four inches in circumference, and *b* is the same circle drawn with a line one-tenth of an inch wide. Now any figure in a thin line

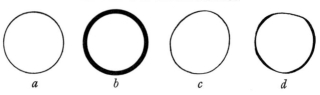

which would, if superimposed on the thickened circle, lie entirely within the thickened line, ranks as a *Circle*. Such figures are legion, and would include those shown at *c* and *d*. A qualification which follows from the *Definitions* is that all approximations to curved figures must curve throughout their length in the same sense (general direction) as the ideal, and contain no appreciably straight lengths.

Precisely the same principle is applied to semicircles, squares, rectangles and parallel lines, but it will seldom be found necessary to use it in connection with other figures. A special extension of this principle is allowed with hand-written scripts, where a stroke intended to be straight is sometimes distinctly curved. In such cases the curve, though perhaps more pronounced than our first principle would allow, may yet be quite clearly not sufficiently pronounced to form a significant feature. Thus, the Chinese brush often produces on a downward stroke a marked but insignificant curvature which we are obliged to ignore.

2. *Nearly Closed Figures.* A figure which is so nearly closed that careful scrutiny is required for the gap to be clearly perceived is regarded as being intended for a closed figure. The rule is that the gap in a nearly closed figure must not measure more than $2\frac{1}{2}$ per cent of its perimeter.

Thus, if *a*, in the following cut, is a circle measuring four inches in circumference, a gap of one-tenth of an inch or less may be ignored. By this rule *b* and *c* are treated as complete circles. Figures with gaps wider than these would be classed as gibbous figures or spirals respectively. The same principle may be applied to rectilinear figures.

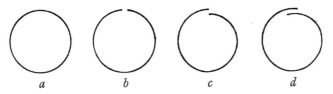

a   b   c   d

3. *Overlapping of Ends.* From Rule 2 it will be found that the limit allowed for the gap in a nearly closed circle is nearly 10 degrees, so that the rule might be restated in the form that approximately 350 degrees are allowed to count for 360. However, the inaccuracies in angular measurements may lie on either side of the true angle, so that the *range* of the latitude permitted amounts to 20 degrees.

Thus, at *d* in the previous cut the two ends of the curve overlap, and this is allowed up to the limit of 20 degrees. If they overlap by more than 20 degrees the figure is classed as a spiral. In other words, 380 degrees are also allowed to count as 360, but it should be recalled that for any such rule to apply the overlapping lines must lie within the width of the 'thickened line' defined in Rule 1.

4. *Semicircles and Arcs.* A curved figure subtending an angle at its centre of less than 350 degrees but more than 190 degrees is defined as a 'gibbous' figure, but this becomes a semicircle when it approaches within 10 degrees of the ideal semicircle (180 degrees). Similarly, the semicircle becomes an arc when it is less than 180 degrees by 10 degrees or more. The limits of a semicircle are therefore from 190 to 170 degrees, and in cases of doubt classification as semicircles is preferred to that as gibbous figures or arcs. These relations are set out in the following cut:

33

5. *Measurement of Angles.* Angles may depart from the 60 or 90 degrees (right angle) specified in the *Definitions* or mentioned in the Key by no more than 10 degrees on either side of the ideal, and any pair of angles may be considered equal if they differ by not more than 10 degrees. It has been found by experiment that there is uncertainty in free estimations of angles within the limit of 10 degrees for small figures, but that outside this limit few people are likely to mistake differences in angles.

6. *Delineation of Angles.* The points of angles, and the corners of all rectilinear figures, are allowed to be rounded to a negligible degree, though, of course, the *sides* of all such figures must consist of lines which are straight within the limits laid down in Rule 1.

The precise rule here is that the curved portion joining two straight lines intended to form an angle must not occupy more than 5 per cent of the total length of the two lines. This is a defection from the otherwise strict distinction between curves and straight lines, and applies chiefly to such manuscript signs as ╱, which few people ever write with a perfectly sharp angle.

SECOND PRINCIPLE. *Very minute elements which might reasonably be considered accidents incident to the process of writing, or those which are clearly finishing marks determining the length of a line (but too small to be likely to have significance of their own), may be ignored.*

1. *Serifs, Brush-flicks, etc.* No figure is to be ignored if it is of a size which suggests intention, unless it belongs to a well-known category of such features as serifs. Flourishes and ornaments often assume large proportions, but the reader is not to be expected to know which of these are significant and which not.

34

Chief among the classes of features which may be ignored are the serifs on printed letters, dots replacing serifs on printed letters, reduplicated lines in 'open-faced' types, dashes at the ends of lines in black-letter, similar features in Hebrew characters, internal ornaments, 'tongues' and reduplicated lines in black-letter, the brush-flicks at the ends of strokes in Chinese characters and the accidental points in cuneiform scripts. Examples of all these are illustrated in the following cut,

J S F G א ヱ ⑾
J S F G ﬡ ヱ ‖·

which shows also how the signs given should be treated for the purpose of classification. It will not, of course, be expected to find all the ornamental Roman letters, though a few are given.

2. *Very Small Loops.* Loops in cursive writing which are so very minute as to be liable to be blotted may be ignored. It may be assumed that if the width of such a loop is no greater than the thickness of the line in which it is drawn, it is either an unintentional loop or one of no moment. Thus, the small loop in 3 is of no significance, but even if it were it could safely be ignored for the purposes of a formal classification.

This rule applies to cursive writing only. The reader is not to ignore loops of any size in printed signs, or in any likely to belong to shorthand systems. In all doubtful cases there are, after all, never more than two alternatives—loop or no loop—and if the sign is not traced through the one it is sure to be found through the other.

3. *Incidental Defects.* The quiverings and inadvertent angles which are generally described as 'accidents of the hand-drawn

line' are always ignored. They will not arise except in obvious examples of handwriting, where they are readily recognized. It is unfortunate that no scheme can be devised to sort out the vagaries of really bad handwriting and reveal the forms intended—that would be asking too much of any merely human classifier!

4. *Ornamental Scripts.* Curved lines taking the place of straight ones in ornamental scripts are, of course, treated as curves. If the reader were already aware that a curved line 'ought' to be straight he might be assumed to have no need to consult the *Glossary*. Thus, although D consists of a semi-circle and a straight line, and is therefore classed among the open curved figures, the curved form of the upright in $\mathcal{D}$ must be taken into account and places this form of the letter in the closed curves containing angles.

5. *Alphabetical Standards.* The variety of type-faces and scripts widely used in most alphabets necessitates the adoption of standards, and those in common use in the standard textbooks of languages have been followed. With the Roman letters, the *Times* type face has been referred to in cases of variable form, but many letters from other common styles of type are also included in the *Glossary*. The cursive letters are taken from 'copybook' hands and seldom differ significantly from 'copperplate' type faces. The connecting strokes between letters are considered as coming *before* the letters but are important only when they are defined as straight. Usually they are curved and make no difference to the classification, so they are not given in the drawings where the italic forms of the letters serve to cover the cursive forms also.

36

ORDERS OF PRECEDENCE

THE lists given under this heading indicate the principles of arrangement followed in compiling the *Glossary*, but though they may be found useful for occasional reference they are not likely to be required in the ordinary use of the *Glossary*. There are three such lists, or *Orders of Precedence*, and of these the second is the most important.

The first gives the general order adopted in the *Classes* and their *Orders*. The second applies within the framework of the *Orders*. This arrangement avoids much repetition, but it may be taken that no term in either list is considered before any of the terms preceding it in the same list.* The third list makes provision for the arrangement of signs possessing no classified differences, their order being based on the disposition or number of their component parts, and similar considerations.

ORDER I

Signs consisting of:

1. Curves only.
2. Curves and straight lines.
3. Curves, straight lines and dots.
4. Curves and dots.
5. Straight lines only.
6. Straight lines and dots.
7. Dots only.

---

* There are, however, some few exceptions, made for the convenience of both the compiler and the reader for reasons it would sometimes be hard to give but which generally concern the advantage of grouping closely similar signs together.

ORDER II

1. *Closed curves.*
2. Re-entrant curves.
3. Circle.
4. Ellipse.
5. Irregular re-entrant curves.
6. Loop.
7. Drop.
8. Almond.
9. Crescent.
10. Other closed curves with two angles.
11. Closed curves with more than two angles.

12. *Open curves.*
13. Gibbous figures.
14. Semicircle.
15. Hoop.
16. Arc.
17. Hook.
18. Complex open curves.
19. Wave (S-shape).
20. Spiral.
21. Irregular open curves.

22. *Closed rectilinear figures.*
23. Right-angled triangle.
24. Equilateral triangle.
25. Isosceles triangle (other than equilateral or right-angled).
26. Scalene triangle (other than right-angled).
27. Square.
28. Rectangle.
29. Other parallelograms.

30. Trapezium.
31. Other quadrilaterals.
32. Regular polygons.
33. Irregular polygons.

34. *Open angles.*
35. One right angle.
36. Two or more right angles.
37. One angle other than a right angle.
38. Two or more angles other than right angles.

39. *Free straight lines.*
40. Single lines.
41. Lines continuous in direction.
42. Parallel lines.
43. Symmetrically converging lines.
44. Asymmetrically converging lines.

45. *Single dots.*
46. Dots with definite size.
47. Circular dots.
48. Three-quarter dots.
49. Semicircular dots.
50. Quarter dots.
51. Square dots.
52. Rectangular dots.
53. Triangular dots.
54. Polygonal dots.
55. Irregular dots.
56. Dots with enclosed figures.
57. Points presumed without size.

58. *Groups of dots.*
59. One to three dots.
60. Four or more dots in definite numbers.
61. Dots in indefinite numbers.

ORDER III

1. Alphabetical order.
2. Numerical order.
3. Size (descending).
4. Number of parts (ascending).
5. Completeness.
6. Position.
7. Equality.
8. Regularity.
9. Symmetry.
10. Complexity.
11. Thickness of line.
12. Colour.

These properties are utilized in the following ways:

1. *Alphabetical Order.* Where letters occur in signs which are otherwise similar, the signs are given in alphabetical order of the letters.

2. *Numerical Order.* Where numerals occur in signs which are otherwise similar, the signs are given in numerical order of their numerals. (Letters take precedence over numerals, other considerations being equal.)

3. *Size.* Large figures take precedence over smaller ones of the same kind, *except* that acute angles take precedence over obtuse angles.

4. *Number.* Signs containing single examples of a figure under consideration take priority over those containing more than one. Ascending numerical order is the rule in all cases. Single signs come before repeated signs.

5. *Completeness.* Closed figures take precedence over nearly closed figures, and arcs or hooks closed internally [⌒] over those closed externally [△]. Again, complete signs take

40

precedence over indefinite signs such as shading conventions or symbolic lines of indeterminate length.

6. *Position.* In signs which are composed of identical parts differently arranged, figures in the centre take priority over all others, those above take priority over those below, and those to the left priority over those to the right. Similarly, diagonal figures sloping upwards to the left [\\ ] take priority over those sloping upwards to the right [╱], and left hand-spirals [(ᴑ)] priority over right-hand spirals [(ᴑ)]. Circles or other curves specifically directed anti-clockwise ('direct') take priority over those directed clockwise ('retrograde').

7. *Equality.* Signs containing two or more equal figures take priority over those containing unequal figures of the same kind.

8. *Regularity.* Signs containing regular figures take priority over those containing irregular figures of the same kind.

9. *Symmetry.* Symmetrical signs take priority over asymmetrical signs of similar form.

10. *Complexity.* When signs are identical save for the degree of complexity of one or more of their figures, the least complex example is given first, and the others in order of increasing complexity. Thus, a spiral consisting of one turn would precede those with two or more turns. Similarly, polygons not already placed are put in ascending order of the number of their sides.

11. *Thickness of line.* Signs with thick lines precede similar forms with thin lines, and signs with lines of constant thickness precede similar signs with lines of variable thickness.

12. *Colour.* Signs may be alike in all respects save for colours indicated in their definitions, in which case black and white take precedence over all other colours. Following white come the primary and secondary colours, but it has not been found necessary to order them.

41

SYSTEM OF CLASSIFICATION

THE basic system of the classification is given here in a simplified form as a matter of interest; it is not intended for the practical use of the *Glossary*. In order to present the scheme in a readily comprehensible way it has been considered advantageous to adopt the familiar pattern of biological nomenclature. Thus, the first broad groupings are labelled Classes, and their subgroups Divisions, Orders, Families and Genera. The numbers in brackets refer to the *Tables of Signs*, and show the degree to which the Genera have been subdivided. It should not be necessary to emphasize that this terminology has been used solely as an expedient.

CLASS I— SIGNS WITH CURVES

DIVISION I—Consisting Solely of Curves

    ORDER I—CLOSED CURVES

        FAMILY I — *Re-entrant Curves*
        GENUS I—Circles (1–11)
        GENUS II—Ellipses, etc. (12–15)
        FAMILY II—*Angular Curves*
        GENUS I—Loops and Drops (16–25)
        GENUS II—Almonds, Crescents, etc. (26–30)

    ORDER II—OPEN CURVES

        FAMILY I—*Simple Curves*
        GENUS I—Gibbous Figures (31–34)
        GENUS II—Semicircles and Hoops (35–41)
        GENUS III—Arcs and Hooks (42–52)

FAMILY II—*Complex Curves*
    GENUS I—Waves or S-shapes (53–61)
    GENUS II—Spirals, etc. (62–64)

DIVISION II—Curves and Straight Lines (With or Without Dots)

  ORDER I—CLOSED CURVES

    FAMILY I—*Re-entrant Curves*
    GENUS I—Circles (65–126)
    GENUS II—Ellipses, etc. (127–136)
    FAMILY II—*Angular Curves*
    GENUS I—Loops and Drops (137–150)
    GENUS II—Almonds, Crescents, etc. (151–152)

  ORDER II—OPEN CURVES

    FAMILY I—*Simple Curves*
    GROUP I—Curves Blocked by Straight Lines
      GENUS I—Gibbous Figures (153–158)
      GENUS II—Semicircles and Hoops (159–167)
      GENUS III—Arcs and Hooks (168–175)
    GROUP II—Curves Not Blocked by Straight Lines
      GENUS I—Gibbous Figures (176–184)
      GENUS II—Semicircles and Hoops (185–201)
      GENUS III—Arcs and Hooks (202–237)
    FAMILY II—*Complex Open Curves*
    GENUS I—Waves or S-shapes (238–245)
    GENUS II—Spirals, etc. (246–247)

DIVISION III—Curves and Dots Only

  ORDER I—CLOSED CURVES

    FAMILY I—*Dots Coincident with Curves*
    GENUS I—Angular Dots (248)
    GENUS II—All Other Dots (249)

FAMILY II—*Dots Enclosed by Curves*
   GENUS I—One Dot (250–251)
   GENUS II—Two or More Dots (252)
FAMILY III—*Dots Outside Curves*
   GENUS I—Re-entrant Curves (253)
   GENUS II—Angular Curves (254)

ORDER II—OPEN CURVES

FAMILY I—*Dots Coincident with Curves*
   GENUS I—One Dot (255–256)
   GENUS II—Two or More Dots (257–258)
FAMILY II—*Dots Not Coincident with Curves*
   GENUS I—One Dot (259)
   GENUS II—Two or More Dots (260)

CLASS II—STRAIGHT LINES WITHOUT CURVES

ORDER I—CONSISTING SOLELY OF STRAIGHT LINES

FAMILY I—*Closed Figures*
   GENUS I—Triangles (261–276)
   GENUS II—Squares and Rectangles (277–287)
   GENUS III—All Other Figures (288–293)
FAMILY II—*Open Angles*
   GENUS I—Right angles (294–329)
   GENUS II—Other Angles (330–365)
FAMILY III—*Free Straight Lines*
   GENUS I—Non-converging (366–386)
   GENUS II—Converging (387–388)

ORDER II—STRAIGHT LINES AND DOTS

FAMILY I—*Closed Figures*
   GENUS I—Triangles (389–390)
   GENUS II—Other Figures (391–393)

FAMILY II—*Open Angles*
    GENUS I—Circular or Curved Dots (394–398)
    GENUS II—Triangular Dots (399–400)
    GENUS III—All Other Dots (401–402)
FAMILY III—*Free Straight Lines*
    GENUS I—With Dots Detached (403–412)
    GENUS II—With Dots Attached (413–417)

CLASS III—SIGNS COMPOSED SOLELY OF DOTS

    GENUS I—Single Dots (418–423)
    GENUS II—Groups of Dots (424–434)

ABBREVIATIONS

a., alphabet
Abbr., abbreviation
Acc., accent, diacritical mark
Aero., aeronautics, aerodynamics
Afr., native African
Alch., alchemy
Alg., algebra
Am., Amerindian
Ant., antiquities
APO, may be used in any position or orientation
Arab., Arabic
Arch., architecture, architectural
Arith., arithmetic
Ass., Assyrian
Astrol/n., astrology or astronomy
Astrol., astrology
Astron., astronomy

Biog., biography
Biol., biology
Bot., botany
Brit., British
Cab., cabalistic
Cal., calculus
Cap., capital or upper case letter
Cart., cartography
Cent., century
Chem., chemistry
Chin., Chinese
Cl., class
Com., commerce
Cop., Coptic
Cret., Cretan
Crys., crystallography
Cun., cuneiform
Cz., Czech

Dan., Danish
Div., division
D/Nor., Danish or Norwegian
Du., Dutch

Egy., Egyptian
EL, Early Latin
Elec., electricity
Eng., English
Engn., engineering
Eq., equivalent or alternative to, form of
Esp., especially
Etr., Etruscan
Ext., extension

Fam., family
Fr., French

Gen., genus
Gr., group
Geol., geology
Geom., geometry
Ger., German
Gk., Greek
G/use, in general use in many contexts

H/mrk, Hall mark
Heb., Hebrew
Her., heraldry
Hier., hieroglyphic
High., highway
Hyd., hydrographic

Ice., Icelandic
Ind., Indian
Insig., insignia
Inter., international
Ir., Irish
It., italic

46

ITA, Initial Teaching Alphabet
Ital., Italian

Jap., Japanese

L., very large; never used less than ten times size printed
Lat., Latin
l.c., lower case or small letter
Log., logic

Mag., magnetism
Math., mathematics
ME, Middle English
Mech., mechanics and properties of matter
Med., Mediaeval
Meteor., meteorology
Mil., military
Min., mineralogy
Mod., modern
Mon., money
MS., manuscript
Mus., music

Nav., navigation and shipping
Nav. Arch., naval architecture
Nor., Norwegian
Num., numeral, number
Numis., numismatics

Obs., obsolete
Obsnt., obsolescent
OE, Old English
Og., Ogham script
Opt., optics
Ord., order
OS, Ordnance Survey

Per., Persian
Ph., Phoenician

Phar., pharmacy
Phila., philately
Philol., philology
Phon., phonetics
Photo., photography
Phys., physics
Pol., Polish
Port., Portuguese
Pot., pottery
Print., printing
Pron., pronounced
Prop., property
Pros., prosody
Punc., punctuation

RC, Roman Catholic
Rec., records (documentary)
Rel., religion
Rep., repeated or continued indefinitely
Rlwy., railway
Rom., Roman
Run., Runic
Rus., Russian

Sem., Semitic
Sh., shorthand
S/Nor., Swedish or Norwegian
Soil/m., soil mechanics
Sp., Spanish
Sw., Swedish

Tel., telecommunications
Therm., thermodynamics
Thick, thick line essential
Thin, thin line essential
Trig., trigonometry
Turk., Turkish

UNS, United Nations Standard
USA, United States of America

† *A dagger following the number of a sign indicates by its position that the sign is either above or below the line.*

'Smogger': *cant for the code of signs which tramps chalk on walls, etc., for the benefit of their brethren.*

KEY TO THE TABLES

IT IS essential to start at paragraph No. 1 and to consider the features described in strict order. Refer to the numbered paragraph as instructed at each step, and resist any temptation to follow a description out of the ordered sequence that may catch the eye. The end of each search is marked by a number in bold type followed by a page number. The number in bold type refers to the Table containing the wanted sign, and the page number indicates where the Table begins.

For example, a search for the letter *O* would begin in paragraph 1 with the instruction to turn to paragraph 2, and thence you would pass to numbers 5, 12, 30 and 61, where you would learn that this alphabetical sign is to be found in Table 12, which begins at page 86. The sequence for the letter *N* would similarly be paragraphs 1, 3, 8, 19, 48, 105, 189 and 269, where the required Table is seen to be No. 342, which begins on page 428.

Boundary lines and other such cartographical signs which may be curved or straight are classified as straight horizontal segments of them.

START HERE—

1	Signs with curves	turn to	2
	Rectilinear signs (without curves)		3
	Signs composed solely of dots (including complex dots. *See* pp. 19 and 21)		4
2	Consisting solely of curves		5
	With curves and straight lines (with or without dots)		6
	Consisting of curves and dots only		7
3	Consisting solely of straight lines		8
	Consisting of straight lines and dots		9

4 Single dots (with or without enclosed
     figures)   10
     Two or more dots   11

5 With closed (or nearly closed) curves   12
     With all curves open *   13

6 With closed (or nearly closed) curves   14
     With all curves open *   15

7 With closed (or nearly closed) curves   16
     With all curves open *   17

> * It should be remembered that the closure by means of a
> straight line of the space embraced by an open curve does not
> make it a closed curve. By definition, a 'curve' may not
> contain any straight elements whatever.

8 With closed (or nearly closed) figures   18
     With open angles   19
     With free straight lines only   20

9 With closed (or nearly closed) figures   21
     With lines forming open angles   22
     With free straight lines   23

10 Without enclosed figures (i.e. simple 'solid'
       dots)   24
     With enclosed figures   25

11 Two dots   26
     Three dots   27
     Four dots   28
     Five or six dots   **432**, p. 541
     Seven or more dots   29

12 Containing re-entrant curves   30
     Containing angles   31

13 Containing simple curves   32
     Consisting solely of complex open curves   33

14 Containing re-entrant curves   34
     Containing curved angles   35

15 Simple curves blocked * by other lines, at
        least one of which is straight   36
    Simple curves not blocked by other lines   37
    With complex open curves   38

    * *Blocked*—enclosing a space with the help of straight lines
    attached to the extremities of the curve. See *Definitions.*

16 Dots coincident with closed curves   39
    Dots enclosed by curved figures   40
    Dots outside closed curves   41

17 Dots coincident with curves   42
    Dots not coincident with curves   43

18 With triangles   44
    With squares or/and rectangles   45
    With other figures   46

19 With right angles   47
    With all angles other than right angles   48

20 Single or non-converging lines (i.e. parallel
        or in straight succession)   49
    Converging lines   50

21 With linear triangles   51
    All other closed figures   52

22 Circular or elliptical dots or points   53
    Triangular dots   54
    All other dots   55

23 With dot, or some dots, detached   56
    All dots attached   57

24 Circular dots   58
    Triangular, square or rectangular dots   **420,** p. 528
    All other dots   **421,** p. 530

25 Circular dots   **422,** p. 531
    All other dots   **423,** p. 532

Note: Lines with optional or uncertain orientation are treated as horizontal.

58 Large and medium dots   418, p. 523
    Points (and very small circular dots)   419, p. 525

59 Forming a right-angled triangle   426, p. 536
    Forming any other triangle   427, p. 537

60 Circles only (no other figures)   120
    Circles with other figures   121

61 Ellipses only (no other figures)   12, p. 86
    Ellipses with other figures   122
    Irregular figures   15, p. 90

62 With closed subsidiary figures   16, p. 91
    With gibbous figures, semicircles or hoops   123
    With arcs or/and hooks only (including
        double hooks)   124
    With complex open curves   125

63 With no more than one free end   23, p. 97
    With two free ends only   24, p. 98
    With three or more free ends   25, p. 99

64 With almonds   26, p. 100
    With crescents   126
    With hearts and other figures containing
        angles directed inwards   29, p. 102
    All other figures   30, p. 103

65 One gibbous figure   127
    Two or more gibbous figures   128

66 One semicircle or hoop (no other figure)   129
    One semicircle or hoop with other curves   39, p. 113
    Two or more semicircles or/and hoops (with
        or without other curves)   130

67 One arc or hook (no other figure)   131
    Two or more arcs or/and hooks * (no other
        figure)   132
    One arc or hook with other figures   133
    Two or more arcs or/and hooks * with other
        figures   52, p. 125

        * Including double hooks.
                        54

* That is to say, signs of variable shape which are not *necessarily* symmetrical, though an individual example may chance to be so. Such chances are likely to be rare.

* No part of the circumscribing circle is to be considered here.

138   With closed subsidiary figures *   **73,** p. 142
One to three right angles   **74,** p. 143
Four or more right angles   214
Other angles   **77,** p. 148
With one straight line only (with or without dots)   215
With two or more straight lines   216

       * No part of the circumscribing circle is to be considered here.

139   With other types of curve (open or closed)   217
With closed rectilinear figures or other subsidiary enclosed areas   218
With right angles   219
With other rectilinear angles   220
One straight line (with or without dots)   220
Two or more straight lines (with or without dots   222

140   With other types of curve   **108,** p. 177
With rectilinear angles   223
Straight lines without dots   224
With dots   **116,** p. 189

141   Not more than one free end   **117,** p. 191
Two or more free ends   **118,** p. 191

142   With one to four right angles   225
With five or more right angles   **121,** p. 194

143   With vertical or diagonal lines   226
With horizontal lines   227

144   With second ellipse or other curves blocked *   **127,** p. 199
With waves, S-shapes or spirals   **128,** p. 200
Other figures   **129,** p. 201

       * See *Definitions.*

145   At least one line vertical   228
At least one line diagonal   229
All lines horizontal   230

       Note: Lines with optional or uncertain orientation are treated as horizontal.

* See *Definitions.*

KEY

228 One straight line only   **130**, p. 202
     Two or more straight lines   **131**, p. 203

229 Line on left side of ellipse only   **132**, p. 204
     Line on right or both sides of ellipse   **133**, p. 205
     All other signs   **134**, p. 206

230 With no free ends   **135**, p. 206
     With free ends   **136**, p. 208

231 With other closed or blocked * areas   286
     With S-shapes or/and spirals   287
     Not more than two free ends   288
     Three free ends only   **144**, p. 214
     Four or more free ends   289
        * See *Definitions*.

232 Containing right angles   **147**, p. 216
     Not containing right angles   **148**, p. 217

233 Line dropping below curve   **156**, p. 225
     Line not dropping below curve   **157**, p. 225

234 No free ends   **159**, p. 227
     With free ends   **160**, p. 228

235 Not more than one free end   **161**, p. 229
     Two free ends only   290
     Three free ends   **164**, p. 232
     Four or more free ends   **165**, p. 232

236 Three free ends (and doubtful cases)   **173**, p. 242
     Four or more free ends   **174**, p. 243

237 Openings of all gibbous figures directed (in
          some degree) to right   **179**, p. 248
     All other signs   **180**, p. 249

238 Not more than two free ends   **185**, p. 253
     Three or more free ends   **186**, p. 254

239 Not more than two free ends   **187**, p. 255
     Three free ends only   **188**, p. 256
     Four or more free ends   **189**, p. 257

69

Note: When disposition seems to be immaterial, treat as horizontal.

279	Not more than four free ends	**87,** p. 156
	Five or more free ends	**88,** p. 157
280	With right angles	**89,** p. 158
	With no right angles	**90,** p. 158
281	Figures completely closed by straight lines	297
	Areas closed only by the circle	**95,** p. 163
282	Line running down from left side of circle	**101,** p. 169
	All other signs	**102,** p. 170
283	Line running from top of circle	**104,** p. 172
	All other signs	**105,** p. 173
284	All angles inside the circle	**109,** p. 178
	Not all angles inside the circle	**110,** p. 180
285	Not more than one free end	**112,** p. 185
	Two or more free ends	**113,** p. 185
286	Not more than one free end	**137,** p. 208
	Two or more free ends	**138,** p. 209
287	With loop or drop at foot of sign	**139,** p. 210
	With loop or drop not at foot of sign	**140,** p. 210
288	Extremities of loop crossed	298
	Extremities of loop not crossed	**143,** p. 214
289	With loop or drop at foot of sign	**145,** p. 215
	With loop or drop not at foot of sign	**146,** p. 215
290	With rectilinear angles	**162,** p. 230
	With no rectilinear angles	**163,** p. 231
291	With at least one vertical line	**204,** p. 271
	With no vertical lines	**205,** p. 272
292	Line vertical	**239,** p. 312
	Line diagonal or horizontal	**240,** p. 313

293	Not more than two free ends	**269,** p. 343
	Three free ends only	**270,** p. 345
	Four or more free ends	**271,** p. 346
294	At least one free end pointing upwards	**304,** p. 387
	Both free ends pointing downwards	**305,** p. 388
295	With thin lines only	**311,** p. 393
	With thick lines	**312,** p. 395
296	With other closed figures	**6,** p. 82
	With no other closed figures	**7,** p. 83
297	One closed area (in addition to the circle)	**93,** p. 161
	Two or more closed areas (in addition to the circle)	**94,** p. 163
298	Loop or drop forming (or level with) highest part of sign	**141,** p. 211
	Loop or drop not forming (or not level with) highest part of sign	**142,** p. 213

TABLES

Cl.I, Div.I, Ord.I, Fam.I, Gen.I

TABLE 1

1 High. (L. Red. Brit.) Pay attention to the directions here exhibited. (Brit. 1964) all vehicles prohibited in both directions; play street.

2 High. (L. Red. Inter.) Road closed; stop.

2·1 High. (L. Brit. Obsnt.) Eq. 1. (Sw.) Keep to the right (since 3rd September, 1967).

3 High. (L. White chalk.) No use calling here. (Tramps' 'smogger'.)

3·1 G/use. 'Ring', drawing attention to what it encloses.

4 Tel. Cavity resonator, double line.

5 Mus. Tempus perfectus; three-metre.

6 Elec. Instrument. (USA) motor or generator.

6·1 Engn. Measuring instrument.

75

6·2		*Geom.* Eq. 3363·7.
6·3		*Meteor.* Sky clear; barometer steady; calm; Beaufort No. o.
6·4		*Rlwy.* (USA.) Sump.
6·5		*Tel.* Circular wave-guide; window.
7	O	*Rom.* Sanserif or 'block' form of O.
8	O	*Geom.* (Co-ordinate.) Origin.
8·1		*Gk.* (Cap.) Omicron, 15th letter of the a., eq. Rom. O (short).
8·2		*Ir.* 13th letter of the a., eq. Rom. O.
8·3		*Mech.* Centre of rotation.
8·4		*Num.* (Arab.) Nought, zero, cipher; preceding one. (By extension) non-existent; worthless.
8·5		*Phar.* Pint (Lat. *octavius*).
8·6		*Phila.* Used.
8·7		*Phys.* Assumed standard; starting-point.
8·8		*Rom.* (Cap.) 15th letter of the a. (Med. ext. of Rom. num.) cardinal number 11. See 102.
8·9		*Rus.* (Cap.) O, 16th letter of the old a., 15th of the mod., eq. Rom. O (short).

TABLE 2

10   ◯   *Alch.* Alum. (*A Compleat Body of Chymistry*, 17th cent.)

10·1   *Astron.* Full moon.

10·2   *Bot.* Annual; monocarpous. (In inheritance chart) female individual.

10·3   *Cart.* (Ant. OS) Minor Rom. settlement.

10·4   *Chem.* Oxygen. (John Dalton's elements, 1806–1807); salt (Bergmann, 1783).

10·5   *Elec.* (In or with 1091, 1536 or 3844) carbon type. (In conjunction with 2484, 3765·1 or 4180) local battery. (On arch. plans. USA) ceiling outlet.

10·6   *Engn.* (Across pipe symbol) soldered or wiped joint. (USA) weld all round.

10·7   *Geom.* Eq. 3363·7.

10·8   *Mech.* Polar axis.

10·9   *Meteor.* Eq. 6·3.

10·01   *Mil.* Quartermaster.

10·02   *Ph.* Moabite (Tyrian). Eq. Rom. A. See also 3649·1.

10·03		*Print.* (Proof correction. USA.) Spell out (a number or abbr.).
10·04		*Rlwy.* (Brit.) Illuminated sign. (Locomotive formulæ) wheel. (USA) oil or gas well; non-stick marker normally not lighted; (locomotive formulæ) driving wheel without driving rod attached.
11	O	*Chem.* Fifteenth.
11·1		*Gk.* (l.c.) Omicron, 15th letter of the a., eq. Rom. o (short).
11·2		*Meteor.* Sky completely covered by cloud.
11·3		*Phon.* Half-close back vowel, o as in go.
11·4		*Rom.* (l.c.) 15th letter of the a. (*ITA*) o as in on.
11·5		*Rus.* (l.c.) O, 16th letter of the old a., 15th of the mod., eq. Rom. o (short).
12	**O**	*Ind. Num.* (Phila.) Nought, zero, eq. Arab. 0.

TABLE 3

15	O	*Astron.* Planet.
15·1		*Cart.* Well, spring; boundary post. (On rlwy. line) eq. 5974. (Rep.) plantation. (Fr.) church.
15·2		*Elec.* Removable terminal or connection.

Engn. Sealing run weld.

15·4   *Hyd.* (Inter.) Chimney, tower. (With descriptive initials) radio station.

15·5   *Min. Cryst.* Atom.

15·6   *Rlwy.* (Locomotive formulæ.) Pilot or trailer wheel.

16   o   *Arab.* The aspirate, the voiced h.

16·1   *Hyd.* Beacon.

16·2   *Mus.* (After a number) diminished.

17[†]   o   *Cz.* (Over the letter u) diacritical mark to lengthen the vowel.

17·1   *Dan.* (Over the letter a) l.c. form of Aa.

17·2   *Fr.* etc. (After a numeral) *-ième* (eq. nd, rd, th), signifying an ordinal number; *numéro.*

17·3   *Jap.* (Katakana syllabary.) Diacritical mark indicating a voiceless sound.

17·4   *Math.* Degrees of arc.

17·5   *Meteor.* Eq. 18.

17·6   *Mus.* (Stringed instruments.) Play as harmonic; play on open string.

17·7		*Phon.* Voiceless, breathed.
17·8		*Photo.* (After a numeral) Din, a system of speed assessment of a film or plate.
17·9		*Phys.* Degrees of temperature; electrically neutral.
17·01		*Print.* (After a numeral) number of folios per sheet.
17·02		*S/Nor.* (Over the letter A.) Diacritical mark to modify sound to long O.
18†	o	*Meteor.* Intensity slight.
18·1		*Mus.* (Stringed instruments.) Eq. 17·6.
18·2		*Phon.* Eq. 17·7.
18·3		*Rlwy.* (Continental locomotive formulæ) wheels not coupled.

TABLE 4

20	◎	*High.* (L. White chalk.) I have gone home. (Scout sign.)
21	◯	*Engn.* (Plumbing. USA.) Wash fountain.
22	◯	*Engn.* Ball or tube mill.

80

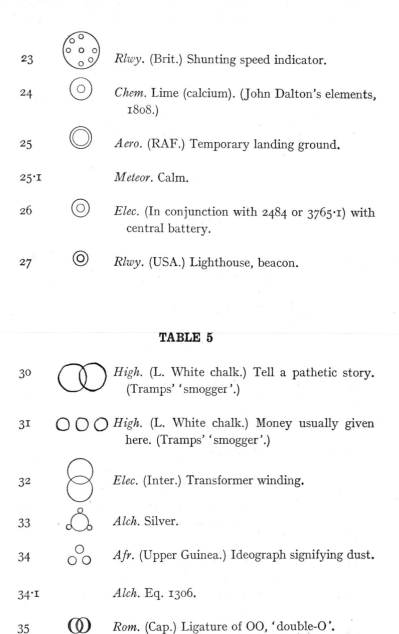

23   *Rlwy.* (Brit.) Shunting speed indicator.

24   *Chem.* Lime (calcium). (John Dalton's elements, 1808.)

25   *Aero.* (RAF.) Temporary landing ground.

25·1   *Meteor.* Calm.

26   *Elec.* (In conjunction with 2484 or 3765·1) with central battery.

27   *Rlwy.* (USA.) Lighthouse, beacon.

TABLE 5

30   *High.* (L. White chalk.) Tell a pathetic story. (Tramps' 'smogger'.)

31   *High.* (L. White chalk.) Money usually given here. (Tramps' 'smogger'.)

32   *Elec.* (Inter.) Transformer winding.

33   *Alch.* Silver.

34   *Afr.* (Upper Guinea.) Ideograph signifying dust.

34·1   *Alch.* Eq. 1306.

35   *Rom.* (Cap.) Ligature of OO, 'double-O'.

36	♂	*Astron.* Eq. 1518.
37	8	*Num.* (Arab.) Eight, the eighth cardinal number.
38		*Geol.* Conglomerate; pebble-bed.
38·1		*Soil/m.* Gravel.

TABLE 6

40		*Alch.* Marcasite, sulphide of iron. (*A Compleat Body of Chymistry*, 17th cent.)
41	Ϙ	*Rom.* (Cap.) See 66·2.
42		*Am.* (Cherokee syllabary.) Eq. Rom. SU.
43	*g*	*Elec.* Conductance.
43·1		*Mech.* Eq. 123·2.
43·2		*Meteor.* Dull.
43·3		*Phon.* Eq. 1922, but used only in languages where 1922 is required particularly to represent an advanced g.
43·4		*Phys.* Vapour in contact with liquid.
43·5		*Rom.* (l.c.) 7th letter of the a.
44	6	*Gk.* (l.c.) Eq. 1697·4.

TABLE 7

45		*Astron.* Eq. 600.
46		*Ind. Num.* (Phila.) Eq. Arab. 7.
47		*Num.* (Arab.) Eq. 3400.
48		*Num.* (Arab.) Eq. 3401.
49		*Am.* (Cherokee syllabary.) Eq. Rom. DA.
50		*Sh., Pitman's.* Thousand, thousandth.
51		*Sh., Pitman's.* (Thin.) Francs.
52		*OE.* (l.c.) Eq. Rom. d.
53		*Cab.* Eq. Heb. vau, 2707.
54†		*ME. MS.* (Abbr.) -us.

TABLE 8

60		*Rel.* Symbol of the Trinity.
61		*Engn.* (Plumbing. USA.) Pedestal-type urinal.
62		*Engn.* (Heating and ventilating. USA.) Rotary compressor with enclosed crank-case, belted.
63		*Rom.* (Cap.) Cursive form of Q.

83

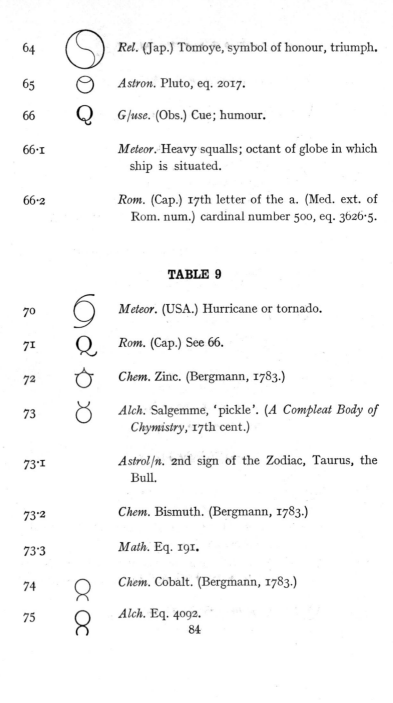

64   *Rel.* (Jap.) Tomoye, symbol of honour, triumph.

65   *Astron.* Pluto, eq. 2017.

66   *G/use.* (Obs.) Cue; humour.

66·1   *Meteor.* Heavy squalls; octant of globe in which ship is situated.

66·2   *Rom.* (Cap.) 17th letter of the a. (Med. ext. of Rom. num.) cardinal number 500, eq. 3626·5.

TABLE 9

70   *Meteor.* (USA.) Hurricane or tornado.

71   *Rom.* (Cap.) See 66.

72   *Chem.* Zinc. (Bergmann, 1783.)

73   *Alch.* Salgemme, 'pickle'. (*A Compleat Body of Chymistry,* 17th cent.)

73·1   *Astrol/n.* 2nd sign of the Zodiac, Taurus, the Bull.

73·2   *Chem.* Bismuth. (Bergmann, 1783.)

73·3   *Math.* Eq. 191.

74   *Chem.* Cobalt. (Bergmann, 1783.)

75   *Alch.* Eq. 4092.

76	♉	*Mil.* 2nd Army Group, Royal Artillery.
77	♉	*Aero.* (RAF.) Aircraft park.
78	♂	*OE.* Eq. 1104·1.

TABLE 10

80	♊	*Nav. Arch.* Section amidships.
81	Ⓒ	*Chem.* Copper. (John Dalton's elements, 1806–1807.)
81·1		*Nav. Arch.* Resistance constant; Froude's coefficient; performance.
81·2		*Print.* (Inter.) Copyright.
82	Ⓢ	*Chem.* Sulphur. (John Dalton's elements, 1806–1807.)
82·1		*Nav. Arch.* Wetted-surface constant.
83	∝	*Gk.* Eq. 1740·5.

TABLE 11

| 90 | ⚬⚬⚬ | *Insig.* (Inter.) Symbol of the Olympic Games. |
| 91 | ⊘ | *Afr.* (Cameroons.) Ideograph signifying food on a plate. |

85

92	⌢⌢	*Alch.* Gold.
93	☍	*Astrol/n.* (Obs.) Eq. 1547.
94	℧℧	*Alch.* Purify. (*A Compleat Body of Chymistry,* 17th cent.)
95	◠ ◯	*Alch.* Sublimate. (*A Compleat Body of Chymistry,* 17th cent.)
96	℧℧	*Astron.* Descending node.
97	☊	*Astron.* Ascending node.
97·1		*Elec.* Eq. 1226·1.
97·2		*Log.* Eq. 2380·1.
97·3		*Mech.* Angular velocity (esp. of gyroscopes).
98	⊙∿∿∿	*Hyd.* (Inter.) Submarine sound signal (not emitted from a light vessel or buoy).

Cl.I, Div.I, Ord.I, Fam.I, Gen.II

TABLE 12

100	◯	*Cart.* Eq. 144.
100·1		*Geol.* Eq. 101·1.
101	◯	*Cart.* Eq. 144.

101·1		*Geol. Roche moutonnée,* not striated.
102	O	*Bot.* Wanting.
102·1		*Log.* Null class.
102·2		*Num.* (Arab.) Eq. 8·4. Cursive form of 8·4.
102·3		*Rom.* (Cap.) 15th letter of the a. See under 8.
103	*O*	*Astron.* Olber's *M.*
103·1		*It.* (Cap.) Eq. Rom. O.
103·2		*Nav. Arch.* Froude's coefficient of friction.
103·3		*Num.* (Arab.) Eq. 8·4. Cursive form of 8·4.
103·4		*Phila.* Eq. 8·6.
104	OO	*Bot.* Eq. 239.
105	⊂⊃	*Mus.* Eq. 107.
106	*O*	*Sh., Gregg's.* Vowel, a.
107	⊂⊃	*Mus.* Semibreve.
108	*o*	*It.* (l.c.) Eq. Rom. o. See 11.
109	*o*	*Sh., Gregg's.* Vowel, e or i.
110†	**0**	*Math.* (Theory of infinite sets.) Null. (Cantor, 1874.)

TABLE 13

115   *Ger.* (Cap.) Cursive form of 2047.

116   *H/mrk.* Silver date mark, 1699.

117   *Mayan Num.* Eq. Arab. 20; to the base 20.

118   *Egy.* (Hier.) Eq. Rom. DJ, S, Z.

119   *Rus.* (Cap.) Cursive form of 1362·6.

120   *It.* (Cap.) Eq. Rom. Q. See 1591.

121   *It.* (Cap.) Eq. Rom. Q. See 1591.

122   *It.* (l.c.) Eq. 1580·1.

123   *Elec.* Conductance; eq. 2251·1.

123·1   *It.* (l.c.) Eq. Rom. g.

123·2   *Mech.* Acceleration due to gravity.

123·3   *Phys.* Osmotic coefficient; gyromagnetic ratio; Lande factor; stati tical weight or degeneracy; Gibbs function per unit mass.

124   *Gk.* (l.c.) Eq. 348·3.

TABLE 14

128	 ⊘	*Am.* (Cherokee syllabary.) Eq. Rom. NA.
128·1		*Rus.* (Cap./l.c. Obs.) Eq. 1676·1.
129	 ϴ	*Rus.* (Cap./l.c. Obs.) Cursive form of 1676·1.
130	𝒶	*Ger.* (Cap.) Cursive form of 314.
131	Ư	*Am.* (Cherokee syllabary.) Eq. Rom. U.
132	 Ơ	*Am.* (Cherokee syllabary.) Eq. Rom. NÖ.
133	 σ	*Print.* Eq. 1725.
134	𝒬	*It.* (Cap.) Eq. Rom. Q. See 1591.
135	∂	*Cal.* Partial derivative.
135·1		*Rom.* (l.c.) Cursive form of d.
135·2		*Rus.* (l.c.) It. and cursive form of 2108·1. See also 1582·1.
136	б	*Rus.* (l.c.) Beh, 2nd letter of the a., eq. Rom. b.
137	۹	*Arab. Num.* Nine, eq. 3400.
138	�	*Gk.* (l.c.) Eq. 165·5.
139	σ	*Gk.* (l.c.) Eq. 1186·4.
140	 Ο	*Ger.* (Cap./l.c.) Cursive form of 311 and 2106.

140·1   *Rom.* (Cap./l.c.) Cursive form of o.

140·2   *Rus.* (Cap./l.c.) Cursive form of 8·9 and **11·5**.

141 †   *ME. MS.* (Abbr.) -ur, -urn.

142   *Gk.* (l.c.) Eq. 1148·5.

142·1   *Phys.* (Nuclear.) Eq. 1148·01.

TABLE 15

144   *Cart.* (Very variable. Associated with a number.) Contour, contour line, connecting together points at the same height above, or depth below, sea-level.

145   *Cart.* (Red. Ant. OS.) Celtic fields.

146   *Engn.* (USA.) Line vibration absorber.

147   *Numis.* Mint mark, eglantine.

148   *Numis.* Mint mark, helmet.

149   *Bot.* Eq. 283.

150   *Mil.* Pack-horse.

151   *Cart.* ('25-inch' map, across stream. OS.) Stepping stones.

TABLE 16

155   *𝒟*   *Rom.* (Cap.) Cursive form of D.

155·1   *Rus.* (Cap.) Cursive form of 2108.

156   *ℛ*   *Ger.* (Cap.) Cursive form of 2212·1.

156·1   *Rom.* (Cap.) Cursive form of R. See 649 and 655.

157   *𝒮*   *Rom.* (Cap.) Cursive form of S.

158   *Egy.* (Hier.) Eq. Rom. H.

TABLE 17

160   *Am.* (Cherokee syllabary.) Eq. Rom. GWÖ.

161   *Am.* (Cherokee syllabary.) Eq. Rom. KA.

162   *Am.* (Cherokee syllabary.) Eq. Rom. WU.

163   *Num.* (Arab.) Cursive form of numeral 8.

164   *Cal.* Eq. 135.

165   *Aero.* Angle of set of control surfaces.

165·1		*Astron.* Declination; differential correction.
165·2		*Chem.* Fourth.
165·3		*Elec.* Dielectric loss angle.
165·4		*Engn.* Specific deflection. (Chemical) volumetric diffusivity.
165·5		*Gk.* (l.c.) Delta, 4th letter of the a., eq. Rom. d; cardinal number 4.
165·6		*Math.* Variation; increment; finite difference operator.
165·7		*Nav. Arch.* Deflection.
165·8		*Opt.* Angle of minimum deviation; *cf.* 3584·7.
165·9		*Phys.* Total elongation; deflection; angle of deviation; deviation difference in phase; frequency deviation; piezoelectric strain constant, modulus. (Heat) total thermal expansion.
165·01		*Tel.* Logarithmic decrement.
166	δ	*Gk.* Eq. 165·5.
167	$\wp$	*Phon.* Voiceless alveolo-palatal fricative consonant, as *si* in Polish *gesia*.
168	δ	*Phon.* Turned-delta, labialized th (soft).
169	ꙍ	*ITA.* (Augmented Rom.) oo as in food.

TABLE 18

175		*Ger.* (Cap.) Cursive form of 2867.
176		*Ger.* (Cap.) Cursive form of 2868.
177		*Ger.* (Cap.) Cursive form of 3211.
178		*Ger.* (Cap.) Cursive form of 618.
179		*Ger.* (Cap.) Cursive form of 561.
180		*Num.* (Arab. 10th cent. Sp.) Eq. mod. 4.
181		*Ger.* (l.c.) Cursive form of 2825.
182		*Ger.* (l.c.) Cursive form of 1606.
182·1		*Rom.* (l.c.) Cursive form of z.

TABLE 19

185		*MS.* (Law.) Mark made on the outside of a barrister's brief to show that the case is concluded.
186		*Ind. Num.* (3rd cent. B.C.) Eq. Arab. 6.
187		*Alch.* Eq. 1251.
188		*Cab.* Eq. Heb. resh, 4119.

189		*Arab.* Ha, 26th letter of the a., eq. Rom. H.
189·1		*Cop.* Eq. Rom. O.
190		*Math.* Varies as; is proportional to.
191		*Math.* The amount by which $Sn > \log n$ when Sn is the sum of n terms of a harmonic progression and n is very large.

TABLE 20

192		*G/use.* (APO. Size and shape very variable.) Balloon, enclosing omitted matter. (On drawings, enclosing words to be taken as spoken.)
193		*Rom.* (l.c.) Cursive form of e.
194		*Print.* Eq. 1725.
195		*Egy.* (Hier.) Eq. Rom. TH.
196		*Alch.* 'Note of distillation'. (*A Compleat Body of Chymistry*, 17th cent.)
197		*Astron.* (Obs.) Eq. 1726.
198		*Ger.* (l.c.) Cursive form of 4647.
198·1		*Rom.* (l.c.) Cursive form of l.
199		*Ger.* (l.c.) Cursive form of 565.

200	φ	*Gk.* (l.c.) Cursive form of 1377·5.
201		*Num.* (Arab.) Cursive form of numeral 6.
202		*Math.* Cursive form of 4753.
203	γ	*Gk.* (l.c.) Eq. 2727·5.
204		*Lat.* (Celtic.) Eq. Rom. D.
204·1		*Math.* Eq. 135.
205		*Sh., Gregg's.* Diphthong oi.
206		*Sh., Gregg's.* Diphthong ow.
207	e	*Astron.* Eccentricity of orbit.
207·1		*Engn.* (Hydraulics. USA.) Elasticity; kinematic K/ρ.
207·2		*It.* (l.c.) Eq. Rom. e.
207·3		*Math.* Base of natural logarithms, 2·71828. . . . (From L. *E*uler, 1707–1783.)
207·4		*Mech.* Direct strain.
207·5		*Nav. Arch.* Elongation.
207·6		*Phys.* Coefficient of restitution, resilience. (With negative sign) electronic charge. (Nuclear) electron.

207·7		*Rom.* (l.c.) Eq. 193.
207·8		*Rus.* (l.c.) Cursive form of 2220·4. (With 6080·4) cursive form of 2224.
208	σ	*Sh., Gregg's.* Diphthong û.

TABLE 21

209		*Ger.* (Cap.) Cursive form of 313·1.
210		*Math.* (Obs.) Equals. (Descartes, 17th cent.)
211		*Com. Mon.* Eq. 1717.
212		*Rom.* (Cap.) Cursive form of L.
213		*Rom.* (Cap./l.c.) Cursive form of V.
214		*Astron.* Coefficient of secondary spectrum.
214·1		*Gk.* (Obs.) Eq. 892.
215		*Rom.* (Cap.) Cursive form of Q.
216		*Gk.* (l.c.) Eq. 2727·5.
217		*It.* (l.c.) Eq. Rom. w. See 2624.
218		*It.* (l.c.) Eq. Rom. a. See 1920·5.

TABLE 22

220		*Ger.* (Cap.) Cursive form of 350.
220·1		*Rom.* (Cap.) Cursive form of Z.
221		*Ger.* (Cap.) Cursive form of 562·1.
222		*Rom.* (Cap.) Cursive form of Q.
223		*Rom.* (Cap.) Cursive form of C.
223·1		*Rus.* (Cap.) Cursive form of 321·1.
224		*Mus.* Eq. 3413.
225		*Math.* Weierstrass's excess function.
226		*Am.* (Cherokee syllabary.) Eq. Rom. GWI.
227		*Am.* (Cherokee syllabary.) Eq. Rom. WO.
228		*Num.* (Arab.) Cursive form of figure 2.

TABLE 23

230		*Pot.* China mark, Limbach, Germany.
231		*Am.* (Cherokee syllabary.) Eq. Rom. DÖ.
232		*Am.* (Cherokee syllabary.) Eq. Rom. WE.
233		*Am.* (Cherokee syllabary.) Eq. Rom. DLA.

234	8	*Num.* (Arab.) Print. and cursive form of eight.
235	♂	*Am.* (Cherokee syllabary.) Eq. Rom. LE.
236	♂	*Gk.* (Obs.) Eq. 1697·4.
237	♂	*Ir. & Rom.* (l.c.) Cursive form of 1951·2.
238	œ	*It.* (l.c.) Eq. 1709·1.
239	∞	*Bot.* Indefinite number of. (Of stamens) more than twenty.
239·1		*Math.* Infinity, an infinite quantity. (First used by Wallis, 1655.)
239·2		*Meteor.* Haze; visibility from 1,100 to 2,200 yards.
240	∞	*Math.* (Or reversed) 'Lazy-8'. Eq. 239·1.

TABLE 24

245	ℒ	*Ger.* (Cap.) Cursive form of 622·1.
245·1		*Rom.* (Cap.) Cursive form of L.
246	ℰ	*Elec.* Electric force.
246·1		*Rom.* (Cap.) Cursive form of E.
246·2		*Rus.* (Cap.) Cursive form of 4385·6. (With 6080·4) cursive form of 5654.

247 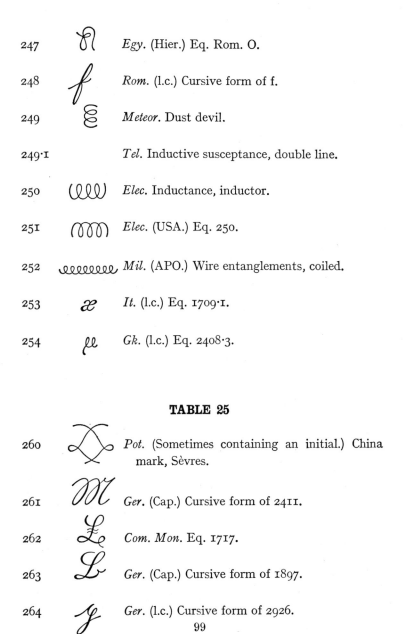 *Egy.* (Hier.) Eq. Rom. O.

248 *Rom.* (l.c.) Cursive form of f.

249 *Meteor.* Dust devil.

249·1 *Tel.* Inductive susceptance, double line.

250 *Elec.* Inductance, inductor.

251 *Elec.* (USA.) Eq. 250.

252 *Mil.* (APO.) Wire entanglements, coiled.

253 *It.* (l.c.) Eq. 1709·1.

254 *Gk.* (l.c.) Eq. 2408·3.

TABLE 25

260 *Pot.* (Sometimes containing an initial.) China mark, Sèvres.

261 *Ger.* (Cap.) Cursive form of 2411.

262 *Com. Mon.* Eq. 1717.

263 *Ger.* (Cap.) Cursive form of 1897.

264 *Ger.* (l.c.) Cursive form of 2926.

99

TABLE 26

270		*Cab.* Virginity.
270·1		*Meteor.* Air clear; exceptional visibility.
271		*Nav.* Eq. 1275.
272		*Math.* Quantic whose terms have the same numerical coefficients as a corresponding expression formed by involution.
273	§	*Bot.* Naturalized. Section of a genus; variety of a species.
273·1		*Print. Punc.* Section mark. (Ger.) Paragraph. Also used as a mark of reference. (A modified S.)
274		*Egy.* (Hier.) Mouth. Eq. Rom. R.
274·1		*Meteor.* (USA.) Visibility reduced by smoke.
275		*Arab. Num.* Five, eq. 2298.
276		*Rel.* Eq. 1880.
277		*Egy.* (Hier.) Moon.
278		*Meteor.* Mirage.

TABLE 27

280	☾	*Cab.* Moon. Sign of the archangel Gabriel.
280·1		*Alch.* Silver. Waxing moon.
280·2		*Astron.* Moon, last quarter.
281		*Astron.* Eq. 282; eq. 3363·2.
282		*Astron.* Quintile; eq. 3363·2.
283		*Bot.* (In floral diagram) petal.
284		*Alch.* Waning moon. (Before 500 A.D.) Mercury.
284·1		*Astron.* Moon, first quarter.
284·2		*Bot.* Biennial.
284·3		*Min.* Silver ore.
285		*Astron.* Moon's longitude.
286		*Astron.* Eq. 285.

TABLE 28

290		*Alch.* Moon. (*Theatrum Chemicum*, Strasbourg, 1659–61.)

101

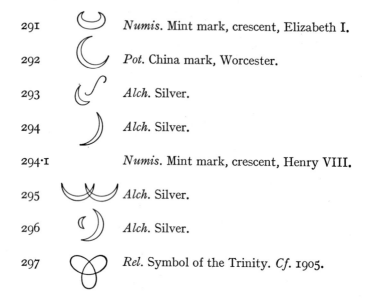

291		*Numis.* Mint mark, crescent, Elizabeth **I.**
292		*Pot.* China mark, Worcester.
293		*Alch.* Silver.
294		*Alch.* Silver.
294·1		*Numis.* Mint mark, crescent, Henry VIII.
295		*Alch.* Silver.
296		*Alch.* Silver.
297		*Rel.* Symbol of the Trinity. *Cf.* 1905.

TABLE 29

300		*Phon.* Close back vowel, oo as in book.
301		*Phon.* (Obs.) Eq. 1580.
302		*Bot.* (In floral diagram) stamen, the dent indicating the position of dehiscence of the anther.
302·1		*Phon.* (Obs.) eq. 1580.
303		*Bot.* Eq. 302.
304		*Sh.*, *Gregg's.* Diphthong, ī.
305		*Arab. Num.* Five, eq. 2298.

305·1		*Numis.* Mint mark, heart.
306	ϖ	*Math.* Eq. 1900.
307		*Egy.* (Hier.) Eq. Rom. SH.
308		*Cart.* ('25-inch' map. OS.) Deciduous tree.

TABLE 30

310	a	*Rom.* (l.c.) 1st letter of the a. See 2153·1.
311	D	*Ger.* (Cap.) 15th letter of the a., eq. Rom. O.
312	D	*Rom.* (Cap.) Cursive form of D.
312·1		*Rus.* (Cap.) Cursive form of 2108.
313	D	*Elec.* & *Mag.* Current intensity in strength per unit cross-section.
313·1		*Ger.* (Cap.) 4th letter of the a., eq. Rom. D.
314	Ω	*Ger.* (Cap.) 17th letter of the a., eq. Rom. Q.
315	{	*Bot.* (In floral diagram) sepal.
316	○	*Engn.* (Terminating pipe symbol, USA.) Bell and spigot bull plug.

TABLE 31

320	**C**	*Elec.* Coulomb. Permittance.
320·1		*Mus.* Quadruple or common time, with four crotchets in a bar.
320·2		*Phar.* Gallon (Lat. *congius*).
320·3		*Rom.* (Cap.) 3rd letter of the a. Cardinal number 100 (Lat. *centum*).
320·4		*Rus.* (Cap.) Eq. 321·1.
321	**Ɔ**	*Rom.* (Cap.) Eq. 320·3.
321·1		*Rus.* (Cap.) Ess, 19th letter of the old a., 18th of the mod., eq. Rom. S.
322	**Ɔ**	*Rom. Num.* (Used in conjunction with I) Turned-C, eq. 1975·1. (Following IƆ) multiply by ten.
323	**C**	*Rlwy.* (On symbol for wicket gate. Brit.) Gate locks.
324	**c**	*ME. MS.* (Abbr.) -s. (Derived from Gk. sigma, 365.)
324·1		*Meteor.* Detached, opening clouds; sky partly visible but more than one-quarter covered.
324·2		*Phon.* Voiceless palatal plosive consonant, as k in Persian yak.

324·3		*Phys.* Velocity of light *in vacuo*, $2 \cdot 9979.10^{10}$ cm./sec.; specific heat; neutral axis.
324·4		*Rom.* (l.c.) 3rd letter of the a. (*ITA*) c hard.
324·5		*Rus.* (l.c.) Eq. 321·1.
325	**C**	*Ir.* 3rd letter of the a., eq. Rom. C.
326†	c	*Math.* Radian, radians.
327	ɔ	*Phon.* 'Turned-c'. Half-open back vowel, as o in pot.
328	ꙍ	*Am.* (Cherokee syllabary.) Eq. Rom. GWE.

TABLE 32

330	*C*	*Chem.* Concentration.
330·1		*Elec.* Capacitance.
330·2		*Engn.* Shear modulus; deflection coefficient; eccentricity coefficient; factor of safety. (Hydraulics) Chezy coefficient of roughness; modulus of rigidity.
330·3		*It.* (Cap.) Eq. Rom. C.
330·4		*Phys.* (Heat) cooling effect.
330·5		*Therm.* Heat capacity per mole.

331   *C*   *It.* (Cap.) Eq. Rom. C.

332   *Ϭ*   *Rus.* (Cap./l.c.) Cursive form of 340 and 342. See also 1788·1.

333   *ȝ*   *Num.* (Arab.) Eq. 3454.

334   *c*   *Astron.* Collimation error of transit instrument.

334·1   *Chem.* Eq. 330.

334·2   *Engn.* Distance of centres of gravity from a given axis. (Structural) intensity of compressive stress. (Hydraulics) coefficient of discharge.

334·3   *It.* (l.c.) Eq. Rom. c.

334·4   *Nav. Arch.* Chord.

334·5   *Phys.* Eq. 324·3. (Heat) co-aggregation volume; specific heat.

334·6   *Rom.* (l.c.) Cursive form of c.

334·7   *Rus.* (l.c.) It. and cursive form of 321·1.

335   *ʋ*   *It.* (l.c.) Swash form eq. Rom. v. See 2696.

336†   *ᴗ*   *Acc.* Eq. 388·4.

337   *&*   *Print.* (Abbr.) Eq. 1710.

338   *ꝫ*   *Rus.* (l.c.) Cursive form of 2295.

TABLE 33

340	Ȝ	*Rus.* (Cap.) Zeh, 8th letter of the a., eq. Rom. Z.
341	Ɜ	*Num.* (Arab.) Eq. 3454.
342	з	*Rus.* (l.c.) Eq. 340.
343	ع	*Arab.* Ayin, 18th letter of the a., a deep guttural or glottal sound with no Rom. eq. See 376 and 2505.
344	з	*Num.* (Arab.) Eq. 3454.
344·1		*Phon.* 'Reversed ϵ'. Half-open central vowel.
345	ε	*Gk.* (l.c.) Eq. 429·5.
345·1		*Phon.* Half-open front vowel, a as in fate.
346 †	³	*Math.* Cubed.
347	ω	*Gk.* (Cap.) Eq. 1226·2.
348	ω	*Astron.* Longitude of perihelion.
348·1		*Chem.* Twenty-fourth. The end (esp. of a chain of carbon atoms).
348·2		*Elec.* Eq. 1226·1.
348·3		*Gk.* (l.c.) Omega, 24th letter of the a., eq. Rom. o (long). Cardinal number 800.

348·4   *ITA*. (Augmented Rom.) oo as in book.

348·5   *Mag*. Specific magnetic rotatory power; Verdet constant.

348·6   *Math*. Solid angle. Cube root of unity. Transfinite ordinal number.

348·7   *Phys*. Angular velocity; angular frequency.

348·8   *Pros*. Two syllables taken together as one mora.

TABLE 34

350   𝔷   *Ger*. (Cap.) 26th letter of the a., eq. Rom. Z.

351   𝔵   *Alch*. 'Reversed *x*', eq. 1001.

352   𝔵   *Chem*. Mole fraction.

352·1   *Elec*. Reactance; mass susceptibility.

352·2   *Engn*. Horizontal axis.

352·3   *G/use*. Unknown or unidentified person, object, quantity, quality, etc.

352·4   *Geom*. (Co-ordinate.) Cartesian co-ordinate.

352·5   *It*. (l.c.) Eq. Rom. x.

352·6   *Log*. Any one of a class; a variable individual.

352·7   *Math.* Unknown quantity.

352·8   *Rom.* (l.c.) Cursive form of x.

352·9   *Rus.* (l.c.) It. and cursive form of 4876·2.

353 † x *Log.* For all values of x.

Cl.I, Div.I, Ord.II, Fam.I, Gen.II

                          TABLE 35

360   ⌣   *High.* (L. White chalk.) Keep away; useless to call. (Tramps' 'smogger'.)

361   (*Mus. Tempus imperfectus,* four-metre. Cf. 320·1.

362   )   *Engn.* (At end of pipe symbol. USA.) Bell and spigot cap. (Across pipe symbol) cross-over.

363   )   *Astron.* Eq. 284·1.

364   (*Astron.* Eq. 280·2.

365   C   *Gk.* (Cap.) Early eq. 4861·1.

366   ɔ   *Phon.* (After a letter.) Lips well rounded.

366·1   *Sh., Pitman's.* Initial w.

367   c   *Phon.* (After a letter.) Lips well spread.

368 †   c   *Phon.* (Under a letter.) Esp. open vowel.

TABLE 36

370   )   *High.* (L. White chalk.) A good haystack or barn for sleeping: 'Greenfields Hotel—no bill and no bell.' (Tramps' 'smogger'.)

371   )   *Print.* Eq. 673.

372   (*Mil.* Gun emplacement (individual).

373   (*Chem.* (With other symbols.) Carbonated (1795).

374   ᲈ   *Sh. Gregg's.* Vowel, oo.

375   ᴗ   *Sh., Gregg's.* Vowel, o.

376 †   ʿ   *Arab.* (Used in Rom. scripts.) Ayin. See 343.

376·1   *Gk.* Asper, an aspirate or spirit indicating pronunciation with an h.

377 †   ˓   *OE. MS.* Diacritical mark used in some MSS. to indicate short vowels.

377·1   *Pol.* Diacritical mark attached to a and e to nasalize the sounds.

378 †   ˒   *Arab.* The hamza or glottal stop.

378·1   *Gk.* Lenis, a negative aspirate or spirit indicating the absence of an h in pronunciation.

379 †   ˀ   *Rus.* (After 2006·1 or 2043.) To be followed by a very short i.

TABLE 37

380	⌣	*Bot.* (In floral diagram.) Bract.
381	‿	*Sh.*, *Pitman's.* (Thin.) n.
382	‿	*Sh.*, *Pitman's.* (Thick.) ng.
383	‿	*Sh.*, *Gregg's.* r.
384	‿	*Sh.*, *Gregg's.* l.
385	⌣	*Math.* (Ital. obs.) See 2439.
385·1		*Mus.* (Between two letters standing for notes.) The interval between the notes indicated is a semitone.
386	∪	*Astron.* Polar distance.
386·1		*Chem.* Twentieth.
386·2		*Gk.* (l.c.) Upsilon, 20th letter of the a., eq. Rom. u. Cardinal number 400.
386·3		*Phys.* (Obsnt.) Neutrino.
387	∪	*Cart.* (Ant. OS.) Rom. shale-workings.
388 †	∪	*Ger.* (Over a cursive diphthong containing an i.) The Umlaut, eq. 6080·1.
388·1		*Log.* Reversal relation between two terms; converse.

111

388·2   *Phon.* Consonantal vowel; the weaker element of a diphthong. (Over a nasal consonant) very short and to be combined with following plosive. (Preceding syllable in Annamese) rising tone, breathy voice variety.

388·3   *Pros.* Mora, the unit of metre; the short foot or syllable.

388·4   *Acc.* Breve, indicating a short vowel.

TABLE 38

390   *High.* (L. Obsnt. Brit.) Hump bridge. Cf. 2740.

391   *Am.* Ideograph signifying sky.

391·1   *Engn.* Seal weld.

391·2   *Meteor.* Rainbow.

392   *Chem.* (Obs.) Phosphorus. (J. H. Hassenfratz and P. A. Adet in *Méthode de nomenclature chimique*, by A. Lavoisier *et al.*, 1787.)

393   *Afr.* (Bamun script.) Stone.

394   *Sh., Pitman's.* Diphthong, ū (as in music) written in the third vowel place. (Note: The actual position depends on the other strokes with which it is used.)

395 [†]   *Gk. Acc.* Circumflex accent, used to denote a rising and falling in a long syllable.

395·1   *Phon.* (Attached to a consonant.) Voiced implosive.

TABLE 39

400   *Num.* (Arab.) Continental equivalent of 2285.

401   *Arab. Num.* Four, eq. 3527.

402   *Ger.* (l.c.) Cursive form of 2632.

403   *Rom.* (Cap.) Gothic form of E.

404   *Cab.* Eq. Rom. Y.

405   *Cab.* Eq. Rom. O.

406   *Astron.* Zenith distance corrected for refraction. (With negative sign) right ascension of north pole of the equator.

406·1   *Chem.* Fourteenth.

406·2   *Elec.* Electrokinetic potential.

406·3   *Gk.* (l.c.) Xi, 14th letter of the a., eq. Rom. x. Cardinal number 60.

406·4   *Math.* Cartesian co-ordinate. Term in Cayley's solution of a general cubic equation.

113

407   Ⴟ   *Gk.* (l.c.) Eq. 406·3.

408   ⟫   *Mus.* Eq. 2709.

409   *Am.* Ideograph signifying rain.

TABLE 40

415   *Alch.* Fire. (*Theatrum Chemicum*, Strasbourg, 1659–61.)

416   *Meteor.* Altocumulus clouds. 'Mackerel', high stratocumulus.

416·1   *Pros.* Two syllables taken together as one and a half moræ.

417   *Pros.* Tribrach.

418   *Meteor.* Altocumulus clouds growing out of cumulus.

419   *Ger.* (l.c.) Cursive form of 2632.

420   *Arab.* Sin, 12th letter of the a., eq. Rom. S.

421 †   *Phon.* Labialization.

TABLE 41

426   ⌇   *Num.* (Arab. 16th century, London and elsewhere.) Eq. mod. numeral 5.

427   ﻉ   *Arab.* Eq. 343.

428   3   *Ger.* (l.c.) Eq. 1606.

428·1   *Num.* (Arab.) Cursive form of numeral 3.

429   ε   *Aero.* Angle of downwash.

429·1   *Astron.* Obliquity of ecliptic; eccentricity; mean longitude in orbit; angle of emergence of diffusely reflected light; production of atomic energy per gramme per second.

429·2   *Chem.* Fifth.

429·3   *Elec.* Dielectric constant; electrode potential; specific inductive capacity.

429·4   *Engn.* Arm of eccentricity.

429·5   *Gk.* (l.c.) 5th letter of the a. eq. Rom. e (short).

429·6   *Log.* Is, denoting membership of a class.

429·7   *Mag.* Permittivity; coefficient of shape.

429·8   *Math.* Eq. 207·3.

429·9   *Nav. Arch.* Elongation per unit length; strain.

| 429·01 | | *Phon.* Half-open front vowel, a as in fate. |
| 430 † |)c | *Gk.* (Obs.) 'Horns'. Lenis (378·1) and asper (376·1), spirits formerly used over double-rho. |

Cl.I, Div.I, Ord.II, Fam.I, Gen.III

TABLE 42

435	)	*Num.* (Arab. 2nd century. Hindu.) Eq. mod. 7.
436	)	*Arab.* Ra, 10th letter of the a., eq. Rom. R.
437	)	*Bot.* Winding to left.
437·1		*Math.* See 490·5.
437·2		*Punc.* See 490·8.
438	)	*Sh., Pitman's.* (Thin.) s.
439	)	*Sh., Pitman's.* (Thick.) z.
440	(	*Bot.* Winding to right.
440·1		*Math.* See 490·5.
440·2		*Punc.* See 490·8.
441	(	*Sh., Pitman's.* (Thin.) th (hard, as in thin). Thousand, thousandth.

442   (*Sh., Pitman's.* (Thick.) th (soft, as in the).

443 †   '   *Punc.* Eq. 3422·3.

TABLE 43

450   *High.* (L. Brit.) Bend in the road.

451   *Sh., Pitman's.* (Thin.) r (terminal sound).

452   *Sh., Pitman's.* (Thin.) sh.

453   *Sh., Pitman's.* (Thick.) zh.

454   *Sh., Pitman's.* (Thin.) f.

455   *Sh., Pitman's.* (Thick.) v.

456   *Arab. Num.* One, eq. 5135.

457   *Sh., Gregg's.* b.

458   *Sh., Pitman's.* (Thin.) l.

459   *Sh.. Gregg's.* v.

460   *Sh., Gregg's.* f.

461   *Sh., Gregg's.* p.

462   *Jap.* (Katakana syllabary.) Eq. Rom. NO.

| 463 | ⌣ | *Sh.*, *Gregg's*. Eq. 464. |

| 464 | ⌐ | *Sh.*, *Gregg's*. th. |

465 † ‹   *Egy.* Sign used when printing ancient Egy. in Rom. characters. *Cf.* 376.

466   ⌐   *Sh.*, *Gregg's*. Eq. 467.

467   ⌐   *Sh.*, *Gregg's*. s.

468 † ‹   *Gk.* Eq. 376·1.

469 † ›   *Gk.* Eq. 378·1.

470 † ⌐   *Phon.* (After a plosive consonant.) Sound consists of the stop only.

TABLE 44

475   ⌣   *Mus.* Eq. 483.

476   ⌣   *Sh.*, *Pitman's*. (Thin.) n. Hundred, hundredth.

477   ⌣   *Sh.*, *Pitman's*. (Thick) ng.

478 † ⌣   *Mus.* Eq. 488·1. (In conjunction with 577) the arpeggio is to be played upwards.

478·1   *Phon.* Link, a mark used to join letters. Synchronic articulation; colouration of one sound by another.

479 ⌣ *Print.* (Proof correction.) Less space; close up.

480 † ⌣ *Pros.* Eq. 388·3.

TABLE 45

483 ⸺ *Mus.* The slur; play smoothly or *legato*. A link or ligature connecting notes of a group or phrase. (Vocal) embracing notes belonging to one syllable of the libretto. (In mus. for strings) embracing notes to be played with one bow.

484 ⌒ *Bot.* Climbing plant.

484·1 *Geom.* Arc.

484·2 *Engn.* (USA.) Weld to have convex contour.

484·3 *Print.* (Proof correction.) Use a ligature.

484·4 *Sh., Pitman's.* (Thin.) m. Million, millionth.

485 ⌒ *Sh., Gregg's.* g.

486 ⌒ *Sh., Gregg's.* k.

487 ⌒ *Sh., Pitman's.* (Thin.) m.

488 † ⌒ *Phon.* Eq. 478·1.

488·1 *Mus.* Tie or bind, a ligature prolonging a note for the value of a second note to which it is

119

linked and which is not sounded separately. (In conjunction with 577) the arpeggio is to be played downwards.

TABLE 46

490   (   ) *Bot.* (In floral formula.) Enclosed parts are joined together.

490·1   *Chem.* (In formulæ.) Used to enclose groups or radicals within a compound.

490·2   *Chess.* Enclose present position of piece.

490·3   *Geom.* Numbers enclosed are to be taken in the order given. (Riemann.)

490·4   *Log.* For all values of enclosed expression.

490·5   *Math.* Brackets, indicating that the expression enclosed is to be treated as a whole; eq. 635·2, 4416·2 and 5169.

490·6   *Meteor.* Enclosed observation within sight of station.

490·7   *Min. Crys.* Used to enclose Millerian symbol.

490·8   *Print.* Marks of parenthesis, parentheses, used to enclose explanatory matter which might be omitted without impairing the syntax; enclosing an interpolation or a reference;

120

enclosing a whole sentence if this is in the nature of an aside. (Proof correction) close up, reduce leading.

491   ) (*Cart. Mil.* (USA.) Road or rlwy bridge.

492   ⌢⌣   *Print.* (Proof correction.) Close up, no space; use ligature.

493 [†]   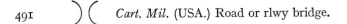   *Jap.* Eq. 5451.

494   ))   *Punc.* (At beginning of line. Fr., etc.) Continuing quotation.

495   ((   ))   *Punc.* (Fr.) Eq. 4784 and 4785.

496   ꞈ꞉ꞈ꞉ꞈ   *Soil/m.* Uncemented calcareous matter (including shells).

TABLE 47

500   ⋎   *Astron.* 1st sign of the Zodiac, Aries, the Ram.

501   ⋎   *Arab. Num.* Seven, eq. 4670.

502   ⋏   *Arab. Num.* Eight, eq. 37.

503   ⌇   *Geol.* Alluvium.

504   ⌒   *Geol.* Marine gravel; shingle.

505   <   *Math.* Of smaller order than.

506   >   *Cart.* Eq. 5679.

506·1   *Math.* Of greater order than.

TABLE 48

510   *Num.* (Arab.) Cursive form of numeral 7. (Modern Arab.) eq. 511.

511   *Arab. Num.* Six, eq. 3401.

512   *Arab. Num.* Two, eq. 3431.

513   *ME.,* late *OE.* (l.c.) Eq. 4269.

514   *Arab. Num.* Three, eq. 3454.

515   *Ger.* (l.c.) 3rd letter of the a., eq. Rom. c.

516   *Gk.* (l.c.) Eq. 429·5.

516·1   *Rom.* (l.c.) The 'Greek e', cursive form of e.

517   *Gk.* (l.c.) Eq. 2727·5.

518   *Gk.* (l.c.) Eq. 2727·5.

519   *Gk.* (l.c.) Eq. 2697·3.

122

TABLE 49

525	$\mathcal{X}$	Gk. (l.c.) Eq. 4169·3.
526	$\mathcal{X}$	It. (l.c.) Eq. Rom. x. See 352.
527		Ger. (l.c.) Cursive form of 2632.
528	$\geqq$	Math. Of order not less than; contains or is equal to.
529	$\leqq$	Math. Of order not greater than; is contained in or equal to.
530		Geol. Brickearth.
531		Meteor. (Red.) State of swell in open sea; average length of waves, 9–10 feet.
532		Pot. China mark, Copenhagen.
533		Numis. Mint mark, Henry VI, the voided cross.

TABLE 50

540	$\mathfrak{G}$	Ger. (Cap.) 7th letter of the a., eq. Rom. G.
541	$\mathfrak{F}$	Elec. Magnetomotive force.
541·1		Ger. (Cap.) 6th letter of the a., eq. Rom F.
542		Sh., Pitman's. Fr. nasal sound.

543	**λ**	*Rom.* (l.c. Obs.) Eq. 5709. ('Breeches Bible', 17th cent.)
544	**ᵹ**	*It.* (l.c. Continental typeface.) Eq. Rom. v. See 2696.
545	**ζ**	*Gk.* (l.c.) Eq. 553·3.
546	**ʋ**	*Rom.* (l.c.) Cursive form of v.

TABLE 51

550	**ƛ**	*Rus.* (Cap./l.c.) Cursive form of 2398.
551	**ᴐ**	*Am.* (Cherokee syllabary.) Eq. Rom. GWU.
552	**γ**	*Gk.* (l.c.) Eq. 2727·5.
553	**ζ**	*Arith.* Riemann's zeta function.
553·1		*Chem.* Sixth.
553·2		*Geom.* Cartesian co-ordinate.
553·3		*Gk.* (l.c.) Zeta, 6th letter of the a., eq. Rom. z. Cardinal num. 7. See also 576.
553·4		*Math.* (Obs.) Unknown quantity. (Diophantus.)
554	**ζ**	*Mus.* Eq. 2709.
555	**ʃ**	*Phon.* Eq. 1186·7.

124

TABLE 52

560	$\mathfrak{H}$	*Ger.* (Cap.) 8th letter of the a., eq. Rom. H.
560·1		*Mag.* Strength of magnetic field.
561	$\mathfrak{C}$	*Ger.* (Cap.) 3rd letter of the a., eq. Rom. C.
562	$\mathfrak{E}$	*Elec. & Mag.* Electric field strength.
562·1		*Ger.* (Cap.) 5th letter of the a., eq. Rom. E.
563	$\mathfrak{M}$	*Ger.* (Cap.) Eq. 2411.
564		*Afr.* (Cameroons.) Ideograph signifying a horse.
565	$\mathfrak{s}$	*Ger.* (l.c.) 19th letter of the a., eq. Rom. s. See also 3105.
566		*Cab.* Eq. Rom. T.
567	ξ	*Gk.* (l.c.) Eq. 406·3.

Cl.I, Div.I, Ord.II, Fam.II, Gen.I

TABLE 53

570	S	*Am.* (Cherokee syllabary.) Eq. Rom. DU.
570·1		*Elec.* Eq. 655.
570·2		*Ir.* 16th letter of the a., eq. Rom. S.

570·3		*Rom.* (Cap.) 19th letter of the a. (Med. ext. of Rom. num.) cardinal number 7 or 70.
571	S	*Elec.* Poynting vector.
571·1		*Rom.* (Cap.) Sanserif form of 570·3.
572	Ƨ	*Etr.* (Late.) Eq. Rom. S.
573	∫	*Cal.* Eq. 2902.
574	S	*Phon.* Voiceless alveolar fricative consonants, s as in so.
574·1		*Rom.* (l.c.) 19th letter of the a. (*ITA*) s as in so.
575	ʔ	*Mus.* Eq. 589.
576	ȝ	*Gk.* (l.c.) Mod. form of 553·3.
577	⸨	*Mus.* Arpeggio: play the notes of the following chord in rapid succession, usually upwards.

TABLE 54

579	∫	*Astron.* Solar constant.
579·1		*Elec.* Apparent power, volt-amperes. Eq. 571.
579·2		*Engn.* Total shear at any section. (Hydrology) storage.

579·3   *It.* (Cap.) Eq. Rom. S.

579·4   *Phys.* Specific gravity.

579·5   *Therm.* Entropy.

580   S *Astron.* Geometrical path in direction of chosen ray. (Astrophysics) measured co-ordinate in spectrum in the direction of dispersion.

580·1   *Engn.* Intensity of shear stress. (Structural) penetration or set in piling; space between webs in steel pillar.

580·2   *Geom.* Length of arc.

580·3   *It.* (l.c.) Eq. Rom. s.

580·4   *Mech.* Linear distance.

580·5   *Nav. Arch.* Length of arc.

580·6   *Opt.* Distance from refracting or reflecting surface of a point on the optical axis.

580·7   *Therm.* Entropy per unit mass.

581   *G/use.* (Or reversed) Eq. 2520.

582   *Rus.* (l.c.) It. and cursive form of 4115·6.

583   *Heb.* Yod, 10th letter of the a., eq. Rom. Y.

584   *Meteor.* (USA.) Barometer unsteady.

TABLE 55

585 ⌢⌣ *Print.* Eq. 4410.

586 ∞ *Meteor.* Glazed frost.

587 ∿ *Elec.* Alternating current.

587·1 *Log.* Negation; not.

587·2 *Math.* Varies as; difference between; similar to; asymptotic to; the complement of.

588 ∼ *Mus.* Turn, *grupetto*, implying a group of four notes: the note above, the note itself, the note below, and the note itself.

589 ∿ *Mus.* Inverted turn, implying a group of four notes: the note below, the note itself, the note above, and the note itself.

590 ∼ *Phon.* (Crossing a consonant, e.g., ŧ, đ, ƶ.) Velarized or pharyngalized.

591 † ∼ *Log.* A member of the class.

591·1 *MS.* Contraction.

591·2 *Phon.* Nasalized.

591·3 *Phys.* See 2596.

591·4 *Port.* Diacritical mark indicating nasalization of a vowel.

591·5   *Sp.* The *tilde*, placed over an *n* to equate it with the Fr. *gn* or the Rom. *ny*.

592   *Geom.* Eq. 5170.

592·1   *Mus.* Eq. 588.

593   *Math.* Is equivalent to, corresponds with.

594   *Afr.* (Upper Guinea.) Ideograph signifying water.

595   *Mus. Tremolo,* in string music a rapid reiteration of a note or notes, in vocal music a rapid but slight variation of pitch. *Vibrato,* in string music a rapid but slight variation of pitch, in vocal music a rapid reiteration of a note.

595·1   *Print.* (Proof correction.) Set in bold-faced type.

595·2   *Sh., Pitman's.* Mark of emphasis.

596   *Mus.* Eq. 5054.

597   *Hyd.* (Inter.) Submarine cable.

TABLE 56

600   *Astrol/n.* 5th sign of the Zodiac, Leo, the Lion.

601   *Num.* (Arab. 2nd century. Hindu.) Eq. mod. 9.

129

602		*Num.* (Arab. 16th century.) Eq. mod. 9.
603		*Ger.* (Cap.) Eq. 618.
603·1		*Math.* Summation.
604		*Astron.* Eq. 96.
605		*Astron.* Eq. 97.

TABLE 57

611		*Print.* (Proof correction. USA.) Transpose to end of preceding line.
612		*Print.* (Proof correction. USA.) Carry over to next line.
613		*Chem.* Eq. 1186·2.
613·1		*Gk.* (l.c.) Sigma, 18th letter of the a., eq. 1186·4 and to Rom. s. Used at the end of a word.
614		*Gk.* (l.c.) Eq. 386·2.
615		*Gk.* (l.c.) Eq. 613·1.
616		*Astron.* Eq. 96.
617		*Astron.* Eq. 97.
618		*Ger.* (Cap.) 19th letter of the a., eq. Rom. S.

130

TABLE 58

620   {   *G/use.* (APO.) 'Curly bracket', used to group related matters together.

620·1   *Mus.* Brace, sound simultaneously; play simultaneously.

620·2   *Math.* See 635·2.

620·3   *Print.* Brace, a device for linking together matter printed on different lines, or (used horizontally) in different columns.

620·4   *Pros.* (Linking three lines.) Triplet, three consecutive rhymed lines.

621   *Num.* (Arab. 10th cent. Sp.) Eq. mod. 5.

622   *Astron.* (Relativity theory.) World-line.

622·1   *Ger.* (Cap.) 12th letter of the a., eq. Rom. L.

623   *Ger.* (Cap.) 9th letter of the a., eq. Rom. I. Also 10th letter of the a., eq. Rom. J.

623·1   *Mag.* Magnetization.

624   *Rel.* Current or 'running' variety of 4521·1.

625   *Geol.* Undulating strata.

626   *It.* (l.c.) Eq. Rom. x. See 352.

131

627   SS   *Phar.* Half. (Lat. *semis.*)

628   ≈   *Elec.* Alternating current of audio-frequency.

628·1   *Math.* Is approximately equal to.

629   }   *Mus.* Eq. 2709.

630   2   *Num.* (Arab.) Eq. 3431.

TABLE 59

634   *z*   *It.* (l.c.) Eq. Rom. z. See 4770.

635   {   }   *Bot.* (In floral formula.) Eq. 490.

635·1   *Chem.* (In formulæ.) Relative activity.

635·2   *Math.* 'Curly' brackets, eq. 490·5, 4416·2 and 5169.

635·3   *Min. Crys.* Brackets indicating that the expression enclosed is a form symbol.

636   𝔗   *Ger.* (Cap.) 20th letter of the a., eq. Rom. T.

637   𝔍   *Rom.* (Cap.) 'Old English', 'Black Letter', eq. I.

638   𝔙   *Ger.* (Cap.) 22nd letter of the a., eq. Rom. V.

639   ≋   *Elec.* Alternating current of superaudio-frequency.

640		*Geol.* (Rep.) Metamorphic rocks.
641		*Hyd.* (Inter.) Overfalls and tide rips.

TABLE 60

644		*Ger.* (Cap.) Eq. 540.
645		*Rus.* (Cap./l.c.) Cursive form of 2008.
646		*Math.* Imaginary part of.
646·1		*Rom.* (Cap.) Cursive form of I. See 2130.
647		*Rus.* (Cap.) Cursive form of 2295.
648		*Rus.* (Cap.) Cursive form of 2009.
649		*Math.* Real part of.
649·1		*Rom.* (Cap.) Cursive form of R. See 655.
650		*Rom.* (Cap.) Cursive form of P. See 681·1.
650·1		*Rus.* (Cap.) Cursive form of 2005·6.
651		*Rom.* (Cap.) Cursive form of B.
651·1		*Rus.* (Cap.) Cursive form of 2084·3.
652		*Num.* (Arab.) Cursive form of numeral 2.
653		*Mus.* Eq. 589.

133

TABLE 61

655   *Elec.* Leduc effect; reluctance.

655·1   *Rom.* (Cap.) Swash and cursive forms of R.

Cl.I, Div.I, Ord.II, Fam.II, Gen.II

TABLE 62

660   *High.* (L. White chalk.) A good workhouse. (Tramps' 'smogger'.)

661   *Arab.* Flourish at ends of words.

662   *Hyd.* (Inter.) Eq. 675.

662·1   *Egy.* (Hier.) Eq. Rom. U.

662·2   *Math.* (Obs.) Eq. 2647·6.

663   *Egy. Num.* Cardinal number 100.

TABLE 63

670   *Rom.* (Cap.) Cursive form of O.

670·1   *Rus.* (Cap.) Cursive form of 8·9.

671   *Rus.* (Cap./l.c.) Cursive form of 2006·1.

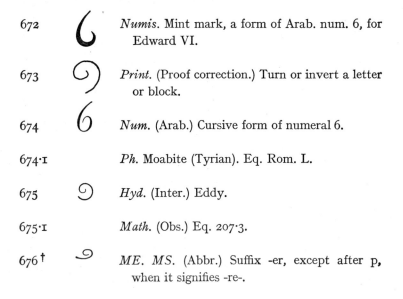

672   *Numis.* Mint mark, a form of Arab. num. 6, for Edward VI.

673   *Print.* (Proof correction.) Turn or invert a letter or block.

674   *Num.* (Arab.) Cursive form of numeral 6.

674·1   *Ph.* Moabite (Tyrian). Eq. Rom. L.

675   *Hyd.* (Inter.) Eddy.

675·1   *Math.* (Obs.) Eq. 207·3.

676 †   *ME. MS.* (Abbr.) Suffix -er, except after p, when it signifies -re-.

TABLE 64

679   *Cart.* (Very variable. Associated with a number.) Eq. 144.

680   *Rom.* (l.c.) Cursive form of d. *Cf.* 135, 164 and 204.

681   *Elec.* Permanence.

681·1   *Rom.* (Cap.) Swash and cursive forms of P.

682   *Ger.* (Cap.) *See* 618.

683   *Am.* (Cherokee syllabary.) Eq. Rom. YA.

135

684   ⟨symbol⟩   *Alch.* Eq. 3884.

684·1   *Rom.* (Cap.) Ornamental form of X.

Cl.I, Div.II, Ord.I, Fam.I, Gen.I

TABLE 65

690   @   *Com.* At; at the rate of.

691   (f)   *Tel.* Frequency meter.

692   (G)   *Chem.* Gold. (John Dalton's elements, 1808.)

692·1   *Tel.* Generator.

693   (P)   *Chem.* Platina (platinum). (John Dalton's elements, 1808.)

693·1   *Nav. Arch.* Speed to prismatic-length constant.

694   (R)   *Engn.* (USA.) Relief valve (pressure or vacuum).

695   (2)   *Astron.* Eq. 710.

695·1   *Bot.* Biennial.

TABLE 66

700   (A)   *Tel.* Ammeter.

701	(I)	*Chem.* Iron. (John Dalton's elements, 1806–7.)
702	(K)	*Rlwy.* (Brit.) Occupation key instrument.
703	(K)	*Nav. Arch.* Speed-to-displacement constant.
704	(L)	*Chem.* Lead. (John Dalton's elements, 1806–7.)
704·1		*Nav. Arch.* Speed-to-length constant.
705	(M)	*Nav. Arch.* Length-to-displacement constant.
705·1		*Tel.* Motor.
706	(↗)	*Prop.* Texas cattle brand, 'Tumbling-T'.
707	(V)	*Tel.* Voltmeter.
708	(W)	*Tel.* Wattmeter.
709	(Z)	*Chem.* Zinc. (John Dalton's elements, 1806–7.)
710	(1)	*Astron.* (Containing any number.) Asteroid.
710·1		*Bot.* Annual.

TABLE 67

715		*High.* (L. Red circle and bar. UNS., 1953.) Parking forbidden.
716		*High.* (L. Red circle and bar. Brit.) Eq. 715.

137

717  *High.* (L. Diagonal and right half red. Du.) Parking on left.

718 ⊕ *Chem.* Gold. (John Dalton's elements, 1806–7.)

TABLE 68

720 *High.* (L. USA.) Level crossing.

721 ⊕ *Pot.* China mark, Crown Derby.

722 ⊕ *Mil.* (L. red on blue ground.) Territorial Army, 51st Highland Division.

723 ⊕ *Prop.* Texas cattle brand, 'Mulkey Ranch'.

724 ⊕ *Prop.* Texas cattle brand, 'Peevy Ranch'.

725 ⊕ *Prop.* Texas cattle brand, 'Katie Barr'.

726 ⊕ *Prop.* Texas cattle brand, 'U-up and U-down'.

727 ⊕ *Prop.* Texas cattle brand, 'Ten in Texas'.

TABLE 69

730   *High.* (L. Red circle. Inter.) Maximum width in metres.

731   *High.* (L. Red circle. Inter.) Maximum height in metres.

732   *High.* (L. Red circle. Inter.) Maximum weight in metric tons.

733   *High.* (L. Red circle. UNS, 1953.) Width limit.

734   *High.* (L. Red circle. UNS, 1953.) Height limit.

735   *High.* (L. Red circle. Brit.) Laden weight limit.

736   *High.* (L. Red circle. Brit.) Axle weight limit.

737   *High.* (L. Red circle. Brit.) Speed limit in miles per hour. (Inter.) speed limit in km. per hour.

TABLE 70

740   *High.* (L. Red on black in red circle. Swiss.) Beginning of postal mountain road.

741	⊕	*Elec.* Automatic contact.
742	⊗	*Engn.* (In pipe symbol. USA.) Blast thermo-static trap.
743	⊗	*Elec.* Street lighting standard.
744	⊙	*Elec.* Master clock.
745	⊙►	*Prop.* Texas cattle brand, 'O-H-triangle'.
746	⊘	*Mil.* Searchlight (anti-aircraft.)
747	⦿	*Meteor.* Sky overcast but calm.
748	⊖	*Chem.* Alkali. (Bergmann, 1783.)
749	⊛	*Prop.* Texas cattle brand, 'Bridle bit'.
750		*Rel.* (RC.) Consecrated.
751	⊛	*Prop.* Texas cattle brand, earliest recorded, 1762.

TABLE 71

755	⃠	*High.* (L. Red circle and bar. UNS, 1953.) U-turn forbidden. *Cf.* 765.
756	ⓡ	*Prop.* Texas cattle brand, 'Keyhole'.
757	⌂	*Prop.* Texas cattle brand, 'Weed hoe'.

140

758   *Prop.* Texas cattle brand, 'Seven Up'.

759   *Prop.* Texas cattle brand, 'Rocking-chair'.

760   *Prop.* Texas cattle brand, 'Bow and arrow'.

761   *Prop.* Texas cattle brand, 'Three D's'.

TABLE 72

764   *High.* (L. Ger.) Turn right.

765   *High.* (L. Red circle and bar. Brit., 1964.) No U-turns. *Cf.* 755.

766   *High.* (L. Red bar and circle. Fr.) Overtaking forbidden.

767   *High.* (L. Red bar and circle. Inter.) Overtaking forbidden.

768   *G/use.* Cursive form of 2510·2.

768·1   *Print.* (Proof correction.) Check for accuracy.

769   *Tel.* Ohmmeter.

770   *Prop.* Texas cattle brand, 'Jew's harp'.

771   *Prop.* Texas cattle brand, 'Seven-six'.

141

772   *Prop.* Texas cattle brand, 'Slashed lazy-S'.

773   *Tel.* Wavemeter.

774   *Prop.* Texas cattle brand, 'Wineglass-H'. (Used inverted during Prohibition.)

775   *Afr.* (Nsibidi.) Ideograph signifying a man lying ill in his house, with three visitors.

776   *Elec.* Synchronous clock outlet.

TABLE 73

779   *High.* (L. White on blue ground. Brit., 1964.) Turn left ahead. (Reversed) turn right.

780   *High.* (L. Red. Brit.) Caution.

781   *High.* (L. Red bar and circle. UNS, 1953.) No left turn.

782   *High.* (L. Red bar and circle. UNS, 1953.) Overtaking forbidden.

783   *Elec.* Steel support (to conductor line). (USA.) 3-phase delta winding of motor or generator.

783·1   *Engn.* (In pipe symbol. USA.) Air eliminator.

784   *Mil.* Headquarters A.A. Group.

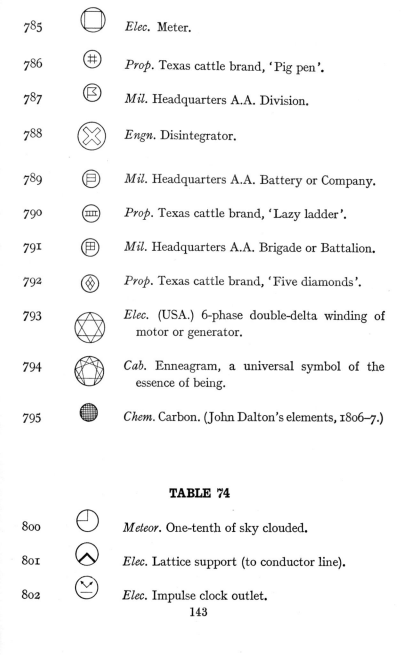

785   *Elec.* Meter.

786   *Prop.* Texas cattle brand, 'Pig pen'.

787   *Mil.* Headquarters A.A. Division.

788   *Engn.* Disintegrator.

789   *Mil.* Headquarters A.A. Battery or Company.

790   *Prop.* Texas cattle brand, 'Lazy ladder'.

791   *Mil.* Headquarters A.A. Brigade or Battalion.

792   *Prop.* Texas cattle brand, 'Five diamonds'.

793   *Elec.* (USA.) 6-phase double-delta winding of motor or generator.

794   *Cab.* Enneagram, a universal symbol of the essence of being.

795   *Chem.* Carbon. (John Dalton's elements, 1806–7.)

TABLE 74

800   *Meteor.* One-tenth of sky clouded.

801   *Elec.* Lattice support (to conductor line).

802   *Elec.* Impulse clock outlet.

803   *Meteor.* More than nine-tenths of sky clouded, but with openings of clear sky.

804   *Rlwy.* See 823.

805   *Rlwy.* (USA.) Inductive train stop; unwound (stop).

806   *Alch.* Animalia. (*Golden Chain of Homer*, Leipzig, 1728.)

807   *Alch.* Mineralia. (*Golden Chain of Homer*, Leipzig, 1728.)

808   *Meteor.* Nine-tenths of sky clouded.

809   *Engn.* (Fire protection.) Main radio station.

810   *Rlwy.* Three-aspect fog repeater signal.

811   *Prop.* Texas cattle brand, 'Walking Y'.

TABLE 75

815   *High.* (L. White on blue ground, UNS, 1938. Red on blue, Brit., 1964.) Waiting forbidden; no stopping on carriageway.

816   *Alch. Viride aeris* or verdigris, basic copper acetate. (*A Compleat Body of Chymistry*, 17th cent.); *Materia prima omniũ concretorum sublunarium immediata seu Azoth.* (*Golden Chain of Homer*, Leipzig, 1728.)

144

816·1		*Astron.* Earth.
816·2		*Bot.* Regular; actinomorphic, radially symmetrical.
816·3		*Chem.* Sulphur. (John Dalton's elements, 1806–1807.)
816·4		*Egy.* (Early.) Probably eq. Rom. th.
816·5		*Elec.* Wooden support (to overhead line).
816·6		*Gk.* (Chalcidian.) Eq. 892.
816·7		*Math.* Abstract addition; direct sum.
816·8		*Meteor.* Solar halo.
816·9		*Mil.* Telegraph station; radio station.
816·01		*Min.* Nickel ore.
816·02		*Ph.* Teth, theth, eq. 892.
816·03		*Rel.* Eq. 4521·1.
816·04		*Rlwy.* (USA.) Salt well.
817	⊗	*Elec.* Signal lamp. (USA.) 2-phase winding of motor or generator.
817·1		*Egy.* Eq. 816·4.

817·2   *Engn.* (In pipe symbol. USA.) Thermostatic trap; automatic expansion valve.

817·3   *Etr.* Eq. 892.

817·4   *Gk.* (Theran, 900 B.C.) Eq. 892.

817·5   *Lat.* (Early.) Eq. th.

817·6   *Math.* Abstract multiplication. (Group theory) plethysm operator.

817·7   *Meteor.* (USA.) Sky obscured by fog, dust, etc., as distinct from cloud.

817·8   *Ph.* Moabite (Tyrian). Eq. 892.

817·9   *Pot.* China mark, early Spode.

817·01   *Print.* Eq. 4363·9.

818   ⊕   *Cart.* (Ant. OS.) Roman signal station.

818·1   *Hyd.* (Inter.) Observation spot.

819   ⊗   *Engn.* (Fire protection.) Chimney or stack.

820   ⊕   *Rlwy.* (Brit.) Two-aspect fog repeater signal.

821   *Rlwy.* (Brit.) Two-aspect single unit searchlight signal, normal green, approach lighted.

822   *Rlwy.* (Brit.) Two-aspect single unit searchlight signal, normal red, approach lighted.

823 *Rlwy.* (Brit.) Three-aspect single unit searchlight signal, normal green, approach lighted.

TABLE 76

825 *High.* (L. White chalk.) A day's work is found. (Tramps' 'smogger'.)

826 *High.* (L. White chalk.) Very hospitable people. (Tramps' 'smogger'.)

827 *High.* (L. Red circle. Sw.) Built-up area ahead.

828 *Insig.* St John Ambulance Association, foundation of the Grand Priory of the Hospital of St John of Jerusalem in England.

829 *Alch.* Vegetabilia; living, organic, matter. (*Golden Chain of Homer*, Leipzig, 1728.)

830 *Math.* Eq. 816·7.

831 *Math.* Eq. 817·6.

832 *Chem.* Positive ion.

832·1 *Phys.* Proton; positive electron (positron).

833 *Prop.* Texas cattle brand, 'Pitchfork'.

834 *Prop.* Texas cattle brand, 'Lazy 4-Y'.

TABLE 77

835   *High.* (L. Red bar and circle. UNS, 1953.) Entry forbidden.

836   *High.* (L. Red circle and small arrow, large arrow black, Brit., 1964. With black circle and arrows reversed, Du.) Give way to traffic approaching.

837   *Cart.* (OS.) Bench-mark likely to remain stable in an area liable to subsidence.

838   *Mil.* Machine-gun (anti-aircraft).

839   *Tel.* Galvanometer.

840   *Elec.* (USA.) 3-phase wye winding of motor or generator (ungrounded). (Brit.) 3-phase star winding of voltage transformer.

841   *Chem.* Phosphorus. (John Dalton's elements, 1806–7.)

842   *Prop.* Signifying the Mercedes motor-car.

843   *Chem.* Magnesia (magnesium). John Dalton's elements, 1806–7.)

844   *Chem.* Lime (calcium). (John Dalton's elements, 1806–7.)

845   *Insig.* Campaign for Nuclear Disarmament.

846   *Mil.* Visual plotting station (anti-aircraft).

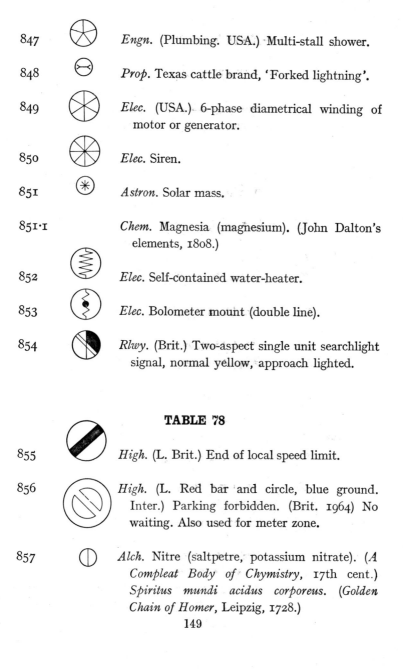

847   *Engn.* (Plumbing. USA.) Multi-stall shower.

848   *Prop.* Texas cattle brand, 'Forked lightning'.

849   *Elec.* (USA.) 6-phase diametrical winding of motor or generator.

850   *Elec.* Siren.

851   *Astron.* Solar mass.

851·1   *Chem.* Magnesia (magnesium). (John Dalton's elements, 1808.)

852   *Elec.* Self-contained water-heater.

853   *Elec.* Bolometer mount (double line).

854   *Rlwy.* (Brit.) Two-aspect single unit searchlight signal, normal yellow, approach lighted.

TABLE 78

855   *High.* (L. Brit.) End of local speed limit.

856   *High.* (L. Red bar and circle, blue ground. Inter.) Parking forbidden. (Brit. 1964) No waiting. Also used for meter zone.

857   *Alch.* Nitre (saltpetre, potassium nitrate). (*A Compleat Body of Chymistry,* 17th cent.) *Spiritus mundi acidus corporeus.* (*Golden Chain of Homer,* Leipzig, 1728.)

149

857·1   *Chem.* Azote (nitrogen). (John Dalton's elements, 1806–7.)

857·2   *Cret.* Prehistoric letter, probably eq. Rom. ph.

857·3   *Gk. & Etr.* (Chalcidian, Athenian and Etruscan.) Eq. 1362·2.

857·4   *Meteor.* Solar corona. (USA.) Eq. 866.

857·5   *Rlwy.* (Brit.) Green light signal. (USA) inductive train stop, set for stop.

858   *Num.* (Arab. 16th cent., London.) Nought, zero, eq. mod. O.

859   *Rlwy.* (Brit.) Yellow or amber light signal.

860   *Rlwy.* (Brit.) Light signal, normal green, approach lighted.

861   *Rlwy.* (Brit.) Light signal, normal yellow, approach lighted.

TABLE 79

865   *High.* (L. Ger.) Keep straight on.

866   *Meteor.* (USA.) Sky one-tenth cloud.

867   *Elec.* (USA.) 1-phase winding of motor or generator. (Circle basic for motor or generator.)

150

867·1   *Meteor.* Two- to three-tenths of sky clouded.

868   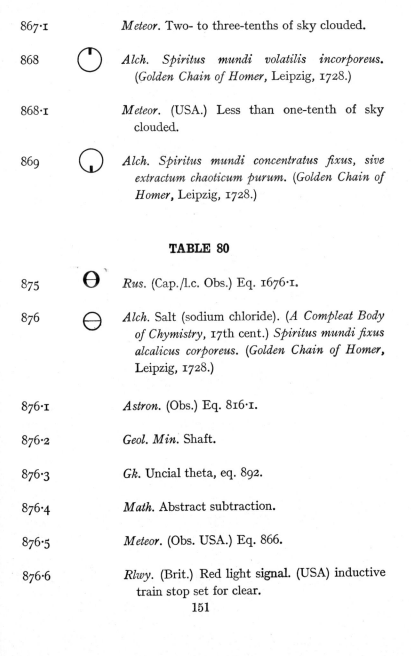 *Alch. Spiritus mundi volatilis incorporeus.* (*Golden Chain of Homer*, Leipzig, 1728.)

868·1   *Meteor.* (USA.) Less than one-tenth of sky clouded.

869   *Alch. Spiritus mundi concentratus fixus, sive extractum chaoticum purum.* (*Golden Chain of Homer*, Leipzig, 1728.)

TABLE 80

875   *Rus.* (Cap./l.c. Obs.) Eq. 1676·1.

876   *Alch.* Salt (sodium chloride). (*A Compleat Body of Chymistry*, 17th cent.) *Spiritus mundi fixus alcalicus corporeus.* (*Golden Chain of Homer*, Leipzig, 1728.)

876·1   *Astron.* (Obs.) Eq. 816·1.

876·2   *Geol. Min.* Shaft.

876·3   *Gk.* Uncial theta, eq. 892.

876·4   *Math.* Abstract subtraction.

876·5   *Meteor.* (Obs. USA.) Eq. 866.

876·6   *Rlwy.* (Brit.) Red light signal. (USA) inductive train stop set for clear.

151

877   **e**   *Rom.* (l.c.) 5th letter of the a. See 2220.

878   ɘ   *Phon.* Half-close central vowel, as u in Sw. dum.

879   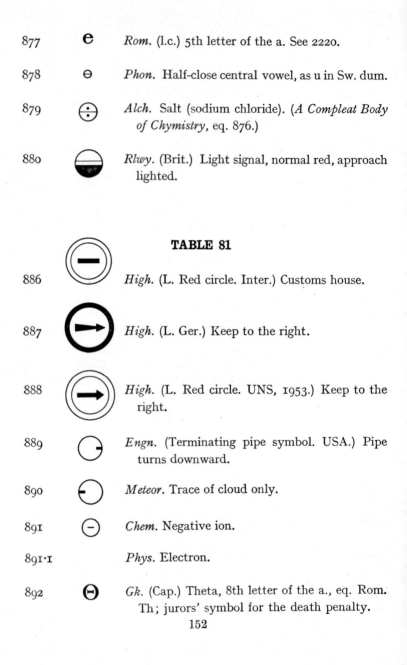   *Alch.* Salt (sodium chloride). (*A Compleat Body of Chymistry*, eq. 876.)

880   *Rlwy.* (Brit.) Light signal, normal red, approach lighted.

TABLE 81

886   *High.* (L. Red circle. Inter.) Customs house.

887   *High.* (L. Ger.) Keep to the right.

888   *High.* (L. Red circle. UNS, 1953.) Keep to the right.

889   *Engn.* (Terminating pipe symbol. USA.) Pipe turns downward.

890   *Meteor.* Trace of cloud only.

891   *Chem.* Negative ion.

891·1   *Phys.* Electron.

892   *Gk.* (Cap.) Theta, 8th letter of the a., eq. Rom. Th; jurors' symbol for the death penalty.

152

892·1   *Mag.* Conversion point.

892·2   *Phys.* Temperature.

TABLE 82

895   *Chem.* Soda (sodium). (John Dalton's elements, 1806–7.)

896   *Rlwy.* (Brit.) Green light signal, normal aspect.

897   *Meteor.* Four- to six-tenths of sky clouded.

898   *Chem.* Potash (potassium). (John Dalton's elements, 1806–7.)

899   *Meteor.* Seven- to eight-tenths of sky clouded.

900   *Mil.* Section (anti-aircraft guns).

901   *Meteor.* Sky completely overclouded.

TABLE 83

904   *High.* (L. White chalk.) Snappy people. (Tramps' 'smogger'.)

905   *Elec.* Reinforced concrete support (to line.)

906   *Rlwy.* (Brit.) Yellow or amber light signal, normal aspect.

153

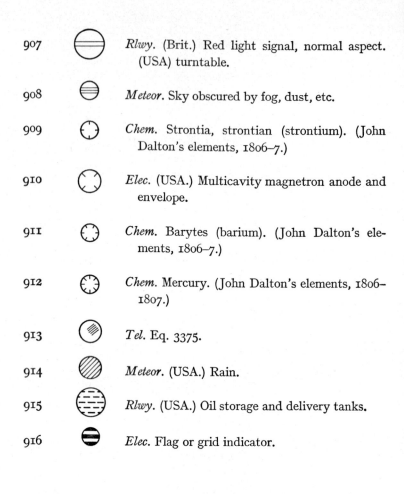

907   *Rlwy.* (Brit.) Red light signal, normal aspect. (USA) turntable.

908   *Meteor.* Sky obscured by fog, dust, etc.

909   *Chem.* Strontia, strontian (strontium). (John Dalton's elements, 1806–7.)

910   *Elec.* (USA.) Multicavity magnetron anode and envelope.

911   *Chem.* Barytes (barium). (John Dalton's elements, 1806–7.)

912   *Chem.* Mercury. (John Dalton's elements, 1806–1807.)

913   *Tel.* Eq. 3375.

914   *Meteor.* (USA.) Rain.

915   *Rlwy.* (USA.) Oil storage and delivery tanks.

916   *Elec.* Flag or grid indicator.

TABLE 84

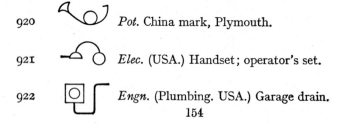

920   *Pot.* China mark, Plymouth.

921   *Elec.* (USA.) Handset; operator's set.

922   *Engn.* (Plumbing. USA.) Garage drain.

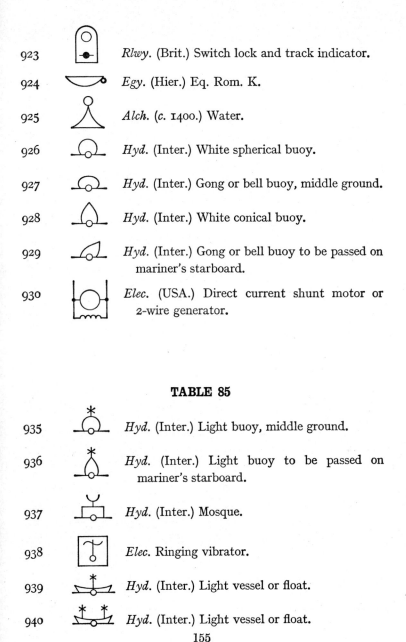

923   *Rlwy.* (Brit.) Switch lock and track indicator.

924   *Egy.* (Hier.) Eq. Rom. K.

925   *Alch.* (*c.* 1400.) Water.

926   *Hyd.* (Inter.) White spherical buoy.

927   *Hyd.* (Inter.) Gong or bell buoy, middle ground.

928   *Hyd.* (Inter.) White conical buoy.

929   *Hyd.* (Inter.) Gong or bell buoy to be passed on mariner's starboard.

930   *Elec.* (USA.) Direct current shunt motor or 2-wire generator.

TABLE 85

935   *Hyd.* (Inter.) Light buoy, middle ground.

936   *Hyd.* (Inter.) Light buoy to be passed on mariner's starboard.

937   *Hyd.* (Inter.) Mosque.

938   *Elec.* Ringing vibrator.

939   *Hyd.* (Inter.) Light vessel or float.

940   *Hyd.* (Inter.) Light vessel or float.

TABLE 86

945   *Elec.* Support in steel socket (for conductor line).

946   *Afr.* (Upper Guinea.) Ideograph signifying flying ants.

947   *Pot.* China mark, Chelsea, *c.* 1750.

948   *Alch.* Electrum (gold-silver alloy).

949   *Hyd.* (Inter.) Buoy with topmark.

950   *Hyd.* (Inter.) Buoy with topmark.

951   *Pot.* China mark, Bow.

952   *Hyd.* (Inter.) Black and white spherical buoy.

TABLE 87

955   *Tel.* Window coupling of cavity resonator to waveguide (single line).

956   *Cab.* Eq. Heb. gimel, 2797.

957   *Am.* (Cherokee syllabary.) Eq. Rom. O.

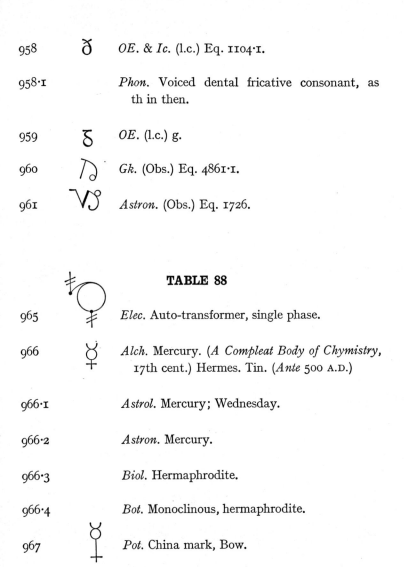

958   *OE.* & *Ic.* (l.c.) Eq. 1104·1.

958·1   *Phon.* Voiced dental fricative consonant, as th in then.

959   *OE.* (l.c.) g.

960   *Gk.* (Obs.) Eq. 4861·1.

961   *Astron.* (Obs.) Eq. 1726.

TABLE 88

965   *Elec.* Auto-transformer, single phase.

966   *Alch.* Mercury. (*A Compleat Body of Chymistry,* 17th cent.) Hermes. Tin. (*Ante* 500 A.D.)

966·1   *Astrol.* Mercury; Wednesday.

966·2   *Astron.* Mercury.

966·3   *Biol.* Hermaphrodite.

966·4   *Bot.* Monoclinous, hermaphrodite.

967   *Pot.* China mark, Bow.

968   *Alch.* Sublimate of quicksilver (corrosive sublimate, mercuric chloride). (*A Compleat Body of Chymistry,* 17th cent.)

157

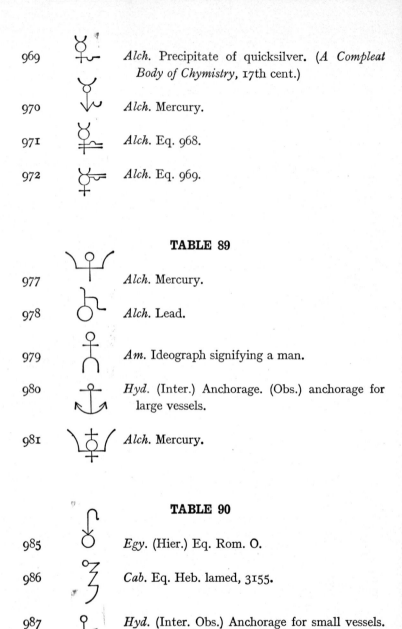

969   *Alch.* Precipitate of quicksilver. (*A Compleat Body of Chymistry*, 17th cent.)

970   *Alch.* Mercury.

971   *Alch.* Eq. 968.

972   *Alch.* Eq. 969.

TABLE 89

977   *Alch.* Mercury.

978   *Alch.* Lead.

979   *Am.* Ideograph signifying a man.

980   *Hyd.* (Inter.) Anchorage. (Obs.) anchorage for large vessels.

981   *Alch.* Mercury.

TABLE 90

985   *Egy.* (Hier.) Eq. Rom. O.

986   *Cab.* Eq. Heb. lamed, 3155.

987   *Hyd.* (Inter. Obs.) Anchorage for small vessels.

158

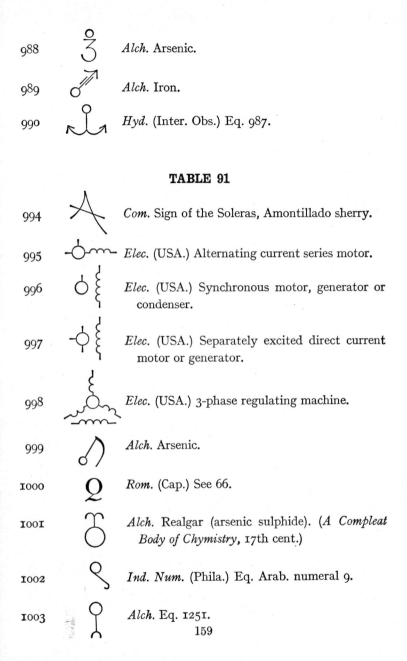

988   *Alch.* Arsenic.

989   *Alch.* Iron.

990   *Hyd.* (Inter. Obs.) Eq. 987.

TABLE 91

994   *Com.* Sign of the Soleras, Amontillado sherry.

995   *Elec.* (USA.) Alternating current series motor.

996   *Elec.* (USA.) Synchronous motor, generator or condenser.

997   *Elec.* (USA.) Separately excited direct current motor or generator.

998   *Elec.* (USA.) 3-phase regulating machine.

999   *Alch.* Arsenic.

1000   *Rom.* (Cap.) See 66.

1001   *Alch.* Realgar (arsenic sulphide). (*A Compleat Body of Chymistry*, 17th cent.)

1002   *Ind. Num.* (Phila.) Eq. Arab. numeral 9.

1003   *Alch.* Eq. 1251.

159

| 1004 | | *Alch.* Mars. (*Theatrum Chemicum*, Strasbourg, 1659–61.) |

1004   *Alch.* Mars. (*Theatrum Chemicum*, Strasbourg, 1659–61.)

1005   *Phon.* Labialized sh.

1006   *Elec.* Gravity switch-hook.

1007   *Gk.* (Obs.) Eq. 1148·5.

1008   *Elec.* Pull-off, single.

1009   *Cab.* Mars; the angel Samael.

1010   *ITA.* See 1933.

1011   *Am.* (Cherokee syllabary.) Eq. Rom. S.

TABLE 92

1015   *Num.* (Arab.) Eq. numeral 8. A form found in funerary and ecclesiastical inscriptions.

1016   *Mil.* Cavalry (individual).

1017   *Phys.* Eq. 1018.

1017·1   *S/Nor.* See 17·02.

1018   *Phys.* Ångström unit, 10^{-8} cm.

1018·1   *S/Nor.* See 17·02.

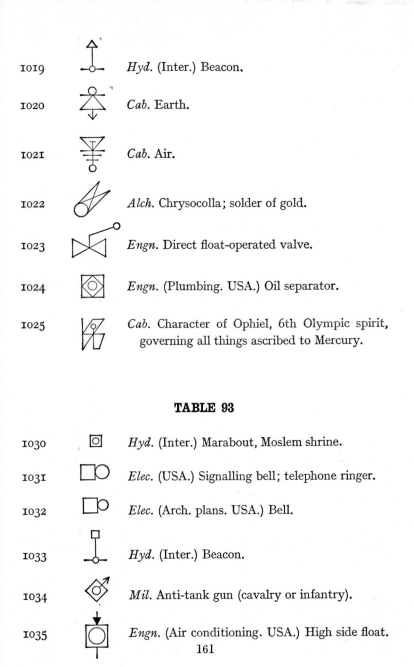

1019   *Hyd.* (Inter.) Beacon.

1020   *Cab.* Earth.

1021   *Cab.* Air.

1022   *Alch.* Chrysocolla; solder of gold.

1023   *Engn.* Direct float-operated valve.

1024   *Engn.* (Plumbing. USA.) Oil separator.

1025   *Cab.* Character of Ophiel, 6th Olympic spirit, governing all things ascribed to Mercury.

TABLE 93

1030   *Hyd.* (Inter.) Marabout, Moslem shrine.

1031   *Elec.* (USA.) Signalling bell; telephone ringer.

1032   *Elec.* (Arch. plans. USA.) Bell.

1033   *Hyd.* (Inter.) Beacon.

1034   *Mil.* Anti-tank gun (cavalry or infantry).

1035   *Engn.* (Air conditioning. USA.) High side float.

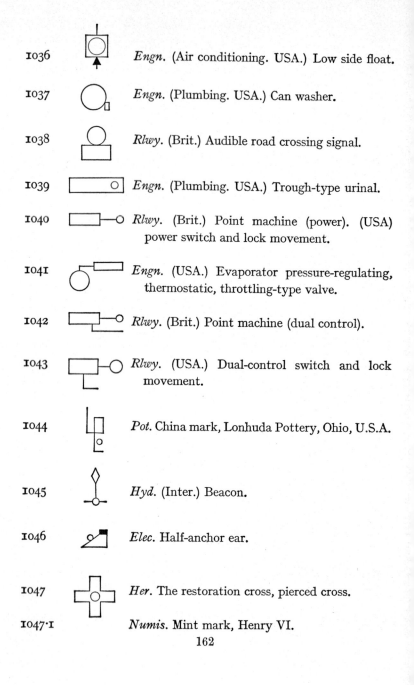

1036   *Engn.* (Air conditioning. USA.) Low side float.

1037   *Engn.* (Plumbing. USA.) Can washer.

1038   *Rlwy.* (Brit.) Audible road crossing signal.

1039   *Engn.* (Plumbing. USA.) Trough-type urinal.

1040   *Rlwy.* (Brit.) Point machine (power). (USA) power switch and lock movement.

1041   *Engn.* (USA.) Evaporator pressure-regulating, thermostatic, throttling-type valve.

1042   *Rlwy.* (Brit.) Point machine (dual control).

1043   *Rlwy.* (USA.) Dual-control switch and lock movement.

1044   *Pot.* China mark, Lonhuda Pottery, Ohio, U.S.A.

1045   *Hyd.* (Inter.) Beacon.

1046   *Elec.* Half-anchor ear.

1047   *Her.* The restoration cross, pierced cross.

1047·1   *Numis.* Mint mark, Henry VI.

TABLE 94

1050		*Elec.* (USA.) Vibrator reed.
1051		*Engn.* (Plumbing. USA.) Water-closet with tank.
1052		*Alch.* Gold leaf.
1053		*Hyd.* (Inter.) Buoy with topmark.
1054		*Hyd.* (Inter.) Tower.
1055		*Rlwy.* (USA.) Bell signal.
1056		*Hyd.* (Inter.) Pillar buoy.
1057		*Hyd.* (Inter.) Buoy with topmark.
1058		*Hyd.* (Inter. Obs.) Bell buoy.

TABLE 95

1060		*Rlwy.* (USA.) Automatic trip train stop, set at stop.
1061		*Alch.* Gold.

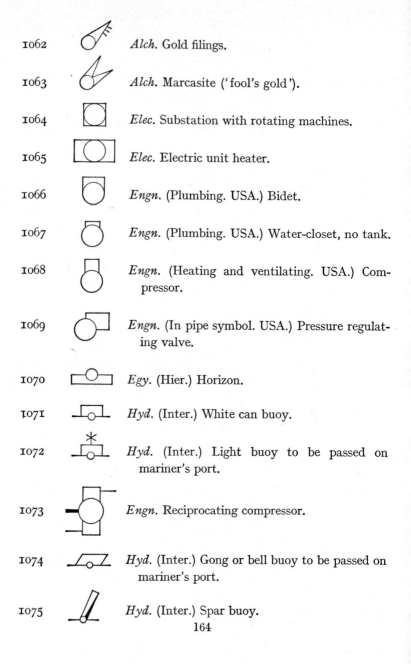

1062   *Alch.* Gold filings.

1063   *Alch.* Marcasite ('fool's gold').

1064   *Elec.* Substation with rotating machines.

1065   *Elec.* Electric unit heater.

1066   *Engn.* (Plumbing. USA.) Bidet.

1067   *Engn.* (Plumbing. USA.) Water-closet, no tank.

1068   *Engn.* (Heating and ventilating. USA.) Compressor.

1069   *Engn.* (In pipe symbol. USA.) Pressure regulating valve.

1070   *Egy.* (Hier.) Horizon.

1071   *Hyd.* (Inter.) White can buoy.

1072   *Hyd.* (Inter.) Light buoy to be passed on mariner's port.

1073   *Engn.* Reciprocating compressor.

1074   *Hyd.* (Inter.) Gong or bell buoy to be passed on mariner's port.

1075   *Hyd.* (Inter.) Spar buoy.

TABLE 96

1081   ♃   *Cart.* (Du.) Cinchona (quinine) tree.

1082   *Rlwy.* (Brit.) Water column. (USA) water or gasoline column.

1083   *Cab.* Eq. Heb. cheth, 4251.

1084   *Bot.* With cotyledons conduplicate and radicle dorsal.

1085   *Elec.* (In valve symbol.) Electrode used either as an anode or as a cold cathode.

1086   *Elec.* Stayed or strutted support (of conductor line).

1087   *Rlwy.* (USA.) Wig-wag.

1088   Ω   *Gk.* (Cap.) Eq. 1226·2.

1089   *Engn.* Rotary vacuum filter.

1090   *Cart.* (Du.) Trigonometrical point.

1091   *Elec.* Microphone or telephone transmitter.

1092   *Pot.* China mark, Chelsea.

1093   *Astron.* (Obs.) Neptune. (L.V. for Le Verrier.)

1094   *Hyd.* (Inter.) Wreck with any part of hull or superstructure visible at low water.

TABLE 97

1099   *Com.* Sign of the Soleras, 'P-X', Pedro Ximenez, a black sweet sherry.

1100   *Alch.* Antimony. (*A Compleat Body of Chymistry,* 17th cent.)

1100·1   *Astron.* (Obs.) Eq. 816·1.

1100·2   *Bot.* (Obs.) Male.

1100·3   *Cart.* Eq. 5617. (Mil. USA) church, mosque, synagogue, cross.

1100·4   *Mil.* Troop leader; platoon commander; company officer. (R.A.) section commander. (R.E.) section leader. (USA) see 1100·3.

1101   *Astrol.* Venus; Friday.

1101·1   *Astron.* Venus.

1101·2   *Biol.* Female, 'Venus's girdle'.

1101·3   *Cab.* Venus; the angel Anael.

1101·4   *Min.* Copper ore.

1102   *Math.* Eq. 5646.

1103   *Alch.* Iron. (F for Latin *ferrum.*)

1104   *ME. MS.* (Abbr.) That.

1104·1		*OE. & Ic.* (l.c.) Eq. 1986.
1105	♂	*Bot.* (Obs.) Eq. 966·4.
1106	♀	*Elec.* (In valve symbol.) Eq. 5352.
1107	☿	*Astron.* (Obs.) Juno.
1108	O┼O	*Rlwy.* (Brit.) Visual road crossing signal, flashing light.

TABLE 98

1110		*Cab.* Character of Och, 4th Olympic spirit, governing all things ascribed to the sun.
1111		*ME. & OE.* Eq. 1104.
1112		*Pot.* China mark, Bow.
1113		*Astron.* (Obs.) Eq. 1114.
1114		*Astron.* Uranus. The H commemorates William Herschel.
1115		*Alch.* Powder. (*A Compleat Body of Chymistry,* 17th cent.)
1116		*Alch.* Eq. 1251.
1117		*Astron.* (Obs.) Eq. 1093. (L for 'Leverrier', a common mis-spelling of Le Verrier.)

167

TABLE 99

1120	♁	*Astron.* (Obs.) Uranus.
1121	♀	*Pot.* China mark, Plymouth; Nottingham.
1122	♂	*Alch.* Iron. (*A Compleat Body of Chymistry*, 17th cent.; Étienne-François Geoffroy, 1718; Torbern O. Bergman, 1795.)
1122·1		*Astrol.* Mars; Tuesday.
1122·2		*Astron.* Mars.
1122·3		*Biol.* Male, 'Mars's arrow'.
1122·4		*Bot.* Biennial.
1122·5		*Min.* Iron ore.
1122·6		*Pot.* China mark, Rogers, Burslem, 1790–1842.
1123		*Alch.* Iron.
1124		*Pot.* China mark, Rogers, Longport, 1780–1825.
1125		*Alch.* Iron.

TABLE 100

1130		*Elec.* (USA.) Ionically-heated cathode with provision for supplementary heating.

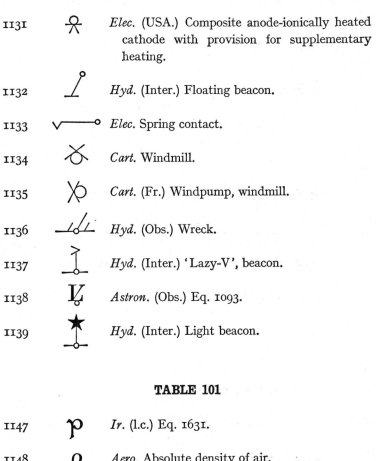

1131   *Elec.* (USA.) Composite anode-ionically heated cathode with provision for supplementary heating.

1132   *Hyd.* (Inter.) Floating beacon.

1133   *Elec.* Spring contact.

1134   *Cart.* Windmill.

1135   *Cart.* (Fr.) Windpump, windmill.

1136   *Hyd.* (Obs.) Wreck.

1137   *Hyd.* (Inter.) 'Lazy-V', beacon.

1138   *Astron.* (Obs.) Eq. 1093.

1139   *Hyd.* (Inter.) Light beacon.

TABLE 101

1147   ***Ir.*** (l.c.) Eq. 1631.

1148   *Aero.* Absolute density of air.

1148·1   *Astron.* Radius of curvature; radius vector; distance from the centre of the earth.

1148·2   *Chem.* Seventeenth.

1148·3   *Elec.* Charge density (volume); resistivity; specific resistance.

1148·4   *Engn.* Steel ratio in reinforced concrete.

1148·5   *Gk.* (l.c.) Rho, 17th letter of the a., eq. Rom. r. cardinal number 100.

1148·6   *Math.* Radius of curvature; radius vector; *semilatus recium*; (obs.) an unknown quantity (A.D. 1559).

1148·7   *Mech.* Density.

1148·8   *Nav. Arch.* Mass per unit volume; specific mass.

1148·9   *Opt.* Coefficient of refraction; refractive power; reflection factor.

1148·01   *Phys.* Density; frequency; cut-off ratio. (Heat) degree of supersaturation. (Light) see 1146·9. (Nuclear) rho meson.

TABLE 102

1155   *Elec.* (USA.) Alternating current generator or motor.

1155·1   *Engn.* (Plumbing. USA.) Head shower.

1156   *Rlwy.* (USA.) Auxiliary air reservoir.

1157   *Mil.* Infantry (individual); officer.

1158   *Rlwy.* (Brit.) Electrical treadle with contacts normally open.

1159		*Gk.* Eq. 2231.
1160		*Tel.* (In valve symbol.) Cold cathode; guide cathode.
1161		*Cab.* Eq. to Heb. ayin (ain), 2633.
1162		*Ir.* 2nd letter of the a., eq. Rom. B.
1163		*Sh., Pitman's.* (Thin.) Dollars.
1164		*Am.* (Cherokee syllabary.) Eq. Rom. dzu.
1165		*Rlwy.* (USA.) Post indicator valve.

TABLE 103

1170		*Rom.* (Cap.) See 66.
1171		*Arab. Num.* Nine, eq. 3400.
1172		*Alch.* Day. (*A Compleat Body of Chymistry*, 17th cent.)
1172·1		*Astron.* Conjunction.
1173		*Alch.* Eq. 1172.
1174		*Alch.* Eq. 1175.
1175		*Alch.* Night. (*A Compleat Body of Chymistry*, 17th cent.)

171

1176	∂	*Sh., Pitman's.* (Thin.) Eq. 1177.
1177	ʔ	*Sh., Pitman's.* (Thin.) H.
1178	9	*Num.* Cursive form of figure 9.
1179	∖ᴑ	*Sh., Pitman's.* (Thin.) Pounds.
1180	⟋ᴑ	*Sh., Samuel Taylor's* (1786). H.
1180·1		*Sh., Pitman's.* (Thin.) Rupees.

TABLE 104

1185	℧	*Ir.* 4th letter of the a., eq. Rom. D.
1186	σ	*Aero.* Relative density of air.
1186·1		*Astron.* Area; angular radius at unit distance.
1186·2		*Chem.* Eighteenth.
1186·3		*Elec.* Charge density (surface); conductivity; current density; specific resistance; specific conductance.
1186·4		*Gk.* (l.c.) Sigma, 18th letter of the a., eq. Rom. s. Cardinal number 200.
1186·5		*Mech.* Poisson's ratio; surface tension.
1186·6		*Nav. Arch.* Cavitation number.

1186·7   *Phon.* Labialized th (hard).

1186·8   *Phys.* Stephan-Boltzmann constant; standard deviation; surface tension; resistivity of a porous substance to flow of air; density; one thousandth of a second.

TABLE 105

1190   *Egy.* (Hier.) Cardinal number 10,000,000.

1191   *Elec.* (USA.) Cold cathode.

1192   *Elec.* (Arch. plans. USA.) Wall outlet.

1193   *Cart.* (Rep. Du.) Forest.

1194   *Mil.* (L. Rep. Naval sleeve and epaulette badge. Gold. Brit.) Sub-Lieutenant.

1195   *Mil.* (L. Rep. Naval sleeve and epaulette badge. Gold. Brit.) Warrant Officer.

1196   *Alch.* Glass. (*A Compleat Body of Chymistry,* 17th cent.)

1197   *Elec.* Contact point.

1198   *Mil.* (L. Rep. Naval sleeve and epaulette badge. Gold. Brit.) Commodore 2nd class.

1199   *Hyd.* Black can buoy.

173

1200	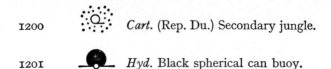	*Cart.* (Rep. Du.) Secondary jungle.
1201		*Hyd.* Black spherical can buoy.
1202		*Hyd.* Black conical can buoy.

TABLE 106

1205		*Rlwy.* (USA.) Electric light location.
1206	O‖	*Bot.* Having cotyledons incumbent and the radicle dorsal.
1207	O‖‖	*Bot.* Having cotyledons folded twice and the radicle dorsal.
1208	O‖‖‖	*Bot.* Having cotyledons folded three times and the radicle dorsal.
1209	O=	*Bot.* Having cotyledons accumbent and the radicle lateral.
1210		*Mil.* Searchlight.
1211		*Alch.* Gold.
1212		*Elec.* Switch.
1213		*Mil.* (L. Rep. Naval sleeve and epaulette badge. Gold. Brit.) Lieutenant.

174

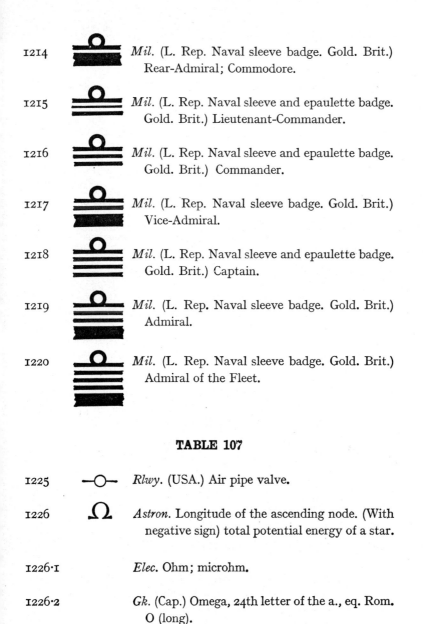

1214   *Mil.* (L. Rep. Naval sleeve badge. Gold. Brit.) Rear-Admiral; Commodore.

1215   *Mil.* (L. Rep. Naval sleeve and epaulette badge. Gold. Brit.) Lieutenant-Commander.

1216   *Mil.* (L. Rep. Naval sleeve and epaulette badge. Gold. Brit.) Commander.

1217   *Mil.* (L. Rep. Naval sleeve badge. Gold. Brit.) Vice-Admiral.

1218   *Mil.* (L. Rep. Naval sleeve and epaulette badge. Gold. Brit.) Captain.

1219   *Mil.* (L. Rep. Naval sleeve badge. Gold. Brit.) Admiral.

1220   *Mil.* (L. Rep. Naval sleeve badge. Gold. Brit.) Admiral of the Fleet.

TABLE 107

1225   —O—   *Rlwy.* (USA.) Air pipe valve.

1226 Ω *Astron.* Longitude of the ascending node. (With negative sign) total potential energy of a star.

1226·1   *Elec.* Ohm; microhm.

1226·2   *Gk.* (Cap.) Omega, 24th letter of the a., eq. Rom. O (long).

175

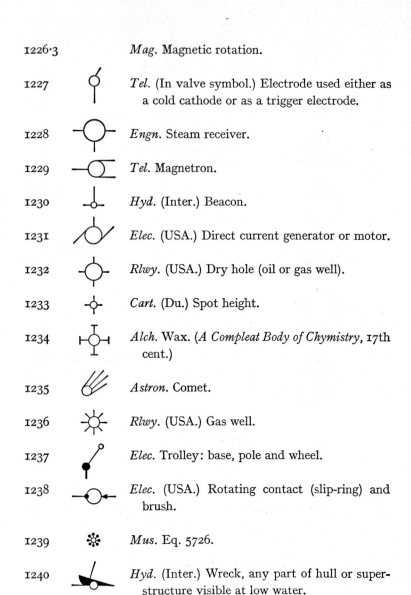

1226·3   *Mag.* Magnetic rotation.

1227   *Tel.* (In valve symbol.) Electrode used either as a cold cathode or as a trigger electrode.

1228   *Engn.* Steam receiver.

1229   *Tel.* Magnetron.

1230   *Hyd.* (Inter.) Beacon.

1231   *Elec.* (USA.) Direct current generator or motor.

1232   *Rlwy.* (USA.) Dry hole (oil or gas well).

1233   *Cart.* (Du.) Spot height.

1234   *Alch.* Wax. (*A Compleat Body of Chymistry*, 17th cent.)

1235   *Astron.* Comet.

1236   *Rlwy.* (USA.) Gas well.

1237   *Elec.* Trolley: base, pole and wheel.

1238   *Elec.* (USA.) Rotating contact (slip-ring) and brush.

1239   *Mus.* Eq. 5726.

1240   *Hyd.* (Inter.) Wreck, any part of hull or super-structure visible at low water.

176

TABLE 108

TABLE 108

§ 1. *Without Dots*

1245   *H/mrk.* Silver date mark, 1713.

1246   *Elec.* Filament lamp.

1247   *Engn.* Centrifugal clarifier.

1248   *Engn.* Air ejector, steam-jet or thermo-compressor type.

1249   *Geol.* Head (drift, esp. in Cornwall).

1250   *Engn.* Centrifugal separator with heavy and light fraction discharges.

1251   *Alch.* Calcinated copper, *crocus veneris*: possibly yellow cuprous oxide. (*A Compleat Body of Chymistry*, 17th cent.)

1252   *Alch.* Common salt (sodium chloride). (*A Compleat Body of Chymistry*, 17th cent.)

1253   *Alch.* Mercury. (*Theatrum Chemicum*, Strasbourg, 1659–61.)

1254   *Elec.* (USA.) Phase-shifter with 1-phase output.

1255   *Elec.* (USA.) Symmetrical photoconductive transducer; selenium cell.

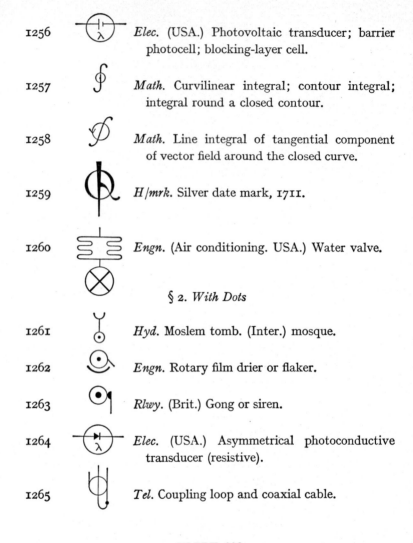

1256   *Elec.* (USA.) Photovoltaic transducer; barrier photocell; blocking-layer cell.

1257   *Math.* Curvilinear integral; contour integral; integral round a closed contour.

1258   *Math.* Line integral of tangential component of vector field around the closed curve.

1259   *H/mrk.* Silver date mark, 1711.

1260   *Engn.* (Air conditioning. USA.) Water valve.

§ 2. *With Dots*

1261   *Hyd.* Moslem tomb. (Inter.) mosque.

1262   *Engn.* Rotary film drier or flaker.

1263   *Rlwy.* (Brit.) Gong or siren.

1264   *Elec.* (USA.) Asymmetrical photoconductive transducer (resistive).

1265   *Tel.* Coupling loop and coaxial cable.

TABLE 109

1269   *Engn.* (Plumbing. USA.) Unit of series of overhead gang showers.

178

1270   *Cart.* (Ant. OS.) Roman villa enclosure.

1271   *Alch.* Vitriol. (*A Compleat Body of Chymistry*, 17th cent.)

1272   *Mil.* (R.A.) Orderly Officer.

1273   *Bot.* Eq. 816·2.

1273·1   *Geol. Min.* Abandoned shaft.

1273·2   *Mus.* (Obsnt.) Sign marking end of passage to be repeated.

1273·3   *Rlwy.* (Brit.) Wagon or coach turntable.

1274   *Rel.* Celtic cross.

1275   *Nav.* Dead flat.

1275·1   *Nav. Arch.* The largest transverse section of a vessel.

1276   *Elec.* (USA.) 1-phase synchronous reluctance motor.

1277   *Elec.* (USA.) 1-phase repulsion-start induction motor.

1278   *Rlwy.* (Brit.) Trip cock test indicator.

1279   *Elec.* Signal lamp.

1279·1   *Geol.* Pebble gravel.

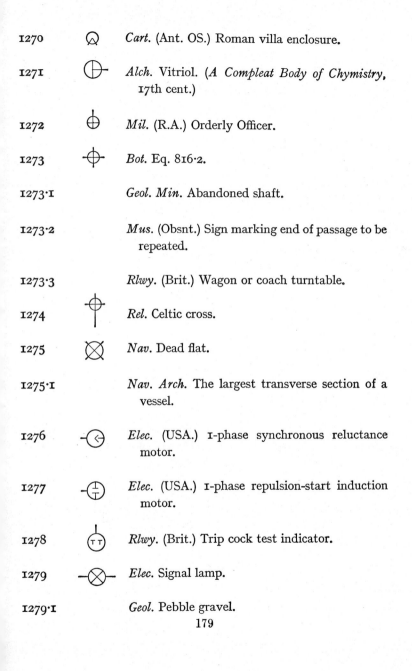

179

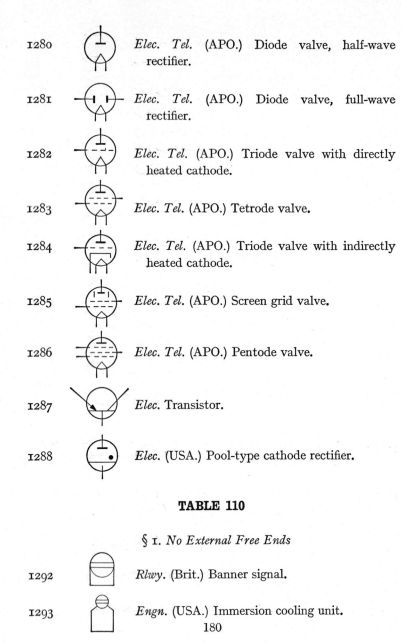

1280   *Elec. Tel.* (APO.) Diode valve, half-wave rectifier.

1281   *Elec. Tel.* (APO.) Diode valve, full-wave rectifier.

1282   *Elec. Tel.* (APO.) Triode valve with directly heated cathode.

1283   *Elec. Tel.* (APO.) Tetrode valve.

1284   *Elec. Tel.* (APO.) Triode valve with indirectly heated cathode.

1285   *Elec. Tel.* (APO.) Screen grid valve.

1286   *Elec. Tel.* (APO.) Pentode valve.

1287   *Elec.* Transistor.

1288   *Elec.* (USA.) Pool-type cathode rectifier.

TABLE 110

§ 1. *No External Free Ends*

1292   *Rlwy.* (Brit.) Banner signal.

1293   *Engn.* (USA.) Immersion cooling unit.

180

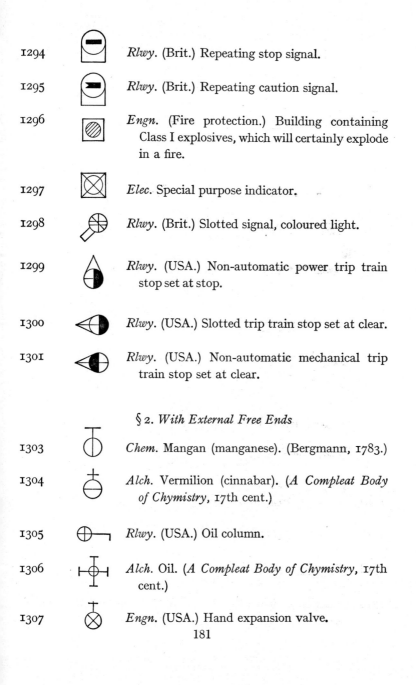

1294	*Rlwy.* (Brit.) Repeating stop signal.
1295	*Rlwy.* (Brit.) Repeating caution signal.
1296	*Engn.* (Fire protection.) Building containing Class I explosives, which will certainly explode in a fire.
1297	*Elec.* Special purpose indicator.
1298	*Rlwy.* (Brit.) Slotted signal, coloured light.
1299	*Rlwy.* (USA.) Non-automatic power trip train stop set at stop.
1300	*Rlwy.* (USA.) Slotted trip train stop set at clear.
1301	*Rlwy.* (USA.) Non-automatic mechanical trip train stop set at clear.

§ 2. *With External Free Ends*

1303	*Chem.* Mangan (manganese). (Bergmann, 1783.)
1304	*Alch.* Vermilion (cinnabar). (*A Compleat Body of Chymistry*, 17th cent.)
1305	*Rlwy.* (USA.) Oil column.
1306	*Alch.* Oil. (*A Compleat Body of Chymistry*, 17th cent.)
1307	*Engn.* (USA.) Hand expansion valve.

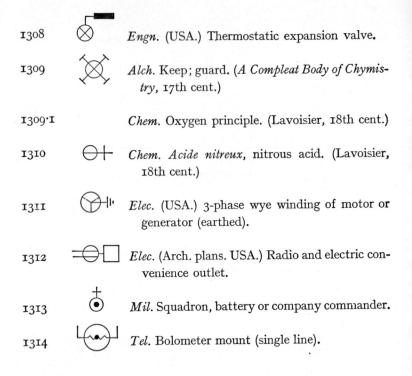

1308   *Engn.* (USA.) Thermostatic expansion valve.

1309   *Alch.* Keep; guard. (*A Compleat Body of Chymistry*, 17th cent.)

1309·1   *Chem.* Oxygen principle. (Lavoisier, 18th cent.)

1310   *Chem. Acide nitreux*, nitrous acid. (Lavoisier, 18th cent.)

1311   *Elec.* (USA.) 3-phase wye winding of motor or generator (earthed).

1312   *Elec.* (Arch. plans. USA.) Radio and electric convenience outlet.

1313   *Mil.* Squadron, battery or company commander.

1314   *Tel.* Bolometer mount (single line).

TABLE 111

§ 1. *Without Dots*

1316   *Math.* Anticlockwise.

1317   *Math.* Clockwise.

1318   *Alch.* Lead.

1319   *Geol.* Plane or flat surface, striated, showing direction of ice-flow.

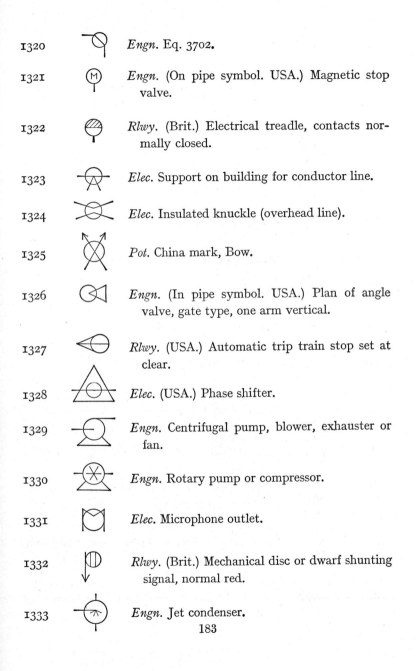

1320   *Engn.* Eq. 3702.

1321   *Engn.* (On pipe symbol. USA.) Magnetic stop valve.

1322   *Rlwy.* (Brit.) Electrical treadle, contacts normally closed.

1323   *Elec.* Support on building for conductor line.

1324   *Elec.* Insulated knuckle (overhead line).

1325   *Pot.* China mark, Bow.

1326   *Engn.* (In pipe symbol. USA.) Plan of angle valve, gate type, one arm vertical.

1327   *Rlwy.* (USA.) Automatic trip train stop set at clear.

1328   *Elec.* (USA.) Phase shifter.

1329   *Engn.* Centrifugal pump, blower, exhauster or fan.

1330   *Engn.* Rotary pump or compressor.

1331   *Elec.* Microphone outlet.

1332   *Rlwy.* (Brit.) Mechanical disc or dwarf shunting signal, normal red.

1333   *Engn.* Jet condenser.

183

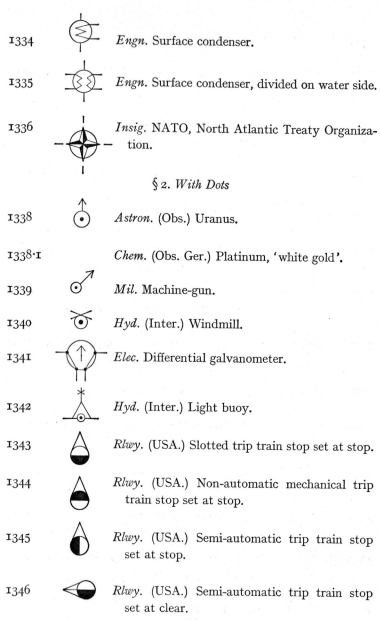

1334   *Engn.* Surface condenser.

1335   *Engn.* Surface condenser, divided on water side.

1336   *Insig.* NATO, North Atlantic Treaty Organization.

§ 2. *With Dots*

1338   *Astron.* (Obs.) Uranus.

1338·1   *Chem.* (Obs. Ger.) Platinum, 'white gold'.

1339   *Mil.* Machine-gun.

1340   *Hyd.* (Inter.) Windmill.

1341   *Elec.* Differential galvanometer.

1342   *Hyd.* (Inter.) Light buoy.

1343   *Rlwy.* (USA.) Slotted trip train stop set at stop.

1344   *Rlwy.* (USA.) Non-automatic mechanical trip train stop set at stop.

1345   *Rlwy.* (USA.) Semi-automatic trip train stop set at stop.

1346   *Rlwy.* (USA.) Semi-automatic trip train stop set at clear.

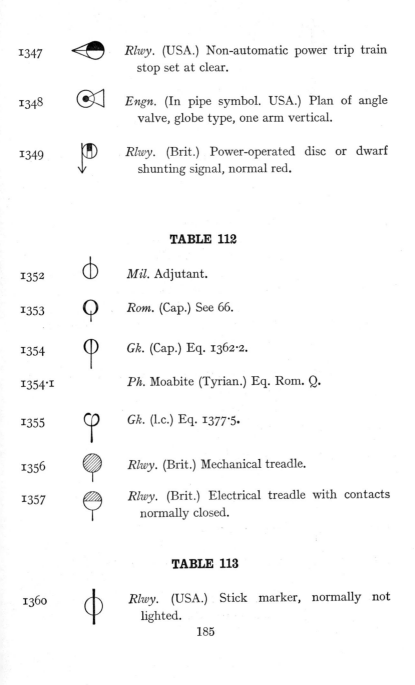

1347		*Rlwy.* (USA.) Non-automatic power trip train stop set at clear.
1348		*Engn.* (In pipe symbol. USA.) Plan of angle valve, globe type, one arm vertical.
1349		*Rlwy.* (Brit.) Power-operated disc or dwarf shunting signal, normal red.

TABLE 112

1352		*Mil.* Adjutant.
1353		*Rom.* (Cap.) See 66.
1354		*Gk.* (Cap.) Eq. 1362·2.
1354·1		*Ph.* Moabite (Tyrian.) Eq. Rom. Q.
1355		*Gk.* (l.c.) Eq. 1377·5.
1356		*Rlwy.* (Brit.) Mechanical treadle.
1357		*Rlwy.* (Brit.) Electrical treadle with contacts normally closed.

TABLE 113

| 1360 | | *Rlwy.* (USA.) Stick marker, normally not lighted. |

185

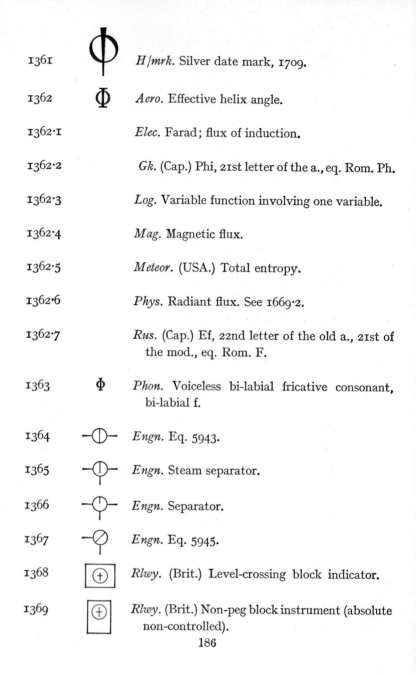

1361   *H/mrk.* Silver date mark, 1709.

1362   *Aero.* Effective helix angle.

1362·1   *Elec.* Farad; flux of induction.

1362·2   *Gk.* (Cap.) Phi, 21st letter of the a., eq. Rom. Ph.

1362·3   *Log.* Variable function involving one variable.

1362·4   *Mag.* Magnetic flux.

1362·5   *Meteor.* (USA.) Total entropy.

1362·6   *Phys.* Radiant flux. See 1669·2.

1362·7   *Rus.* (Cap.) Ef, 22nd letter of the old a., 21st of the mod., eq. Rom. F.

1363   *Phon.* Voiceless bi-labial fricative consonant, bi-labial f.

1364   *Engn.* Eq. 5943.

1365   *Engn.* Steam separator.

1366   *Engn.* Separator.

1367   *Engn.* Eq. 5945.

1368   *Rlwy.* (Brit.) Level-crossing block indicator.

1369   *Rlwy.* (Brit.) Non-peg block instrument (absolute non-controlled).

1370   ⊞   *Rlwy.* (Brit.) Non-peg block instrument (absolute controlled).

TABLE 114

1375   Ø   *D/Nor.* (Cap.) Modified Rom. O, having the sound eu.

1376   ø   *D/Nor.* (l.c.) Eq. 1375.

1376·1   *Math.* (Theory of sets.) Null set, empty set.

1376·2   *Phon.* Half-close back vowel, as in Fr. peu.

1377   ϕ   *Aero.* Angle of roll or bank.

1377·1   *Astron.* Geographical latitude; angle of eccentricity; altitude of north pole; absolute gradient.

1377·2   *Chem.* Twenty-first; the phenyl group C_6H_5; volume fraction.

1377·3   *Elec.* Phase difference; electronic exit work function. (Photo-electric emission) latent energy.

1377·4   *Engn.* Angle of repose; shear strain in radians. (Hydraulics) speed in revolutions per minute.

1377·5   *Gk.* (l.c.) Phi, 21st letter of the a., eq. Rom. ph. Cardinal number 500.

1377·6		*Math.* Polar co-ordinate; function; any angle from the vertical.
1377·7		*Mech.* Angle of friction; fluidity.
1377·8		*Nav. Arch.* Angle of inclination of ship; potential function.
1377·9		*Phys.* Phase; angular phase difference; potential; peripheral speed.
1377·01		*Therm.* Entropy.
1378		*Elec.* (USA.) 1-phase shaded-pole motor.

TABLE 115

1384		*Insig.* (L.) London Transport Board, esp. with reference to the Underground Rlwy.
1385		*Elec.* (USA.) 1-phase hysteresis motor.
1386		*Alch.* Spirit. (*A Compleat Body of Chymistry*, 17th cent.)
1386·1		*Astron.* Sun's centre.
1386·2		*Engn.* Eq. 3700.
1387		*Geol.* Plane or flat surface, striated.
1388		*Elec.* Flag or grid indicator with alarm contact.

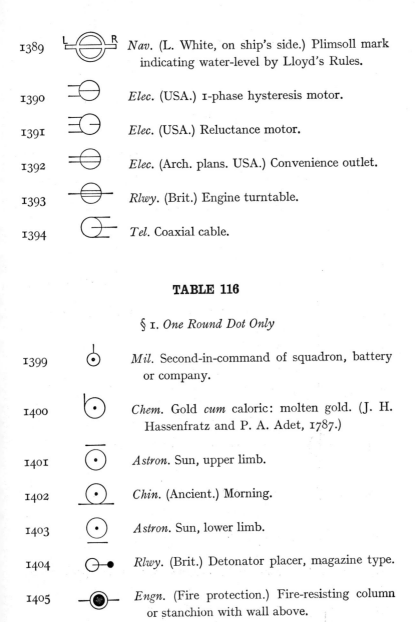

1389   *Nav.* (L. White, on ship's side.) Plimsoll mark indicating water-level by Lloyd's Rules.

1390   *Elec.* (USA.) 1-phase hysteresis motor.

1391   *Elec.* (USA.) Reluctance motor.

1392   *Elec.* (Arch. plans. USA.) Convenience outlet.

1393   *Rlwy.* (Brit.) Engine turntable.

1394   *Tel.* Coaxial cable.

TABLE 116

§ 1. *One Round Dot Only*

1399   *Mil.* Second-in-command of squadron, battery or company.

1400   *Chem.* Gold *cum* caloric: molten gold. (J. H. Hassenfratz and P. A. Adet, 1787.)

1401   *Astron.* Sun, upper limb.

1402   *Chin.* (Ancient.) Morning.

1403   *Astron.* Sun, lower limb.

1404   *Rlwy.* (Brit.) Detonator placer, magazine type.

1405   *Engn.* (Fire protection.) Fire-resisting column or stanchion with wall above.

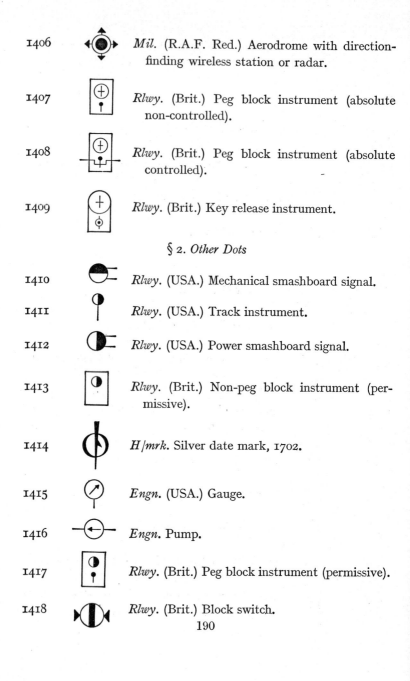

1406   *Mil.* (R.A.F. Red.) Aerodrome with direction-finding wireless station or radar.

1407   *Rlwy.* (Brit.) Peg block instrument (absolute non-controlled).

1408   *Rlwy.* (Brit.) Peg block instrument (absolute controlled).

1409   *Rlwy.* (Brit.) Key release instrument.

§ 2. *Other Dots*

1410   *Rlwy.* (USA.) Mechanical smashboard signal.

1411   *Rlwy.* (USA.) Track instrument.

1412   *Rlwy.* (USA.) Power smashboard signal.

1413   *Rlwy.* (Brit.) Non-peg block instrument (permissive).

1414   *H/mrk.* Silver date mark, 1702.

1415   *Engn.* (USA.) Gauge.

1416   *Engn.* Pump.

1417   *Rlwy.* (Brit.) Peg block instrument (permissive).

1418   *Rlwy.* (Brit.) Block switch.

1419   *High.* (L. White chalk.) Kind lady lives here. (Tramps' 'smogger'.)

1420   *Rlwy.* (Brit.) Block switch with control.

TABLE 117

1425   *Egy.* (Hier.) Eq. Rom. Th.

1426   *Alch.* Arsenic.

1427   *Cab.* Eq. Heb. aleph, 3206.

1428   *Cab.* Eq. Heb. schin, 2635.

1429   *Alch.* (Egy.) Copper.

1430   *Cab.* Character of Phul, 7th Olympic spirit, governing all things ascribed to the Moon.

TABLE 118

1435   *Gk.* (Obs.) Eq. 348·3. See 1900.

1436   *Elec.* (USA.) Telephone receiver.

1437   *Elec.* U-link.

1438   *Elec.* (USA.) Feed-through capacitor.

191

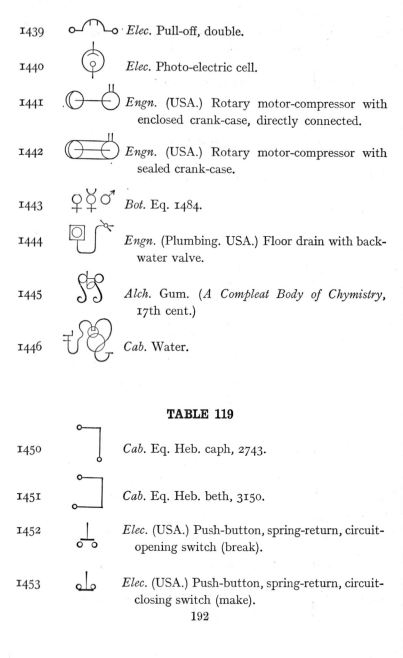

1439	*Elec.* Pull-off, double.
1440	*Elec.* Photo-electric cell.
1441	*Engn.* (USA.) Rotary motor-compressor with enclosed crank-case, directly connected.
1442	*Engn.* (USA.) Rotary motor-compressor with sealed crank-case.
1443	*Bot.* Eq. 1484.
1444	*Engn.* (Plumbing. USA.) Floor drain with back-water valve.
1445	*Alch.* Gum. (*A Compleat Body of Chymistry*, 17th cent.)
1446	*Cab.* Water.

TABLE 119

1450	*Cab.* Eq. Heb. caph, 2743.
1451	*Cab.* Eq. Heb. beth, 3150.
1452	*Elec.* (USA.) Push-button, spring-return, circuit-opening switch (break).
1453	*Elec.* (USA.) Push-button, spring-return, circuit-closing switch (make).

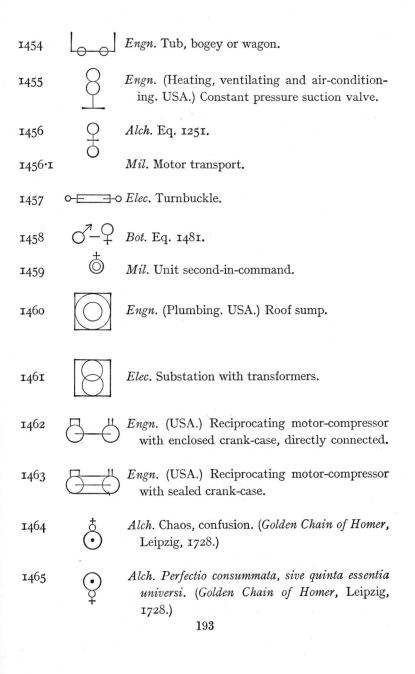

1454   *Engn.* Tub, bogey or wagon.

1455   *Engn.* (Heating, ventilating and air-condition-ing. USA.) Constant pressure suction valve.

1456   *Alch.* Eq. 1251.

1456·1   *Mil.* Motor transport.

1457   *Elec.* Turnbuckle.

1458   *Bot.* Eq. 1481.

1459   *Mil.* Unit second-in-command.

1460   *Engn.* (Plumbing. USA.) Roof sump.

1461   *Elec.* Substation with transformers.

1462   *Engn.* (USA.) Reciprocating motor-compressor with enclosed crank-case, directly connected.

1463   *Engn.* (USA.) Reciprocating motor-compressor with sealed crank-case.

1464   *Alch.* Chaos, confusion. (*Golden Chain of Homer*, Leipzig, 1728.)

1465   *Alch. Perfectio consummata, sive quinta essentia universi.* (*Golden Chain of Homer*, Leipzig, 1728.)

TABLE 120

1470   *Alch.* Sulphur.

1471   *Cab.* Eq. Heb. teth, 2881.

1472   *Alch.* Mercury.

1472·1   *Cart.* ('6-inch' and '25-inch' maps. OS.) Antiquity.

1473   *Mil.* See 1520.

1474   *Cab.* Eq. Heb. pe, 2871.

1475   *Elec.* Substation with transformers and rotating machines.

TABLE 121

1480   *Bot.* Diclinous.

1481   *Bot.* Monoecious.

1482   *Bot.* Dioecious.

1483   *Alch.* Black sulphur (black mercuric sulphide). (*A Compleat Body of Chymistry*, 17th cent.)

1484   *Bot.* Polygamous.

194

1485		*Mil.* Motor transport unit.
1486		*Egy.* (Hier.) Eq. Rom. S.
1487		*Elec.* Oil breaker.
1488		*Engn.* (USA.) Manifolded, bare-tube evaporator, gravity air.
1489		*Engn.* (USA.) Manifolded, finned evaporator, gravity air.

TABLE 122

1495		*Alch.* Lodestone. (*A Compleat Body of Chymistry,* 17th cent.)
1496		*Cab.* Eq. Heb. nun, 2796.
1497		*Cab.* Eq. Heb. zayin, 4684.
1498		*Cab.* Eq. Heb. samek, 2126.
1499		*Com.* Cursive form of 1530.
1500		*Engn.* Roll crusher.
1501		*Elec.* (APO.) Fuse.
1502		*Hyd.* Buoy with topmark.

195

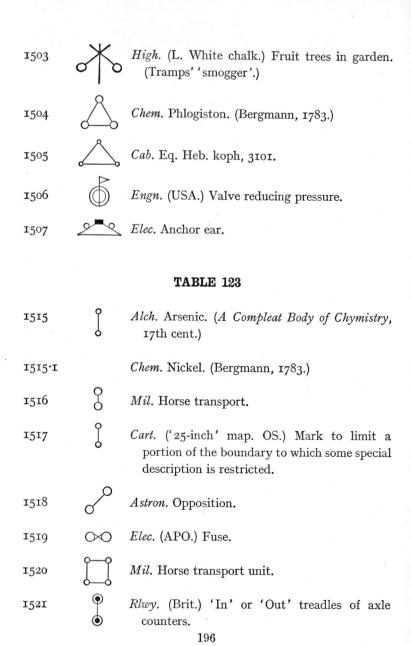

1503   *High.* (L. White chalk.) Fruit trees in garden. (Tramps' 'smogger'.)

1504   *Chem.* Phlogiston. (Bergmann, 1783.)

1505   *Cab.* Eq. Heb. koph, 3101.

1506   *Engn.* (USA.) Valve reducing pressure.

1507   *Elec.* Anchor ear.

TABLE 123

1515   *Alch.* Arsenic. (*A Compleat Body of Chymistry,* 17th cent.)

1515·1   *Chem.* Nickel. (Bergmann, 1783.)

1516   *Mil.* Horse transport.

1517   *Cart.* ('25-inch' map. OS.) Mark to limit a portion of the boundary to which some special description is restricted.

1518   *Astron.* Opposition.

1519   *Elec.* (APO.) Fuse.

1520   *Mil.* Horse transport unit.

1521   *Rlwy.* (Brit.) 'In' or 'Out' treadles of axle counters.

196

1522   *Rlwy.* (Brit.) 'In' and 'Out' treadles of axle counters.

TABLE 124

1528   *Elec.* (USA.) Toggle switch, circuit-closing.

1529   *Elec.* (USA.) Toggle switch, circuit-opening.

1530   *Com.* Per cent., per hundred. (Lat. *per centum.*)

1531   *Com.* Per thousand.

1532   *Elec.* Air circuit-breaker.

1533   *Engn.* (On pipe symbol. USA.) Bushing, soldered.

1534   *Elec.* (USA.) Wound-rotor induction motor; synchronous induction motor; induction generator.

1535   *Elec.* (USA.) Synchro characteristic.

1536   *Elec.* Microphone or telephone transmitter, push-pull.

1537   *Cab.* Fire.

1538   *Elec.* (USA.) Speed regulator.

1539   *Tel.* Key.

197

TABLE 125

1545	O–O	*Chess.* Castles with King's Rook.
1546	<u>OO</u>	*Meteor.* (USA.) Smoky atmosphere.
1547	⊙──O	*Astrol/n.* 4th sign of the Zodiac, Cancer, the Crab.
1548	O–O–O	*Chess.* Castles with Queen's Rook.
1549	— ꙍ	*Pros.* Trochaic dactyl.
1550	–o—o—o	*Elec.* (Rep. APO.) Circuit connection.
1551	—⦶—	*Elec.* Tumbler switch.
1552		*Soil/m.* (Rep.) Boulder clay.
1553		*Soil/m.* (Rep.) Hoggin (a rough gravel of large and small stones, with some sand).

TABLE 126

1565	O——O	*Alch.* Arsenic. (*A Compleat Body of Chymistry,* 17th cent.)
1565·1		*Chem.* Arsen (arsenic). (Bergmann, 1783.)
1566	⊂▬⊃	*Alch.* Auripigmentum, orpiment (sulphide of arsenic). *A Compleat Body of Chymistry,* 17th cent.)

1567	—o——o—	*Engn.* (USA.) Branch and lead sprinkler system.
1568	—⊕—	*Rlwy.* (USA.) Main air reservoir.
1569	o——o	*Engn.* Band, belt or shaker conveyeor.
1570	o⊖o	*Geol.* Plateau gravel.
1571	-o—o—o-	*Rlwy.* (USA.) Compressed air pipe line.
1572	8̶8̶8̶8̶8̶	*Rlwy.* (USA.) Flood-lighting tower.
1573		*Hyd.* Mooring buoy.
1574		*Hyd.* Mooring buoy.
1575		*Hyd.* Mooring buoy.

Cl.I, Div.II, Ord.I, Fam.I, Gen.II

TABLE 127

1580	œ	*Phon.* Half-open front vowel, as in Fr. peur.
1580·1		*Rom.* (l.c.) Eq. 1634. (*ITA*) o as in go.
1581	æ	*Rom.* (l.c.) Eq. 3541·3.
1582	*g*	*Rom.* (l.c.) Cursive form of Rom. g.
1582·1		*Rus.* (l.c.) Cursive form of 2108·1. See also 135·2.
1583	*G*	*Ger.* (Cap./l.c.) Cursive form of 540.

199

TABLE 128

1589	𝓗𝓞	*Rus.* (Cap.) Cursive form of 1633.
1590	𝑜	*Rus.* (l.c.) Cursive form of 136.
1591	𝒬	*Aero.* Torque.
1591·1		*Elec.* Electric charge; reactive power; Nernst effect; Q-factor, magnification factor; ratio of the inductive reactance of a tuned circuit at the resonant frequency to its radio-frequency resistance.
1591·2		*Engn.* Factor of safety. (Hydraulics) rate of flow.
1591·3		*It.* (Cap.) Eq. Rom. Q.
1591·4		*Mech.* Statical moment of any area about a given axis.
1591·5		*Nav. Arch.* Torque.
1591·6		*Therm.* Quantity of heat; partition function.
1592	ℛ	*Ir.* 15th letter of the a., eq. Rom. R.
1593	⌐o	*Numis.* Mint mark, a grapple.
1594	𝒲	*Ger.* (Cap.) Cursive form of 638.
1595	ℛ𝒫	*Pot.* China mark, Rookwood Pottery, Cincinnati, Ohio.

1596		*Am.* (Cherokee syllabary.) Eq. Rom. MA.

TABLE 129

1598		*Com.* Sign of the Soleras, Oloroso, a sweet golden sherry.
1599	*a*	*Rom.* (Cap.) Cursive form of A.
1600	*a*	*It.* (l.c.) Eq. Rom. a. See 1920.
1601	*d*	*Astron.* Angular distance.
1601·1		*Elec.* Current density at an electrode surface.
1601·2		*It.* (l.c.) Eq. Rom. d.
1601·3		*Mech.* Relative density.
1601·4		*Nav. Arch.* Moulded draught.
1602	*b*	*Rus.* (l.c.) It. form of 2008.
1603	*a*	*Rom.* (l.c.) Cursive form of a.
1603·1		*Rus.* (l.c.) Cursive form of 2153·2.
1604	*Q*	*It.* (Cap.) Eq. Rom. Q. See 1591.
1605		*Mil.* Motor-cycle.
1606	*з*	*Ger.* (l.c.) 26th letter of the a., eq. Rom. z.

201

1607	*Ol*	*Ger.* (Cap./l.c.) Cursive form of 2582.
1608	ᵹ	*OE.* Anglo-Saxon yogh, eq. 4269.
1609	*ɔ*	*Ger.* (l.c.) Cursive form of 2135.
1610	*ɔ̸*	*Ger.* (l.c.) Cursive form of 2127.
1611	ou	*ITA.* (Augmented Rom.) ou as in out.
1612	*no*	*Ger.* (l.c.) Cursive form of 2137.
1613	*ɪo*	*Rus.* (l.c.) Cursive form of 1633.
1614	*ɑ*	*Ger.* (l.c.) Cursive form of 2128.
1615	*oj*	*Ger.* (l.c.) Cursive form of 2140.

TABLE 130

1618	⏀	*Engn.* (In pipe symbol. USA.) Line filter.
1619	q	*Num.* (Arab.) Cursive form of numeral 9.
1620	q	*Rom.* (l.c.) 17th letter of the a. See 1941.
1621	p	*Rom.* (l.c.) 16th letter of the a. See 1942.
1622	ρ	*Mus.* Eq. 1624.
1623	d	*Rom.* (l.c.) 4th letter of the a.
1624	♩	*Mus.* Minim.

202

1625	b	*Rom.* (l.c.) 2nd letter of the a.
1626	Φ	*Gk.* (Cap.) Eq. 1362·2.
1627	ℐ	*Mil.* (RAF.) Balloon.

TABLE 131

1630		*Am.* (Cherokee syllabary.) Eq. Rom. WI.
1631	p	*Ir.* 14th letter of the a., eq. Rom. P.
1632		*Am.* (Cherokee syllabary.) Eq. Rom. ME.
1633	Ю	*Rus.* (Cap./l.c.) Yoo, 33rd letter of the old a., 31st of the mod., eq. Rom. Yu.
1634	Œ	*Rom.* (Cap.) Ligature of O and E; the diphthong formed by the union of O and E.
1635	oi	*ITA.* (Augmented Rom.) oi as in oil.
1636	‖◁‖	*Mus.* Breve.
1637		*Am.* (Cherokee syllabary.) Eq. Rom. HA.
1638		*Pot.* China mark, New Milford Pottery, Connecticut, USA.
1639	℔	*Com.* Eq. 1963.
1640		*Mus.* Repeat the notes indicated at semiquaver intervals.

203

TABLE 132

1645   *b*   *Astron.* Heliocentric latitude; galactic latitude; planetographic latitude; semi-axis minor of meridian ellipse of the earth; horizontal flexure.

1645·1   *Elec.* Susceptance.

1645·2   *Engn.* Width of rectangular beam or of rib of T-beam. (Hydraulics) surface width of channel.

1645·3   *It.* (l.c.) Eq. Rom. b.

1645·4   *Phys.* Co-volume.

1646   *p*   *Astron.* Precession; position angle, reckoned from north towards east.

1646·1   *Elec.* Resistivity.

1646·2   *Engn.* Pitch. (Structural) longitudinal pitch of rivets; percentage of reinforcement. (Hydraulics) height of weir-crest above up-stream bed.

1646·3   *It.* (l.c.) Eq. Rom. p.

1646·4   *Log.* Variable proposition.

1646·5   *Mech.* Pressure; intensity of normal stress.

1646·6   *Nav. Arch.* Pitch ratio.

1646·7		*Phys.* (Relativity.) Momentum.
1646·8		*Rus.* (l.c.) It. form of 1942·3.
1647	**7b**	*Rus.* (l.c.) It. form of 2043.

TABLE 133

1655	q	*Num.* (Arab.) Cursive form of numeral 9.
1656	q	*Astron.* Perihelion distance. (Astrophotometry) direction of analyser.
1656·1		*It.* (l.c.) Eq. Rom. q.
1656·2		*Log.* Variable proposition.
1656·3		*Math.* Quaternion.
1656·4		*Mech.* Intensity of shear stress.
1656·5		*Nav. Arch.* Quantity of flow.
1656·6		*Phys.* Dryness of fraction.
1656·7		*Therm.* Quantity of heat.
1657	q	*Rom.* (Cap./l.c.) Cursive form of q.
1658	*Œ*	*It.* (Cap.) Eq. 1634.

205

TABLE 134

1665	Q	*Rom.* (Cap.) See 66.
1666	$\mathcal{O}$	*It.* (Cap.) Eq. Rom. Q. See 1591.
1667	$\emptyset$	*D/Nor. It.* (Cap.) Eq. 1375.
1668	$\emptyset$	*D/Nor. It.* (l.c.) Eq. 1376.
1669	$\mathcal{P}$	*Gk.* (Cap.) Eq. 1362·2.
1669·1		*Mag.* Magnetic flux.
1669·2		*Phys.* (Light.) Luminous flux. See 1362·6.
1670	ϕ	*Gk.* (l.c.) Eq. 1377·5.
1671		*Afr.* (Cameroons.) Ideograph signifying a fowl.

TABLE 135

1676	θ	*Am.* See 129.
1676·1		*Rus.* (Cap./l.c. Obs.) Feeta, the old 35th letter of the a., eq. Rom. PH, F.
1677	e	*Rom.* (l.c.) 5th letter of the a.
1678	θ	*Aero.* Angle of pitch.
1678·1		*Astron.* Co-latitude; sidereal time; position angle of proper motion, measured from north

towards east; angle with positive direction of normal; longitude in circular orbit.

1678·2   *Chem.* Eighth.

1678·3   *Elec.* Angular phase difference.

1678·4   *Engn.* Angle in radians of lap of belt on a pulley.

1678·5   *Gk.* (l.c.) Theta, 8th letter of the a., eq. Rom. th. Cardinal number 9.

1678·6   *Math.* Polar co-ordinate; degrees of arc; any angle from the horizontal; angle between polar axis and radius vector; cylindrical co-ordinate.

1678·7   *Mech.* Angle of twist; torsional strain.

1678·8   *Meteor.* Absolute temperature of a column of air.

1678·9   *Opt.* Critical Angle.

1678·01   *Phon.* Voiceless dental fricative consonant, as th in thick.

1678·02   *Phys.* Absolute temperature; Curie point; angular displacement in radians; angle between direction of view and the normal to a surface.

1678·03   *Rus.* (l.c.) 35th letter of the a., eq. Rom. f.

1678·04   *Therm.* Empirical temperature.

1679 θ *Gk.* (l.c.) Eq. 1678·5.

TABLE 136

1685		*Mil.* Tree. (Rep.) wood.
1686		*Cart.* (Du.) Teak.
1687		*Geol.* Roche moutonnée, striated.
1688		*Pot.* China mark, Turner, Longton.

Cl.I, Div.II, Ord.I, Fam.II, Gen.I

TABLE 137

1695   *Num.* (Arab. 17th cent.) Eq. mod. 8.

1696   *Phon.* Voiced bi-labial fricative consonant, b as in Spanish Saber.

1697   *Aero.* Angle of stabilizer with reference to lower wing.

1697·1   *Astron.* Geocentric latitude; celestial latitude.

1697·2   *Chem.* Second.

1697·3   *Engn.* (Hydraulics.) Angle between relative velocity of water and tangential velocity of wheel.

1697·4   *Gk.* (l.c.) Beta, 2nd letter of the a., eq. Rom. b. Cardinal number 2.

| 1697·5 | | *Min. Crys.* Intermediate refractive index of a crystal, or the corresponding axis (Y) of the optical indicatrix. |

1697·5   *Min. Crys.* Intermediate refractive index of a crystal, or the corresponding axis (Y) of the optical indicatrix.

1697·6   *Nav. Arch.* Block coefficient.

1697·7   *Phys.* Coefficient of pressure change in a gas; ratio of a given velocity to the velocity of light. (Atomic) beta-rays, beta particles; Bohr's magnetron. (Heat) coefficient of cubical expansion. (Light) luminescence factor.

1698   *H/mrk.* Silver date mark, 1715.

1699   *Alch.* Sulphur. *Cf.* 3638.

1700   *Alch.* Sulphur. *Cf.* 3638.

TABLE 138

1705   *Rom.* (Cap./l.c.) Cursive form of S.

1706   *Rom.* (Cap.) Cursive form of A.

1707   *Abbr.* Eq. 1710. *Cf.* 1708.

1707·1   *Am.* (Cherokee syllabary.) Eq. Rom. DLO.

1708   *Abbr.* Eq. 1710.

1709   *Phon.* Open central vowel, a as in man.

1709·1   *Rom.* (l.c.) See 2874.

1710	&	*Abbr.* (Rom.) 'Ampersand', eq. Lat. *et*, and.
1711		*Mus.* Eq. 3413.
1712		*Mus.* (Obs.) Eq. 1732.

TABLE 139

1715		*Rom.* (Cap./l.c.) Cursive form of Y.
1715·1		*Rus.* (l.c.) Cursive form of 3037·8.
1716		*Ger.* (Cap.) Cursive form of 623, eq. Rom. J.
1717	£	*Com. Mon.* 'Crossed-L', pound or pounds (sterling), a modified cursive L (Lat. *Libra*, pound).
1718		*Rus.* (Cap.) Cursive form of 4396.
1719		*Rus.* (Cap.) Cursive form of 4485.
1720		*Egy.* (Hier. Pen and ink.) Eq. Rom. P.

TABLE 140

1725		*Print.* (Proof correction.) Delete. (A cursive d, 135·1, followed by a finishing-stroke, 5214·5.)

1726	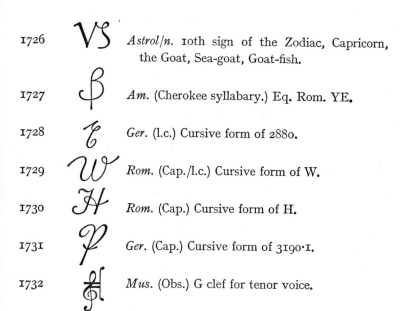	*Astrol/n.* 10th sign of the Zodiac, Capricorn, the Goat, Sea-goat, Goat-fish.
1727		*Am.* (Cherokee syllabary.) Eq. Rom. YE.
1728		*Ger.* (l.c.) Cursive form of 2880.
1729		*Rom.* (Cap./l.c.) Cursive form of W.
1730		*Rom.* (Cap.) Cursive form of H.
1731		*Ger.* (Cap.) Cursive form of 3190·1.
1732		*Mus.* (Obs.) G clef for tenor voice.

TABLE 141

| 1740 | α | *Aero.* Angle of attack. |

1740·1   *Astron.* Right ascension; phase angle; compression of the earth; mass ratio; intensity-deficiency in units of intensity-deficiency at complete eclipse; mean distance; semi-axis major of meridian ellipse of the earth, or of orbit; absorption coefficient in interstellar space in magnitudes per thousand parsecs; Stefan's constant $\times$ 4/*c*.

1740·2   *Chem.* First, beginning with; degree of dissociation; relative activity.

211

1740·3   *Elec.* Degree of electrolytic dissociation; phase-difference between voltage and current; angle of lag.

1740·4   *Engn.* Arm of resistance. (Chemical. USA) absorptivity for radiation; relative distribution of two components between two phases at equilibrium; thermal diffusivity. (Hydraulics) angle of batter; angle between absolute velocity of water and tangential velocity of wheel.

1740·5   *Gk.* (l.c.) Alpha, 1st letter of the a., eq. Rom. a. Cardinal number 1.

1740·6   *Math.* Eq. 190.

1740·7   *Mech.* Angular acceleration.

1740·8   *Min. Crys.* Smallest refractive index of a crystal; the corresponding axis (X) of the optical indicatrix.

1740·9   *Nav. Arch.* Angle of attack.

1740·01   *Phys.* Acceleration; coefficient of linear expansion; temperature coefficient; alternation coefficient; Sommerfeld, fine-structure, constant; optical rotation; refraction angle of prism; observed angle of optical rotation. (Atomic) alpha-rays; alpha particles.

1740·02   *Tel.* Decay coefficient.

1741   *ℓ*   *Ger.* (l.c.) Cursive form of 4647.

1741·1		*Rom.* (l.c.) Cursive form of l.
1742	$\mathcal{e}$	*Rom.* (l.c.) Cursive form of e.
1743	$\mathcal{J}$	*ME. MS.* (Abbr.) -es or -is.
1744	φ	*Gk.* (l.c.) Eq. 1377·5.
1745	φ	*Phys.* Electron affinity. (A form of 1744.)
1746	$\mathcal{J}.$	*Math.* Cursive form of 4753.
1747	$\mathcal{N}^{\varrho}$	*Ger.* (l.c.) Cursive form of 3154.
1748	$\mathcal{r}$	*Rom.* (l.c.) Cursive form of r.

TABLE 142

1750		*High.* (L. Swiss.) Postal mountain road.
1751	α	*Gk.* (l.c.) Cursive form of 1740·5.
1752	γ	*Gk.* (l.c.) Cursive form of 2727·5.
1753	γ	*Num.* (Arab.) Cursive form of numeral 8.
1754		*Phon.* Palatalized sh.
1755		*Elec.* (With 3844.) Electro-dynamic type.
1756		*Elec.* Series winding (relays and releases). (With 1091) electro-dynamic type.
1757	$\mathfrak{z}$	*Phon.* Palatalized zh.

213

TABLE 143

1765	*a*	*It.* (l.c.) Eq. Rom. a. See 1920.
1766	*e*	*Ir.* (Cap.) Cursive form of 2221.
1767		*Arab.* Ṭa, 16th letter of the a., eq. Rom. Ṭ.
1768		*Arab.* Ẓa, 17th letter of the a., eq. Rom. Ẓ.
1769	*a*	*It.* (l.c.) Eq. Rom. a. See 1920.
1770		*Ind. Num.* (Phila.) Eq. Arab. 1; unity.
1771		*Arab.* Ṣad, 14th letter of the a., eq. Rom. Ṣ.
1772		*Am.* (Cherokee syllabary.) Eq. Rom. WÖ.

TABLE 144

1779		*Rom.* (Abbr.) Cursive form of 1708 and 4323·01.
1780	*h*	*Rom.* (l.c.) Cursive form of h.
1781		*Ind. Num.* (3rd cent. Hindu.) Eq. Arab. 6.
1782	*k*	*It.* (l.c.) Eq. Rom. k. Also the cursive form. See 3204.
1783		*Am.* (Cherokee syllabary.) Eq. Rom. HO.
1784		*Am.* (Cherokee syllabary.) Eq. Rom. DLU.

214

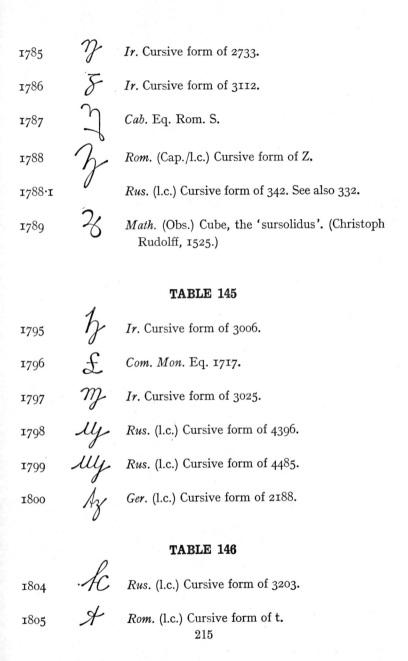

1785		*Ir.* Cursive form of 2733.
1786		*Ir.* Cursive form of 3112.
1787		*Cab.* Eq. Rom. S.
1788		*Rom.* (Cap./l.c.) Cursive form of Z.
1788·1		*Rus.* (l.c.) Cursive form of 342. See also 332.
1789		*Math.* (Obs.) Cube, the 'sursolidus'. (Christoph Rudolff, 1525.)

TABLE 145

1795		*Ir.* Cursive form of 3006.
1796		*Com. Mon.* Eq. 1717.
1797		*Ir.* Cursive form of 3025.
1798		*Rus.* (l.c.) Cursive form of 4396.
1799		*Rus.* (l.c.) Cursive form of 4485.
1800		*Ger.* (l.c.) Cursive form of 2188.

TABLE 146

| 1804 | | *Rus.* (l.c.) Cursive form of 3203. |
| 1805 | | *Rom.* (l.c.) Cursive form of t. |

215

1806		*Ger.* (l.c.) Cursive form of 3162.
1807		*Num.* (Arab.) Cursive form of 4952.
1808		*Elec.* Current Transformer.
1809		*Ger.* (l.c.) Cursive form of 1911.
1810		*Cab.* Mercury; sign of the angel Raphael.
1811		*Ger.* (l.c.) Cursive form of 2197.

TABLE 147

1815		*MS.* (Law.) Eq. 185.
1816		*Phon.* Half-close back vowel in Asiatic languages.
1817		*Phon.* Voiceless alveolar lateral fricative consonant, ll as in Welsh Llangollen.
1818		*Am.* (Cherokee syllabary.) Eq. Rom. TE.
1819		*Rel.* The Ankh, *Crux ansata*, handled, hafted cross. (Cop.) symbol for Christianity. (Egy.) symbol for life, male and female in conjugation.
1820		*OE.* & *Ic.* (l.c.) Eq. 1986.
1821		*Egy.* (Hier.) Eq. Rom. N.

216

TABLE 148

1824		*Ind. Num.* (Phila.) Eq. Arab. 4.
1825		*Arab. Num.* Eq. 275.
1826		*Phon.* Voiced velar fricative consonant, g as in Sp. luego.
1827		*Rel.* Eq. 1880.
1828		*OE., ME. & Ic.* (l.c.) Eq. 2168.
1829		*Ger.* (l.c.) Cursive form of 5736.
1829·1		*Rom.* (l.c.) Cursive form of j.
1830		*It.* (l.c.) Eq. Rom. k. See 3204.
1831		*Phon.* Voiced alveolo-palatal fricative consonant, z as in Pol. Ziarno.

TABLE 149

1835		*Engn.* Mechanical stirrer.
1836		*Ir. & Rom.* (l.c.) Cursive form of d.
1837		*Rom.* (Cap.) Cursive form of J.
1838		*Ger.* (l.c.) Cursive form of 2824.

217

1838·1		*Rom.* (Obs.) Cursive form of the 'long s', 2903·2, used generally at the beginning or in the middle of a word.
1839		*Ger.* (l.c.) Cursive form of 2142.
1839·1		*Rom.* (l.c.) Cursive form of b.
1839·2		*Rus.* (l.c.) Cursive form of 2084·3.
1840		*Am.* (Cherokee syllabary.) Eq. Rom. YI.
1841		*Alch.* Silver.
1842		*Ger.* (l.c.) Cursive form of 2189.
1843		*Tel.* Inductive susceptance (single line).
1844		*Tel.* Inductance; inductive reactance.
1845		*Elec.* Shunt winding (relays and releases).
1846		*Numis.* Mint mark, Edward III.
1847		*Geol.* (Rep.) 'Mussel' band.
1848		*Rlwy. Cart.* (Rep. USA.) Vineyard.

TABLE 150

§ 1. *Not More Than Two Loops*

1855		*Rom.* (Cap.) Cursive form of 2230·1.

218

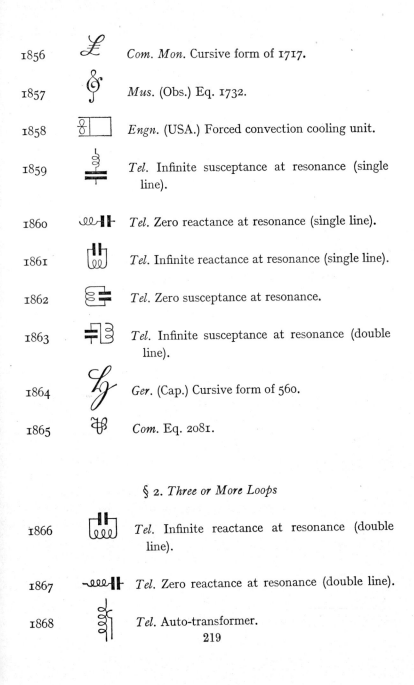

1856   *Com. Mon.* Cursive form of 1717.

1857   *Mus.* (Obs.) Eq. 1732.

1858   *Engn.* (USA.) Forced convection cooling unit.

1859   *Tel.* Infinite susceptance at resonance (single line).

1860   *Tel.* Zero reactance at resonance (single line).

1861   *Tel.* Infinite reactance at resonance (single line).

1862   *Tel.* Zero susceptance at resonance.

1863   *Tel.* Infinite susceptance at resonance (double line).

1864   *Ger.* (Cap.) Cursive form of 560.

1865   *Com.* Eq. 2081.

§ 2. *Three or More Loops*

1866   *Tel.* Infinite reactance at resonance (double line).

1867   *Tel.* Zero reactance at resonance (double line).

1868   *Tel.* Auto-transformer.

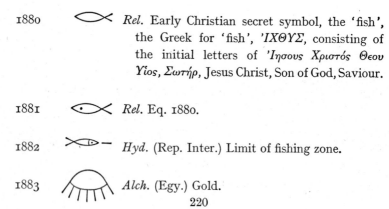

1869   *Tel.* Eq. 1868.

1870   *Engn.* Eq. 1890.

1871   *Elec.* Current transformer; inductor with iron core.

1872   *Elec.* Transformer.

1873   *Elec.* Transformer with iron core.

1874   *Elec.* Screened transformer with iron core.

Cl.I, Div.II, Ord.I, Fam.II, Gen.II

TABLE 151

§ 1. *Almonds*

1880   *Rel.* Early Christian secret symbol, the 'fish', the Greek for 'fish', *'IXΘΥΣ*, consisting of the initial letters of *'Ιησους Χριστός Θεου Υίος, Σωτήρ*, Jesus Christ, Son of God, Saviour.

1881   *Rel.* Eq. 1880.

1882   *Hyd.* (Rep. Inter.) Limit of fishing zone.

1883   *Alch.* (Egy.) Gold.

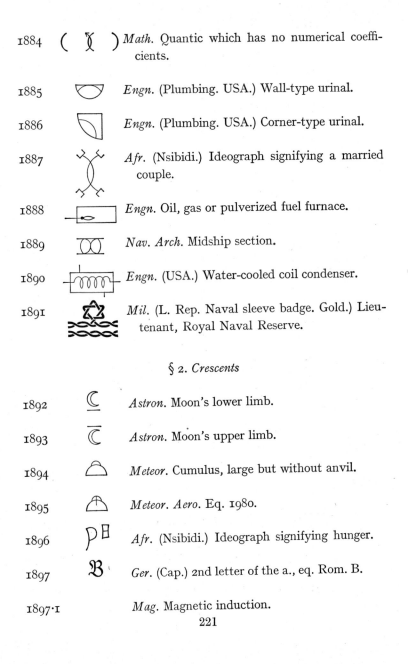

1884 (𝕏) *Math.* Quantic which has no numerical coefficients.

1885 *Engn.* (Plumbing. USA.) Wall-type urinal.

1886 *Engn.* (Plumbing. USA.) Corner-type urinal.

1887 *Afr.* (Nsibidi.) Ideograph signifying a married couple.

1888 *Engn.* Oil, gas or pulverized fuel furnace.

1889 *Nav. Arch.* Midship section.

1890 *Engn.* (USA.) Water-cooled coil condenser.

1891 *Mil.* (L. Rep. Naval sleeve badge. Gold.) Lieutenant, Royal Naval Reserve.

§ 2. *Crescents*

1892 ℂ *Astron.* Moon's lower limb.

1893 ℂ *Astron.* Moon's upper limb.

1894 △ *Meteor.* Cumulus, large but without anvil.

1895 △ *Meteor. Aero.* Eq. 1980.

1896 ꝓꞞ *Afr.* (Nsibidi.) Ideograph signifying hunger.

1897 ℬ *Ger.* (Cap.) 2nd letter of the a., eq. Rom. B.

1897·1 *Mag.* Magnetic induction.

221

TABLE 152

1900	⭓	*Math.* The 'tilde omega'. Arbitrary constant used in solving equations in elliptic motion.
1900·1		*Phys.* The 'pomega', wave-number, eq. 2596.
1901	⭓	*Math.* Eq. 1900.
1902		*Pot.* China mark, Bow.
1903		*Cart.* Deciduous tree.
1904		*High.* or elsewhere. (L. Often cut into bark of tree, etc.) 'Cupid's arrow'; loves.
1905		*Rel.* Triquetra, emblem of the Trinity.

Cl.I, Div.II, Ord.II, Fam.I, Gr.I, Gen.I

TABLE 153

1910		*ME. MS.* (Abbr.) Pro-.
1911		*Ger.* (l.c.) Ligature of 3105 and 1606, eq. Rom. sz.
1912		*Egy. Num.* Eq. Arab. number 1,000.
1913		*Phon.* Ligature denoting the affricate dzh.
1914		*Rus.* (l.c.) Ef, 22nd letter of the old a., 21st of the mod., eq. Rom. f.

1915	ϕ	*Rus.* (l.c.) Cursive form of 1914.
1916	ϕ	*Rus.* (l.c.) It. form of 1914.
1917	ϖ	*Math.* See 1900.

TABLE 154

| 1919 | d | *It.* (l.c.) Eq. Rom. d. See 1601·2. |
| 1920 | a | *Aero.* Aerodynamic. |

1920·1   *Astron.* Semi-axis major of meridian ellipse of the earth, or of orbit; absorption coefficient in interstellar space in magnitudes per thousand parsecs; Stefan's constant $\times 4/c$.

1920·2   *Chem.* Relative activity.

1920·3   *Engn.* Arm of Resistance.

1920·4   *Gk.* (l.c.) Eq. 1740·5.

1920·5   *It.* (l.c.) Eq. Rom. a.

1920·6   *Log.* (Between two symbols.) All the former is the latter; universal affirmative proposition.

1920·7   *Mech.* Acceleration.

223

1920·8		*Phys.* Van der Waal's volume constant.
1920·9		*Rus.* (l.c.) It. form of 2153·2.
1921[†]	ɑ	*ME. MS.* (Abbr.) -ra-.
1922	g	*Phon.* Voiced velar plosive consonant, g as in get.
1922·1		*Rom.* (l.c.) Eq. 43·5. (*ITA*) g as in get.
1923	*g*	*Rom.* (l.c.) Cursive form of g.
1924	ɖ	*Phon.* Voiced retroflex plosive consonant, rd as in Sw. bord.
1925	@	*Com.* See 690.

TABLE 155

1929	*Ꭿ*	*Rus.* (Cap./l.c.) Cursive form of 2031.
1930	picture	*Phon.* (Obs.) Eq. 1826.
1931	picture	*Phon.* (Obs.) Eq. 1826.
1932	*k*	*It.* (l.c.) Eq. Rom. k. See 3204.
1933	ŋ	*ITA.* (Augmented Rom.) ng as in king.
1934	C	*Geol.* Coombe deposits.

TABLE 156

1939	$\mathcal{G}$	*Num.* (Arab.) Cursive form of numeral 9.
1940	d	*ITA.* (Augmented Rom.) d as in doll.
1941	q	*Meteor.* Squalls.
1941·1		*Phon.* Voiceless uvular plosive consonant, modified k.
1941·2		*Rom.* (l.c.) 17th letter of the a. (In the Umbrian a.) eq. rs.
1942	p	*Phon.* Voiceless bi-labial plosive consonant, p as in pot.
1942·1		*Phys.* Pico-, eq. to micro-micro-, 10^{-12}; position.
1942·2		*Rom.* (l.c.) 16th letter of the a. (*ITA*) p as in pot.
1942·3		*Rus.* (l.c.) Er, 18th letter of the old a., 17th of the mod., eq. to Rom. r.
1943	ρ	*Gk.* (l.c.) Eq. 1148·5.

TABLE 157

1950	a	*Phon.* Open back vowel, a as in car.
1950·1		*Rom.* (l.c.) Eq. 2153·1. (*ITA*) a as in arm.

| 1951 | d | *Cal.* Differential. |

1951·1   *Phon.* Voiced dental plosive consonant, d as in do.

1951·2   *Rom.* (l.c.) 4th letter of the a.

1952   b   *Meteor.* At least one quarter of sky clear of cloud, but sky may be blue or hazy.

1952·1   *Phon.* Voiceless bi-labial plosive consonant, b as in bed.

1952·2   *Rom.* (l.c.) 2nd letter of the a. (ITA) b as in bed.

1953   ɒ   *Phon.* 'Turned-ɑ', open back vowel, o as in southern (Eng.) hot.

TABLE 158

1960   Œ   *Rom.* (Cap.) Eq. 1634.

1961   *Œ*   *It.* (Cap.) Eq. 1634.

1962   ꝑ   *ME. MS.* (Abbr.) par- *or* per-.

1963   ℔   *Com.* Pound or pounds (weight). (Lat. *libra.*)

1964   ʣ   *Phon.* Ligature denoting the affricate, dz.

Cl.I, Div.II, Ord.II, Fam.I, Gr.I, Gen.II

TABLE 159

1970 ⌒ *Egy.* (Hier.) Eq. Rom. T.

1970·1 *Engn.* (Brit.) Edge weld. (USA) bead weld.

1970·2 *Meteor.* Small cumulus, 'fair-weather' cumulus.

1970·3 *Phys.* (Illumination. Following the letter I.) Mean hemispherical candle-power (upper).

1971 ⌒ *Geom.* Semi-circle.

1972 ⌣ *Meteor.* Lunar halo.

1972·1 *Phys.* (Illumination. Following the letter I.) Mean hemispherical candle-power (lower).

1973 ▽ *Engn.* Butt weld.

1974 ⊂ *Engn.* (Across pipe symbol.) Spigot and socket joint.

1975 D *Cal.* Differential coefficient.

1975·1 *Rom.* (Cap.) 4th letter of the a. Cardinal number 500, a ligature of IϽ. (See 2303.)

1976 **D** *Elec.* Electrostatic flux density; current intensity; electric displacement.

1976·1 *Rom.* (Cap.) Sanserif form of D.

227

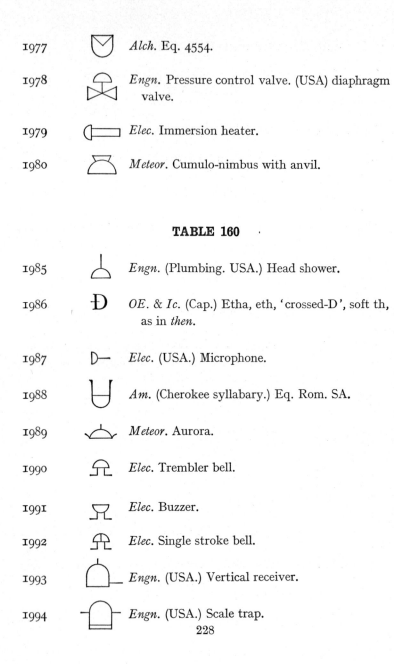

1977   *Alch.* Eq. 4554.

1978   *Engn.* Pressure control valve. (USA) diaphragm valve.

1979   *Elec.* Immersion heater.

1980   *Meteor.* Cumulo-nimbus with anvil.

TABLE 160   ·

1985   *Engn.* (Plumbing. USA.) Head shower.

1986   *OE.* & *Ic.* (Cap.) Etha, eth, 'crossed-D', soft th, as in *then.*

1987   *Elec.* (USA.) Microphone.

1988   *Am.* (Cherokee syllabary.) Eq. Rom. SA.

1989   *Meteor.* Aurora.

1990   *Elec.* Trembler bell.

1991   *Elec.* Buzzer.

1992   *Elec.* Single stroke bell.

1993   *Engn.* (USA.) Vertical receiver.

1994   *Engn.* (USA.) Scale trap.

1995	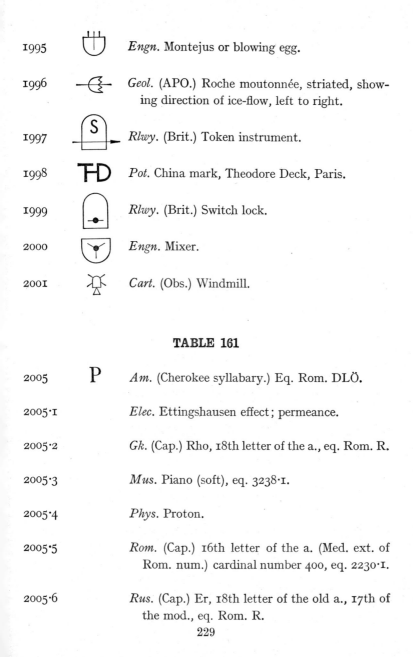	*Engn.* Montejus or blowing egg.
1996		*Geol.* (APO.) Roche moutonnée, striated, showing direction of ice-flow, left to right.
1997		*Rlwy.* (Brit.) Token instrument.
1998		*Pot.* China mark, Theodore Deck, Paris.
1999		*Rlwy.* (Brit.) Switch lock.
2000		*Engn.* Mixer.
2001		*Cart.* (Obs.) Windmill.

TABLE 161

2005	P	*Am.* (Cherokee syllabary.) Eq. Rom. DLÖ.
2005·1		*Elec.* Ettingshausen effect; permeance.
2005·2		*Gk.* (Cap.) Rho, 18th letter of the a., eq. Rom. R.
2005·3		*Mus.* Piano (soft), eq. 3238·1.
2005·4		*Phys.* Proton.
2005·5		*Rom.* (Cap.) 16th letter of the a. (Med. ext. of Rom. num.) cardinal number 400, eq. 2230·1.
2005·6		*Rus.* (Cap.) Er, 18th letter of the old a., 17th of the mod., eq. Rom. R.

229

2006	Ь	*Am.* (Cherokee syllabary.) Eq. Rom. SI.
2006·1		*Rus.* (Cap./l.c.) Yer', 30th letter of the old a., 29th of the mod., the 'soft sign' (no Rom. eq.).
2007	Ρ	*Astron.* Pluto.
2008	Ъ	*Rus.* (Cap./l.c.) Yer, 28th letter of the old a., 27th of the mod., the 'hard sign' (no Rom. eq.).
2009	Б	*Rus.* (Cap.) Beh, 2nd letter of the a., eq. Rom. B.
2010		*Engn.* (Plumbing. USA.) Stall-type urinal.
2011		*Engn.* (In pipe symbol. USA.) Boiler return trap.

TABLE 162

2015	R	*Am.* (Cherokee syllabary.) Eq. Rom. E.
2015·1		*Rom.* (Cap.) Sanserif form of 2032·3.
2016	¶	*Print.* (USA.) Eq. 5715.
2017	R	*Astron.* (Obs.) Pluto.
2018		*Ph.* Sidonian koph, eq. Rom. Q.
2019	HP	*Aero.* Horse-power.
2020	NP	*Prop.* National Physical Laboratory (Teddington, England).

| 2021 | ℞ | *Nav.* Lloyd's Register. |

| 2022 | ⌇ | *Rlwy.* (Brit.) Ground telephone. |

TABLE 163

2029   ⌒   *Meteor.* Dew.

2030   Ᵽ   *Run.* Fehe, love.

2031   Я   *Rus.* (Cap./l.c.) Yah, 34th letter of the old a., 32nd of the mod., eq. Rom. Ya.

2032   R   *Elec.* Hall effect.

2032·1   *Log.* Relation.

2032·2   *Phys.* Gas constant.

2032·3   *Rom.* (Cap.) 18th letter of the a. (Med. ext. of Rom. num.) cardinal number 80.

2033   R   *Rom.* (Cap.) Eq. R, 2032·3.

2034   R   *Phon.* Uvular rolled consonant, uvular flapped consonant, variety of Parisian Fr. r.

2035   ʁ   *Phon.* 'Turned Russian ya', voiced uvular fricative consonant, variety of Parisian Fr. r.

2036   ⌒   *Cart.* (Ant. OS.) Farm or similar site of probably Rom. date.

TABLE 164

2040	⊅⊢	*Elec.* Socket outlet.
2041	⟊	*Rel.* Eq. 2054.
2042	**Ы**	*Rus.* (Cap./l.c.) Yerü, 29th letter of the old a., 28th of the mod., the dark 'l', (no Rom. eq.).
2043	**Ѣ**	*Rus.* (Cap./l.c. Obs.) Yat', 31st letter of the old a., eq. to Rom. YEH.
2044	℞	*Phar.* Eq. 2055·1.
2045	ⲫ	*Cop.* Eq. Rom. P.
2046	𝒜R	*Astron.* (Obs.) Right ascension.
2046·1		*Numis.* Silver (Lat. *argentum*).
2047	𝔚𝔅	*Ger.* (Cap.) Vay, 23rd letter of the a., eq. Rom. W.

TABLE 165

2050	₵	*H/mrk.* Silver date mark, 1698.
2051	⏛	*Engn.* (Terminating pipe symbol. USA.) Flanged bull plug.
2052	⋎⋏	*Hyd.* (Inter.) Watermill.
2053	₱	*Com. Mon.* (Sp.) 'Crossed-P', peso or pesos.

232

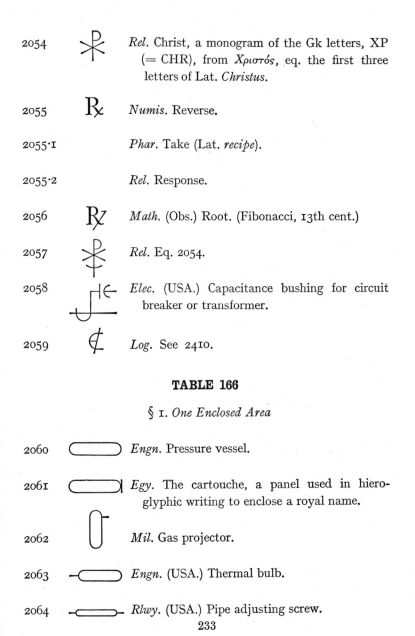

2054		*Rel.* Christ, a monogram of the Gk letters, XP (= CHR), from Χριστός, eq. the first three letters of Lat. *Christus.*
2055	℞	*Numis.* Reverse.
2055·1		*Phar.* Take (Lat. *recipe*).
2055·2		*Rel.* Response.
2056		*Math.* (Obs.) Root. (Fibonacci, 13th cent.)
2057		*Rel.* Eq. 2054.
2058		*Elec.* (USA.) Capacitance bushing for circuit breaker or transformer.
2059		*Log.* See 2410.

TABLE 166

§ 1. *One Enclosed Area*

2060		*Engn.* Pressure vessel.
2061		*Egy.* The cartouche, a panel used in hieroglyphic writing to enclose a royal name.
2062		*Mil.* Gas projector.
2063		*Engn.* (USA.) Thermal bulb.
2064		*Rlwy.* (USA.) Pipe adjusting screw.

233

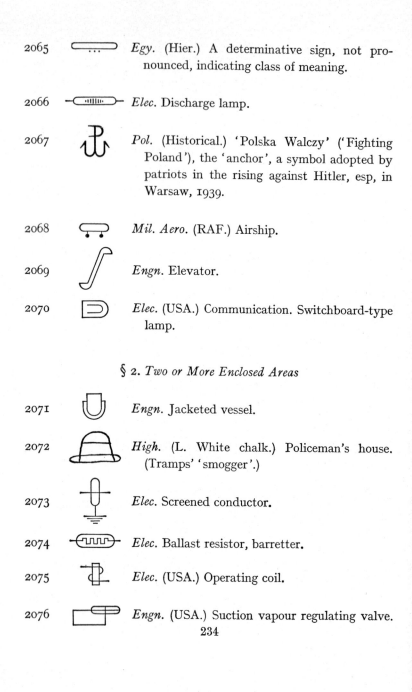

2065   *Egy.* (Hier.) A determinative sign, not pronounced, indicating class of meaning.

2066   *Elec.* Discharge lamp.

2067   *Pol.* (Historical.) 'Polska Walczy' ('Fighting Poland'), the 'anchor', a symbol adopted by patriots in the rising against Hitler, esp, in Warsaw, 1939.

2068   *Mil. Aero.* (RAF.) Airship.

2069   *Engn.* Elevator.

2070   *Elec.* (USA.) Communication. Switchboard-type lamp.

§ 2. *Two or More Enclosed Areas*

2071   *Engn.* Jacketed vessel.

2072   *High.* (L. White chalk.) Policeman's house. (Tramps' 'smogger'.)

2073   *Elec.* Screened conductor.

2074   *Elec.* Ballast resistor, barretter.

2075   *Elec.* (USA.) Operating coil.

2076   *Engn.* (USA.) Suction vapour regulating valve.

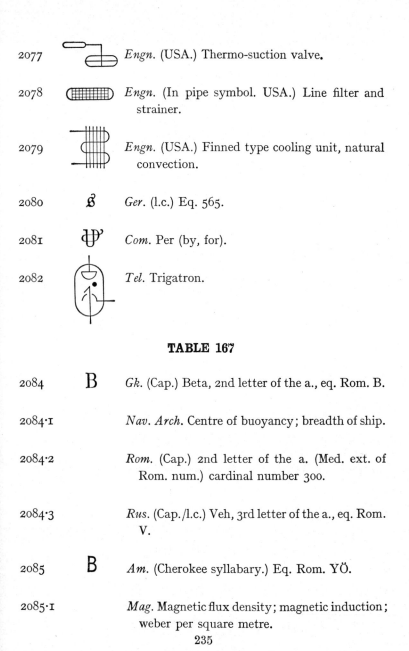

2077   *Engn.* (USA.) Thermo-suction valve.

2078   *Engn.* (In pipe symbol. USA.) Line filter and strainer.

2079   *Engn.* (USA.) Finned type cooling unit, natural convection.

2080   *Ger.* (l.c.) Eq. 565.

2081   *Com.* Per (by, for).

2082   *Tel.* Trigatron.

TABLE 167

2084   B   *Gk.* (Cap.) Beta, 2nd letter of the a., eq. Rom. B.

2084·1   *Nav. Arch.* Centre of buoyancy; breadth of ship.

2084·2   *Rom.* (Cap.) 2nd letter of the a. (Med. ext. of Rom. num.) cardinal number 300.

2084·3   *Rus.* (Cap./l.c.) Veh, 3rd letter of the a., eq. Rom. V.

2085   B   *Am.* (Cherokee syllabary.) Eq. Rom. YÖ.

2085·1   *Mag.* Magnetic flux density; magnetic induction; weber per square metre.

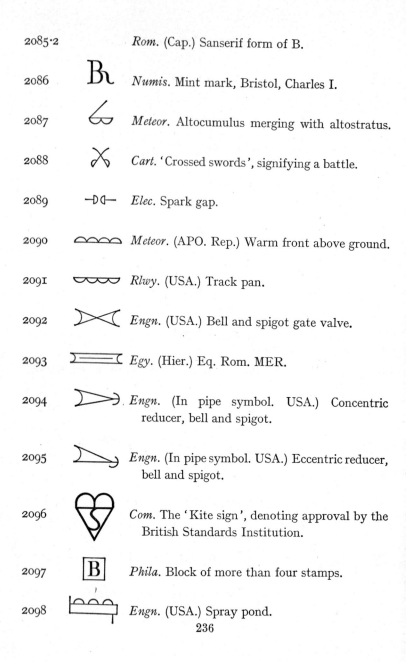

2085·2   *Rom.* (Cap.) Sanserif form of B.

2086   *Numis.* Mint mark, Bristol, Charles I.

2087   *Meteor.* Altocumulus merging with altostratus.

2088   *Cart.* 'Crossed swords', signifying a battle.

2089   *Elec.* Spark gap.

2090   *Meteor.* (APO. Rep.) Warm front above ground.

2091   *Rlwy.* (USA.) Track pan.

2092   *Engn.* (USA.) Bell and spigot gate valve.

2093   *Egy.* (Hier.) Eq. Rom. MER.

2094   *Engn.* (In pipe symbol. USA.) Concentric reducer, bell and spigot.

2095   *Engn.* (In pipe symbol. USA.) Eccentric reducer, bell and spigot.

2096   *Com.* The 'Kite sign', denoting approval by the British Standards Institution.

2097   *Phila.* Block of more than four stamps.

2098   *Engn.* (USA.) Spray pond.

236

TABLE 168

2105		*Geom.* Quadrant.
2106	D	*Ger.* (l.c.) 15th letter of the a., eq. Rom. o.
2107		*Rlwy.* (USA.) Manual skate machine.
2108		*Rus.* (Cap. With or without the dot.) Deh, 5th letter of the a., eq. Rom. D.
2108·1		*Rus.* (l.c. Without dot.) Eq. 2108.
2109		*Engn.* (compressing plant.) Bursting disc.
2110		*Hyd.* (Inter.) Ferry.
2111		*Cart.* Radio aerial mast.
2112		*Meteor.* (Two mid lines, USA.) Zodiacal light.
2113		*Chem.* Regulus, gold. (Bergmann, 1783.)
2114		*Meteor.* (APO. Rep.) Cold front above ground.
2115	*D*	*Astron.* Star density as a multiple of the density in the sun's immediate neighbourhood.
2115·1		*Chem.* Diffusion coefficient.
2115·2		*Engn.* (Hydraulics.) Depth of water in channel. (Hydrology) day's storage.

237

| 2115·3 | | *It.* (Cap.) Eq. Rom. D. |

2115·3   *It.* (Cap.) Eq. Rom. D.

2115·4   *Nav. Arch.* Moulded depth; drag; diameter of propeller.

2116   *B*   *Astron.* Parabolic time argument in Barker's equation; the sun's geocentric latitude with regard to the ecliptic; coefficient of rotational term in proper motions.

2116·1   *Elec.* Susceptance.

2116·2   *Engn.* (Chemical. USA.) Thickness.

2116·3   *It.* (Cap.) Eq. Rom. B.

2116·4   *Phys.* (Light.) Luminance, photometric brightness.

2117   *g*   *It.* (l.c.) Eq. Rom. g. See 123.

2118   ☐   *Num.* (Magnetic ink E 13 B font) Nought, zero, eq. 8·4.

TABLE 169

2125   *g*   *Rom.* (l.c.) Cursive form of g. See 43 and 123.

2126   ☐   *Heb.* Samek, 15th letter of the a., eq. Rom. S. Cardinal number 60.

2127   ℊ   *Ger.* (l.c.) 7th letter of the a., eq. Rom. g.

2128	α	*Ger.* (l.c.) 1st letter of the a., eq. Rom. a.
2129	$\mathfrak{B}$	*H/mrk.* Eq. 2814.
2130	$\mathcal{I}$	*Rom.* (Cap.) Cursive form of I. See 646.
2131	$\mathfrak{G}$	*Rom.* (Cap.) 'Old English', 'Black Letter', eq. G.
2132	$\mathfrak{s}$	*Ger.* (l.c.) Eq. 565.

TABLE 170

2134	$\flat$	*Mus.* Flat, an 'accidental' instructing to play (or read) a semitone below the note indicated. (Following another, similar sign) double-flat, play (or read) a whole tone below the note.
2135	$\mathfrak{v}$	*Ger.* (l.c.) 22nd letter of the a., eq. Rom. v.
2136	$\big\rangle$	*Egy.* & *Cop.* (Hier.) Eq. Rom. short a, e or i.
2137	$\mathfrak{w}$	*Ger.* (l.c.) 23rd letter of the a., eq. Rom. w.
2138	P	*OE.* Eq. Run. W. See 3615.
2139	b	*It.* (l.c.) Eq. Rom. b. See 1645.
2140	q	*Ger.* (l.c.) 17th letter of the a., eq. Rom. q.
2141	P	*Astron.* Parallax; orbital period; degree of polarization. (Of variable stars) period.

2141·1		*Engn.* Tensile or compressive force. (Hydraulics) wetted perimeter. (Hydrology) percolation.
2141·2		*It.* (Cap.) Eq. Rom. P.
2141·3		*Mech.* Pressure; power; force; aggregate normal force.
2141·4		*Nav. Arch.* Pitch of propeller.
2142	♭	*Ger.* (l.c.) 2nd letter of the a., eq. Rom. b.
2143	℔	*Alch.* Vapour bath. (*A Compleat Body of Chymistry*, 17th century.)
2144	ℳ℔	*Alch.* Sea-water bath. (*A Compleat Body of Chymistry*, 17th century.)

TABLE 171

2150	ℓ	*Ger.* (l.c.) Cursive form of 4647.
2150·1		*Rom.* (l.c.) Cursive form of l.
2151	⌒	*Cop.* Eq. Rom. DJ.
2152	Д	*Rus.* See 2108.
2153	a	*Phon.* Open front vowel, a as in northern Eng. pan.
2153·1		*Rom.* (l.c.) 1st letter of the a.

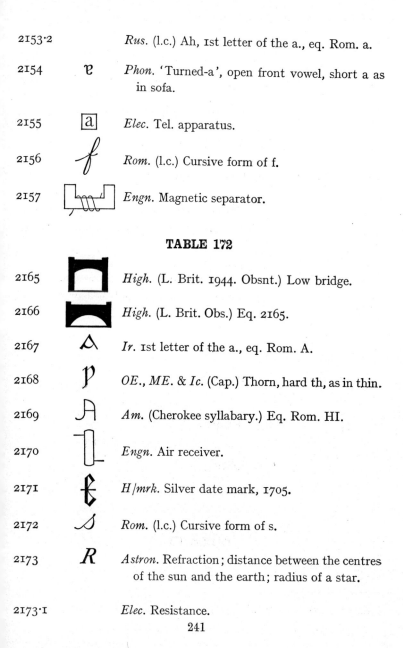

2153·2		*Rus.* (l.c.) Ah, 1st letter of the a., eq. Rom. a.
2154	ɐ	*Phon.* 'Turned-a', open front vowel, short a as in sofa.
2155	a	*Elec.* Tel. apparatus.
2156	ƒ	*Rom.* (l.c.) Cursive form of f.
2157		*Engn.* Magnetic separator.

TABLE 172

2165		*High.* (L. Brit. 1944. Obsnt.) Low bridge.
2166		*High.* (L. Brit. Obs.) Eq. 2165.
2167	ᚨ	*Ir.* 1st letter of the a., eq. Rom. A.
2168	Þ	*OE., ME.* & *Ic.* (Cap.) Thorn, hard th, as in thin.
2169	Ꭷ	*Am.* (Cherokee syllabary.) Eq. Rom. HI.
2170		*Engn.* Air receiver.
2171		*H/mrk.* Silver date mark, 1705.
2172		*Rom.* (l.c.) Cursive form of s.
2173	R	*Astron.* Refraction; distance between the centres of the sun and the earth; radius of a star.
2173·1		*Elec.* Resistance.

241

2173·2		*Engn.* Resultant load. (Hydraulics) resistance per unit of wetted area. (Hydrology) total rainfall.
2173·3		*It.* (Cap.) Eq. Rom. R.
2173·4		*Mech.* Moment of resistance; resultant.
2173·5		*Nav. Arch.* Resistance.
2173·6		*Phys.* Gas constant per mole; Rhydberg's constant. (Light) luminous radiance. (Heat) reheat factor.
2174	♭♭	*Mus.* Double flat, an 'accidental' instructing to play or read a whole tone below the note indicated.
2175	℞	*Alch.* Eq. 3141.
2176		*Egy.* (Hier.) Eq. Rom. G.
2177		*Engn.* Evaporator.
2178		*Elec.* Splicing ear.

TABLE 173

2184		*Engn.* Bursting disc.
2185	fl	*Rom.* (l.c.) Ligature of f and l.

2186	♂	*H/mrk.* Silver date mark, 1714.
2187	ℛ	*Astron.* Gas constant.
2187·1		*Rom.* (Cap.) Form of 'Black Letter' R.
2188	ß	*Ger.* (l.c.) Ligature of 4431 and 1606, eq. Rom. tz.
2189	ch	*Ger.* (l.c.) Ligature of 515 and 2824, eq. Rom. ch.
2190	ℓ	*Ger.* (l.c.) Cursive form of 4454.
2191		*Rlwy.* (Brit.) Shunting signal, position light.
2192		*Rlwy.* (Brit.) Shunting signal, position light, three aspect.

TABLE 174

2194		*Egy.* (Hier.) Eq. Rom. M, MER.
2195		*Rus.* (With or without dot.) See 2108.
2196	ʉ	*Phon.* Crossed-u. Close central vowel, u as in Nor. hus.
2197	ck	*Ger.* (l.c.) Ligature of 515 and 4454, eq. Rom. ck.
2198	ff	*Rom.* (l.c.) Ligature of f and f, double-f.

2199	ff	*H/mrk.* Silver date mark, 1701.
2200	ffl	*Rom.* (l.c.) Ligature of f, f and l, double-f l.
2201	ffi	*Rom.* (l.c.) Ligature of f, f and i, double-f i.
2202	þ	*ME. MS.* (Abbr.) That.
2203	au	*ITA.* (Augmented Rom.) au as in author.
2204		*Engn.* Pressure filter.
2205		*Engn.* Evaporator.

TABLE 175

2210	fl	*It.* (l.c.) Eq. 2185.
2211	ʧ	*Phon.* Ligature denoting the affricate tsh.
2212	ℜ	*Elec.* Eq. 655.
2212·1		*Ger.* (Cap.) 18th letter of the a., eq. Rom. R.
2213	ff	*It.* (l.c.) Eq. 2198.
2214	ffl	*It.* (l.c.) Eq. 2200.
2215	ffi	*It.* (l.c.) Eq. 2201.

TABLE 176

| 2220 | e | *Math.* Eq. 207·3. |

2220·1   *Meteor.* Wet air without rain.

2220·2   *Phon.* Half-close front vowel, e as in bet.

2220·3   *Rom.* (l.c.) 5th letter of the a. (*ITA*) e as in egg.

2220·4   *Rus.* (l.c.) (Y)eh, 6th letter of the a., eq. Rom. (y)e (short). See 2224.

2221   e   *Ir.* 5th letter of the a., eq. Rom. E.

2222   *e*   *It.* (l.c.) Eq. Rom. e. See 207.

2223   ə   *Phon.* 'Turned-e'. Half-close central vowel, the neutral vowel or 'schwa', as a in about, e in err, or o in wagon.

2224   ё   *Rus.* (l.c.) Modified yeh, 6th letter of the a., eq. Rom. yo (short). See 2220·4.

TABLE 177

2230   G   *Phys.* Graviton. (Elec.) See 2335.

2230·1   *Rom.* (Cap.) 7th letter of the a. (Med. ext. of Rom. num.) cardinal number 400, eq. 2005·5.

2231	ꟼ	*Gk.* Cardinal number 90.
2232	ʕ	*Phon.* Voiced pharyngeal fricative consonant, as the Arab. letter ayn, 343.
2233	ʔ	*Phon.* Glottal plosive consonant, the Arab. hamza.
2234	ʖ	*Phon.* Lateral click, Zulu x.
2235	G	*Phon.* Voiced uvular plosive consonant, one value of Per. gaf.
2236	G̃	*Am.* (Cherokee syllabary.) Eq. Rom. YU.
2237	?	*Punc.* Eq. 2510·2.

TABLE 178

2245	Ω	*Gk.* (Cap.) Eq. 1226·2.
2246	ʊ	*Phon.* (Obsnt.) 'Turned-Omega'. Eq. 300.
2247	ϸ	*Elec.* (USA.) Air circuit breaker.
2248	℧	*Math.* Eq. 2502. *Cf.* 3224.
2249	℧	*ME. MS.* (Abbr. Rare.) com- or con-.
2250	5	*Bot.* Large shrub; small tree.
2250·1		*Num.* (Arab.) Eq. 2298.

246

2251	*G*	*Astron.* Gravity; gravitational constant, $6.67.10^{-8} cm^3/g^2$.
2251·1		*Elec.* Conductance; resistance change in transverse field. See also 2335.
2251·2		*It.* (Cap.) Eq. Rom. G, 2230·1.
2251·3		*Mech.* Rigidity.
2251·4		*Nav. Arch.* Centre of gravity.
2251·5		*Therm.* Gibbs function.
2252		*Am.* (Cherokee syllabary.) Eq. Rom. MO.
2252·1		*Num.* (Arab.) Eq. 3454.
2253	3	*Phon.* Voiced palato-alveolar fricative consonant, s as in pleasure.
2254		*Ind. Num.* (Phila.) Eq. Arab. 2.
2255		*Phon.* (Obsnt.) Eq. 3096.
2256	æ	*Rom.* (l.c.) See 2874.
2257		*Tel.* Window coupling of cavity resonator to waveguide (double line).
2258		*Tel.* Inductor or choke.

247

2259		*Am.* (Cherokee syllabary.) Eq. Rom. DZO.
2260		*Ind. Num.* (Phila.) Eq. Arab. 6.
2261		*Ind. Num.* (Phila.) Eq. Arab. 3.

TABLE 179

2265	Є	*Log.* Eq. 2396.
2265·1		*Rom.* (Cap.) 'Celtic' form of E, 4385·5.
2266	G	*Am.* (Cherokee syllabary.) Eq. Rom. NAH.
2266·1		*Rom.* (Cap.) Ornamental form of G, 2230·1.
2267	·G	*Rom.* (Cap.) 7th letter of the a. See 2230.
2268	C	*Tel.* Rotating joint.
2269	Ϲ	*Ir.* 17th letter of the a., eq. Rom. T.
2269·1		*OE.* (l.c.) Eq. Rom. T.
2270	Ⴀ	*Numis.* Mint mark, T.C., Henry VIII.
2271	ç	*Fr.* Softened c. See 2711.
2271·1		*Phon.* Voiceless palatal fricative consonant, ch as in Ger. ich.

248

2272	𝕮	*Rom.* (Cap.) 'Old English', 'Black Letter', eq. C.
2273	𝕰	*Rom.* (Cap.) 'Old English', 'Black Letter', eq. E.

TABLE 180

2280	ꟼ	*Gk.* Eq. 2231.
2281	p	*It.* (l.c.) Eq. Rom. p. See 1646.
2282	h	*It.* (l.c.) Eq. Rom. h. See 3008.
2283	♋	*Astron.* Mean distance.
2284	Ɍ	*Am.* (Cherokee syllabary.) Eq. Rom. SO.
2284·1		*Rom.* (Cap.) Ornamental form of R.
2285	5	*Num.* (Arab.) Cursive form of numeral 5.
2286†	5	*Turk.* Eq. 2711·1.
2287	5	*Bot.* Tree.
2288	℥	*Phar.* Fluid ounce.

TABLE 181

2295	Э	*Rus.* (Cap./l.c.) Eh, 32nd letter of the old a., 30th of the mod., eq. Rom. E (short), or a as in may.

2296	3	*Num.* (Arab.) Eq. 3454.
2296·1		*Phar.* Drachm.
2297	3	*ITA.* (Augmented Rom.) zh as s in treasure.
2298	5	*Num.* (Arab.) Five, the fifth cardinal number.
2299	ie	*ITA.* (Augmented Rom.) i as in tie.
2300		*Elec.* (USA.) Rheostat.
2301		*Insig.* (Br.) 'Giro' national banking service.

TABLE 182

2303	IƆ	*Rom. Num.* Eq. D, Arab. 500.
2304	₵	*Mus.* Simple duple time with two minims in a bar (sometimes incorrectly used for the quadruple *alla breve*).
2305	¢	*Com. Mon.* 'Crossed-c', cent or cents.
2306	₡	*Com. Mon.* Colon or colons, monetary unit of Costa Rica and El Salvador.
2307		*Am.* (Cherokee syllabary.) Eq. Rom. HE.
2308	ch	*ITA.* (Augmented Rom.) ch as in chair.
2309	ue	*ITA.* (Augmented Rom.) u as in due.
2310	₵	*Bot.* Clone, a plant propagated vegetatively.

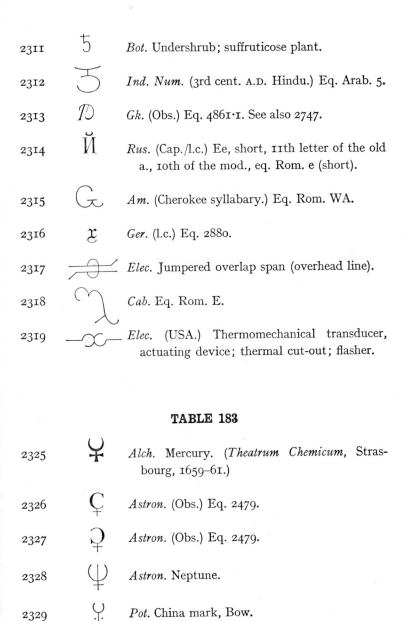

2311	ꝫ	*Bot.* Undershrub; suffruticose plant.
2312		*Ind. Num.* (3rd cent. A.D. Hindu.) Eq. Arab. 5.
2313		*Gk.* (Obs.) Eq. 4861·1. See also 2747.
2314	Й	*Rus.* (Cap./l.c.) Ee, short, 11th letter of the old a., 10th of the mod., eq. Rom. e (short).
2315		*Am.* (Cherokee syllabary.) Eq. Rom. WA.
2316	ꭓ	*Ger.* (l.c.) Eq. 2880.
2317		*Elec.* Jumpered overlap span (overhead line).
2318		*Cab.* Eq. Rom. E.
2319		*Elec.* (USA.) Thermomechanical transducer, actuating device; thermal cut-out; flasher.

TABLE 183

2325	☿	*Alch.* Mercury. (*Theatrum Chemicum*, Strasbourg, 1659–61.)
2326		*Astron.* (Obs.) Eq. 2479.
2327		*Astron.* (Obs.) Eq. 2479.
2328	♆	*Astron.* Neptune.
2329		*Pot.* China mark, Bow.

251

2330	⸸	*Bot.* Shrub.
2331	♄	*Alch.* Lead.
2332	𝄡	*Mus.* Eq. 3207.

TABLE 184

2334	$\mathcal{H}$	*Rom.* (Cap.) Cursive form of H.
2334·1		*Rus.* (Cap.) Cursive form of 4374·4.
2335	G′	*Elec.* Electromotive force of magnetization.
2336	∉	*Log.* 'Crossed-E'. Eq. 2410.
2337	⊃	*Elec.* Brush and ring distributor.
2338	$\mathcal{U}$	*Rus.* (l.c.) Cursive form of 2042.
2339	$\mathcal{G}$	*Geol.* Clay-with-flints.
2340	ⱻR	*Prop.* (L.) British Railways.
2341	$\mathcal{X}$	*Ger.* (Cap.) Cursive form of 2880.
2341·1		*Rom.* (Cap.) Cursive form of X.
2342	$\mathcal{H}$	*Rus.* (Cap./l.c.) Eq. 3061.
2343	CIↃ	*Rom. Num.* Eq. M, Arab. 1,000.

252

TABLE 185

2345	ﺝ	*Arab.* Lam, 23rd letter of the a., eq. Rom. L.
2346	J	*Elec.* Current density; Joule.
2346·1		*Rom.* (Cap.) 10th letter of the a., a modified I.
2347†	ᴶ	*Phon.* (Attached to a consonant, as ʈ, ɖ.) Palatalized.
2348†	ᶷ	*Phon.* (Attached to a vowel, as ɒ, ɛ, ə,) 'Re-coloured', formed with retroflex tongue or in some other way.
2349	✓	*Sh., Pitman's.* (Thin.) w.
2350	⟋	*Sh., Pitman's.* (Thin.) y.
2351	⟋	*Meteor.* Cirrus with tufts or upturned 'hooks'.
2352	⸺⟍	*Meteor.* Cirrus, isolated wisps.
2353	⌐⟍	*Meteor.* Cirrus, anvil form; cirrostratus.
2354	ɩ	*Phon.* Close front vowel, as i in it.
2355	⟋	*Meteor.* (USA.) Cirrus or cirrostratus advancing to more than 45 degrees above horizon.
2356	2	*Meteor.* Intensity high; severe.

2356·1		*Num.* (Arab.) Eq. 3431.
2357	J	*D/Nor.* (Cap.) Eq. Rom. J.
2358	L	*Num.* (Arab. 10th cent. Sp.) Eq. mod. 6.
2359		*Tel.* Coupling loop.
2360		*Rlwy.* (Brit.) Token receiver.
2361		*Rlwy.* (Brit.) Token exchanger.

TABLE 186

2365	Υ	*Gk.* (Cap.) Eq. 2523·1.
2366		*Meteor.* Cirrus, abundant but not continuous.
2367	$\mathcal{V}$	*Rom.* (Cap.) Eq. 4814·4.
2367·1		*Rus.* (Cap.) Oo, 21st letter of the old a., 20th of the mod., eq. Rom. U (oo).
2368		*Geol.* (APO.) Strike and dip of overturned beds.
2369		*Egy.* (Hier.) Eq. Rom .S.
2370		*Alch.* Tin; electrum, a gold-silver alloy.
2370·1		*Astrol.* Jupiter; Thursday.
2370·2		*Astron.* Jupiter.

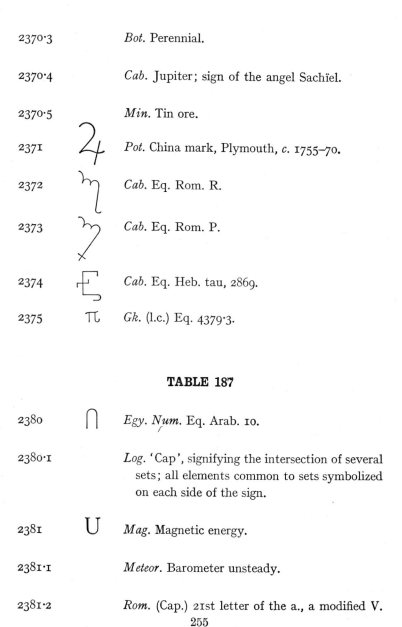

2370·3   *Bot.* Perennial.

2370·4   *Cab.* Jupiter; sign of the angel Sachïel.

2370·5   *Min.* Tin ore.

2371   *Pot.* China mark, Plymouth, *c.* 1755–70.

2372   *Cab.* Eq. Rom. R.

2373   *Cab.* Eq. Rom. P.

2374   *Cab.* Eq. Heb. tau, 2869.

2375   *Gk.* (l.c.) Eq. 4379·3.

TABLE 187

2380   *Egy. Num.* Eq. Arab. 10.

2380·1   *Log.* 'Cap', signifying the intersection of several sets; all elements common to sets symbolized on each side of the sign.

2381   *Mag.* Magnetic energy.

2381·1   *Meteor.* Barometer unsteady.

2381·2   *Rom.* (Cap.) 21st letter of the a., a modified V.

2382	∪	*Log.* 'Cup', signifying the union of sets.
2382·1		*Meteor.* Eq. 2381·1.
2383	⊂	*Log.* Is implied by; is included in; is a proper subset of.
2384	⊃	*Log.* Implies; includes; contains properly. (USA.) if . . . . then, the sign being placed between the two propositions referred to.
2384·1		*Math.* Has the operational form of.
2385	⋒	*Log.* The class of a well-ordered series.
2386	⋃	*Cab.* Eq. Rom. I.
2387	⨆	*Engn.* Single-U butt weld.
2388	Ü	*Rom.* (Cap. Ger.) Space-saving form of Ü, eq. U with an Umlaut.
2389	╠	*Elec.* Blow-out coil.

TABLE 188

2395	U	*Rom.* (Cap.) See 2381.
2396	∈	*Log.* Belongs to; is a member of; is an element of.
2397	˙h	*Phon.* Voiceless glottal fricative consonant, h as in hot.

2397·1		*Phys.* Eq. 3008·3.
2397·2		*Rom.* (l.c.) 8th letter of the a. (*ITA*) h as in hat.
2398	Ч	*Rus.* (Cap.) Cheh, 25th letter of the old a., 24th of the mod., eq. Rom. CH.
2399	Ч	*Phon.* 'Turned-h', bi-labial semi-vowel, as u in Fr. nuit.
2399·1		*Rus.* (l.c.) Eq. 2398.
2400	n	*Phon.* Dental nasal consonant, n as in nut.
2400·1		*Rom.* (l.c.) 14th letter of the a. (*ITA*) n as in nut.
2401	ɦ	*Phon.* Voiced glottal fricative consonant, the voiced h as in behave.

TABLE 189

2405	h	*High.* (L. Brit. *Obs.*) Dual carriage-way.
2406	⊆	*Log.* Is included in, is contained in; is a subset of.
2407	⊇	*Log.* Includes, contains.
2408	μ	*Astron.* Mean daily motion; mean angular motion in unit time; total proper motion in seconds of arc per year.

2408·1		*Chem.* Twelfth; middle position; chemical potential.
2408·2		*Elec.* Amplification factor; dipole moment.
2408·3		*Gk.* (l.c.) Mu, 12th letter of the a., eq. Rom. m. Cardinal number 12.
2408·4		*Mag.* Magnetic permeability; dipole moment.
2408·5		*Mech.* Coefficient of friction.
2408·6		*Nav. Arch.* Coefficient of viscosity.
2408·7		*Opt.* Refractive index.
2408·8		*Phys.* Modulus; molar conductance; micro-; micron, microns (1/1,000 mm, or 1/25,400 inch). (Nuclear) muon, a lepton.
2408·9		*Therm.* Joule-Thomson coefficient.
2409	ℏ	*ME. MS.* (Abbr.) -esu (from Gk. η, eta).
2409·1		*Phon.* 'Crossed-h'. Voiceless pharyngeal fricative consonant, j as in Arab. jim.
2409·2		*Phys.* Eq. 3011.
2410	∉	*Log.* 'Crossed-E'. Does not belong to; is not a member of; is not an element of.
2411	𝔐	*Ger.* (Cap.) 13th letter of the a., eq. Rom. **M.**

| 2411·1 | | *Mag.* Magnetic field. |
| 2412 | | *Astron.* Eq. 2328. |

TABLE 190

2416		*Egy.* (Hier.) Eq. Rom. S.
2417		*Phon.* Jap. syllabic nasal consonant.
2418		*Phon.* (Obsnt.) Eq. 3096.
2419		*Phon.* Velar nasal consonant, ng as in thing.
2420		*Phon.* Retroflex nasal consonant, a close n.
2421		*Aero.* Propeller efficiency.
2421·1		*Astron.* Parallactic angle.
2421·2		*Chem.* Seventh.
2421·3		*Elec.* Electrolytic polarization; overpotential.
2421·4		*Gk.* (l.c.) Eta, 7th letter of the a., eq. Rom. e (long). Cardinal number 8.
2421·5		*Math.* Cartesian co-ordinate.
2421·6		*Phys.* Efficiency; coefficient of viscosity.
2422		*OE.* (l.c.) Eq. Rom. r.

2423	ɲ	*Phon.* Palatal nasal consonant; the Fr. 'n-mouillé'.
2424		*Am.* (Cherokee syllabary.) Eq. Rom. HNA.
2425		*Rom.* (Cap.) Cursive form of Y.
2425·1		*Rus.* (Cap.) Cursive form of 2367·1.
2426		*Cab.* Eq. Rom. D.
2427		*Cab.* Eq. Rom. X.

TABLE 191

2430		*Tel.* Photo-voltaic cell.
2431		*Geol.* (APO.) Glacial drainage channel.
2432		*Jap.* (Katakana syllabary.) Eq. Rom. KE ('kay'). (With 5248) GE ('gay').
2433		*Alch.* Mercury, quicksilver.
2433·1		*Astrol.* (Medieval.) Mercury.
2434		*Alch.* Lead.
2435		*Cab.* Eq. Rom. N.

260

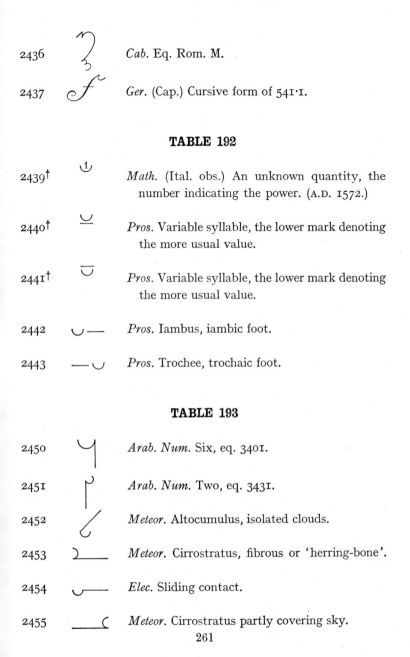

2436		*Cab.* Eq. Rom. M.
2437		*Ger.* (Cap.) Cursive form of 541·1.

TABLE 192

2439†		*Math.* (Ital. obs.) An unknown quantity, the number indicating the power. (A.D. 1572.)
2440†		*Pros.* Variable syllable, the lower mark denoting the more usual value.
2441†		*Pros.* Variable syllable, the lower mark denoting the more usual value.
2442		*Pros.* Iambus, iambic foot.
2443		*Pros.* Trochee, trochaic foot.

TABLE 193

2450		*Arab. Num.* Six, eq. 3401.
2451		*Arab. Num.* Two, eq. 3431.
2452		*Meteor.* Altocumulus, isolated clouds.
2453		*Meteor.* Cirrostratus, fibrous or 'herring-bone'.
2454		*Elec.* Sliding contact.
2455		*Meteor.* Cirrostratus partly covering sky.

TABLE 194

2460	⋎	*Engn.* (USA.) U-weld.
2461	⋎	*Ph.* Moabite (Tyrian). Eq. to Rom. W.
2462	⋎	*Elec.* Socket.
2463	⊃—	*High.* (L. White chalk.) The 'cleft stick': go in this direction—it is better than the other road. (Tramps' 'smogger'.)
2464	—⊂	*Elec.* (USA.) Photocathode.
2465	¢	*Mus. Tempus Duplex* or two-metre; eq. 2304.
2466	⊔	*Meteor.* Lunar corona.
2467	∈	*Gk.* (l.c.) Eq. 429·5.
2468	∃	*Phar.* Scruple.
2469	Ψ	*Gk.* (Cap.) Eq. 3089·1.
2470	ψ	*Aero.* Angle of yaw.
2470·1		*Astron.* Geocentric angle between the sun and the object; angle with negative direction of normal; latitude on a globular planetary surface.
2470·2		*Chem.* Twenty-third; pseudo.
2470·3		*Gk.* (l.c.) Psi, 23rd letter of the a., eq. Rom. ps. Cardinal number 700.

2470·4		*Mag.* Kundt constant; coefficient of rotation.
2470·5		*Nav. Arch.* Stream function.
2471	4	*Num.* (Arab.) Cursive form of 4.

TABLE 195

2475		*Engn.* (Terminating pipe symbol. USA.) Bell and spigot pipe plug.
2476		*Tel.* Dinode, dynode.
2477		*High.* (L. White chalk.) Call here—if you have what they want they will buy. (Tramps' 'smogger'.)
2478		*Alch.* Saturn. (*Theatrum Chemicum*, Strasbourg, 1659–61.)
2479		*Astron.* Ceres.
2480		*Ph.* Sidonian. Teth, eq. to Rom. TH.
2481		*Sh., Pitman's. Punc.* Note of interrogation.
2482		*Alch.* Quicklime. (*A Compleat Body of Chymistry,* 17th cent.)
2482·1		*Astron.* Eq. 2328.
2482·2		*Chem.* Chalx, lime. (Bergmann, 1783.)

263

2483		*Mil.* Lorry.

2484		*Elec.* Subscriber's telephone set.

TABLE 196

2490		*Meteor.* Altocumulus castellatus.

2491		*Meteor.* Stratus; stratocumulus.

2492		*Pros.* Cretic foot.

2493		*Astrol/n.* 7th sign of the Zodiac, Libra, the Scales.

2493·1		*Math.* Is approximately equal to; difference between.

2494		*Alch.* Precipitate. (*A Compleat Body of Chymistry*, 17th cent.)

2495		*Engn.* (On pipe symbol. USA.) Bushing, bell and spigot.

2496		*Rlwy.* (Brit.) Relaying or cut section in track current, the arrow indicating the direction of control. (Here, track circuit on right controls track circuit on left.)

2497		*Elec.* (APO.) Conductors crossing without contact.

2498		*Ph.* Sidonian. Mem, eq. to Rom. M.

2499		*Am.* (Cherokee syllabary.) Eq. Rom. DLI.
2500		*Ger.* (l.c.) Cursive form of 3039.
250т		*Math.* Eq. 3224.
2502		*Math.* Ultraradical.
2503		*Alch.* Gold.
2504		*Hyd.* (Inter.) Minaret.
2505		*Arab.* Eq. 343.

TABLE 197

2509		*Cop.* Eq. Rom. F.
2510		*Bot.* & *G/use.* Uncertainty.
2510·1		*Chess.* Move of doubtful value; bad move.
2510·2		*Punc.* Note of interrogation, 'query', question-mark, indicating that the preceding sentence or phrase asks a question or is of doubtful validity; uncertainty.
2511		*Punc. Sp.* Note of interrogation preceding a question or statement of doubtful validity.
2512		*Elec.* Plug and socket.

2513	Heb. Mem, 13th letter of the a., eq. Rom. M.
2514	H/mrk. Silver date mark, 1708.
2515	Cart. Mohammedan church, mosque.
2516	Arab. Eq. 3475.

TABLE 198

2519	Print. (Proof correction. Between paragraphs.) Run on without a break.
2520	G/use. (Or reversed.) 'Pothook', a figure used in learning to write.
2521†	Acc. Eq. 388·4.
2522	Phon. Retroflex click, Zulu q.
2523	Astron. Eq. 500.
2523·1	Gk. (Cap.) Upsilon, 20th letter of the a., eq. Rom. U.
2524	Geom. Is a part of.
2525	Meteor. Eq. 3113.
2526	Am. (Cherokee syllabary.) Eq. Rom. YO.
2527	Phon. Combined x and sh, as in Sw. tj.

266

2528		*H/mrk.* Eq. 2199.
2529		*Meteor.* Cirrocumulus with wisps of cirrus.
2530		*Cab.* Eq. Rom. G.

TABLE 199

2535		*Log.* Contains or is contained in.
2536		*Arab.* Kaf, 22nd letter of the a., eq. Rom. K.
2537	m	*Phon.* Bi-labial nasal consonant, m as in man.
2537·1		*Rom.* (l.c.) 13th letter of the a. See 3017.
2537·2		*Trig.* Direction cosine.
2538	ɯ	*Phon.* 'Turned-m', close back vowel, unrounded u.
2539		*Phar.* Drop, minim.
2540	ɱ	*Phon.* Labio-dental nasal consonant, n as in Ital. invidia.
2541		*Am.* (Cherokee syllabary.) Eq. Rom. NU.
2542	π	*Gk.* (l.c.) Eq. 4379·3.
2543		*Cab.* Eq. Rom. K.

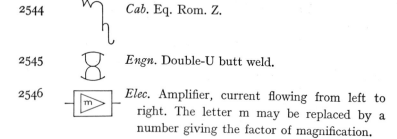

2544   *Cab.* Eq. Rom. Z.

2545   *Engn.* Double-U butt weld.

2546   *Elec.* Amplifier, current flowing from left to right. The letter m may be replaced by a number giving the factor of magnification.

TABLE 200

2550   *Pros.* Cyclic anapæst.

2551   *Pros.* Cyclic dactyl.

2552   *Meteor.* Cirrostratus covering sky.

2553   *Arab. Num.* Three, eq. 3454.

2554   *Meteor.* Altocumulus in bands.

2555   *Chem.* Eq. 5363.

2555·1   *Math.* Is equivalent to, applied to magnitudes; geometrically equivalent to.

2556   *Am.* (Cherokee syllabary.) Eq. Rom. SO.

2557   *Meteor.* Stratocumulus.

2558   *Elec.* (USA.) Inductor winding.

2559		*High.* (L. White chalk.) Rough-house; beware of dog. (Tramps' 'smogger'.)
2560		*Cart.* (Rep. '25-inch' map. OS.) Orchard.
2561		*Elec.* (USA.) Shunt inductor.

TABLE 201

2564	Œ	*ITA.* (Augmented Rom.) e as in eel.
2565	∪ — ∪	*Pros.* Amphibrach, amphibrach foot.
2566	— ∪∪ —	*Pros.* Choriambus, choriambic foot.
2567	∪∪∪ —	*Pros.* Eq. 2550.
2568	∪∪ —	*Pros.* Anapæst, anapæstic foot.
2569	— ∪∪∪	*Pros.* Eq. 2551.
2570	— ∪∪	*Pros.* Dactyl, dactylic foot.
2571		*Am.* Ideograph signifying night.
2572		*Elec.* (USA.) 1-phase 2-winding transformer.
2573		*Elec.* (USA.) Magnetic core inductor.
2574		*Pot.* China mark, late 19th cent., Volkstedt, Germany.
2575		*Astron.* (Obs.) Vesta.

269

TABLE 202

2580		*Rom.* (Cap.) Cursive form of T.
2581		*Rom.* (Cap.) Eq. 2580.
2581·1		*Rus.* (Cap. Obs.) Cursive form of 5125·3.
2582	𝔄	*Ger.* (Cap.) 1st letter of the a., eq. Rom. A.
2583		*Numis.* Mint mark, W.S., Henry VIII.
2584		*Min.* Lead ore.
2585	ʂ	*Phon.* Voiceless retroflex fricative consonant, rs as in Sw. tvars.
2586	*y*	*It.* (l.c.) Eq. Rom. y. See 3037.
2587		*Am.* (Cherokee syllabary.) Eq. Rom. LÖ.
2588		*Am.* (Cherokee syllabary.) Eq. Rom. GWO.

TABLE 203

2594	𝒦	*Rom.* (Cap.) Cursive form of K.
2594·1		*Rus.* (Cap.) Cursive form of 3203.

2595   𝒜   *Rom.* (Cap.) Cursive form of A.

2595·1   *Rus.* (Cap.) Cursive form of 3626·6.

2596 $\tilde{\nu}$ *Phys.* Wave number.

2597   𝓕   *Rom.* (Cap.) Cursive form of F.

2598   𝓎   *Ger.* (Cap.) Cursive form of 636.

2599   𝓂𝓎   *Astrol/n.* Eq. 2982.

2600   *k*   *It.* (l.c.) Eq. Rom. k. See 3204.

2601   *k*   *It.* (l.c.) Rom. k. See 3204.

TABLE 204

2605   ⌠   *Arab.* Mim, 24th letter of the a., eq. Rom. **M.**

2606   J   *Am.* (Cherokee syllabary.) Eq. Rom. GU.

2606·1   *Rom.* (Cap.) 10th letter of the a., a modified I. See 2346·1.

2607   Л   *Rus.* (Cap./l.c.) El, 13th letter of the old a., 12th of the mod, eq. Rom. L.

2608   ſ   *OE.* (l.c.) Eq. Rom. s.

| 2609 | ɹ | *Phon.* A sound between r and l. |

| 2610 | ř | *Phon.* Alveolar rolled fricative consonant, r as in Czech breh. |

| 2611 | f | *Rom.* (l.c.) 6th letter of the a. See 2770·1. |

| 2612 | ʈ | *Phon.* Voiceless retroflex plosive consonant, rt as in Sw. kort. |

| 2613 | r | *Phon.* Alveolar rolled consonant, r as in red. (*ITA*) r as in run; *cf.* 2907. |

| 2613·1 | | *Rom.* (l.c.) 18th letter of the a. |

| 2614 | ᏒᎵ | *Am.* (Cherokee syllabary.) Eq. Rom. DI. |

| 2615 | ɾ | *Phon.* 'Turned-J'. Alveolar flapped consonant, r as in Sp. pero. |

| 2616 | ɹ | *Phon.* 'Turned-r'. Alveolar frictionless continuant, or fricative consonant, r as in southern Eng. dry. |

TABLE 205

| 2620 | *J* | *It.* (Cap.) Eq. Rom. J. See 2676. |

| 2621 | V | *Rus.* (Cap./l.c. Obs.) Ízhütsa, a Slavonic V rarely used to represent the Gk. upsilon (2523·1) but omitted from the mod. a.; replaced by 4737. |

272

| 2622 | $\mathcal{V}$ | *It.* (l.c.) Eq. Rom. v. See 2696. |

2622 $\mathcal{V}$ *It.* (l.c.) Eq. Rom. v. See 2696.

2623 $\mathcal{V}$ *Gk.* (l.c.) Eq. 2697·3.

2624 $\mathcal{W}$ *Chem.* Weight fraction.

2624·1   *Engn.* (Hydraulics.) Tangential component of absolute velocity of water.

2624·2   *G/use.* Weight.

2624·3   *It.* (l.c.) Eq. Rom. w.

2624·4   *Mech.* Work.

2624·5   *Nav. Arch.* Density; specific weight.

2625   *Meteor.* Drizzle with fog.

TABLE 206

2630   *High.* (L. UNS, 1953.) Bend in road.

2631 $\mathcal{L}$ *Min.* Eq. 4766·1.

2631·1   *Rom.* (l.c.) 'Old English', 'Black Letter', eq. c.

2632 $\mathfrak{x}$ *Ger.* (l.c.) 18th letter of the a., eq. Rom. r.

2633   *Heb.* Ayin, 16th letter of the a., a pharyngeal voiced fricative sound often passed over in pron.

| 2634 | 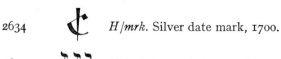 | *H/mrk.* Silver date mark, 1700. |

2635   ⟍⟨⟩⟋   . *Heb.* Shin, 21st letter of the a., eq. Rom. Sh. Cardinal number 300.

TABLE 207

2640	j	*Phon.* Palatal semi-vowel, y as in yes, or fricative consonant.
2640·1		*Rom.* (l.c.) 10th letter of the a. (*Num.*) used instead of i in l.c. numerals, esp. in the final position.
2641	ɩ	*Ger.* (l.c.) 9th letter of the a., eq. Rom. i.
2642	j	*Rom.* (l.c.) Eq. 2640. (*ITA*) j as in jam; g soft.

TABLE 208

2645	*j*	*Engn.* The square-root of minus one.
2645·1		*It.* (l.c.) Eq. Rom. j.
2645·2		*Math.* Unit vector along y axis; unit vector along axes in a right-handed system.
2645·3		*Phys.* Inner quantum number.
2646	*j*	*It.* (l.c.) Eq. Rom. j. See 2645.

2647	*i*	*Aero.* Angle of setting.
2647·1		*Astron.* Inclination to ecliptic; angle of incidence; level error of transit instrument.
2647·2		*Elec.* Current.
2647·3		*Engn.* (Structural.) Inset of reinforcement. (Hydraulics) hydraulic gradient. (Hydrology) intensity of rainfall.
2647·4		*It.* (l.c.) Eq. Rom. i.
2647·5		*Mag.* Magnetic flux.
2647·6		*Math.* The square root of minus one (Euler).
2647·7		*Mech.* Slope.
2647·8		*Opt.* Angle of incidence.
2647·9		*Rom.* (l.c.) Cursive form of i.
2647·01		*Rus.* (l.c.) It. and cursive form of 5737·3.
2648	$\ddot{y}$	*Cal.* Second derivative.

TABLE 209

2655	خ	*Arab.* Kha, 7th letter of the a., eq. Rom. KH.
2656	ج	*Arab.* Jim, 5th letter of the a., eq. Rom. J.

275

| 2657 | $\overset{\cdot}{C}$ | *Arab.* Eq. 3475. |

| 2658 | ﺩ | *Arab.* Dhal, 9th letter of the a., eq. Rom. ḌH. |

TABLE 210

| 2665 | ⌡ | *Print.* (Proof correction. USA.) Eq. 4199·3. |

| 2666 | ⫽ | *Jap.* (Katakana syllabary.) Eq. Rom. KU. (With 5249) GU. |

| 2667 | ⧸⧹ | *Chin. Num.* Eq. Arab. 8. |

TABLE 211

| 2670 | (| *Com.* Sign of the Soleras, The Palma; fino sherry. |

| 2671 | (| *Com.* Sign of the Soleras, The Raya, used to indicate that a sherry has passed its preliminary test; a second grade sherry. |

| 2672 | ʅ | *Phon.* Retroflex lateral non-fricative consonant, a close l. |

| 2673 | J | *Rom.* (Cap.) 10th letter of the a., a modified I. See 2346. |

| 2674 | ſ | *Rom.* (l.c. Obs.) The 'long s', used generally in the middle of a word. |

276

2675	I	*Ir.* 9th letter of the a., eq. to Rom I.
2676	J	*Elec.* Eq. 2346.
2676·1		*It.* (Cap.) Eq. Rom. J.
2676·2		*Mag.* Intensity of magnetization.
2676·3		*Mech.* Polar moment of inertia.
2676·4		*Phys.* Mechanical equivalent of heat, Joule.
2677	*l*	*Com. Mon.* (Obs.) Pound or pounds (sterling). See 1717.
2677·1		*It.* (l.c.) Eq. Rom. l.
2678	℧	*Phon.* Labio-dental frictionless continuant, as Du. w.
2679	ﺩ	*Arab.* Dal, 8th letter of the a., eq. Rom. D.
2680	ι	*Aeron.* Angle of setting.
2680·1		*Chem.* Ninth.
2680·2		*Gk.* (l.c.) Iota, 9th letter of the a., eq. Rom. i. Cardinal number 10.
2681	ι	*Gk.* (l.c.) Eq. 2680·2.
2682†	ι	*ME. MS.* (Abbr.) -ri-.

277

2683† ι *Gk.* Iota subscript, a small iota (2680·2) written below a long vowel at the end of a word (except when in caps.).

TABLE 212

2690 ⟍ *Ph.* Moabite (Tyrian). Eq. Rom. P.

2691 ⟍ *Jap.* (Katakana syllabary.) Eq. Rom. FHU. (With 17·3) PU. (With 5248) BU.

2692 V *Jap.* (Katakana syllabary.) Eq. Rom. RE (pron. ray). Cardinal number 2.

2693 L *Ind. Num.* (*Phila.*) Eq. Arab. 8.

2694 ⋂ *Run.* Eq. Rom. U.

2695 h *Cart.* (Green. Gold Coast.) Coconut palm.

2696 ν *Astron. Veratio saecularis*; true anomaly.

2696·1 *Elec.* Phase velocity of electromagnetic waves.

2696·2 *Engn.* Inclined axis of minimum moment of inertia. (Structural) unit shear stress of concrete. (Hydraulics) absolute velocity of water.

2696·3 *It.* (l.c.) Eq. Rom. v.

2696·4 *Math.* Volume.

278

| 2696·5 | | *Mech.* Velocity; final, resultant velocity; radial velocity; velocity component along the y axis; final energy per unit weight. |

2696·5   *Mech.* Velocity; final, resultant velocity; radial velocity; velocity component along the y axis; final energy per unit weight.

2696·6   *Nav. Arch.* Speed of current in feet per second.

2696·7   *Phys.* (Wave mechanics.) Group velocity.

2696·8   *Tel.* Wave velocity.

2697 ν *Astron.* Longitude of ascending node.

2697·1   *Chem.* Thirteenth; stoichiometric number of molecules.

2697·2   *Elec.* Electric tension; reluctivity.

2697·3   *Gk.* (l.c.) Nu, 13th letter of the a., eq. Rom. n. Cardinal number 50.

2697·4   *Mech.* Kinematic viscosity.

2697·5   *Nav. Arch.* Coefficient of kinematic viscosity.

2697·6   *Phys.* Frequency. (With tilde) wave number. (Nuclear, with subscript e) neutrino; (with subscript μ) neutretto.

TABLE 213

2700 1 *Num.* (Arab.) Cursive form of numeral 1.

2701 7 *Num.* (Arab.) Cursive form of numeral 7.

2701·1		*Print.* (Proof correction.) Insert in superior position.
2702		*Print.* (Proof correction.) Eq. 2725.
2703		*Arab. Num.* Four, eq. 3527.
2704		*Arab.* Ḥa, 6th letter of the a., eq. Rom. Ḥ.
2705		*Ind. Num.* (*Phila.*) Eq. Arab. 5.
2706		*Arab. Num.* Two, eq. 3431.
2707		*Heb.* Vau, Waw, 6th letter of the a., eq. Rom. W. Cardinal number 6.
2708		*Mus.* Quaver rest.
2709		*Mus.* Crotchet rest.
2710		*Ger.* Sign indicating Lat. et, as in **ɔc**, etc.
2711†		*Fr.* Cedilla, a diacritical mark placed under the letter c to soften it before a, o or u.
2711·1		*Turk.* Diacritical mark placed under the letter c to give it the sound ch, or under s to give it the sound sh.
2712†		*Fr.* Eq. 2711.

280

TABLE 214

2715 ⊻̅ *High.* (L. White chalk.) Work before you eat. (Tramps' 'smogger'.)

2716 ⅃ *Rlwy.* (USA.) Pipe anchor.

2717 ⟋ *Jap.* (Katakana syllabary.) Eq. Rom. ME (pron. may). Cardinal number 18.

2718 ┼ *Jap.* (Katakana syllabary.) Eq. Rom. NA (pron. nah). Cardinal number 21.

2719 ε *Gk.* (l.c.) Eq. 429·5.

TABLE 215

2725 γ̸ *Print.* (Proof correction.) Insert in inferior position.

2726 ↑ *Ir.* (l.c.) See 2799.

2727 γ *Aero.* Dihedral angle.

2727·1 *Astron.* Effective ratio of specific heats.

2727·2 *Chem.* Third; activity coefficient.

2727·3 *Elec.* Conductivity; specific conductance; stoichiometric activity coefficient.

2727·4 *Engn.* (Hydraulics.) Bazin coefficient of roughness.

281

2727·5	*Gk.* (l.c.) Gamma, 3rd letter of the a., eq. Rom. g. Cardinal number 3.
2727·6	*Mag.* Unit intensity of magnetic field, 0·00001 gauss.
2727·7	*Math.* Eulerian constant, $\equiv$ 0·5772175.
2727·8	*Mech.* Surface tension.
2727·9	*Min. Crys.* Largest refractive index of a crystal, or the corresponding axis (Z) of the optical indicatrix.
2727·01	*Nav. Arch.* Prismatic coefficient; adiabatic index; unital shear.
2727·02	*Phys.* Surface tension; ionization; microgram; gamma-rays; photon; coefficient of absolute expansion; ratio of specific heat of a gas at constant pressure to its specific heat at constant volume.
2727·03	*Therm.* Ratio of specific heats.

TABLE 216

2730	⊔	*Engn.* (USA.) J-weld.
2731	⊓	*Engn.* Square butt weld.
2732	C⧧	*Com.* Hundredweight.

2733	ח	*Ir.* 12th letter of the a., eq. Rom. N.
2734	u	*Ir.* 18th letter of the a., eq. to Rom. U.
2735	n	*Rom.* (l.c.) 14th letter of the a. See 2400.1.
2736	u	*Meteor.* Threatening sky.
2736·1		*Phon.* Close back vowel, u as in push.
2736·2		*Rom.* (l.c.) 21st letter of the a. (*ITA*) u as in up.
2737	リ	*Jap.* (Katakana syllabary.) Eq. Rom. RI (pron. ree). Cardinal number 9.

TABLE 217

2740	⌒	*High.* (L. Brit., 1944.) Hump bridge.
2741	⌒	*Elec.* (APO. USA.) Circuit breaker.
2742	*U*	*It.* (Cap.) Eq. Rom. U.
2742·1		*Phys.* Thermal parameter; thermal transmittance per unit area; mobility.
2742·2		*Therm.* Internal energy.
2743	כ	*Heb.* Kaf, caph, 11th letter of the a., eq. Rom. K.
2744	ヲ	*Jap.* (Katakana syllabary.) Eq. Rom. WO. Cardinal number 12.

2745   Jap. (Katakana syllabary.) Eq. Rom. RA (pron, rah). Cardinal number 22.

2746   Jap. (Katakana syllabary.) Eq. Rom. TE (pron. tay). (With 5248) DE (pron. day).

2747   Gk. (Obs.) Eq. 4861·1. Cardinal number 900.

2748   Gk. Eq. 2747.

2749   Math. Equal or containing.

TABLE 218

2755   Ger. (l.c.) Cursive form of 4431.

2756   Jap. (Katakana syllabary.) Eq. Rom. NU. Cardinal number 10.

2757   Jap. (Katakana syllabary.) Eq. Rom. SA (pron. sah). (With 5248) ZA (pron. zah).

2758   Jap. (Katakana syllabary.) Eq. Rom. CHI (pron. chee). (With 5248 DI) (pron. dee); cardinal number 8.

2759   Jap. (Katakana syllabary.) Eq. 2758.

TABLE 219

2765   Com. Sign of the Soleras, Palma cortado, a fino sherry in process of becoming an Amontillado.

284

2766	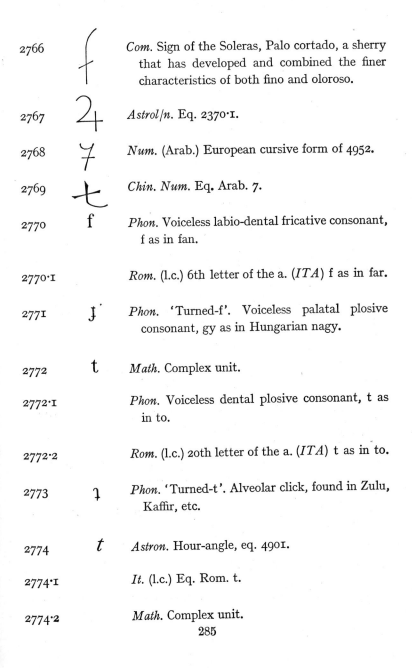	*Com.* Sign of the Soleras, Palo cortado, a sherry that has developed and combined the finer characteristics of both fino and oloroso.
2767		*Astrol/n.* Eq. 2370·1.
2768		*Num.* (Arab.) European cursive form of 4952.
2769		*Chin. Num.* Eq. Arab. 7.
2770	f	*Phon.* Voiceless labio-dental fricative consonant, f as in fan.
2770·1		*Rom.* (l.c.) 6th letter of the a. (*ITA*) f as in far.
2771	ʄ	*Phon.* 'Turned-f'. Voiceless palatal plosive consonant, gy as in Hungarian nagy.
2772	t	*Math.* Complex unit.
2772·1		*Phon.* Voiceless dental plosive consonant, t as in to.
2772·2		*Rom.* (l.c.) 20th letter of the a. (*ITA*) t as in to.
2773	ʇ	*Phon.* 'Turned-t'. Alveolar click, found in Zulu, Kaffir, etc.
2774	*t*	*Astron.* Hour-angle, eq. 4901.
2774·1		*It.* (l.c.) Eq. Rom. t.
2774·2		*Math.* Complex unit.

285

2774·3		*Nav. Arch.* Thrust deduction fraction.
2774·4		*Therm.* Empirical temperature.
2775	t	*Pol.* (l.c.) Eq. 4151.
2776	$\mathfrak{z}$	*Phon.* The affricate ts.

TABLE 220

2780		*Engn.* Single-V butt weld.
2781		*Engn.* Bevel butt weld.
2782		*Am.* (Cherokee syllabary.) Eq. Rom. DZE.
2783		*Ph.* Moabite (Tyrian). Eq. Rom. B.
2784		*Ph.* Moabite (Tyrian). Eq. Rom. N.
2785		*Jap.* (Katakana syllabary.) Eq. Rom. TA (pron. tah). (With 5248) DA (pron. dah).
2786		*Jap.* (Katakana syllabary.) Eq. Rom. WA (pron. wah). Cardinal number 13.
2787	y	*Rom.* (l.c.) 25th letter of the a. (*ITA*) y as in yonder.
2788	λ	*Gk.* (l.c.) Eq. 3038·4.
2789	Λ	*Phon.* 'Turned-y'. Palatal lateral non-fricative consonant, gl as in Ital. egli.

286

| 2790[†] | ⅂ | *ME. MS.* (Abbr.) -and or -ant. |

| 2791 | *T* | *Gk.* (l.c.) Eq. 3040·2. |

| 2792 | ℇ | *Ger.* (l.c.) 5th letter of the a., eq. Rom. e. |

TABLE 221

| 2795 | ⅃ | *Am.* (Cherokee syllabary.) Eq. Rom. TI. |

| 2796 | ⟅ | *Heb.* Nun, 14th letter of the a., eq. Rom. N. |

| 2797 | ⟅ | *Heb.* Gimel, 3rd letter of the a., eq. Rom. G. Cardinal number 3. |

| 2798 | Ⲛ | *Cop.* Eq. Rom. N. |

| 2799 | ɼ | *Ir.* (l.c.) Eq. Rom. s. |

| 2800 | 5 | *Num.* (Arab.) Eq. 2298. |

| 2801 | 2 | *Num.* (Arab.) Eq. 3431. |

| 2802 | 又 | *Jap.* (Katakana syllabary.) Eq. Rom. SU. (With 5248) ZU. |

| 2803 | ∢ | *Math.* Angle. |

| 2804 | γ | *Gk.* (l.c.) Eq. 2727·5. |

| 2805 | ↜ | *Math.* Is transformed into; has for an image; yields; passage from an element to its image. (APO) direction of rotation. |

2806	↘	*G/use.* (APO.) Direction of attention; direction of motion.
2806·1		*Mech.* (APO.) Direction of rotation.
2807	*k*	*It.* (l.c.) Eq. Rom. k. See 3204.
2808†	²	*Math.* The power of 2; squared.
2808·1		*Meteor.* Intensity high; severe.
2809	*V*	*Rus.* (Cap./l.c. Obs.) Cursive form of 2621.

TABLE 222

2810		*Jap.* (Katakana syllabary.) Eq. Rom. WI.
2811		*Elec.* Fan regulator.
2812		*Elec.* Automatic telephone exchange.
2813		*Bot.* Tree.
2814		*H/mrk.* Silver date mark, 1712.
2815		*H/mrk.* Silver date mark, 1707.
2816		*Min.* Eq. 4874·5.
2816·1		*Rom.* (l.c.) 'Old English', 'Black Letter', eq. a.

TABLE 223

2820	ζ	*Num.* (Arab. 10th cent. Sp.) Eq. mod. 3.
2821	ς	*Num.* (Arab. 17th cent.) Eq. mod. 7.
2822	$\mathbf{3}$	*ME.* & late *OE.* (l.c.) Eq. 4269.
2822·1		*Num.* (Arab.) Eq. 3454.
2823		*Jap.* (Katakana syllabary.) Eq. Rom. U.
2824	$\mathfrak{h}$	*Ger.* (l.c.) 8th letter of the a., eq. Rom. h.
2825	$\mathfrak{y}$	*Ger.* (l.c.) 25th letter of the a., eq. Rom. y.
2826		*Am.* (Cherokee syllabary.) Eq. Rom. NI.
2827	fi	*Rom.* (l.c.) Ligature of f and i.
2828		*Ph.* Moabite (Tyrian). Eq. Rom. M.
2829		*Mus.* Direct turn followed by a shake.
2830		*Mus.* Shake followed by a direct turn.
2831		*Mus.* Inverted turn followed by a shake.
2832	$\mathbf{z}$	*Phon.* Voiced retroflex fricative consonant, a variety of the sound zh.

TABLE 224

2835   *Engn.* Gasholder.

2836   *Cab.* Eq. Rom. H.

2837   *Cab.* Eq. Rom. F.

2838   *Com.* Sign of the Soleras, Dos cortados, similar to Palo cortado; see 2766.

2839   *Alch.* Sulphur.

2840   *Pot.* China mark, Nottingham.

2841   *Pot.* (USA.) China mark, McLaughlin, Cincinnati, Ohio.

2842   *Elec.* (USA.) Capacitor.

2843   *Elec.* (USA.) Switch with horn gap.

2844   *Jap.* (Katakana syllabary.) Eq. Rom. O.

2845   *D/Nor.* (Cap.) Eq. Rom. K.

2846   *Am.* (Cherokee syllabary.) Eq. Rom. DZI.

2847   *Ind. Num.* (3rd cent. Hindu.) Eq. Arab. 4.

2848   *Ir.* 6th letter of the a., eq. Rom. F.

2849	$\overline{\mathcal{J}}$	*Jap.* (Katakana syllabary.) Eq. Rom. NE (pron. nay). Cardinal number 20.
2850	wh	*ITA.* (Augmented Rom.) wh as in wheel.
2851	$\int$	*Ir.* Cursive form of 2848.
2852	π	*Gk.* (l.c.) Eq. 4379·3.
2853	π	*Gk.* (l.c.) Eq. 4379·3.
2854		*Elec.* (USA.) Shunt capacitor.
2855		*Elec.* (USA.) Adjustable or variable differential capacitor.

TABLE 225

2857	$\mathcal{X}$	*Rom.* (Cap.) Cursive form of X.
2857·1		*Rus.* (Cap.) Cursive form of 4874·9.
2858	$\mathcal{H}$	*Rom.* (Cap.) Cursive form of H.
2858·1		*Rus.* (Cap.) Eq. 2334·1.
2859	$\mathcal{H}$	*Rus.* (Cap.) Cursive form of 2607.
2860	$\mathcal{U}$	*Rom.* (Cap.) Cursive form of U.

291

2860·1		*Rus.* (Cap.) Cursive form of 4737. (With 388·4) cursive form of 2314.
2861		*Rus.* (Cap.) Cursive form of 4250·5.
2862		*Rus.* (Cap.) Cursive form of 2042.
2863		*Ger.* (Cap.) Cursive form of 3039.
2864		*Rus.* (Cap.) Cursive form of 4395.
2865		*Rus.* (Cap.) Cursive form of 4191·3.
2866		*Rom.* (Cap.) 'Old English', 'Black Letter', eq. V.
2867		*Ger.* (Cap.) 25th letter of the a., eq. Rom. Y.
2868		*Ger.* (Cap.) 14th letter of the a., eq. Rom. N.
2869		*Heb.* Tau, 22nd letter of the a., eq. Rom. T.
2870		*Heb.* Eq. 2881.
2871		*Heb.* Pe, 17th letter of the a., eq. Rom. P.
2872		*Hyd.* (Inter.) Beacon.
2873		*It.* (l.c.) Eq. Rom. x. See 352.
2874		*Rom.* (l.c.) Eq. 3541·3. (*ITA*) a as in angel.
2875		*Rus.* (l.c.) It. form of 4396.
2876		*Rus.* (l.c.) It. form of 4485.

TABLE 226

2880   ꭕ   *Ger.* (Cap./l.c.) 24th letter of the a., eq. Rom. X. See also 2316.

2881   ᗡ   *Heb.* Teth, 9th letter of the a., eq. Rom. Ṭ.

2882   Υ   *Gk.* (Cap.) Eq. 2523·1.

2883   *r*   *Astron.* Diurnal clock rate; revolution value; radius vector from centre of the sun; distance in parsecs; coefficient of diffuse reflection; distance from centre of star.

2883·1   *Elec.* Resistivity, specific resistance; specific reluctance.

2883·2   *Engn.* (Structural.) Ratio of area of steel reinforcements to area of concrete.

2883·3   *It.* (l.c.) Eq. Rom. r.

2883·4   *Math.* Radius; radius vector; polar co-ordinate; cylindrical co-ordinate. (Statistics) correlation coefficient.

2883·5   *Phys.* Cut-off ratio. (Heat) compression ratio; pressure ratio.

2884   ɽ   *Phon.* Retroflex flapped consonant, the 'thick l', as in eastern Nor. Ola.

2885   Ⴟ   *Mil.* (RAF.) Port depot.

293

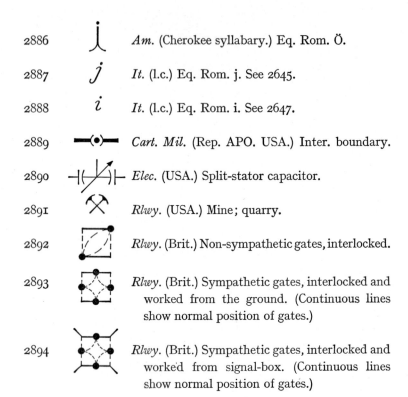

2886   *Am.* (Cherokee syllabary.) Eq. Rom. Ö.

2887   *It.* (l.c.) Eq. Rom. j. See 2645.

2888   *It.* (l.c.) Eq. Rom. i. See 2647.

2889   *Cart. Mil.* (Rep. APO. USA.) Inter. boundary.

2890   *Elec.* (USA.) Split-stator capacitor.

2891   *Rlwy.* (USA.) Mine; quarry.

2892   *Rlwy.* (Brit.) Non-sympathetic gates, interlocked.

2893   *Rlwy.* (Brit.) Sympathetic gates, interlocked and worked from the ground. (Continuous lines show normal position of gates.)

2894   *Rlwy.* (Brit.) Sympathetic gates, interlocked and worked from signal-box. (Continuous lines show normal position of gates.)

TABLE 227

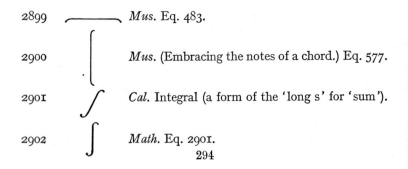

2899   *Mus.* Eq. 483.

2900   *Mus.* (Embracing the notes of a chord.) Eq. 577.

2901   *Cal.* Integral (a form of the 'long s' for 'sum').

2902   *Math.* Eq. 2901.

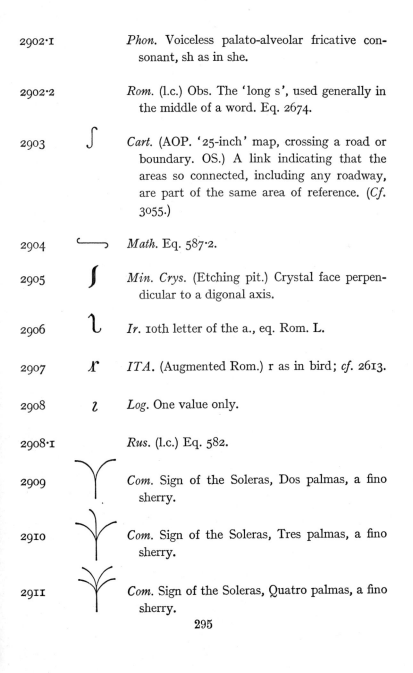

2902·1   *Phon.* Voiceless palato-alveolar fricative consonant, sh as in she.

2902·2   *Rom.* (l.c.) Obs. The 'long s', used generally in the middle of a word. Eq. 2674.

2903   *Cart.* (AOP. '25-inch' map, crossing a road or boundary. OS.) A link indicating that the areas so connected, including any roadway, are part of the same area of reference. (*Cf.* 3055.)

2904   *Math.* Eq. 587·2.

2905   *Min. Crys.* (Etching pit.) Crystal face perpendicular to a digonal axis.

2906   *Ir.* 10th letter of the a., eq. Rom. L.

2907   *ITA.* (Augmented Rom.) r as in bird; *cf.* 2613.

2908   *Log.* One value only.

2908·1   *Rus.* (l.c.) Eq. 582.

2909   *Com.* Sign of the Soleras, Dos palmas, a fino sherry.

2910   *Com.* Sign of the Soleras, Tres palmas, a fino sherry.

2911   *Com.* Sign of the Soleras, Quatro palmas, a fino sherry.

2912 Υ *It.* (Cap.) Eq. Rom. Y. See 4815.

2913 $\uparrow$ *Cart. Rlwy.* (USA.) Corn.

2914 Υ *Gk.* (l.c.) Eq. 2727·5.

2915 ν *Gk.* (l.c.) Eq. 2727·5.

2916 r *It.* (l.c.) Eq. Rom. r. See 2883.

2916·1   *Log.* Variable proposition. (Used, apparently, for its resemblance to a v.)

2917 λ *Cart.* (Ant. OS.) Roman milestone.

2918 λ *Rus.* (l.c.) Cursive form of 2607.

2919 $\int$ *Gk.* (l.c. Obs.) Eq. 2727·5.

2920 υ *It.* (l.c.) Eq. Rom. v. See 2696.

2921 γ *Rom.* (l.c.) Cursive form of r.

TABLE 228

2925 $\lbrace$ *Mus.* Eq. 620·1.

2926 $\mathfrak{p}$ *Ger.* (l.c.) 16th letter of the a., eq. Rom. p.

2927 γ *Mus.* Semiquaver rest.

2928 χ *Mus.* Eq. 2709.

| 2929 | Œ | *Ger.* (Cap.) Eq. 562·1. |

| 2930 | 𝒱 | *It.* (l.c.) Eq. Rom. v. See 2696. |

| 2931 | 𝒰 | *Rom.* (Cap./l.c.) Cursive form of V. |

TABLE 229

| 2935 | ⊥ | *Engn. Nav.* Eq. 5111·2. |

| 2936 | ⨝ | *Astrol/n.* Eq. 2953. |

2937 力 *Jap.* (Katakana syllabary.) Eq. Rom. KA (pron. kah). (With 5248) GA (pron. gah). Cardinal number 14.

| 2938 | ケ | *Jap.* Eq. 2432. |

| 2939 | ル | *Jap.* Eq. 4663. |

2940 *Meteor.* Altocumulus, confused or in several layers.

| 2941 | ᛃ | *Mus.* Demisemiquaver rest. |

| 2942 | 𝒳 | *Gk.* Eq. 4169·3. |

| 2943 | ⨯ | *Mus.* Eq. 2709. |

TABLE 230

2950 ♀ *Engn.* (Across pipe symbol.) Flexible joint.

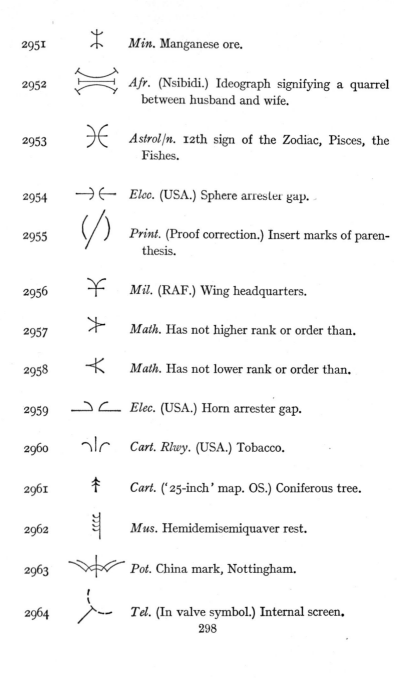

2951   *Min.* Manganese ore.

2952   *Afr.* (Nsibidi.) Ideograph signifying a quarrel between husband and wife.

2953   *Astrol/n.* 12th sign of the Zodiac, Pisces, the Fishes.

2954   *Elec.* (USA.) Sphere arrester gap.

2955   *Print.* (Proof correction.) Insert marks of parenthesis.

2956   *Mil.* (RAF.) Wing headquarters.

2957   *Math.* Has not higher rank or order than.

2958   *Math.* Has not lower rank or order than.

2959   *Elec.* (USA.) Horn arrester gap.

2960   *Cart. Rlwy.* (USA.) Tobacco.

2961   *Cart.* ('25-inch' map. OS.) Coniferous tree.

2962   *Mus.* Hemidemisemiquaver rest.

2963   *Pot.* China mark, Nottingham.

2964   *Tel.* (In valve symbol.) Internal screen.

TABLE 231

2969		*Mil.* (RAF.) Group headquarters.
2970		*Mil.* (RAF.) Army co-operation squadron.
2971		*Engn.* Double-V butt weld.
2972		*Elec.* Multiplex distributor.
2973		*Rlwy.* (USA.) Water-closet, privy, latrine.
2974		*Mil.* (RAF.) Aircraft depot.
2975		*Math.* Integration of a quaternion.
2976		*Engn.* Rotary drier, kiln or calciner.
2977	æ	*Rom.* (l.c.) See 2874.
2978		*Rom.* (Abbr.) 'Old English', 'Black Letter', eq. 1710.
2979		*Rom.* (Cap.) 'Old English', 'Black Letter', eq. U.
2980		*Egy.* (Hier.) Eq. Rom. A.
2981		*Engn.* J butt weld.
2982		*Astrol/n.* 6th sign of the Zodiac, Virgo, the Virgin.
2983		*Astrol/n.* (Obs.) Eq. 3886.

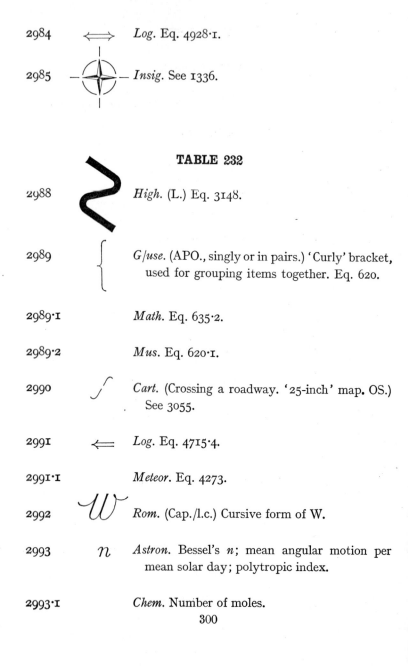

2984   *Log.* Eq. 4928·1.

2985   *Insig.* See 1336.

TABLE 232

2988   *High.* (L.) Eq. 3148.

2989   *G/use.* (APO., singly or in pairs.) 'Curly' bracket, used for grouping items together. Eq. 620.

2989·1   *Math.* Eq. 635·2.

2989·2   *Mus.* Eq. 620·1.

2990   *Cart.* (Crossing a roadway. '25-inch' map. OS.) See 3055.

2991   *Log.* Eq. 4715·4.

2991·1   *Meteor.* Eq. 4273.

2992   *Rom.* (Cap./l.c.) Cursive form of W.

2993   *Astron.* Bessel's n; mean angular motion per mean solar day; polytropic index.

2993·1   *Chem.* Number of moles.

2993·2   *Engn.* Distance from extreme fibre of section
                to neutral axis. (Hydraulics) Kutter coefficient
                of roughness.

2993·3   *It.* (l.c.) Eq. Rom. n.

2993·4   *Math.* Any number; number of terms.

2993·5   *Mech.* Revolutions or rotations per second;
                rigidity; shear modulus of elasticity.

2993·6   *Nav. Arch.* Variable index.

2993·7   *Op.* Eq. 2408·7.

2993·8   *Phys.* Molecular concentration, molecules per
                unit volume; number of components; principal
                quantum number.

2993·9   *Trig.* Direction cosine.

2993·01   *Rom.* (l.c.) Cursive form of n.

2993·02   *Rus.* (l.c.) It. and cursive form of 4250·5.

2994   𝖓   *Ger.* (l.c.) 14th letter of the a., eq. Rom. n.

2995   𝓊   *Astron.* Coefficient of darkening.

2995·1   *Engn.* Inclined axis of maximum moment of
                inertia. (Frame structure) force exerted by
                unit load applied at any point in any direction.
                (Hydraulics) tangential velocity of wheel.

2995·2		*It.* (l.c.) Eq. Rom. u.
2995·3		*Mech.* Initial velocity; circumferential velocity, tangential velocity; velocity component along the x axis; initial energy per unit weight.
2995·4		*Phys.* Eq. 2995·3. (Wave mechanics) phase velocity.
2995·5		*Rom.* (l.c.) Cursive form of u.
2995·6		*Rus.* (l.c.) It. and cursive form of 4737.
2996	$\breve{u}$	*Rus.* (l.c.) It. and cursive form of 2314.
2997	π	*Gk.* (l.c.) Eq. 4379·3.
2998	$\mathcal{H}$	*Rus.* (l.c.) Cursive form of 4374·4.
2999	$\dagger$ $\dagger$	*Sh., Gregg's. Punc.* Parentheses.
3000		*Rlwy.* (Brit.) Non-sympathetic gates, occupation crossing.

TABLE 233

3005	ς	*Gk.* (Obs.) Hard k., kappa; cardinal number 6.
3006	$\mathfrak{h}$	*Ir.* 8th letter of the a., eq. Rom. H.
3007	$\mathcal{p}$	*Rom.* (l.c.) Cursive form of p.

302

3007·1		*Rus.* (l.c.) Cursive form of 2005·6.
3008	h	*Engn.* (Hydraulics.) Head.
3008·1		*It.* (l.c.) Eq. Rom. h.
3008·2		*Nav. Arch.* Depth.
3008·3		*Phys.* Planck's constant, $6·6252.10^{-27}$ erg-seconds, approximately.
3008·4		*Therm.* Heat function.
3009	η	*Gk.* (l.c.) Eq. 2421·4.
3010	μ	*Gk.* (l.c.) Eq. 2408·3.
3011	$\hbar$	*Phys.* 'Crossed-h'. The quotient of Planck's constant divided by 2π, $h/2\pi$.
3012	$\hbar$	*It.* (l.c.) Eq. 2827.
3013	半	*Chin. Num.* One-half.

TABLE 234

3015	$\left\{\ \right\}$	*Math.* Eq. 490·5 and 5169.
3016	m	*Rom.* (l.c.) 13th letter of the a. (*ITA*) m as in man.
3017	m	*Astron.* Bessel's m; mass in units of the solar

mass; apparent magnitude; order of spectrum; molecular weight.

3017·1		*Chem.* Molality, molar concentration.
3017·2		*Engn.* Modular ratio. (Hydraulics) hydraulic mean depth.
3017·3		*It.* (l.c.) Eq. Rom. m.
3017·4		*Mech.* Mass.
3017·5		*Phys.* Mass of electron.
3017·6		*Tel.* Amplification factor.
3017·7		*Rom.* (Cap. l.c.) Cursive form of m.
3017·8		*Rus.* (l.c.) It. and cursive forms of 4191·3.
3018	*ɰɰ*	*Rus.* (l.c.) It. and cursive forms of 4395.
3019	*μμ*	*Phys.* Pico- or micro-micro-, 10^{-12}.
3020	ţh	*ITA.* (Augmented Rom.) th as in three.
3021	ɟh	*ITA.* (Augmented Rom.) th as in mother.
3022	ʃh	*ITA.* (Augmented Rom.) sh as in ship.
3023	⑂	*Egy.* (Hier.) Eq. Rom. MES.
3024	m	*Ger.* (l.c.) 13th letter of the a., eq. Rom. m.

3025	ℳ	*Ir.* 11th letter of the a., eq. Rom. M.
3026	♏	*Astrol/n.* 8th sign of the Zodiac, Scorpio, Scorpius, the Scorpion.
3027		*Mus.* Inverted turn followed by a shake and a direct turn.
3028		*Mus.* Direct turn followed by a shake and another direct turn; appoggiatura followed by a shake.
3029		*Rlwy.* (Brit.) Floodlit shunting signal.
3030		*Rlwy.* (Brit.) Non-sympathetic gates, not inter-locked.
3031		*Rlwy.* (Brit.) Sympathetic gates marked by gateman and not interlocked.
3032		*Soil/m.* (Rep.) Calcareous clay; marl.

TABLE 235

3033	𝒥	*Rom.* (Cap.) Cursive form of T.
3033·1		*Rus.* (Cap.) Cursive form of 4115·6.
3034		*G/use.* Eq. 2989.
3034·1		*Math.* Eq. 635·2.
3034·2		*Mus.* Eq. 620·1.
3035	⋎	*Gk.* (Cap.) Eq. 2523·1.

3036	$\mathcal{Y}$	*Am.* (Cherokee syllabary.) Eq. Rom. GI.
3037	$\mathcal{y}$	*Alg.* The second unknown.
3037·1		*Elec.* Admittance; deflection.
3037·2		*Engn.* Vertical axis. (Structural) distance from extreme fibre of section to neutral axis.
3037·3		*Geom.* Cartesian co-ordinate.
3037·4		*It.* (l.c.) Eq. Rom. y.
3037·5		*Mech.* General deflection; lateral displacement.
3037·6		*Meteor.* Dry air, humidity less than 10 per cent.
3037·7		*Phon.* Close front vowel, u as in Fr. du.
3037·8		*Rus.* (l.c.) Oo, 21st letter of the old a., 20th of the mod., eq. Rom. u (oo).
3037·9		*Tel.* Contact made after other contacts in same relay.
3038	λ	*Aero.* Damping coefficient; logarithmic increment or decrement of amplitude.
3038·1		*Astron.* Geocentric longitude; cosmical constant.
3038·2		*Chem.* Eleventh; absolute activity.
3038·3		*Geol.* Seat-earth.

3038·4		*Gk.* (l.c.) Lambda, 11th letter of the a., eq. Rom. 1. Cardinal number 30.
3038·5		*Mech.* Angle of friction; Young's modulus; damping coefficient.
3038·6		*Nav. Arch.* Water-line coefficient; scale ratio.
3038·7		*Phys.* Wave-length; Ångström unit(s); area ratio; latitude; radioactive constant; micro-litre.
3038·8		*Therm.* Thermal conductivity.
3039	𝔘	*Ger.* (Cap./l.c.) 21st letter of the a., eq. Rom. U.
3040	𝒯	*Astron.* Component of proper motion towards assumed apex plus 90°; optical depth; Milne's time-scale.
3040·1		*Chem.* Nineteenth.
3040·2		*Gk.* (l.c.) Tau, 19th letter of the a., eq. Rom. t. Cardinal number 300.
3040·3		*Math.* (Statistics.) Standard deviation.
3040·4		*Phys.* Volume; temperature. (Light) transmission factor. (Nuclear. Obs.) tau meson.

TABLE 236

| 3044 | ✕ | *Tel.* Directional coupler (double line). |

307

3045	*M*	*Rom.* (Cap.) Cursive form of M.
3045·1		*Rus.* (Cap./l.c.) Cursive form of 4857·3.
3046	*N*	*Rom.* (Cap.) Cursive form of N.
3047		*Com.* Sign of the Soleras, Pata de galena, a style of cortado sherry.
3048		*Mus.* Eq. 3207.
3049		*Am.* (Cherokee syllabary.) Eq. Rom. GWA.
3050	Ʈ	*Geol.* (Obs.) Taele gravels (glacial solifluction).
3051	χ	*Chem.* Twenty-second.
3051·1		*Gk.* (l.c.) Chi, 22nd letter of the a., eq. Rom. ch. Cardinal number 600.
3051·2		*Min.* Eq. 4874·5.
3051·3		*Phys.* (Nuclear.) Chi meson.
3052		*Alch.* Iron.
3053	*f*	*Astron.* Phase coefficient; mass function.
3053·1		*Cal.* Function.
3053·2		*Chem.* Activity coefficient.
3053·3		*Elec.* Frequency.

3053·4   *Engn.* (Hydraulics.) General friction factor; radial component of absolute velocity of water.

3053·5   *It.* (l.c.) Eq. Rom. f.

3053·6   *Mech.* Linear acceleration; modulus of rupture; limiting intensity of stress. (Kinematics) frequency.

3053·7   *Phys.* Saturated liquid at saturation temperature and pressure, liquid in contact with vapour.

3054   *Rom.* (l.c.) Cursive form of t.

3055   *Cart.* ('25-inch' map. Crossing a roadway. OS.) A link indicating that, though the spaces on either side of the roadway are included in the same area of reference, the roadway itself is excluded. *Cf.* 2903.

TABLE 237

3059   *Rel.* Eq. 4521·1.

3060   *Engn.* (Fire protection.) Revolving door.

3061   *Rus.* (Cap./l.c.) Cursive form of 3188.

3062   *Alch.* Water.

3063   *Cart.* (Du.) Swamp palm.

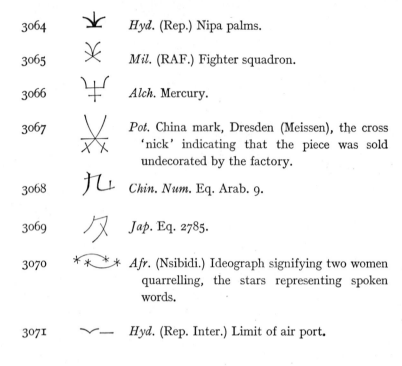

3064   *Hyd.* (Rep.) Nipa palms.

3065   *Mil.* (RAF.) Fighter squadron.

3066   *Alch.* Mercury.

3067   *Pot.* China mark, Dresden (Meissen), the cross 'nick' indicating that the piece was sold undecorated by the factory.

3068   *Chin. Num.* Eq. Arab. 9.

3069   *Jap.* Eq. 2785.

3070   *Afr.* (Nsibidi.) Ideograph signifying two women quarrelling, the stars representing spoken words.

3071   *Hyd.* (Rep. Inter.) Limit of air port.

Cl.I, Div.II, Ord.II, Fam.II, Gen.I

TABLE 238

3075   *Com. Mon.* Eq. 3129.

3076   *Rlwy.* (USA.) Spring switch.

3077   *Engn.* (Fire protection.) Salvage access; exit point.

3078		*Am.* (Cherokee syllabary.) Eq. Rom. GA.
3079		*Sh., Pitman's.* Guttural ch or gh.
3080		*Mus.* Eq. 589.
3081		*Chess.* Check.
3082		*Mus.* Eq. 589.
3083		*Gk.* (Cap.) Eq. 4874·3.
3083·1		*Mag.* Specific magnetism; susceptibility (mass).
3083·2		*Min. Crys.* Bisectrix.
3084		*Phon.* Voiceless uvular fricative consonant. (A modification of Arab letter kha, 2655.)
3085		*Phon.* Velarized or 'dark' l, as in table.
3086		*Gk.* (l.c.) Eq. 2470·3.
3087		*H/mrk.* Silver date mark, 1710.
3088		*Mus.* Segno, denoting the beginning or end of a passage to be repeated; marking the introduction of a vocal part.
3089		*Elec.* Dielectric flux; electrostatic flux.
3089·1		*Gk.* (Cap.) Psi, 23rd letter of the a., eq. Rom. Ps.
3089·2		*Log.* Variable function involving one variable.

311

3089·3   *Phys.* Psi waves.

3089·4   *Psychic research.* Psi-function. The operation of a paranormal faculty; extrasensory perception.

3090   *Gk.* (l.c.) Eq. 2470·3.

3091   *Geol.* Contorted beds.

3092   *Afr.* (Nsibidi.) Ideograph signifying two witnesses contradicting each other, the straight line representing the man telling the truth.

TABLE 239

3095   *Alch.* Lead.

3095·1   *Astrol.* Saturn; Saturday.

3095·2   *Astron.* Saturn.

3095·3   *Bot.* Woody-stemmed plant.

3095·4   *Cab.* Saturn; sign of the angel Cassïel.

3096   *Phon.* Voiced alveolar lateral fricative consonant, dhl as in Zulu dhla.

3097   *Sh., Pitman's.* Preceding remark to be taken humorously.

3098   *Gk.* (l.c.) Eq. 3040·2.

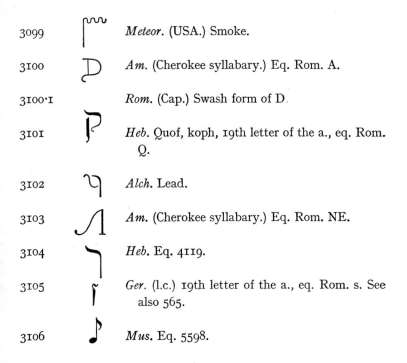

3099		*Meteor.* (USA.) Smoke.
3100		*Am.* (Cherokee syllabary.) Eq. Rom. A.
3100·1		*Rom.* (Cap.) Swash form of D.
3101		*Heb.* Quof, koph, 19th letter of the a., eq. Rom. Q.
3102		*Alch.* Lead.
3103		*Am.* (Cherokee syllabary.) Eq. Rom. NE.
3104		*Heb.* Eq. 4119.
3105		*Ger.* (l.c.) 19th letter of the a., eq. Rom. s. See also 565.
3106		*Mus.* Eq. 5598.

TABLE 240

3110		*Ger.* (Cap.) Eq. 313·1.
3111		*Ger.* (Cap.) Cursive form of 623, eq. Rom. I.
3112		*Ir.* 7th letter of the a., eq. Rom. G.
3113		*Meteor.* Cirrus, thundery type.
3114		*It.* (l.c.) Eq. Rom. y. See 3037.

3114·1		*Log.* Variable individual.
3115		*Ir.* (l.c.) Cursive form of 2799.
3115·1		*Rom.* (l.c.) Cursive form of p.
3116		*Ir.* (l.c.) Cursive form of 2726.
3116·1		*Rom.* (l.c.) Cursive form of r.
3117	≃	*Geom.* Is similarly ordered.
3117·1		*Math.* Is approximately equal to.
3118		*Elec.* Pendant switch.

TABLE 241

3125	*f*	*It.* (l.c.) Eq. Rom. f. See 3053.
3126	2	*Phon.* The affricate dz.
3127		*Geol.* Undulating dip.
3128		*Geol.* Undulating strike.
3129	$	*Com. Mon.* (Esp. USA.) Dollar, dollars.
3130		*Com. Mon.* (Port.) Reis.
3131		*Alch.* Eq. 1306.
3132		*Math.* (Obs.) Is divisible by.

314

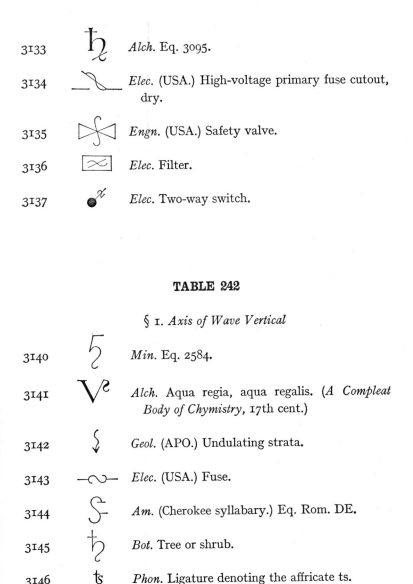

3133		*Alch.* Eq. 3095.
3134		*Elec.* (USA.) High-voltage primary fuse cutout, dry.
3135		*Engn.* (USA.) Safety valve.
3136		*Elec.* Filter.
3137		*Elec.* Two-way switch.

TABLE 242

§ 1. *Axis of Wave Vertical*

3140		*Min.* Eq. 2584.
3141		*Alch.* Aqua regia, aqua regalis. (*A Compleat Body of Chymistry*, 17th cent.)
3142		*Geol.* (APO.) Undulating strata.
3143		*Elec.* (USA.) Fuse.
3144		*Am.* (Cherokee syllabary.) Eq. Rom. DE.
3145		*Bot.* Tree or shrub.
3146		*Phon.* Ligature denoting the affricate ts.
3147		*Phon.* Labialized zh.

315

§ 2. *Axis of Wave Diagonal*

3148 **High.** (L. Inter.) Dangerous bend.

3149 *Tel.* Twisted waveguide.

3150 *Heb.* Beth, 2nd letter of the a., eq. Rom. B. Cardinal number 2.

3151 *Geol.* (APO.) General dip of undulating beds.

3152 *It.* (l.c.) Eq. Rom. k. See 3204.

3153 *Heb.* Tsadek, 18th letter of the a., eq. Rom. S, (T)S.

3154 *Ger.* (l.c.) 4th letter of the a., eq. Rom. d.

3155 *Heb.* Lamed, 12th letter of the a., eq. Rom. L.

3156 *Gk.* (l.c.) Eq. 4169·3.

3157 *Geol.* (APO.) Contorted strata.

§ 3. *Axis of Wave Horizontal*

3158 *It.* (l.c.) Eq. Rom. z. See 4770.

3159 *Hyd.* (APO. Inter.) Current.

3160 *Gk.* (l.c.) Eq. 4379·3.

3161 *Num.* (Arab.) Cursive form of numeral 7.

316

3162	$\mathfrak{f}$	*Ger.* (l.c.) 6th letter of the a., eq. Rom. f.
3163	$\mathcal{J}$.	*It.* (Cap.) Eq. Rom. J. See 2676.
3164		*Am.* (Cherokee syllabary.) Eq. Rom. MU.
3165		*Tel.* Standing wave indicator (double line).
3166		*Tel.* Flexible guide.
3167		*Engn.* Siphon drain.

TABLE 243

3170	$\pm$	*Math.* Sum or difference of.
3171		*Alch.* Spirits of wine (alcohol). (*A Compleat Body of Chymistry,* 17th cent.)
3172	$\lesssim$	*Math.* Equivalent to or less than.
3173	$\gtrsim$	*Math.* Equivalent to or greater than.
3174		*Tel.* (In flange joint.) Gasket.
3175	$\equiv S \equiv$	*Meteor.* (USA.) Sand or dust storm.
3176	$\cong$	*Geom.* Eq. 5363·2.
3177		*Elec.* Modulator.
3178		*Alch.* Mercury.

317

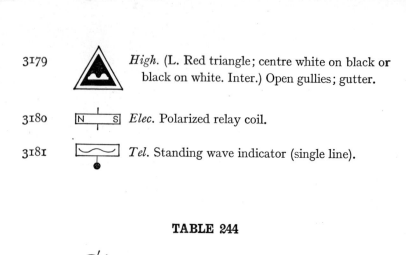

3179   *High.* (L. Red triangle; centre white on black or black on white. Inter.) Open gullies; gutter.

3180   *Elec.* Polarized relay coil.

3181   *Tel.* Standing wave indicator (single line).

TABLE 244

3185   *Elec.* Alternating current of subaudio frequency.

3186   *Math.* Of the form of.

3187   *Chess.* Takes and checks.

3188   *Rus.* (Cap./l.c.) Zheh, 7th letter of the a., eq. Rom. ZH.

3189   *Alch.* Eq. 1304.

3190   *Elec.* Eq. 681.

3190·1   *Ger.* (Cap.) 16th letter of the a., eq. Rom. P.

3191   *Tel.* Band-pass filter.

3192   *Geol.* Contorted dip and strike.

3193   *Elec.* High-pass filter.

3194   *Elec.* Low-pass filter.

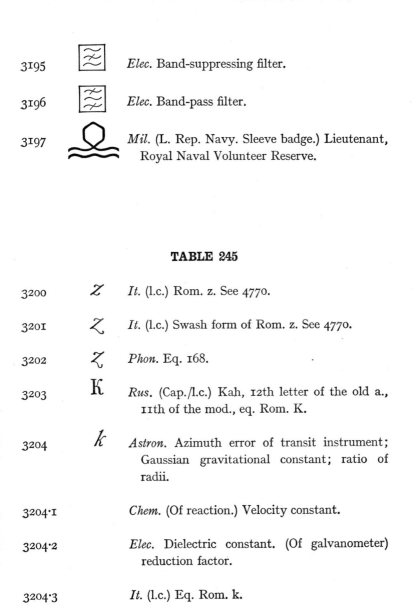

3195   *Elec.* Band-suppressing filter.

3196   *Elec.* Band-pass filter.

3197   *Mil.* (L. Rep. Navy. Sleeve badge.) Lieutenant, Royal Naval Volunteer Reserve.

TABLE 245

3200 z *It.* (l.c.) Rom. z. See 4770.

3201 z *It.* (l.c.) Swash form of Rom. z. See 4770.

3202 z *Phon.* Eq. 168.

3203   К   *Rus.* (Cap./l.c.) Kah, 12th letter of the old a., 11th of the mod., eq. Rom. K.

3204 k *Astron.* Azimuth error of transit instrument; Gaussian gravitational constant; ratio of radii.

3204·1   *Chem.* (Of reaction.) Velocity constant.

3204·2   *Elec.* Dielectric constant. (Of galvanometer) reduction factor.

3204·3   *It.* (l.c.) Eq. Rom. k.

3204·4   *Mag.* Magnetic susceptibility.

3204·5		*Math.* Unit vector along the axes in a right-handed system.
3204·6		*Mech.* Radius of gyration; coefficient of viscosity.
3204·7		*Phys.* Boltzmann's constant; thermal conductivity; specific heat ratio.
3204·8		*Tel.* Coupling coefficient.
3204·9		*Therm.* Thermal conductivity.
3205	*z*	*It.* (l.c.) Eq. Rom. z. See 4770.
3206		*Heb.* Aleph, 1st letter of the a., eq. Rom. A. Cardinal number 1.
3206·1	·	*Math.* Transfinite cardinal number (Cantor).
3206·2		*MS.* Codex Sinaiticus.
3207		*Mus.* C clef, placed on a stave so that the line or space representing the note middle-C falls between the two hooks.
3208		*Soil/m.* (Rep.) Weathered clay.
3209		*High.* (L. Fr.) Moving or swing bridge.
3210		*Egy.* (Hier.) Eq. Rom. K.
3211		*Ger.* (Cap.) 11th letter of the a., eq. Rom. K.

3212   𝕭   *Ger.* (Cap.) Eq. 1897.

3213   *Engn.* (USA.) Evaporator, plate coils, headered or manifold.

3214   *High.* (L. UNS., 1953.) Lifting or bascule bridge.

Cl.I, Div.II, Ord.II, Fam.II, Gen.II

TABLE 246

3220   P   *Rom.* (Cap.) 16th letter of the a. See 2005.

3221   *Num.* (Arab.) Continental cursive numeral 5.

3222   2   *Num.* (Arab.) Eq. 3431.

3223   *Num.* (Arab. 10th cent. Sp.) Eq. mod. 2.

3223·1   *Rom.* (Cap.) Ornamental form of 4191·2.

3224   *Math.* Fifth root. *Cf.* 2248.

TABLE 247

3227   *Am.* (Cherokee syllabary.) Eq. Rom. LI.

3228   *Am.* (Cherokee syllabary.) Eq. Rom. THA.

3229	⎍	*Am.* (Cherokee syllabary.) Eq. Rom. LO.
3230	⎍	*Am.* (Cherokee syllabary.) Eq. Rom. DZA.
3231	⎔	*Cab.* Eq. Rom. Q.
3232	⎔	*Rus.* (Cap. Obs.) Cursive form of 2043.
3233	⎔	*Cab.* Eq. Rom. A.
3234	⎔	*Cab.* Eq. Rom. C.
3235	⎔	*Rus.* (l.c. Obs.) Cursive form of 2043.
3236	$+_2$	*Math.* Nim addition.
3237	⎔	*Astron.* Eq. 2283.
3238	⎔	*It.* (l.c.) Eq. Rom. p. See 1646.
3238·1		*Mus.* Piano (soft).

Cl.I, Div.III, Ord.I, Fam.I, Gen.I

TABLE 248

3340	⎔	*Cart.* (Ant. OS.) Roman spa.
3341	⎔	*Meteor.* (USA.) Sky from two- to three-tenths cloud.

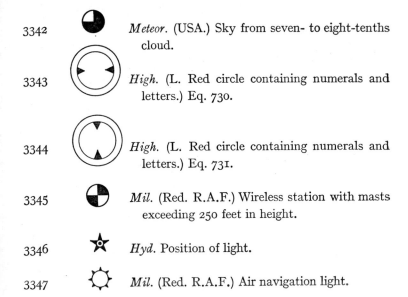

3342	*Meteor.* (USA.) Sky from seven- to eight-tenths cloud.
3343	*High.* (L. Red circle containing numerals and letters.) Eq. 730.
3344	*High.* (L. Red circle containing numerals and letters.) Eq. 731.
3345	*Mil.* (Red. R.A.F.) Wireless station with masts exceeding 250 feet in height.
3346	*Hyd.* Position of light.
3347	*Mil.* (Red. R.A.F.) Air navigation light.

Cl.I, Div.III, Ord.I, Fam.I, Gen.II

TABLE 249

3350   *Meteor.* (USA.) Sky from four- to six-tenths cloud.

3350·1   *Rlwy.* (Brit.) Point indicator.

3351   *Meteor.* (USA.) Sky nine-tenths cloud.

3352   *High.* (L. Red disc, white bar. On motor vehicle. Swiss.) Another motor vehicle is following.

3353 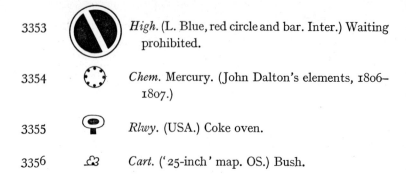 *High.* (L. Blue, red circle and bar. Inter.) Waiting prohibited.

3354 *Chem.* Mercury. (John Dalton's elements, 1806–1807.)

3355 *Rlwy.* (USA.) Coke oven.

3356 *Cart.* ('25-inch' map. OS.) Bush.

Cl.I, Div.III, Ord.I, Fam.II, Gen.I

TABLE 250

3360 *High.* (L. White chalk.) Be careful, temperamental people. (Tramps' 'smogger'.)

3361 *Mus.* Tempus minimus.

3362 *Engn.* (Fire protection.) Sub-divisional police station. (Terminating pipe symbol. USA.) pipe turns upwards.

3363 *Alch.* Gold. (*A Compleat Body of Chymistry*, 17th cent.) Sun. (*Theatrum Chemicum*, Strasbourg, 1659–61.)

3363·1 *Alg.* Eq. 817·6.

3363·2 *Astron.* Sun; sun's longitude; eq. 282.

3363·3   *Bot.* Eq. 10·2.

3363·4   *Cab.* Sun; sign of the archangel Michael.

3363·5   *Chem.* Hydrogen. (John Dalton's elements, 1806–7.)

3363·6   *Geol.* (Often very small.) Borehole.

3363·7   *Geom.* Circle; circumference.

3363·8   *Meteor.* Sunshine.

3363·9   *Mil.* (Red. R.A.F.) Landing ground.

3363·01   *Min.* Gold ore; native gold.

3363·02   *Print.* (Proof correction.) Full-stop, period.

3363·03   *Rlwy.* (USA.) Locomotive formula. Driving-wheel to which driving-rod is attached.

3364   ⊙   *Cart.* (Ant. OS.) Major Roman settlement other than a walled town.

3365   ◉   *Elec.* (Arch. plans. USA.) Floor outlet.

3365·1   *Hyd.* (Inter.) Semaphore, signal or telegraph station.

3365·2   *Mil.* (USA.) Quarry, clay, gravel or sand pit.

3366   ⊙   *Cart.* (Fr.) Church and trigonometrical point. (Rep. Du.) coffee plantation.

3366·1   *Hyd.* Beacon.

3366·2   *Mil.* Observation post; range-taker.

TABLE 251

3370   *High.* (L. Black in red circle. Swiss.) End of postal mountain road.

3371   *Cart.* (Ant. OS.) Roman colony.

3372   *Elec.* Eq. 2040.

3373   *Mil.* (R.A.F.) Aerodrome.

3374   *Elec.* Bell-push outlet.

3375   *Tel.* Gas-filled envelope.

3376   *Elec.* (Arch plans. USA.) Special purpose outlet.

3377   *Meteor.* (USA.) Sky less than one-tenth cloud.

3378   *Engn.* (Fire protection.) Divisional police station.

3379   *Elec.* Fire push.

3380   *Hyd.* (Inter.) Radio station.

3381   *Mil.* (Red. R.A.F.) Seaplane station.

3382   *Chem.* Platinum. (Bergmann, 1783.)

3383   *Alch.* Gold.

3384   *Numis.* Mint mark, 'Eye', Edward IV.

Cl.I, Div.III, Ord.I, Fam.II, Gen.II

TABLE 252

3390   *High.* (L. White chalk.) Dangerous; people here are likely to run you in. (Tramps' 'smogger'.)

3391   *High.* (L. Dan.) General sign indicating restrictions.

3392   *High.* (L. Red on white, mounted on black and white post. Brit.) Limit of carriage-way; edge of road or track.

3393   *Elec.* (In conjunction with 2484.) Dial.

3394   *Alch.* Gold.

3395   *Chem.* Alumine (alumina, aluminium). (John Dalton's elements, 1810.)

3396   *Bot.* Biennial.

3397   *Print.* (Proof correction.) Colon required.

3398   *Print.* (Proof correction.) Insert leader.

3399   *Com.* (L.) Eq. 6129 or 6130.

327

Cl.I, Div.III, Ord.I, Fam.III, Gen.I

TABLE 253

3400	9	*Num.* (Arab.) Nine, the ninth cardinal number.
3401	6	*Num.* (Arab.) Six, the sixth cardinal number.
3402		*Elec.* Support in concrete or iron socket for conductor line.
3403		*Alch.* Eq. 1001.
3404	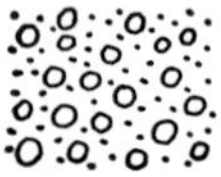	*Engn.* (Rep. Structural.) Concrete.
3404·1		*Geol.* (Rep.) Sandy pebble-bed.
3404·2		*Soil/m.* (Rep.) Sandy gravel.

Cl.I, Div.III, Ord.I, Fam.III, Gen.II

TABLE 254

3410	ض	*Arab.* Ḍad, 15th letter of the a., eq. Rom. Ḍ.
3411		*Mus.* Eq. 3088.
3412	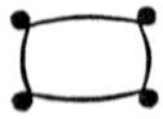	*Numis.* Mint mark, Woolpack.

3413		*Mus.* G clef, placed on a stave so that the spiral encircles the first G above middle C. (Following another, similar clef, esp. in short score) tenor voice.
3414		*Astron.* Eq. 280·2.
3415		*Astron.* Eq. 284·1.

Cl.I, Div.III, Ord.II, Fam.I, Gen.I

TABLE 255

3420		*Arab.* Waw, 27th letter of the a., eq. Rom. W.
3421		*Meteor.* Drizzle.
3422†		*Cz.* Diacritical mark modifying the sounds of the letters d and t.
3422·1		*Mus.* (Vocal score.) Breath mark. (Sol-fa notation) sub-divided beat.
3422·2		*Phon.* Glottal stop.
3422·3		*Punc.* Apostrophe, indicating the omission of a letter or letters, esp. in the possessive case. (After a word ending in s) possessive case. Used after the initial O' in Ir. names, but not in Scottish (see 3424·1). 'Single quote', eq. 3443.

329

3423	**,**	*Chem.* (Obs.) One equivalent of sulphur.

3423·1   *Math.* (Fr. & Continental) Decimal point, eq. 5984·1.

3423·2   *Punc.* Comma, virgule, indicating a brief pause, terminating a phrase or clause within a sentence, introducing or closing a parenthesis. (Ger.) quotation mark introducing a quotation within a quotation.

3424†   **'**   *Phon.* (After p, t, etc.) Slight aspiration.

3424·1   *Punc.* Inverted comma, eq. 3442. Used after the initial M' in Scottish names, but not in Ir. (see 3422·3). 'Single quote', eq. 3442. (Ger.) quotation mark closing a quotation within a quotation.

3425†   **,**   *Turk.* (Beneath cap.) Eq. 2711·1.

3426   *Arab.* Fa, 20th letter of the a., eq. Rom. F.

TABLE 256

3430   *Ger.* (Cap.) Eq. 541·1.

3431   **2**   *Num.* (Arab.) Two, the second cardinal number.

3432   *Mus.* F clef, placed on a stave so that the two dots fall on either side of the line or space representing F.

3433 𝄢 *Mus.* Eq. 3432.

3434 ⌒ *Mus.* Eq. 3432.

Cl.I, Div.III, Ord.II, Fam.I, Gen.II

TABLE 257

3440 ,
, *Meteor.* Intermittent moderate drizzle.

3441 , , *Meteor.* Continuous slight drizzle.

3442† “ *Punc.* Inverted commas, quotation marks, ‘double quotes’, used to introduce quoted matter. (Ger.) quotation marks terminating quoted matter.

3443† ” *Punc.* Quotation marks, ‘double quotes’, (incorrect) ‘double apostrophe’, used to terminate quoted matter.

3444 ,, *Punc.* Double commas, ‘ditto marks’, indicating a repetition of matter immediately above.

3445† „ *Punc.* (Ger.) Quotation marks introducing quoted matter.

TABLE 258

3450 ⁏ *Punc. ME. MS.* Semicolon, full stop, period or mark of interrogation.

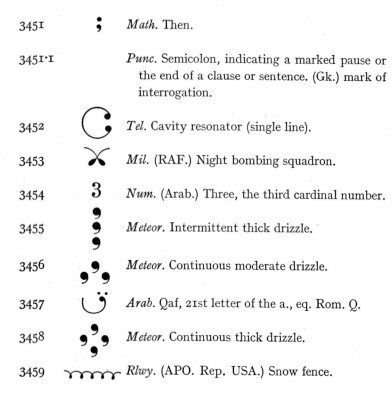

3451	**;**	*Math.* Then.
3451·1		*Punc.* Semicolon, indicating a marked pause or the end of a clause or sentence. (Gk.) mark of interrogation.
3452		*Tel.* Cavity resonator (single line).
3453		*Mil.* (RAF.) Night bombing squadron.
3454	**3**	*Num.* (Arab.) Three, the third cardinal number.
3455		*Meteor.* Intermittent thick drizzle.
3456		*Meteor.* Continuous moderate drizzle.
3457		*Arab.* Qaf, 21st letter of the a., eq. Rom. Q.
3458		*Meteor.* Continuous thick drizzle.
3459		*Rlwy.* (APO. Rep. USA.) Snow fence.

Cl.I, Div.III, Ord.II, Fam.II, Gen.I

TABLE 259

§ 1. *One Simple Curve and Round Dot*

3466   *Log.* Eq. 2380·1.

3466·1   *Mus.* Corona, a pause for a period to be decided by the performer; sometimes marking the end of a passage to be repeated.

3467   ⌣̇   *Arab.* Nun, 25th letter of the a., eq. Rom. N.

3468   ⌣̣   *Log.* Eq. 2382.

3468·1   *Mus.* Eq. 3466·1.

3469   (•   *Log.* Eq. 2383.

3470   •)   *Log.* Eq. 2384.

3471   ⌣̣   *Arab.* Ba, 2nd letter of the a., eq. Rom. B.

3472   )   *Arab.* Za, 11th letter of the a., eq. Rom. Z.

3473   •/   *Jap.* (Katakana syllabary.) Eq. Rom. SO. (With 5248) ZO.

3474   ♉   *Cart.* Eq. 2515.

§ 2. *All Other Signs*

3475   غ   *Arab.* Ghain, 19th letter of the a., eq. Rom. GH or K (guttural).

3476   (●)   *Meteor.* Precipitation within sight, near to but not at station.

3477   )●(*Meteor.* Precipitation within sight, distant from station.

3478   ∿   *Geom.* Eq. 5170.

3479   ⸮   *Punc.* (Sp.) Eq. 2511.

3480   ⸮   *Punc.* It. form of 2510.

3481   ⸮   *Punc.* (Sp.) It form. of 2511.

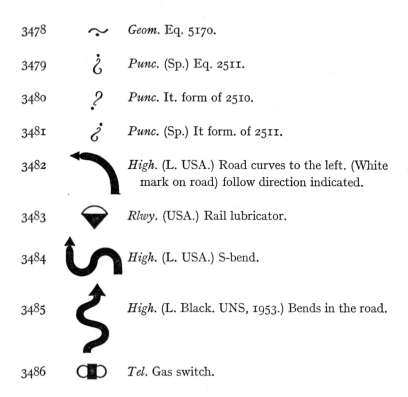

3482   *High.* (L. USA.) Road curves to the left. (White mark on road) follow direction indicated.

3483   *Rlwy.* (USA.) Rail lubricator.

3484   *High.* (L. USA.) S-bend.

3485   *High.* (L. Black. UNS, 1953.) Bends in the road.

3486   *Tel.* Gas switch.

Cl.I, Div.III, Ord.II, Fam.II, Gen.II

TABLE 260

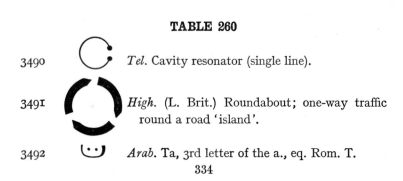

3490   *Tel.* Cavity resonator (single line).

3491   *High.* (L. Brit.) Roundabout; one-way traffic round a road 'island'.

3492   *Arab.* Ta, 3rd letter of the a., eq. Rom. T.

3493   *Arab.* Tha, 4th letter of the a., eq. Rom. TH.

3494   *Arab.* Shin, 13th letter of the a., eq. Rom. SH.

3495   *Jap.* (Katakana syllabary.) Eq. Rom. TSU. (With 5248) DU. Cardinal number 19.

3496   *Cart.* (Rep. '6-inch' map. OS.) Reeds.

3497   *Arab.* Ya, 28th letter of the a., eq. Rom. Y.

3498   *Geol.* (APO. Rep.) Base of lava flow.

Cl.II, Ord.I, Fam.I, Gen.I

TABLE 261

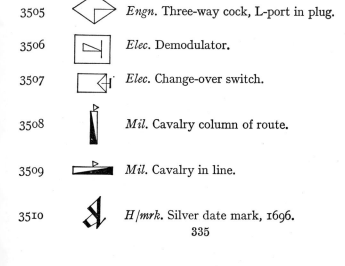

3505   *Engn.* Three-way cock, L-port in plug.

3506   *Elec.* Demodulator.

3507   *Elec.* Change-over switch.

3508   *Mil.* Cavalry column of route.

3509   *Mil.* Cavalry in line.

3510   *H/mrk.* Silver date mark, 1696.

335

3511   *Alch.* Eq. 876.

3512   *Rlwy.* (USA.) Drawbridge pipe coupler.

TABLE 262

3517   *Rlwy.* (Brit.) Traction system dead section indicator.

3518   *Engn.* Fillet weld.

3519   *Gk.* (Cap.) Eq. 3584·5.

3520   *Tel.* Wedge termination.

3521   *Run.* Eq. Rom. W.

3522   *Run.* Eq. Rom. TH.

3523   *Engn.* (In pipe symbol. USA.) Eccentric reducer, screwed.

3524   *Jap.* (Katakana syllabary.) Eq. Rom. A, as in ah.

3525   *Run.* Eq. Rom. R.

3526   *Am.* (Cherokee syllabary.) Eq. Rom. SE.

3527   *Num.* (Arab.) Four, the fourth cardinal number.

3528   *Alch.* Eq. 4554.

3529   _A_/   *Numis.* It. form of 3630.

3530   _W_   *It.* (Cap.) Ornamental form of 4846·3.

TABLE 263

3535   *Elec.* Resistor with non-linear current-voltage.

3536   *Engn.* (In pipe symbol. USA.) Eccentric reducer, flanged.

3537   *Elec.* (USA.) Sector switch.

3538   *Pot.* China mark, Moscow.

3539   *Meteor. Aero.* Eq. 4315.

3540   *Rlwy.* (USA.) Two-way reversed motion crank.

2541   Æ   *Dan.* (Cap.) The long A, as in hay.

3541·1   *Numis.* Eq. 3652.

3541·2   *OE.* (Cap.) The short A, as in hat.

3541·3   *Rom.* (Cap.) Ligature of A and E, indicating a diphthong.

3542   Æ   *Nav.* Third-class vessel.

337

TABLE 264

3547   *Meteor.* Threatening sky.

3548   *Elec.* (USA.) Antenna, aerial.

3549   *Elec.* Frequency changer; main control.

3550   *Mil.* (APO.) Troops, nature and disposition unspecified.

3551   *Engn.* (In pipe symbol. USA.) Float and thermostatic trap.

3552   *Engn.* (Heating and ventilating. USA.) Exhaust or return duct section.

3553   *Cart.* (Ant. OS.) Roman training or practice camp.

3554   *H/mrk.* Silver date mark, 1698.

3555   *Run.* Eq. Rom. B.

3556   *Engn.* Three-way cock, T-port in plug.

3557   *Elec.* Amplifier.

3558   *Elec.* Echo suppressor.

TABLE 265

3565   *Elec.* Symmetrical element (resistor) with non-linear current-voltage.

3566   *Phar.* 'Crossed-M'. Mix. (Lat. *misce.*)

3567   *Alch.* Month. (*A Compleat Body of Chymistry*, 17th cent.)

3567·1   *Astron.* Station mark.

3568   *Mil.* Cavalry section leader. (R.A.) No. 1. (R.E., R.T.C. and R.A.S.C.) subsection commander.

3569   *Elec.* Cooker control unit.

3570   *Engn.* (Plumbing. USA.) Grease separator.

3571   *Elec.* Slow operating relay coil.

3572   *Mil.* Kettle-drum.

3573   *Pot.* China mark, Worcester.

3574   *Mil.* G.H.Q., general headquarters.

TABLE 266

3580   *High.* (L. Red.) Danger; caution.

3580·1   *Mil.* 1st Infantry Division.

3581	△	*High.* (L. Red, enclosing a specific sign in black on white. UNS.) European traffic sign plate, demanding attention to enclosed sign.
3582	△	*Tel.* Single line discontinuity symbol.
3583	△	*Alch.* Fire; sand. (*A Compleat Body of Chymistry*, 17th cent.)
3583·1		*Astrol.* Trine.
3583·2		*Bot.* Evergreen.
3583·3		*Elec.* Internal telephone point.
3583·4		*Engn.* Projection weld.
3583·5		*Geom.* Triangle.
3583·6		*Meteor.* Small hail, soft hail, graupel.
3583·7		*Nav. Arch.* Eq. 3584·6.
3583·8		*Phila.* Used stamp 'on piece', i.e., on a sufficient part of the envelope, card or wrapper to show complete postmark.
3584	Δ	*Astron.* Nutation; distance from the centre of the earth. *Cf.* 3587.
3584·1		*Cal.* Increment; finite difference.
3584·2		*Chem.* Double bond, esp. between carbon atoms.

340

3584·3   *Elec.* 3-phase winding.

3584·4   *Engn.* Maximum or total deflection. (Structural) deflection of a panel point of a truss.

3584·5   *Gk.* (Cap.) Delta, 4th letter of the a., eq. Rom. D.

3584·6   *Nav. Arch.* Displacement by weight.

3584·7   *Opt.* Angle of deviation.

3584·8   *Phys.* Coefficient of diffusion; lowering of freezing-point; heat drop.

3584·9   *Therm.* Heat drop at constant entropy.

3585   *Cart.* (Ant. OS.) Roman building other than temple, villa or bath. (Fr.) camping site.

3586   *Engn.* (Fire protection.) Inaccessible roof space or blind attic.

3586·1   *Rlwy.* (Brit.) Automatic train control inductor.

3587   *Astron.* Mean density of the earth.

3587·1   *Gk.* (Cap.) It. form of 3584·5.

TABLE 267

3595   *High.* (L. Black triangle, red centre. UNS, 1953.) Priority route.

3596   *High.* (L. Red. Inter.) Priority route. (Du) major road ahead.

3597   *High.* (L. Red. triangle, yellow centre. Inter). Major road ahead.

3598   *High.* (L. White chalk.) Spoilt—too many callers. (Tramps' 'smogger'.)

3599   *Alch.* Water. (*A Compleat Body of Chymistry*, 17th cent.)

3599·1   *Cal.* Nabla (incorrectly 'nabula') or del. Laplace's operator; the 'curl' of a vector; symbolic vector; backward finite difference operator. (Heb. *nebel*, a triangular musical instrument.)

3599·2   *Chem.* Water. (Bergmann, 1783.)

3599·3   *Nav.* Displacement by volume.

3600   *Rlwy.* (USA.) Check valve.

3601   *Meteor.* Showers.

3602   *Pot.* China mark, Chelsea; Derby (Joseph Hills).

TABLE 268

3605   *High.* (L. Red triangle and black symbol. Brit., 1964.) T-junction.

342

3606   *High.* (L. Red triangle and black symbol. Brit., 1964.) Side road to right. *Symbol reversed:* side road to left.

3607   *High.* (L. Red triangle and black symbol, or *vice versa.* Inter.) Dangerous bends.

3608   *High.* (L. Red triangle and black symbol. Brit., 1964.) Cross-roads.

3609   *High.* (L. Red triangle, black cross. Inter.) Cross-roads. (Same colours or black triangle, red cross. Sw.) junction of two priority (*sic*) roads.

3610   *High.* (L. Red triangle and black symbol. Brit., 1964.) Two-way traffic.

3611   *High.* (L. Red triangle and black symbol. Brit., 1964.) Dual carriageway ends.

3612   *High.* (L. Red triangle and black symbol. Brit., 1964.) Road narrows on both sides.

3613   *High.* (L. Red triangle, black line. Inter.) Danger. (Sw.) school; end of priority.

TABLE 269

3615   ⊳   *ME. MS.* Eq. W. (Borrowed from the Run.)

3615·1		*Mil.* Brigade.
3616	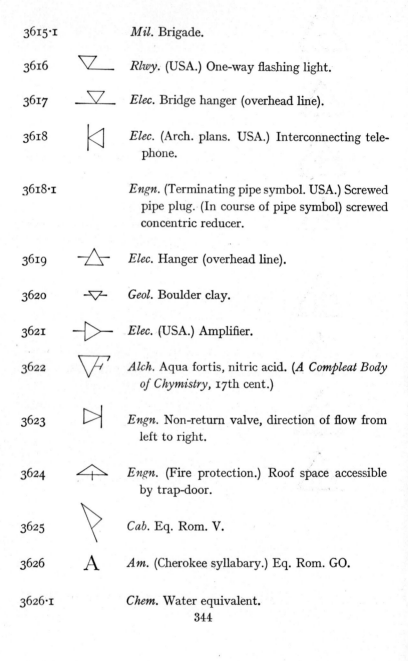	*Rlwy.* (USA.) One-way flashing light.
3617		*Elec.* Bridge hanger (overhead line).
3618		*Elec.* (Arch. plans. USA.) Interconnecting telephone.
3618·1		*Engn.* (Terminating pipe symbol. USA.) Screwed pipe plug. (In course of pipe symbol) screwed concentric reducer.
3619		*Elec.* Hanger (overhead line).
3620		*Geol.* Boulder clay.
3621		*Elec.* (USA.) Amplifier.
3622		*Alch.* Aqua fortis, nitric acid. (*A Compleat Body of Chymistry*, 17th cent.)
3623		*Engn.* Non-return valve, direction of flow from left to right.
3624		*Engn.* (Fire protection.) Roof space accessible by trap-door.
3625		*Cab.* Eq. Rom. V.
3626	A	*Am.* (Cherokee syllabary.) Eq. Rom. GO.
3626·1		*Chem.* Water equivalent.

344

3626·2		*Elec.* Ampere.
3626·3		*Gk.* (Cap.) Alpha, 1st letter of the a., eq. Rom. A.
3626·4		*Log.* Universal affirmative.
3626·5		*Rom.* (Cap.) 1st letter of the a. (Med. ext. of Rom. num.) cardinal numbers 50 or 500 (eq. 66·2).
3626·6		*Rus.* (Cap.) Ah, 1st letter of the a., eq. Rom. A.
3627	A	*Mag.* Magnetic vector potential.
3627·1		*Rom.* (Cap.) Sanserif form of A, 3626·5.
3628	V	*Log.* 'Turned-A'. For all; universal quantifier.
3629		*Engn.* (Fire protection.) Roof space accessible by stairs or fixed ladder.
3630		*Rlwy.* (USA.) Cable post.
3631		*Numis.* Gold.
3632	W	*Rom.* (Cap.) Ornamental form of 4845·2.

TABLE 270

3635		*Am.* Ideograph signifying a man.
3636		*Cart.* (OS.) Beacon.

345

3637		*Am.* Ideograph, signifying an abode, dwelling.
3638		*Alch.* Sulphur.
3638·1		*Astron.* (Obs.) Eq. 4007.
3639		*Alch.* Philosopher's stone.

TABLE 271

3645		*Meteor.* Soft hail.
3646		*Engn.* Controllable or screw-down non-return valve.
3647		*Egy.* (Hier.) Eq. Rom. CH.
3648		*Elec.* (USA.) Eq. 3621.
3649		*Math.* (Obsnt.) Is not less than, eq. 4615.
3649·1		*Ph.* Moabite (Tyrian). Eq. Rom. A, E.
3650		*Math.* Vector subtraction.
3651		*Math.* (Obsnt.) Is not greater than, eq. 4601.
3652		*Numis.* Bronze, copper.
3653		*Alch.* Arsenic.
3654		*Meteor.* Snow showers.

346

3655 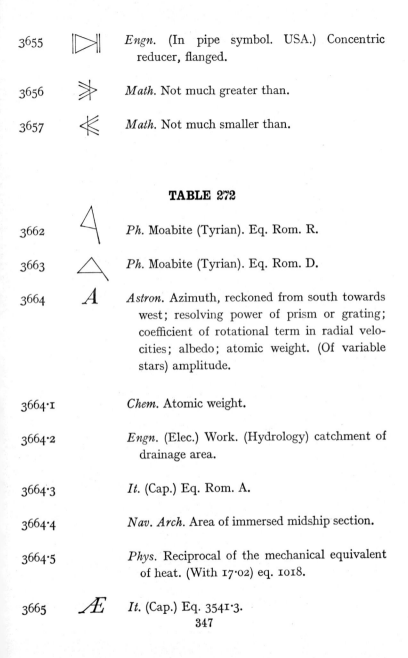 *Engn.* (In pipe symbol. USA.) Concentric reducer, flanged.

3656 *Math.* Not much greater than.

3657 *Math.* Not much smaller than.

TABLE 272

3662 *Ph.* Moabite (Tyrian). Eq. Rom. R.

3663 *Ph.* Moabite (Tyrian). Eq. Rom. D.

3664 *A* *Astron.* Azimuth, reckoned from south towards west; resolving power of prism or grating; coefficient of rotational term in radial velocities; albedo; atomic weight. (Of variable stars) amplitude.

3664·1 *Chem.* Atomic weight.

3664·2 *Engn.* (Elec.) Work. (Hydrology) catchment of drainage area.

3664·3 *It.* (Cap.) Eq. Rom. A.

3664·4 *Nav. Arch.* Area of immersed midship section.

3664·5 *Phys.* Reciprocal of the mechanical equivalent of heat. (With 17·02) eq. 1018.

3665 *Æ* *It.* (Cap.) Eq. 3541·3.

TABLE 273

3670   *High.* (L. Red triangle and black symbol, or *vice versa.* Inter.) Level crossing.

3671   *Elec.* Telephone board, internal.

3672   *Elec.* Amplifying equipment.

3673   *Elec.* (USA.) One-way repeater.

3674   *Elec.* Eq. 2546.

3675   *Mil.* Trumpeter; drummer; orderly.

3676   *Mil.* Drum-major (bugles or pipes).

3677   *Elec.* Feeder pillar.

3678   *Mil.* Armoured car unit.

3679   *Elec.* (Arch. plans. USA.) Telephone switch-board.

3680   *Mil.* Armoured car column of route.

TABLE 274

3685   *Alch.* Air. (*A Compleat Body of Chymistry,* 17th cent.)

3685·1   *Meteor.* (USA.) Frozen drizzle; granular snow.

348

3686	▽	*Alch.* Earth. (*A Compleat Body of Chymistry,* 17th cent.)
3687	◁	*Tel.* Sealed horn.
3688	△⊦	*Chem.* Nitrous air. (Lavoisier, 18th cent.)
3689	⋇▽	*Meteor.* (USA.) Heavy snow showers.
3690	⊏▭	*Rlwy.* (Brit.) Sand hump.
3691	Ａ	*Alch.* Eq. 3916.

TABLE 275

§ 1. *Triangles and No More than Two Other Lines*

3695	◁▷	*Engn.* Straight through cock, direction of flow at right-angles to the diagonal.
3696	▷◁	*Engn.* Control valve.
3697	▷◁	*Run.* Eq. Rom. M.
3698	▷◁	*Engn.* Reducing valve.
3699	▷⊦	*Rlwy.* (USA.) Flashing lights, both ways.
3700	▷◁	*Engn.* Valve, open. (USA) gate valve.
3701	▷ ◁	*Elec.* (USA.) Protective arrester gap.

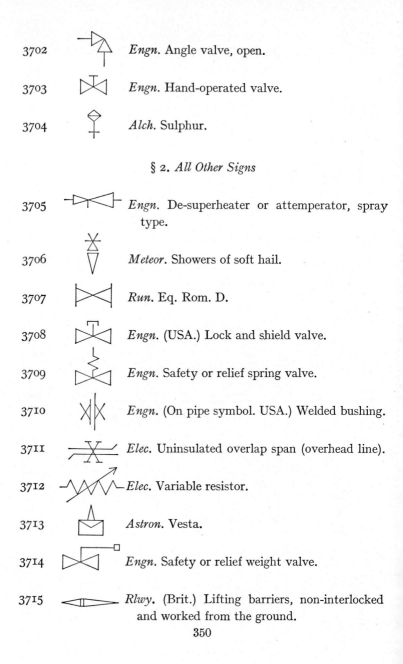

3702   *Engn.* Angle valve, open.

3703   *Engn.* Hand-operated valve.

3704   *Alch.* Sulphur.

§ 2. *All Other Signs*

3705   *Engn.* De-superheater or attemperator, spray type.

3706   *Meteor.* Showers of soft hail.

3707   *Run.* Eq. Rom. D.

3708   *Engn.* (USA.) Lock and shield valve.

3709   *Engn.* Safety or relief spring valve.

3710   *Engn.* (On pipe symbol. USA.) Welded bushing.

3711   *Elec.* Uninsulated overlap span (overhead line).

3712   *Elec.* Variable resistor.

3713   *Astron.* Vesta.

3714   *Engn.* Safety or relief weight valve.

3715   *Rlwy.* (Brit.) Lifting barriers, non-interlocked and worked from the ground.

3716   *Engn.* (USA.) Motor-operated valve.

3717   *Engn.* (USA.) Quick-opening valve.

TABLE 276

3722   *High.* (L. White on blue. Brit.) Vehicle testing station.

3723   *Alch.* Arsenic.

3724   *Elec.* Fixed radiator, heating panel. (Arch. plans. USA) controller.

3724·1   *Engn.* (Heating and ventilating. USA.) Supply duct section.

3724·2   *Phila.* Used stamp on complete envelope, card or wrapper.

3725   *High.* (L. White chalk.) Woman with children: tell tale about own children. (Tramps' 'smogger'.)

3726   *Meteor.* (APO. Rep.) Eq. 2114.

3727   *Hyd.* (Inter.) Temple; pagoda. (Du.) Shinto shrine.

3728   *Engn.* Multi-way valve.

3729   *Cab.* Pentacle, pentagram, an early symbol of the five virtues.

351

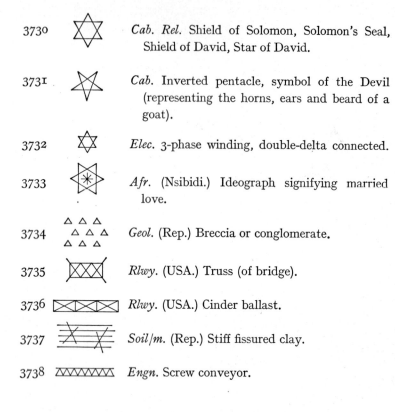

| 3730 | | *Cab. Rel.* Shield of Solomon, Solomon's Seal, Shield of David, Star of David. |

3731   *Cab.* Inverted pentacle, symbol of the Devil (representing the horns, ears and beard of a goat).

3732   *Elec.* 3-phase winding, double-delta connected.

3733   *Afr.* (Nsibidi.) Ideograph signifying married love.

3734   *Geol.* (Rep.) Breccia or conglomerate.

3735   *Rlwy.* (USA.) Truss (of bridge).

3736   *Rlwy.* (USA.) Cinder ballast.

3737   *Soil/m.* (Rep.) Stiff fissured clay.

3738   *Engn.* Screw conveyor.

Cl.II, Ord.I, Fam.I, Gen.II

TABLE 277

3745   *Elec.* Substation.

3745·1   *Tel.* Double line discontinuity symbol; window.

3746   *Astron.* (Obs.) Eq. 3886.

352

3746·1   *Bot.* (In inheritance charts.) Male individual.

3746·2   *Cal.* D'Alembertian operator; mean operator (finite differences).

3746·3   *Egy.* (Hier.) Eq. Rom. P.

3746·4   *Geom.* Square.

3746·5   *Mil.* Rank and file; crew.

3746·6   *Print.* (Proof correction.) Em quad space; indent one em.

3747   □   *Cart.* (Ant. OS.) Roman fort.

3747·1   *Rlwy.* (USA.) Stone monument.

3748   *High.* (L. Border any colour, centre white. Ger., Austrian.) Priority route.

3749   *High.* (L. White chalk.) Generous people, but don't presume too much. (Tramps' 'smogger'.)

3750   *Elec.* (USA.) Visual signalling device, annunciator.

3750·1   *Num.* (Arab.) Early form of 2298. Cf. 426 and 275.

3750·2   *Rom.* Early Lat. form of O.

3751   ▢   *Elec.* Manhole.

3752   *Cart.* (Ant. OS.) Minor Roman legionary fortress.

3753   *Mil.* Tank trap.

3754   *High.* (L. White chalk.) People here are afraid of tramps. (Tramps' 'smogger'.)

3755   *Alch.* Eq. 3171.

TABLE 278

3760   *High.* (L. White chalk.) Eq. 3390. (Tramps' 'smogger'.)

3761   *G/use.* (Proportions variable.) 'Box', enclosing information for special attention.

3761·1   *Math.* (Ger.) 'Büchse', enclosing a significant formula or equation.

3762   *Elec.* (Arch. plans. USA.) Interconnection box.

3762·1   *Engn.* Closed vessel or tank.

3763   *Jap.* (Katakana syllabary.) Eq. Rom. RO.

3764   *Alch.* Powder of bricks. (*A Compleat Body of Chymistry*, 17th cent.)

3764·1   *Elec.* Generating station; switchboard; distribution board, fuseboard; telephone exchange.

3764·2		*Engn.* (In pipe symbol. USA.) Float trap.
3764·3		*Geom.* Rectangle, parallelogram.
3764·4		*Mil.* Eq. 3746·5.
3764·5		*Rlwy.* (Associated with electrified track symbols.) Impedance bond.
3765	⌐	*Cart.* (APO.) Eq. 6017. (Ant. OS) temporary Roman camp. ('25-inch' map. OS) water trough.
3765·1		*Elec.* (USA.) Eq. 4180.
3765·2		*Mil.* Hutment.
3765·3		*Mus.* (Obs.) Eq. 1636.
3766	☐	*Engn.* Unpacked tower.
3767	☐	*Elec.* Relay; integrating meter.
3768	▯	*Tel.* Rectangular waveguide.
3768·1		*Engn.* (On pipe symbol. USA.) Thermometer.
3769	▭	*Engn.* (USA.) Unit ventilator.

TABLE 279

3774	⊟	*Num.* (Magnetic ink E 13 B font.) Eight, eq. 37.

3775		*Rlwy.* (USA.) Section house.
3776		*Rlwy.* (USA.) Coastguard station.
3777		*Rlwy.* (On light signal symbol. Brit.) Automatic.
3778		*Meteor.* Ground frozen hard and dry.
3779		*Engn.* (USA.) Unit heater (propeller).
3780		*Engn.* (USA.) Pressure switch.
3781		*Engn.* (USA.) Pressure switch with high-pressure cut-out.
3782		*Engn.* Closed tank, steam-sealing type.
3783		*Elec.* Contactor.
3783·1		*Phila.* Block of four or more stamps.
3784		*Mil.* Hospital clearing station or aid post.
3785		*Alch.* Water.

TABLE 280

§ 1. *With Squares*

3790		*Phila.* Eq. 2097.
3791		*Elec.* Detector.

3792   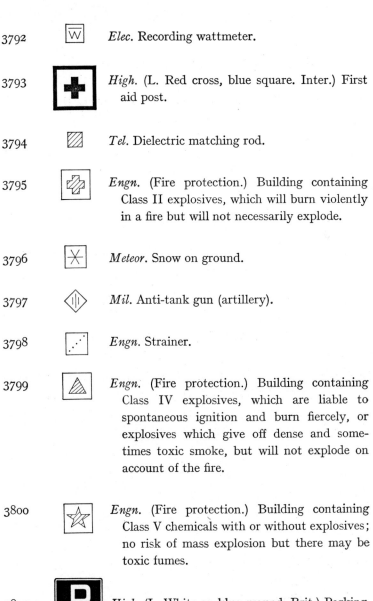 *Elec.* Recording wattmeter.

3793   *High.* (L. Red cross, blue square. Inter.) First aid post.

3794   *Tel.* Dielectric matching rod.

3795   *Engn.* (Fire protection.) Building containing Class II explosives, which will burn violently in a fire but will not necessarily explode.

3796   *Meteor.* Snow on ground.

3797   *Mil.* Anti-tank gun (artillery).

3798   *Engn.* Strainer.

3799   *Engn.* (Fire protection.) Building containing Class IV explosives, which are liable to spontaneous ignition and burn fiercely, or explosives which give off dense and some-times toxic smoke, but will not explode on account of the fire.

3800   *Engn.* (Fire protection.) Building containing Class V chemicals with or without explosives; no risk of mass explosion but there may be toxic fumes.

3801   *High.* (L. White on blue ground. Brit.) Parking.

357

3805   *Engn.* Sight flow indicator.

3806   *Rlwy.* (On light signal symbol, Brit.) Semi-automatic.

3807   *Rlwy.* (USA.) Ground levers.

3808   *Engn.* (In pipe symbol. USA.) Expansion joint.

3809   *Egy.* (Hier.) Eq. Rom. SH.

3810   *Rlwy.* (Brit.) Junction indicator, repeater or subsidiary.

3811   *Elec.* Demodulator-detector.

3812   *Elec.* Convection heater.

3813   *High.* (L. White chalk.) Brutal owner or tenant. (Tramps' 'smogger'.)

3814   *Engn.* Electric furnace.

3815   *Elec.* Correcting network.

3816   *Engn.* (Fire protection.) Home Office regional radio station.

3817   *Elec.* (APO.) Relay-set.

3818   *Engn.* Batch drier.

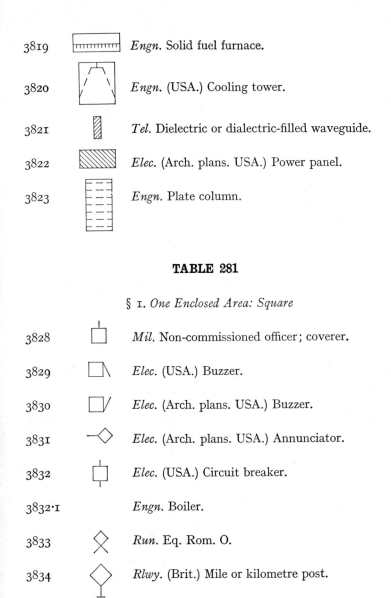

3819   *Engn.* Solid fuel furnace.

3820   *Engn.* (USA.) Cooling tower.

3821   *Tel.* Dielectric or dialectric-filled waveguide.

3822   *Elec.* (Arch. plans. USA.) Power panel.

3823   *Engn.* Plate column.

TABLE 281

§ 1. *One Enclosed Area: Square*

3828   *Mil.* Non-commissioned officer; coverer.

3829   *Elec.* (USA.) Buzzer.

3830   *Elec.* (Arch. plans. USA.) Buzzer.

3831   *Elec.* (Arch. plans. USA.) Annunciator.

3832   *Elec.* (USA.) Circuit breaker.

3832·1   *Engn.* Boiler.

3833   *Run.* Eq. Rom. O.

3834   *Rlwy.* (Brit.) Mile or kilometre post.

3835   *Elec.* Loop aerial.

359

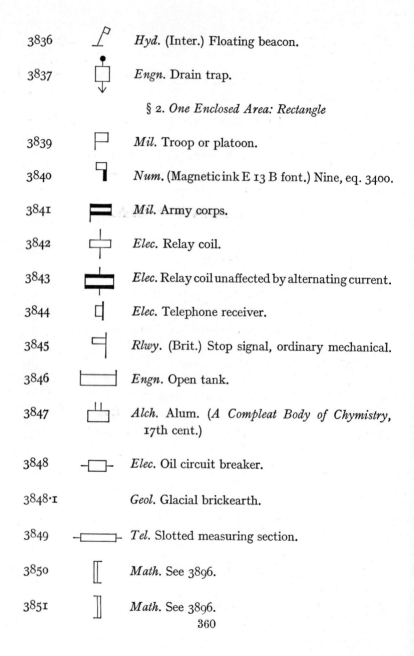

3836		*Hyd.* (Inter.) Floating beacon.
3837		*Engn.* Drain trap.

§ 2. *One Enclosed Area: Rectangle*

3839		*Mil.* Troop or platoon.
3840		*Num.* (Magnetic ink E 13 B font.) Nine, eq. 3400.
3841		*Mil.* Army corps.
3842		*Elec.* Relay coil.
3843		*Elec.* Relay coil unaffected by alternating current.
3844		*Elec.* Telephone receiver.
3845		*Rlwy.* (Brit.) Stop signal, ordinary mechanical.
3846		*Engn.* Open tank.
3847		*Alch.* Alum. (*A Compleat Body of Chymistry,* 17th cent.)
3848		*Elec.* Oil circuit breaker.
3848·1		*Geol.* Glacial brickearth.
3849		*Tel.* Slotted measuring section.
3850		*Math.* See 3896.
3851		*Math.* See 3896.

360

3852   *Engn.* (USA.) Reciprocating compressor, with crank-case belted.

3853   *Elec.* (Arch. plans, USA.) Isolating switch.

3854   *Rlwy.* (USA.) Boom crane.

3855   *Num.* (Magnetic ink E 13 B font.) Six, eq. 3401.

3856   *Rlwy.* (Brit.) Crank handle release instrument.

3857   *Elec.* Compole winding.

3858   *Elec.* (USA.) Eq. 3877.

§ 3. *More Than One Enclosed Area*

3860   *Rlwy.* (USA.) Section tool house.

3861   *Rlwy.* (Brit.) Stop signal, fixed arm.

3862   *Mus.* Long, eq. two breves. (15th cent.)

3863   *Mus.* Large, eq. two longs or four breves. (15th cent.)

3864   *Mil.* Visual signalling station.

3865   *Elec.* (USA.) Carbon block arrester gap.

3866   *Rlwy.* (Across track symbols. Brit.) Cattle guard crossing.

361

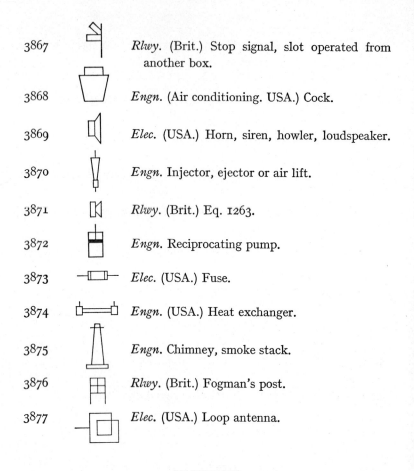

3867   *Rlwy.* (Brit.) Stop signal, slot operated from another box.

3868   *Engn.* (Air conditioning. USA.) Cock.

3869   *Elec.* (USA.) Horn, siren, howler, loudspeaker.

3870   *Engn.* Injector, ejector or air lift.

3871   *Rlwy.* (Brit.) Eq. 1263.

3872   *Engn.* Reciprocating pump.

3873   *Elec.* (USA.) Fuse.

3874   *Engn.* (USA.) Heat exchanger.

3875   *Engn.* Chimney, smoke stack.

3876   *Rlwy.* (Brit.) Fogman's post.

3877   *Elec.* (USA.) Loop antenna.

TABLE 282

§ 1. *One Enclosed Area*

3882   *Engn.* Flash box.

3883   *Mil.* (R.A., R.E., & R.T.C.) Troop, section sergeant. (R.A.S.C.) platoon, subsection sergeant.

362

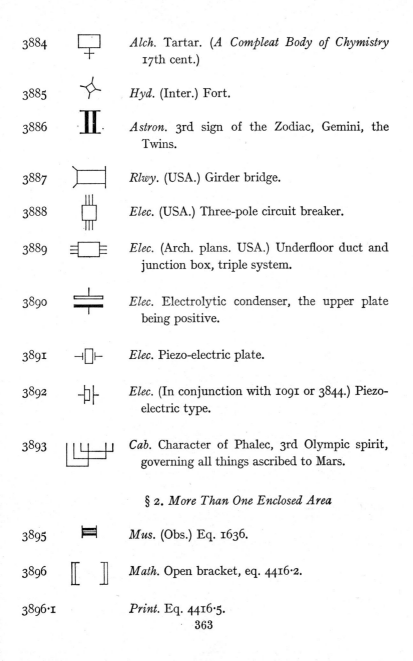

3884   *Alch.* Tartar. (*A Compleat Body of Chymistry* 17th cent.)

3885   *Hyd.* (Inter.) Fort.

3886   *Astron.* 3rd sign of the Zodiac, Gemini, the Twins.

3887   *Rlwy.* (USA.) Girder bridge.

3888   *Elec.* (USA.) Three-pole circuit breaker.

3889   *Elec.* (Arch. plans. USA.) Underfloor duct and junction box, triple system.

3890   *Elec.* Electrolytic condenser, the upper plate being positive.

3891   *Elec.* Piezo-electric plate.

3892   *Elec.* (In conjunction with 1091 or 3844.) Piezo-electric type.

3893   *Cab.* Character of Phalec, 3rd Olympic spirit, governing all things ascribed to Mars.

§ 2. *More Than One Enclosed Area*

3895   *Mus.* (Obs.) Eq. 1636.

3896   *Math.* Open bracket, eq. 4416·2.

3896·1   *Print.* Eq. 4416·5.

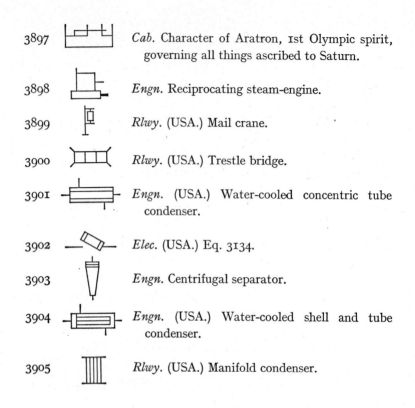

3897   *Cab.* Character of Aratron, 1st Olympic spirit, governing all things ascribed to Saturn.

3898   *Engn.* Reciprocating steam-engine.

3899   *Rlwy.* (USA.) Mail crane.

3900   *Rlwy.* (USA.) Trestle bridge.

3901   *Engn.* (USA.) Water-cooled concentric tube condenser.

3902   *Elec.* (USA.) Eq. 3134.

3903   *Engn.* Centrifugal separator.

3904   *Engn.* (USA.) Water-cooled shell and tube condenser.

3905   *Rlwy.* (USA.) Manifold condenser.

TABLE 283

3910   *Pot.* China mark, Dresden (Meissen).

3911   *Alch.* Lead.

3911·1   *Chess.* Check; takes; moves to.

3911·2   *Math.* Form a complete ordered field.

3911·3   *Pros.* Diaeresis.

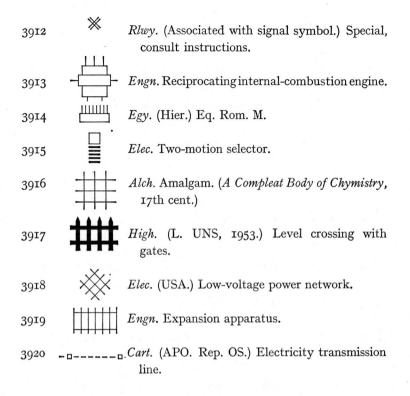

3912	※	*Rlwy.* (Associated with signal symbol.) Special, consult instructions.
3913		*Engn.* Reciprocating internal-combustion engine.
3914		*Egy.* (Hier.) Eq. Rom. M.
3915		*Elec.* Two-motion selector.
3916		*Alch.* Amalgam. (*A Compleat Body of Chymistry,* 17th cent.)
3917		*High.* (L. UNS, 1953.) Level crossing with gates.
3918		*Elec.* (USA.) Low-voltage power network.
3919		*Engn.* Expansion apparatus.
3920		*Cart.* (APO. Rep. OS.) Electricity transmission line.

TABLE 284

§ 1. *One or Two Free Ends* (*Internal and External*)

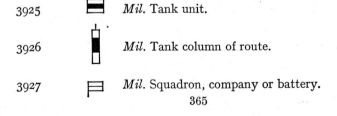

3925		*Mil.* Tank unit.
3926		*Mil.* Tank column of route.
3927		*Mil.* Squadron, company or battery.

365

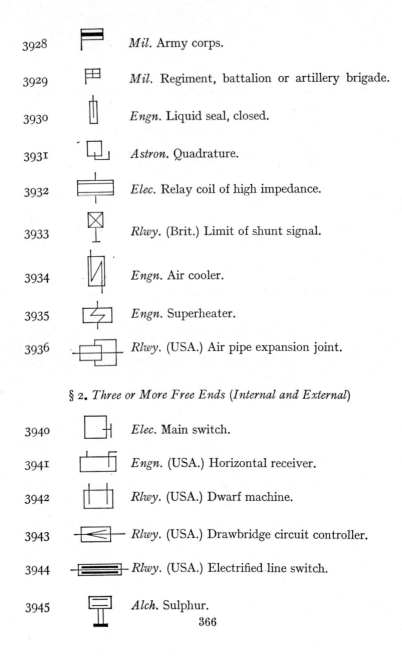

3928   *Mil.* Army corps.

3929   *Mil.* Regiment, battalion or artillery brigade.

3930   *Engn.* Liquid seal, closed.

3931   *Astron.* Quadrature.

3932   *Elec.* Relay coil of high impedance.

3933   *Rlwy.* (Brit.) Limit of shunt signal.

3934   *Engn.* Air cooler.

3935   *Engn.* Superheater.

3936   *Rlwy.* (USA.) Air pipe expansion joint.

§ 2. *Three or More Free Ends (Internal and External)*

3940   *Elec.* Main switch.

3941   *Engn.* (USA.) Horizontal receiver.

3942   *Rlwy.* (USA.) Dwarf machine.

3943   *Rlwy.* (USA.) Drawbridge circuit controller.

3944   *Rlwy.* (USA.) Electrified line switch.

3945   *Alch.* Sulphur.

366

3946   *Engn.* Filter, strainer.

3947   *Rlwy.* (Brit.) Sand drag or sanded track.

3948   *Engn.* (USA.) Evaporative condenser.

TABLE 285

3955   *Engn.* (Heating and ventilating, USA.) Reciprocating compressor with open crank-case, direct drive.

3956   *Engn.* Liquid separator.

3957   *Mil.* (R.A.S.C.) Warrant officer, Class I.

3958   *Mil.* Regimental sergeant-major. (R.A.) brigade sergeant-major.

3959   *Mil.* Squadron, battery or company sergeant-major.

3960   *Engn.* Feed-water heater, contact type.

3961   *Engn.* Combustion chamber.

3962   *Rlwy.* (USA.) One-way bolt lock.

3963   *Hyd.* (*Cart.*) Buddhist temple.

3964   *Elec.* Relay coil with two windings.

3965   *Elec.* Insulated circuit crossing (overhead line).

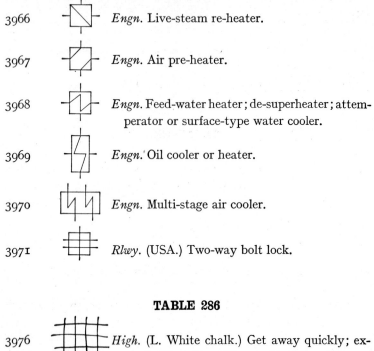

3966   *Engn.* Live-steam re-heater.

3967   *Engn.* Air pre-heater.

3968   *Engn.* Feed-water heater; de-superheater; attemperator or surface-type water cooler.

3969   *Engn.* Oil cooler or heater.

3970   *Engn.* Multi-stage air cooler.

3971   *Rlwy.* (USA.) Two-way bolt lock.

TABLE 286

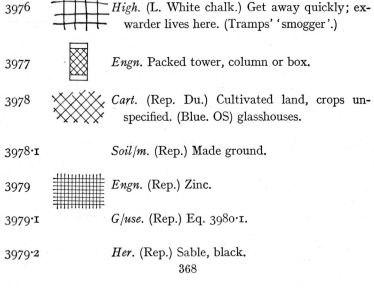

3976   *High.* (L. White chalk.) Get away quickly; ex-warder lives here. (Tramps' 'smogger'.)

3977   *Engn.* Packed tower, column or box.

3978   *Cart.* (Rep. Du.) Cultivated land, crops unspecified. (Blue. OS) glasshouses.

3978·1   *Soil/m.* (Rep.) Made ground.

3979   *Engn.* (Rep.) Zinc.

3979·1   *G/use.* (Rep.) Eq. 3980·1.

3979·2   *Her.* (Rep.) Sable, black.

368

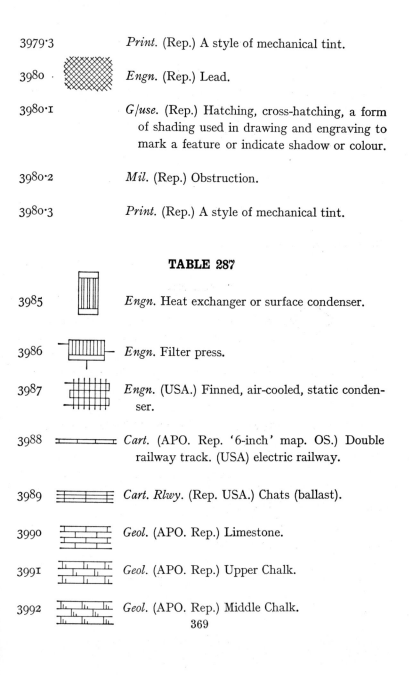

3979·3   *Print.* (Rep.) A style of mechanical tint.

3980   *Engn.* (Rep.) Lead.

3980·1   *G/use.* (Rep.) Hatching, cross-hatching, a form of shading used in drawing and engraving to mark a feature or indicate shadow or colour.

3980·2   *Mil.* (Rep.) Obstruction.

3980·3   *Print.* (Rep.) A style of mechanical tint.

TABLE 287

3985   *Engn.* Heat exchanger or surface condenser.

3986   *Engn.* Filter press.

3987   *Engn.* (USA.) Finned, air-cooled, static condenser.

3988   *Cart.* (APO. Rep. '6-inch' map. OS.) Double railway track. (USA) electric railway.

3989   *Cart. Rlwy.* (Rep. USA.) Chats (ballast).

3990   *Geol.* (APO. Rep.) Limestone.

3991   *Geol.* (APO. Rep.) Upper Chalk.

3992   *Geol.* (APO. Rep.) Middle Chalk.

369

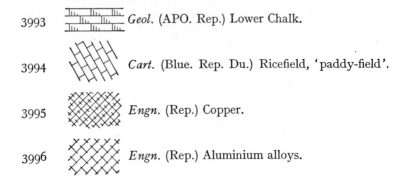

3993   *Geol.* (APO. Rep.) Lower Chalk.

3994   *Cart.* (Blue. Rep. Du.) Ricefield, 'paddy-field'.

3995   *Engn.* (Rep.) Copper.

3996   *Engn.* (Rep.) Aluminium alloys.

Cl.II, Ord.I, Fam.I, Gen.III

TABLE 288

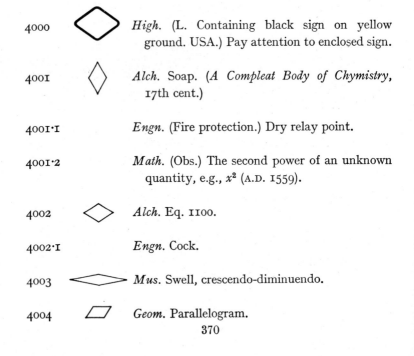

4000   *High.* (L. Containing black sign on yellow ground. USA.) Pay attention to enclosed sign.

4001   *Alch.* Soap. (*A Compleat Body of Chymistry,* 17th cent.)

4001·1   *Engn.* (Fire protection.) Dry relay point.

4001·2   *Math.* (Obs.) The second power of an unknown quantity, e.g., x^2 (A.D. 1559).

4002   *Alch.* Eq. 1100.

4002·1   *Engn.* Cock.

4003   *Mus.* Swell, crescendo-diminuendo.

4004   *Geom.* Parallelogram.

370

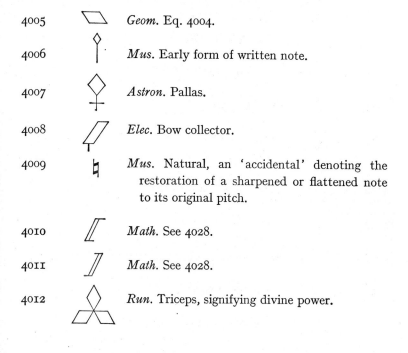

4005		*Geom.* Eq. 4004.
4006		*Mus.* Early form of written note.
4007		*Astron.* Pallas.
4008		*Elec.* Bow collector.
4009		*Mus.* Natural, an 'accidental' denoting the restoration of a sharpened or flattened note to its original pitch.
4010		*Math.* See 4028.
4011		*Math.* See 4028.
4012		*Run.* Triceps, signifying divine power.

TABLE 289

4018		*Ph.* Moabite (Tyrian). Eq. Rom. CH.
4019		*Math.* Homothetically equal to.
4020		*Com.* (Esp. USA.) A mark of emphasis; item. (Preceding a numeral) number. (Following a numeral) pounds weight.
4021		*Math.* Eq. 3911·2.
4021·1		*Print.* (Proof correction.) Space; more space.

4022	♯	*Mus.* Sharp, an 'accidental' instructing to play (or read) a semitone above the note indicated.
4023		*Mus.* Eq. 3207.
4024		*Mus.* Eq. 3207.
4025		*Alch.* Alembic, still. (*A Compleat Body of Chymistry*, 17th cent.)
4026		*Chin. Num.* Eq. Arab. 5.
4027		*Math.* Congruent and parallel.
4028		*Math.* Inclined open square brackets, eq. 4416·2.
4029		*Engn.* Seam weld.
4030		*Engn.* Mashed seam weld.
4031		*G/use.* (Rep.) Eq. 3980·1.
4031·1		*Print.* (Rep.) A style of mechanical tint.

TABLE 290

§ 1. *Not More Than One Right-angle*

| 4035 | | *Engn.* (USA.) Plug or slot weld. |
| 4036 | | *Engn.* (On pipe symbol. USA.) Bushing, screwed. |

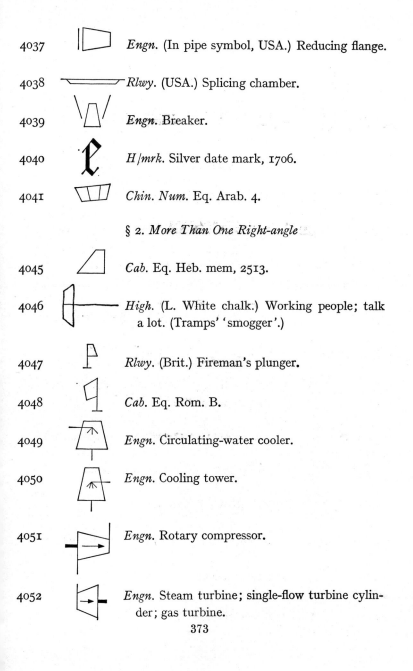

4037   *Engn.* (In pipe symbol, USA.) Reducing flange.

4038   *Rlwy.* (USA.) Splicing chamber.

4039   *Engn.* Breaker.

4040   *H/mrk.* Silver date mark, 1706.

4041   *Chin. Num.* Eq. Arab. 4.

§ 2. *More Than One Right-angle*

4045   *Cab.* Eq. Heb. mem, 2513.

4046   *High.* (L. White chalk.) Working people; talk a lot. (Tramps' 'smogger'.)

4047   *Rlwy.* (Brit.) Fireman's plunger.

4048   *Cab.* Eq. Rom. B.

4049   *Engn.* Circulating-water cooler.

4050   *Engn.* Cooling tower.

4051   *Engn.* Rotary compressor.

4052   *Engn.* Steam turbine; single-flow turbine cylinder; gas turbine.

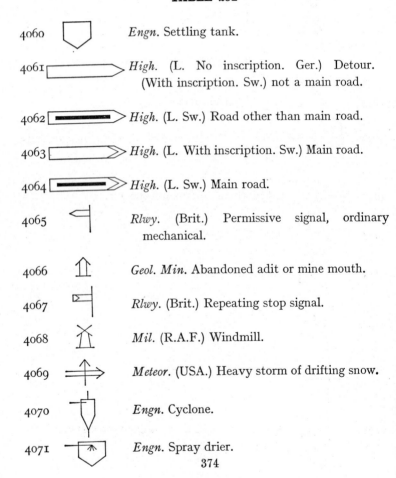

4053   *Rlwy.* (Brit.) Distant signal, fixed arm.

4054   *H/mrk.* Silver date mark, 1703.

4055   *H/mrk.* Silver date mark, 1704.

TABLE 291

4060   *Engn.* Settling tank.

4061   *High.* (L. No inscription. Ger.) Detour. (With inscription. Sw.) not a main road.

4062   *High.* (L. Sw.) Road other than main road.

4063   *High.* (L. With inscription. Sw.) Main road.

4064   *High.* (L. Sw.) Main road.

4065   *Rlwy.* (Brit.) Permissive signal, ordinary mechanical.

4066   *Geol. Min.* Abandoned adit or mine mouth.

4067   *Rlwy.* (Brit.) Repeating stop signal.

4068   *Mil.* (R.A.F.) Windmill.

4069   *Meteor.* (USA.) Heavy storm of drifting snow.

4070   *Engn.* Cyclone.

4071   *Engn.* Spray drier.

374

TABLE 292

4075	⬡	*Chem.* Benzene ring.
4076	⬡	*Elec.* 6-phase winding, mesh connected.
4077	⬡	*Engn.* (Across pipe symbol.) Flow restrictor.
4078	⬡	*Chem.* Benzene ring showing double bonds.
4079	⟺	*Log.* Is equivalent to; implies and is implied by.
4080	ƀ	*Min.* Eq. 4814·2.
4080·1		*Rom.* (l.c.) 'Old English', 'Black Letter', eq. b.

TABLE 293

§ 1. *With No Free Ends*

4085	✕	*High.* (L. Red outline. Fr.) Level crossing.
4086	✛	*Meteor.* (USA.) Mixture of air masses.
4087	☆	*Phila.* Unused stamp.
4088	⋈	*Tel.* (APO.) Screw coupling.
4089	⋈	*Engn.* (With pipe symbol running through centre.) Screwed sleeve joint.
4090	⊐⊏	*Egy.* Pictograph signifying the sky.

375

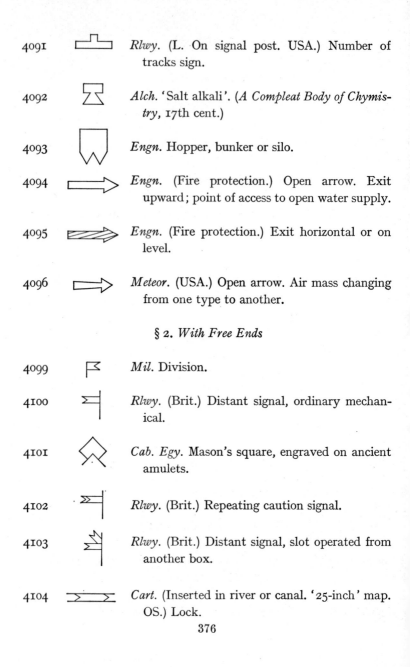

4091   *Rlwy.* (L. On signal post. USA.) Number of tracks sign.

4092   *Alch.* 'Salt alkali'. (*A Compleat Body of Chymistry*, 17th cent.)

4093   *Engn.* Hopper, bunker or silo.

4094   *Engn.* (Fire protection.) Open arrow. Exit upward; point of access to open water supply.

4095   *Engn.* (Fire protection.) Exit horizontal or on level.

4096   *Meteor.* (USA.) Open arrow. Air mass changing from one type to another.

§ 2. *With Free Ends*

4099   *Mil.* Division.

4100   *Rlwy.* (Brit.) Distant signal, ordinary mechanical.

4101   *Cab. Egy.* Mason's square, engraved on ancient amulets.

4102   *Rlwy.* (Brit.) Repeating caution signal.

4103   *Rlwy.* (Brit.) Distant signal, slot operated from another box.

4104   *Cart.* (Inserted in river or canal. '25-inch' map. OS.) Lock.

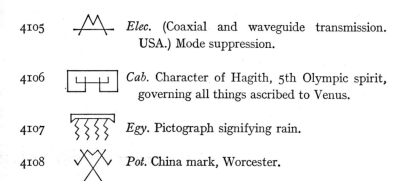

4105		*Elec.* (Coaxial and waveguide transmission. USA.) Mode suppression.
4106		*Cab.* Character of Hagith, 5th Olympic spirit, governing all things ascribed to Venus.
4107		*Egy.* Pictograph signifying rain.
4108		*Pot.* China mark, Worcester.

Cl.II, Ord.I, Fam.II, Gen.I

TABLE 294

4115   Γ   *Am.* (Cherokee syllabary.) Eq. Rom. HU.

4115·1   *Chem.* Surface concentration.

4115·2   *Gk.* (Cap.) Gamma, 3rd letter of the a., eq. Rom. G.

4115·3   *Mag.* Gauss.

4115·4   *Math.* Gamma function.

4115·5   *Nav. Arch.* Circulation.

4115·6   *Rus.* (Cap./l.c.) Geh, 4th letter of the a., eq. Rom. G.

4116   ⌐   *Print.* Eq. 4126·2. (USA) eq. 612.

4116·1   *Rlwy.* (Cutting across symbol for rail, assumed horizontal on page. Brit.) Insulating rail joint with track circuit on right, none on left.

4117   *Print.* Eq. 4128·1.

4117·1   *Rlwy.* (Cutting across symbol for rail, assumed horizontal on page. Brit.) Insulating rail joint with track circuit on left, none on right.

4118   *Heb.* Daleth, 4th letter of the a., eq. Rom. D. Cardinal number 4.

4119   *Heb.* Resh, 20th letter of the a., eq. Rom. R. Cardinal number 200.

4120   *Mus.* Early form of 3863.

4121   *Log.* Not.

4122†   *Phon.* Eq. 5204.

TABLE 295

4125   L   *Am.* (Cherokee syllabary.) Eq. Rom. DLE.

4125·1   *Elec.* Thermal force in cross magnetic and non-magnetic materials. *Cf.* 4150.

4125·2   *Mon.* Pound or pounds sterling.

4125·3   *Rom.* (Cap.) 12th letter of the a. Cardinal number 50.

378

4126	└	*Geom.* Right-angle.
4126·1		*Math.* (Obsnt.) Factorial.
4126·2		*Print.* (Proof correction.) Carry farther to the left; begin new paragraph. (With 4021·1 in margin) reduce space, make spaces equal.
4126·3		*Rlwy.* Eq. 4116·1.
4127	└	*Elec.* 2-phase 3-wire winding.
4128	┘	*Math.* (Obs.) Eq. 4126·1.
4128·1		*Print.* (Proof correction.) Carry farther to the right. (USA) eq. 611.
4128·2		*Rlwy.* Eq. 4117·1.
4129	└─	*Pros.* Triseme; protraction of a syllable to three moræ.
4130†	˪	*Acc.* (Gk.) Early form of 376·1.
4131†	˩	*Acc.* (Gk.) Early form of 378·1.
4131·1		*Phon.* Eq. 5230·1.

TABLE 296

4135	∧	*Elec.* (USA.) Directly heated filament cathode.
4136	∨	*Engn.* (USA.) V-weld.

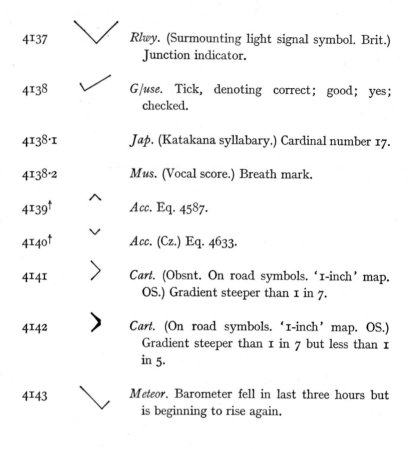

4137   *Rlwy.* (Surmounting light signal symbol. Brit.) Junction indicator.

4138   *G/use.* Tick, denoting correct; good; yes; checked.

4138·1   *Jap.* (Katakana syllabary.) Cardinal number 17.

4138·2   *Mus.* (Vocal score.) Breath mark.

4139†   *Acc.* Eq. 4587.

4140†   *Acc.* (Cz.) Eq. 4633.

4141   *Cart.* (Obsnt. On road symbols. '1-inch' map. OS.) Gradient steeper than 1 in 7.

4142   *Cart.* (On road symbols. '1-inch' map. OS.) Gradient steeper than 1 in 7 but less than 1 in 5.

4143   *Meteor.* Barometer fell in last three hours but is beginning to rise again.

TABLE 297

4150 L' *Elec.* Thermal force in longitudinal magnetic and non-magnetic materials. *Cf.* 4125·1.

4151   Ł   *Pol.* (Cap.) Letter of the a. sounded like a suppressed L and often approximately eq. WL.

380

4152	⊓	*Heb.* He, 5th letter of the a., eq. Rom. E. Cardinal number 5.
4153	↳ ·	*Jap.* (Katakana syllabary.) Eq. Rom. FHI (pron. f'hee). (With 17·3) PI (pron. pee). (With 5248) BI (pron. bee).
4154	⊥⁄	*Jap.* (Katakana syllabary.) Eq. Rom. SE (pron. say). (With 5248) ZE (pron. zay).
4155	⅄	*Cart.* (Du.) Sago palm.

TABLE 298

4160	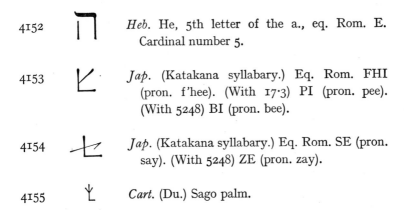	*Engn.* Screen or classifier.
4161	⅄	*Cart.* (Du.) Sugar palm.
4162	⚹	*Cart.* (Du.) Coconut palm.
4163	⌐⚹	*Meteor.* Ground partly covered with snow or hail.

TABLE 299

4167	Y	*High.* (L. UNS, 1953.) 'Y-sign'. Road forks.
4168	K	*Am.* (Cherokee syllabary.) Eq. Rom. DZO.
4168·1		*Gk.* (Cap.) Kappa, 10th letter of the a. eq. Rom. K.

4168·2		*Phys.* Constant. (Temperature) Kelvin scale, absolute. (Nuclear) kaon, a meson.
4168·3		*Rom.* (Cap.) 11th letter of the a. (Med. ext. of Rom. num.) cardinal number 250, eq. 4385·5.
4169	K	*Astron.* Mass continuous absorption coefficient; mass opacity.
4169·1		*Chem.* Tenth.
4169·2		*Elec.* Conductivity; specific conductance.
4169·3		*Gk.* (l.c.) Kappa, 10th letter of the a., eq. Rom. k. Cardinal number 20.
4169·4		*Mag.* Susceptibility (volume).
4169·5		*Mech.* Compressibility.
4169·6		*Nav. Arch.* Surface tension.
4169·7		*Phys.* Constant; specific heat ratio; modulus of elasticity; kappa meson.
4170	⟩|	*Rlwy.* (Brit.) Eq. 4210.
4171	k	*Phon.* Voiceless velar plosive consonant, k as in keep.
4171·1		*Rom.* (l.c.) 11th letter of the a. (*ITA*) k as in kitten.
4172	ʞ	*Phon.* 'Turned-k'. Velar click.

TABLE 300

4178 K *Astron.* Semi-amplitude of radial velocity curve.

4178·1   *Chem.* (Of reaction.) Equilibrium constant.

4178·2   *Elec.* Cathode; cathode glow; conductivity; dielectric constant.

4178·3   *It.* (Cap.) Eq. Rom. K.

4178·4   *Mech.* Bulk modulus of elasticity; moment of inertia.

4178·5   *Nav. Arch.* (Obsnt.) Speed of vessel in knots.

4178·6   *Phys.* (Heat.) Coefficient of thermal conductivity; centuple or rational calorie. (Light) foot-lambert; visibility factor.

4178·7   *Tel.* Modulation percentage.

4179   *Numis.* Nickel.

4180   *Elec.* (USA.) Female contact, socket, receptacle.

4181   *Elec.* (In valve diagrams.) Hot cathode.

4182   *Meteor.* Lightning.

4183   *Elec.* Thermoelement.

4184   *Geol. Min.* Adit or mine mouth.

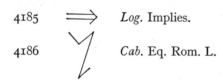

| 4185 | | *Log.* Implies. |
| 4186 | | *Cab.* Eq. Rom. L. |

TABLE 301

4190		*High.* (L. UNS, 1953.) 'T-sign'. Road junction.
4191	T	*Am.* (Cherokee syllabary.) Eq. Rom. I.
4191·1		*Gk.* (Cap.) Tau, 19th letter of the a., eq. Rom. T.
4191·2		*Rom.* (Cap.) 20th letter of the a. (Med. ext. of Rom. num.) cardinal number 160.
4191·3		*Rus.* (Cap./l.c.) Teh, 20th letter of the old a., 19th of the mod., eq. Rom. T.
4192	⊤	*Geom.* Vertical.
4193	⊤	*Elec.* (Coaxial and waveguide diagrams. USA.) Mode transducer.
4194	⊤	*Tel.* Mode changer.
4195	·⊤	*Engn.* (Fire protection.) Receiving-only radio station.
4196	⊤	*Phon.* (Under or after a letter.) Tongue slightly lowered; eq. 366.

384

4197	▬▬	*Mil.* Infantry in line.
4198	▬▬▬	*Geol.* (APO. Rep.) Fault, short stroke on down-throw side.
4199	⊥	*Engn.* Stud weld.
4199·1		*Geom.* Is perpendicular to.
4199·2		*Math.* (Obs.) Divided by.
4199·3		*Print.* (Proof correction.) Attend to mark made by rising quadrat, space or other metal.
4200	⊥	*Elec. Tel.* (APO.) See 4209.
4201	⊥	*Hyd.* (Rep.) Fishing stakes.
4201·1		*Phon.* (Under or after a letter.) Tongue slightly raised; eq. 5988·1, q.v.

TABLE 302

4208	⊢	*High.* (L. UNS, 1953.) Road junction.
4209	⊣	*Elec. Tel.* (APO. In valve diagrams.) Anode.
4210	⊣	*Rlwy.* (Brit.) Fogman's repeater.
4211	⊣	*Gk.* Early form of 378·1.
4212	╱	*Geol.* Cleavage.

385

4213	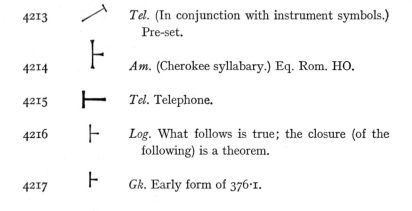	*Tel.* (In conjunction with instrument symbols.) Pre-set.
4214		*Am.* (Cherokee syllabary.) Eq. Rom. HO.
4215		*Tel.* Telephone.
4216		*Log.* What follows is true; the closure (of the following) is a theorem.
4217		*Gk.* Early form of 376·1.

TABLE 303

4224		*Print.* (Proof correction.) Eq. 4126·2.
4225		*Math.* Eq. 4611·1.
4226		*Print.* (Proof correction.) Transpose a letter or word from the end of one line to the beginning of the next.
4227		*Math.* See 4416·2. (Obs.) equals. (A.D. 1559).
4227·1		*Print.* See 4416·5.
4228		*Astron.* (Obs.) Eq. 3931.
4228·1		*Print.* (Proof correction.) Eq. 4128·1.
4229		*Math.* Eq. 4598·2.

4230   *Print.* (Proof correction.) Transpose a letter or word from the beginning of one line to the end of the preceding line.

4231   *Math.* See 4416·2.

4231·1   *Meteor.* Occurred during previous hour but not at time of observation.

4231·2   *Print.* See 4416·5.

4232   *Engn.* (At end of pipe symbol. USA.) Screw cap.

4233   *Jap.* (Katakana syllabary.) Eq. Rom. KO. (With 5248) GO.

TABLE 304

4239   *High.* (L. White chalk.) Invalids—be sympathetic. (Tramps' 'smogger'.)

4240   *Engn.* Open vessel or tank.

4241   *Rlwy.* (Attached to symbol for rail. Brit.) Depression bar.

4242†   *Mus.* Eq. 4734.

4243†   *Chem.* Eq. 4253.

4243·1   *Meteor.* Hoar frost.

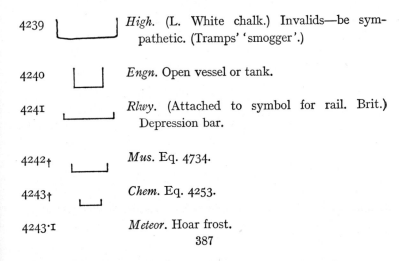

387

4243·2		*Print.* (Proof correction.) Lower.
4243·3		*Pros.* Tetraseme; protraction of a syllable to four moræ.
4244	⊔	*Hyd.* (Containing a number. Inter.) Wire drag has been used to depth indicated.
4245	⊔	*Mus.* (Stringed instruments.) Up-bow.

TABLE 305

4250	Π	*Astron.* Longitude of the ascending node of the ecliptic; eq. 348.
4250·1		*Chem.* Osmotic pressure.
4250·2		*Gk.* (Cap.) Pi, 16th letter of the a., eq. Rom. P.
4250·3		*Math.* Product.
4250·4		*Phys.* Pressure.
4250·5		*Rus.* (Cap./l.c.) Peh, 17th letter of the old a., 16th of the mod., eq. Rom. P.
4251	Π	*Heb.* Cheth, 8th letter of the a., eq. Rom. Ḥ, KH. Cardinal number 8.
4252	⌐¬	*Mus.* Eq. 483.
4253	⌐¬	*Chem.* (In formulae.) Tie, indicating that atoms at extremities are joined.

388

4253·1		*Print.* (Proof correction.) Raise.
4254	⌐⌐	*Elec.* (USA.) Indirectly heated cathode.
4255	◗	*Mus.* (Stringed instruments.) Down-bow.
4256 †	⊓	*Phon.* Dental articulation.

TABLE 306

4260		*Elec.* (APO. USA.) Dipole antenna.
4261	❭ ❭	*Cart.* (Crossing river or canal. '1-inch' map. OS.) Lock.
4262	❭❭	*Cart.* (On roads. '1-inch' map. OS.) Gradient at least 1 in 5.

TABLE 307

4268	Y	*Astron.* Light-year.
4269	⌇	*ME* & *late OE.* (Cap.) Yogh, 'yod', pron. g, gh or y according to period, locality and position in word.
4270	Ͱ	*Am.* (Cherokee syllabary.) Eq. Rom. GE.
4271		*Jap.* (Katakana syllabary.) Eq. Rom. MA (pron. MAH).

389

4272	⁷	*Num.* (Magnetic ink E 13 B font.) Seven, eq. 4670.
4273	⟹	*Meteor.* Open arrow. Warm winds.
4274	⚡	*Ph.* (Sidonian.) Samek, eq. Rom. S.

TABLE 308

§ 1. *Containing Parallel Lines*

4278		*Geom.* Equilateral.
4279		*Engn.* Suction filter.
4280		*Engn.* Liquid seal, open.
4281		*Elec.* (USA.) The chassis or frame is not necessarily at ground potential.
4282		*Elec.* Earth, ground.
4283		*Cart. Hyd.* Beacon.
4284	W	*Tel.* Wattmeter, double line.

§ 2. *With No Lines Parallel*

4286	K	*Rom.* (Cap.) Eq. 4168·3.
4287	↑	*Rlwy.* (Brit.) Trip cock tester.

390

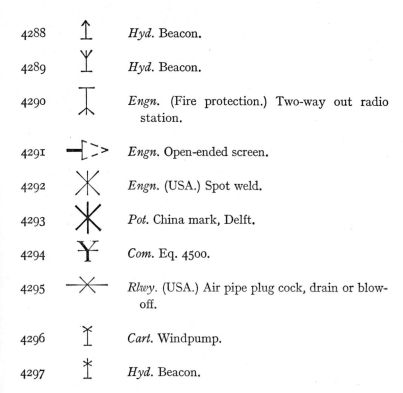

4288		*Hyd.* Beacon.
4289		*Hyd.* Beacon.
4290		*Engn.* (Fire protection.) Two-way out radio station.
4291		*Engn.* Open-ended screen.
4292		*Engn.* (USA.) Spot weld.
4293		*Pot.* China mark, Delft.
4294		*Com.* Eq. 4500.
4295		*Rlwy.* (USA.) Air pipe plug cock, drain or blow-off.
4296		*Cart.* Windpump.
4297		*Hyd.* Beacon.

TABLE 309

4302	F	*Cal.* Eq. 3053·1.
4302·1		*Elec.* Farad; change in thermal conductivity in a cross field. *Cf.* 4316.
4302·2		*Rom.* (Cap.) 6th letter of the a. (Med. ext. of Rom. num.) cardinal number 40.

4303	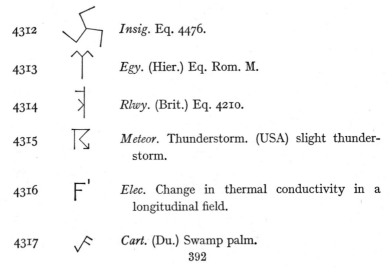	*Gk.* (Obs.) Æolic digamma, 6th letter of early Gk. a., eq. Rom. W (consonant).
4304		*Gk.* Eq. 4816.
4305		*Cab.* Eq. Heb. daleth, 4118.
4306		*Jap.* (Katakana syllabary.) Eq. Rom. YU.
4307		*Num.* (Magnetic ink E 13 B font.) One, eq. 5135.
4308		*Num.* (Arab.) Continental cursive numeral 4.
4309		*Num.* (Magnetic ink E 13 B font.) Four, eq. 3527.

TABLE 310

4312		*Insig.* Eq. 4476.
4313		*Egy.* (Hier.) Eq. Rom. M.
4314		*Rlwy.* (Brit.) Eq. 4210.
4315		*Meteor.* Thunderstorm. (USA) slight thunderstorm.
4316		*Elec.* Change in thermal conductivity in a longitudinal field.
4317		*Cart.* (Du.) Swamp palm.

TABLE 311

4322	$+$	*Chin. Num.* Eq. 4883.
4322·1		*Ind. Num.* (3rd cent. B.C.) Eq. Arab. 4.
4323	$+$	*Alch.* Vinegar. (*A Compleat Body of Chymistry,* 17th cent.)
4323·1		*Astron.* North.
4323·2		*Biog.* Died.
4323·3		*Bot.* Graft-chimaera, graft hybrid; occurrence of particular feature. (In floral diagram) side of flower nearest main stem, the posterior side.
4323·4		*Chem.* Combined with, added to. (Placed over a symbol) vegetable base or alkaloid. (Obs.) acid (Bergmann, 1783).
4323·5		*Elec.* Positive charge; positive ion; anode.
4323·6		*Geol.* Horizontal strata.
4323·7		*Her.* Greek cross.
4323·8		*Log.* Logical sum. (Between two disjoined or alternative propositions) to be considered together.
4323·9		*Mag.* Paramagnetic; north-seeking (pole).

4323·01   *Math.* Plus, add, added to. (First appeared in print, 1489; first used in math. by M. Stifel, 1544.)

4323·02   *Meteor.* Barometer rising. (USA) pressure is higher than three hours ago.

4323·03   *MS.* Eq. 4361·1.

4323·04   *Mus.* Augmented; (stringed instruments) pluck strings with the left hand; (between two letters standing for notes) a tone and a half.

4323·05   *Nav.* North of the equator.

4323·06   *Op.* (Polar.) Dextrorotation.

4323·07   *Phys.* Proton; positively charged particle; positive charge.

4323·08   *Pot.* China mark, Bristol.

4323·09   *Rel.* (RC.) Sign of the Cross to be made.

4324   +   *Cart.* ('1-inch' map. OS.) Ant. ('25-inch' map. OS) surface level obtained by spirit levelling.

4324·1   *Numis.* Eq. 4335·1.

4325   +   *Cart.* (OS.) Church with neither tower nor spire; chapel. (*Rom.* OS.) barrow or mausoleum. (*Hyd.*) rock awash at mean sea-level or covered by less than 6 feet of water at mean sea-level.

394

4325·1		*Chem.* Positive ion.
4325·2		*Phon.* (After or under a letter.) Advanced variety; sometimes eq. 4256.

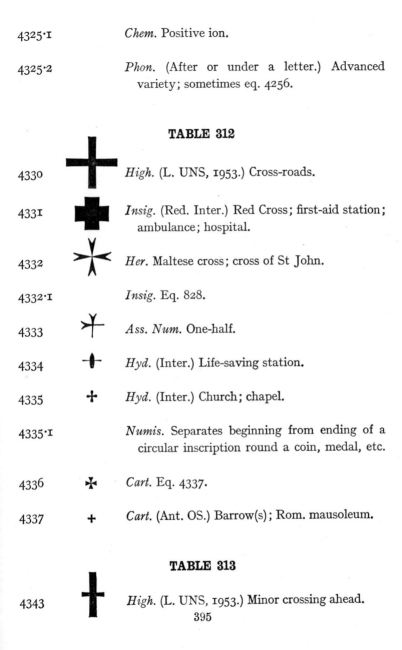

TABLE 312

4330		*High.* (L. UNS, 1953.) Cross-roads.
4331		*Insig.* (Red. Inter.) Red Cross; first-aid station; ambulance; hospital.
4332		*Her.* Maltese cross; cross of St John.
4332·1		*Insig.* Eq. 828.
4333		*Ass. Num.* One-half.
4334		*Hyd.* (Inter.) Life-saving station.
4335		*Hyd.* (Inter.) Church; chapel.
4335·1		*Numis.* Separates beginning from ending of a circular inscription round a coin, medal, etc.
4336		*Cart.* Eq. 4337.
4337		*Cart.* (Ant. OS.) Barrow(s); Rom. mausoleum.

TABLE 313

4343		*High.* (L. UNS, 1953.) Minor crossing ahead.

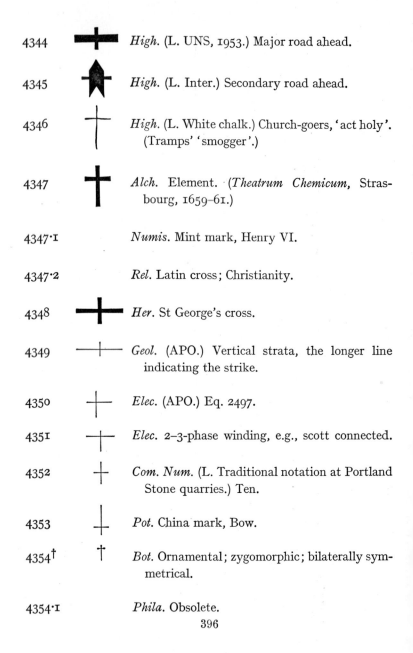

4344   *High.* (L. UNS, 1953.) Major road ahead.

4345   *High.* (L. Inter.) Secondary road ahead.

4346   *High.* (L. White chalk.) Church-goers, 'act holy'. (Tramps' 'smogger'.)

4347   *Alch.* Element. (*Theatrum Chemicum*, Strasbourg, 1659–61.)

4347·1   *Numis.* Mint mark, Henry VI.

4347·2   *Rel.* Latin cross; Christianity.

4348   *Her.* St George's cross.

4349   *Geol.* (APO.) Vertical strata, the longer line indicating the strike.

4350   *Elec.* (APO.) Eq. 2497.

4351   *Elec.* 2–3-phase winding, e.g., scott connected.

4352   *Com. Num.* (L. Traditional notation at Portland Stone quarries.) Ten.

4353   *Pot.* China mark, Bow.

4354[†]   *Bot.* Ornamental; zygomorphic; bilaterally symmetrical.

4354·1   *Phila.* Obsolete.

396

4354·2   *Punc.* Obelus, 'obelisk', 'dagger', a mark of reference used to indicate a point in a text to which a footnote bearing the same mark refers. (Before a proper name) deceased, destroyed.

TABLE 314

(See also Table 350)

4359   *High.* (L. Inter.) Cross-roads.

4360   *High.* (L. White chalk.) Not this way. (Scout sign). Do not call here. (Tramps' 'smogger'.)

4361   *G/use.* Cross. Wrong; bad; not wanted; cancelled; delete; ignore.

4361·1   *MS.* 'His mark', a form of signature for the illiterate.

4362   *Elec.* 2-phase 4-wire winding.

4362·1   *Engn.* (In pipe symbol. USA.) Anchor; hanger or support.

4362·2   *Her.* Saltire cross.

4363   *Alch.* Eq. 4323.

4363·1   *Bot.* Hybrid; crossed with.

4363·2		*Chess.* Takes.
4363·3		*G/use.* (Between measurements in different dimensions.) By.
4363·4		*Math.* Multiplied by. (First used by William Oughtred, *c,* 1620.)
4363·5		*Mil.* Road block.
4363·6		*Mus.* Eq. 5656·1. See also 4364.
4363·7		*Opt.* Magnified by, usually in diameters.
4363·8		*Ph.* Moabite (Tyrian). Eq. Rom. T.
4363·9		*Print.* (Proof correction.) Imperfect type face; blemish on block.
4363·01		*Rlwy.* (Mines.) Prospect; test opening. (USA) crossing sign.
4363·02		*Run.* Eq. Rom. G.
4363·03		*Tel.* Directional coupler (single line).
4364	✕	*Mus.* Double-sharp, an 'accidental' instructing to play or read a whole tone above the note indicated.
4365	✕	*Sh., Gregg's.* Punc. Note of interrogation.
4366†	✕	*Com.* Yard, yards.

4366·1†   *Sh., Pitman's.* Position of accent.

4367†   ✕   *Sh., Pitman's.* Punc. Full-stop.

TABLE 315

4372   *High.* (L. White chalk.) There is more than one tramp on this road. (Tramps' 'smogger'.)

4373   H   *Mag.* Magnetic field strength, intensity of magnetic force.

4373·1   *Rom.* (Cap.) Sanserif form of H, 4374.

4374   H   *Am.* (Cherokee syllabary.) Eq. Rom. MI.

4374·1   *Elec.* Henry.

4374·2   *Gk.* (Cap.) Eta, 7th letter of the a., eq. Rom. E (long).

4374·3   *Rom.* (Cap.) 8th letter of the a. (Med. ext. of Rom. num.) cardinal number 200.

4374·4   *Rus.* (Cap./l.c.) En, 15th letter of the old a., 14th of the mod., eq. Rom. N.

4375   I   *Rlwy.* (Across rail symbols. Brit.) Signal bridge.

4376   *Jap.* (Katakana syllabary.) Eq. Rom. YE (pron. yea) or WE (pron. way), the vowel-sound varying from the Fr. e to the Eng. a, as in fate.

4377	⊢——⊣	*Print.* (Proof correction.) Insert dash.
4378	⊢—⊣	*Mus.* (With a number above.) Bar rest, denoting a rest for the number of bars indicated.
4379	π	*Aero.* (Obs.) Propeller efficiency.
4379·1		*Astron.* Annual change in the inclination of the ecliptic; longitude of perihelion; parallax in seconds of arc.
4379·2		*Chem.* Sixteenth.
4379·3		*Gk.* (l.c.) Pi, 16th letter of the a., eq. Rom. p. Cardinal number 80.
4379·4		*Math.* Ratio of the circumference of a circle to its diameter, 3·14159.
4379·5		*Phys.* Osmotic pressure. (Nuclear) pion, a meson.
4380	⊢⊣	*Phon.* Eq. 5332·3.

TABLE 316

4384	E	*Elec.* Electromotive force; electric field strength.
4384·1		*Rom.* (Cap.) Sanserif form of E, 4385·5.
4385	E	*Am.* (Cherokee syllabary.) Eq. Rom. GO.
4385·1		*Gk.* (Cap.) Epsilon, 5th letter of the a., eq. Rom. E (short).

4385·2   *Log.* Universal negative.

4385·3   *Math.* Replace x by $x + 1$.

4385·4   *Nav.* Vessel fit to carry goods not liable to sea damage.

4385·5   *Rom.* (Cap.) 5th letter of the a. (Med. ext. of Rom. num.) cardinal number 250, eq. 4168·3.

4385·6   *Rus.* (Ca.) Yeh, 6th letter of the a., eq. Rom. (Y)E (short). See 5654.

4386   Ⅎ   *Log.* (Enclosed in brackets with an expression of a variable.) 'Reversed-E'. There is a value of this expression such that; there exists at least one — such that.

4387   ☰   *Jap.* (Katakana syllabary.) Eq. Rom. YO. Cardinal number 15.

4388   Ⴈ   *Log.* Eq. 4389.

4389   ∃   *Log.* There exists at least one. See 4386.

TABLE 317

4395   Ⅲ   *Rus.* (Cap./l.c.) Shah, 26th letter of the old a., 25th of the mod., eq. Rom. SH.

4396   Ц   *Rus.* (Cap./l.c.) Tseh, 24th letter of the old a., 23rd of the mod., eq. Rom. TS.

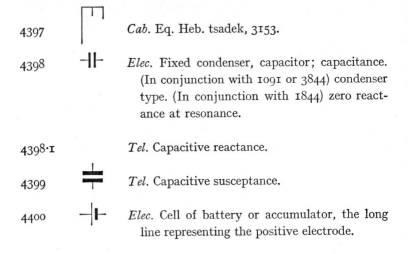

4397	*Cab.* Eq. Heb. tsadek, 3153.
4398	*Elec.* Fixed condenser, capacitor; capacitance. (In conjunction with 1091 or 3844) condenser type. (In conjunction with 1844) zero reactance at resonance.
4398·1	*Tel.* Capacitive reactance.
4399	*Tel.* Capacitive susceptance.
4400	*Elec.* Cell of battery or accumulator, the long line representing the positive electrode.

TABLE 318

4405	*Egy.* (Hier.) Eq. Rom. H.
4406	*Egy.* (Hier.) Abode; eq. Rom. P.
4407	*Num.* (Magnetic ink E 13 B font.) Five, eq. 2298.
4408	*Num.* (Magnetic ink E 13 B font.) Two, eq. 3431.
4409	*Num.* (Magnetic ink E 13 B font.) Three, eq. 3454.
4410	*Print.* (Proof correction.) Transpose.
4411	*Print.* (Proof correction.) Move lines to right.
4412	*Print.* (Proof correction.) Move lines to left.

TABLE 319

4415   *Rel.* 'Open cross', eq. 4521·1.

4416   [   ]   *Chem.* The concentration of (the substance indicated between the brackets); molar concentration. (In formulae) elements enclosed to the inner sphere of attraction.

4416·1   *Log.* Enclosed expression must be taken as a whole in relation to any symbol immediately preceding.

4416·2   *Math.* Absolute value (of enclosed expression); eq. 490·5 or 635·2. (Higher algebra) generated by (the number enclosed).

4416·3   *Min. Crys.* Zone symbol (enclosed).

4r16·4   *Phys.* Dimensions of (enclosed).

4416·5   *Print.* Square brackets, used to enclose explanatory phrases or words in preference to the use of footnotes; to enclose matter inserted in a quotation as a correction and not as part of the author's text. (Proof correction) limits of required position.

4417   *Tel.* Attenuator, cut-off.

4418   *Tel.* Choke coupling.

TABLE 320

4424	✕	*Engn.* (USA.) Projection weld.
4425		*Cab.* Eq. Gk. omega, 1226·2.
4426		*Min.* Zinc ore.
4427		*Meteor.* (USA.) Moderate thunderstorm.
4428		*Num.* (Arab.) Cursive form of 3527.
4429		*Com. Num.* (L. Traditional notation at Portland Stone quarries.) Eq. Arab. 15.
4430		*Com. Num.* (L.) Eq. 4429.
4431	t	*Ger.* (l.c.) 20th letter of the a., eq. Rom. t.

TABLE 321

§ 1. *With Arrow-heads*

4436	+→	*Log.* Does not imply.
4436·1		*Math.* Does not tend to.
4437		*Geol.* (APO.) Steeply inclined strata.
4438		*Geol.* (APO.) Gently inclined strata.
4439		*Geol.* (APO.) Anticlinal axis, anticline.

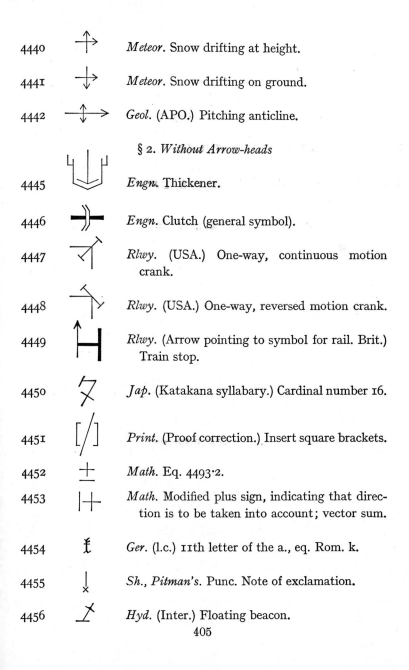

4440		*Meteor.* Snow drifting at height.
4441		*Meteor.* Snow drifting on ground.
4442		*Geol.* (APO.) Pitching anticline.

§ 2. *Without Arrow-heads*

4445		*Engn.* Thickener.
4446		*Engn.* Clutch (general symbol).
4447		*Rlwy.* (USA.) One-way, continuous motion crank.
4448		*Rlwy.* (USA.) One-way, reversed motion crank.
4449		*Rlwy.* (Arrow pointing to symbol for rail. Brit.) Train stop.
4450		*Jap.* (Katakana syllabary.) Cardinal number 16.
4451		*Print.* (Proof correction.) Insert square brackets.
4452		*Math.* Eq. 4493·2.
4453		*Math.* Modified plus sign, indicating that direction is to be taken into account; vector sum.
4454		*Ger.* (l.c.) 11th letter of the a., eq. Rom. k.
4455		*Sh., Pitman's. Punc.* Note of exclamation.
4456		*Hyd.* (Inter.) Floating beacon.

405

TABLE 322

4460   *Rlwy.* (USA.) 2-way continuous motion crank.

4461   *Mil.* (R.A.F.) Eq. 5700.

4462   *Prop.* Bridge House Estates, the company which (originally) owned the house-property on old London Bridge.

4463   *Astron.* Juno.

4464   *Meteor.* Snowstorm.

4465   *Elec.* Arc lamp.

4466   *Jap.* (Katakana syllabary.) Eq. Rom. FHO. (With 17·3) PO. (With 5248) BO. Cardinal number 5.

4467   *Elec.* (USA.) Valve or film element arrester gap.

4468   *Elec.* Quenched spark gap.

TABLE 323

4473   *Cab.* Eq. Heb. he, 4152.

4474   *Alch.* Borax. (*A Compleat Body of Chymistry*, 17th cent.)

4475   *Meteor.* (USA.) Heavy thunderstorm.

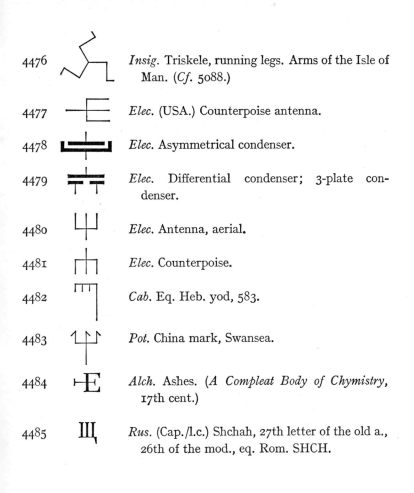

4476   *Insig.* Triskele, running legs. Arms of the Isle of Man. (*Cf.* 5088.)

4477   *Elec.* (USA.) Counterpoise antenna.

4478   *Elec.* Asymmetrical condenser.

4479   *Elec.* Differential condenser; 3-plate condenser.

4480   *Elec.* Antenna, aerial.

4481   *Elec.* Counterpoise.

4482   *Cab.* Eq. Heb. yod, 583.

4483   *Pot.* China mark, Swansea.

4484   *Alch.* Ashes. (*A Compleat Body of Chymistry*, 17th cent.)

4485   *Rus.* (Cap./l.c.) Shchah, 27th letter of the old a., 26th of the mod., eq. Rom. SHCH.

TABLE 324

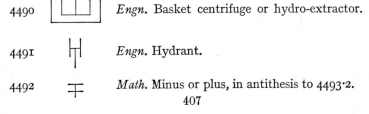

4490   *Engn.* Basket centrifuge or hydro-extractor.

4491   *Engn.* Hydrant.

4492   *Math.* Minus or plus, in antithesis to 4493·2.

4493	Chem. Inactive, particularly of amino acids and their derivatives.
4493·1	Elec. Midwire (direct current).
4493·2	Math. Plus or minus.
4494	Jap. (Katakana syllabary.) Eq. Rom. MO.
4495	Ind. Num. (2nd cent. A.D.) Eq. Arab. 4.
4496	Cart. Telegraph or telephone post.
4497	Hyd. (Inter.) Fixed beacon.
4498	Elec. Shielded condenser.
4499	Engn. (In pipe symbol. USA.) Pump.
4500	Com. Mon. (Chin.) Yen.
4501	Rel. Calvary.

TABLE 325

4507	Insig. (Fr.) Cross of Lorraine; cf. 4508. Symbol of Joan of Arc, adopted by the Free Fr. forces during the 1939–45 war.
4507·1	Rel. Double-beam cross; patriarchal or archiepiscopal cross; Gk. Orthodox Church.

408

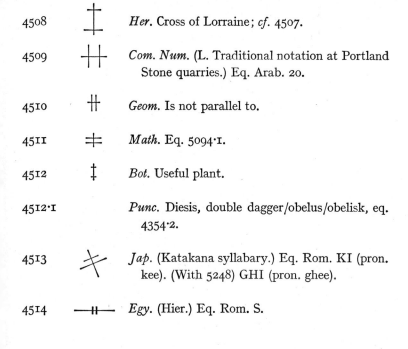

4508   *Her.* Cross of Lorraine; *cf.* 4507.

4509   *Com. Num.* (L. Traditional notation at Portland Stone quarries.) Eq. Arab. 20.

4510   *Geom.* Is not parallel to.

4511   *Math.* Eq. 5094·1.

4512   *Bot.* Useful plant.

4512·1   *Punc.* Diesis, double dagger/obelus/obelisk, eq. 4354·2.

4513   *Jap.* (Katakana syllabary.) Eq. Rom. KI (pron. kee). (With 5248) GHI (pron. ghee).

4514   *Egy.* (Hier.) Eq. Rom. S.

TABLE 326

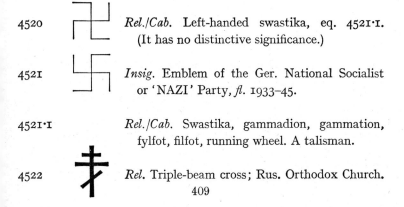

4520   *Rel./Cab.* Left-handed swastika, eq. 4521·1. (It has no distinctive significance.)

4521   *Insig.* Emblem of the Ger. National Socialist or 'NAZI' Party, *fl.* 1933–45.

4521·1   *Rel./Cab.* Swastika, gammadion, gammation, fylfot, filfot, running wheel. A talisman.

4522   *Rel.* Triple-beam cross; Rus. Orthodox Church.

4523   *Mil.* (Red.) Territorial Army, 50th (Northumbrian) Division.

4524   *Tel.* Shim.

4525   *Com.* Eq. 2732.

4526   *Alch.* Pot ashes. (*A Compleat Body of Chymistry,* 17th cent.)

4527   *Elec.* Fixed condenser.

TABLE 327

4532   *High.* (L. White chalk.) People here will telephone police. (Tramps' 'smogger'.)

4533   *Rel.* (RC.) Papal cross.

4534   *Her.* Cross crosslet.

4535   *Sem.* Samek, eq. Rom. S.

4536   *Hyd.* (Inter.) Submerged wreck not dangerous to surface shipping, exact depth unknown but exceeding 10 fathoms or 18 metres.

4537   *Rlwy.* (APO. Rep. USA.) Intertrack fence.

4538   *Cart.* (APO. Rep. OS.) Tramway; mineral railway.

410

4539   + + + +   *Cart.* (APO. Rep. '6-inch' map. OS.) Ridings boundary.

4539·1   *Hyd.* (APO. Rep. Inter.) International boundary.

4540   + — + — +   *Hyd.* (APO. Rep. Inter.) Customs boundary.

4541   + + — + + — *Hyd.* (APO. Rep. Inter.) Limit of sovereignty, territorial waters.

4542   × × × × × × *Mil.* (APO. Rep.) Wire entanglements on posts.

4543   × — × — × — *Elec.* (APO. Rep.) Circuit connection.

4543·1   *Mil.* (APO. Rep.) Chevaux, cheval, de frise.

4544   *Geol.* (Rep.) Igneous rock.

4544·1   *Soil/m.* (Rep.) Silt.

4545   *Soil/m.* (Rep.) Silty clay.

4546   *Soil/m.* (Rep.) Silty peat.

TABLE 328

4551   *High.* (L. UNS, 1953.) Level crossing without gates.

4552   *Cab.* Character of Bethor, 2nd Olympic spirit, governing all things ascribed to Jupiter.

4553   *Rel.* Symbol of divinity; Christianity.

4554   *Alch.* Crucible. (*A Compleat Body of Chymistry*, 17th cent.)

4554·1   *Her.* Cross potent; cross of Jerusalem; cross of St Cross.

4554·2   *MS.* As in 6132·2.

4554·3   *Nav.* (In shipping lists.) A special survey was carried out by Lloyd's during construction.

4554·4   *Numis.* Mint mark, Edward III.

4555   *Ph.* Moabite (Tyrian). Eq. Rom. S.

4556   *Chin. Num.* (In combination with other num.) Eq. Arab. 20.

4557   *Com. Mon.* Eq. 1717.

TABLE 329

4562   *Nav.* (L. White. On hull of a ship, esp. at the bow.) Plimsoll mark, indicating safe water-levels for loading in various circumstances. The horizontal arms may bear the following letters, reading downwards: TF (tropical fresh water), F (fresh water), T (tropical), S (summer), W (winter), WNA (winter North Atlantic).

4563   ⋀⋀⋀⋀   *Alch.* Water.

4563·1   *Astrol/n.* 11th sign of the Zodiac, Aquarius, the Water-bearer.

4564   ⌐∪⌐∪⌐   *Elec.* Non-reactive resistor.

4565   ∪⌐∪⌐∪   *Cart.* (APO. Rep. Ant. OS.) Rom. frontier works.

4566   ⁓⋀⋀⁓   *Meteor.* (Blue. APO. Rep.) Instability front.

4567   ⊥⊥⊥⊥   *Cart.* (APO. Rep. Ant. OS.) Roman canal.

4568   ⊥⊥⊥⊥⊥   *Hyd.* (APO. Rep. Inter.) Fishing stakes.

4569   ⊤⊤⊤⊤⊤   *Cart.* (APO. Rep. Ant. OS.) Eq. 5964.

4570   ⊤⊥⊥⊤   *Rlwy.* (APO. Rep. USA.) Narrow-gauge railway.

4571   ⊤⊥⊥⊤   *Cart.* (APO. Rep. OS.) Light railway; narrow-gauge track.

4572   ⊕   *Alch.* See 5049.

Cl.II, Ord.I, Fam.II, Gen.II

TABLE 330

4576   ⋀   *Mil.* (L. Army/R.A.F. Brit.) Sleeve badge denoting good conduct.

4577   ⋀   *Engn.* (Fire protection.) Span roof.

4578 Λ *Am.* (Cherokee syllabary.) Eq. Rom. DO.

4578·1   *Elec.* Equivalent conductivity.

4578·2   *Gk.* (Cap.) Lambda, 11th letter of the a., eq. Rom. L.

4578·3   *Phys.* (Nuclear.) Lambda particle, a hyperon, 'V-particle'.

4579 $\wedge$ *Arab. Num.* Eight, eq. 37.

4580 $\bigwedge$ *Engn.* (Fire protection.) Skylight or lantern.

4580·1   *Log.* And; product of two sets; symmetric difference of two sets.

4581† $\frown$ *Geom.* (Placed over three letters.) Angle, the apex being indicated by the middle letter; eq. 4673·1.

4582 $\bigwedge$ *Arab. Num.* Eq. 4579.

4582·1   *Elec.* U-point; jacking-in point.

4582·2   *Math.* Multiplication of vector quantities.

4582·3   *Meteor.* Squally weather.

4582·4   *Mus.* Stress mark, sforzando. (Vocal music) breath mark.

4582·5   *Print.* (Proof correction. USA.) Insert in inferior position.

414

4583	∧	*Mus.* (Stringed instruments.) Down-bow.
4584	∧	*Mus.* Eq. 4582·4.
4585	∧	*Phon.* 'Turned-v', half-open back vowel, u as in bun.
4586	∧	*Sh., Pitman's.* Diphthong ow, as in how.
4587†	∧	*Acc.* Circumflex. (Arab. and Egy. printed in Rom. letters) eq. 5303·1, which is to be preferred. (Fr.) lengthen vowel (usually indicates the omission of an obs. s following the accented vowel). (Gk.) eq. 395.
4587·1		*Log.* Propositional function; all values constituting a class.
4587·2		*Phon.* Rise/fall in tone or pitch.
4587·3		*Pros.* Pause of one mora.
4588†	∧	*Print. & G/use.* Caret, indicating where words, letters or other marks are to be inserted.
4589	⩯	*Math.* Estimates; is estimated by.

TABLE 331

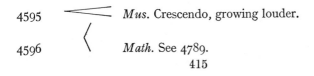

| 4595 | | *Mus.* Crescendo, growing louder. |
| 4596 | ⟨ | *Math.* See 4789. |

4597	∠	*Jap.* (Katakana syllabary.) Eq. Rom. MU. Cardinal number 23.
4598	<	*Chem.* Bivalent.
4598·1		*Log.* Is included in. (Boole.)
4598·2		*Math.* Is less than. (First used by Harriot, 1621).
4598·3		*Mus.* Stress mark.
4599	∠	*Meteor.* Thin altostratus.
4600†	·<	*Phon.* Eq. 366.
4601	≤	*Math.* Is equal to or less than.
4602	≾	*Math.* (Obs.) Eq. 4601.

TABLE 332

4607	＼	*Rlwy.* (Over light signal symbol. Brit.) Junction indicator.
4608	＞	*Mus.* Diminuendo, growing softer.
4609	＞	*Tel.* Tapering waveguide.
4610	⟩	*Math.* See 4789.
4611	＞	*Chem.* Eq. 4598.

416

4611·1		*Math.* Is greater than. (First used by Harriot, 1621); rarely eq. 4673·1.
4611·2		*Mus.* Stress mark; sforzato-piano.
4611·3		*Print.* (Proof correction.) Eq. 4588.
4611·4		*Pros.* Irrational syllable.
4612	>	*Math.* (Obs.) Eq. 4673·1.
4613	>	*Sh., Pitman's.* Diphthong oi.
4613·1		*Sh., Gregg's.* Paragraph.
4614†	>	*Phon.* Pron. with inhaled breath.
4615	≧	*Math.* Is equal to or greater than.
4616	>	*Math.* (Obs.) Eq. 4615.

TABLE 333

4622	∨	*Mil.* (L. Navy. Brit.) Sleeve-badge denoting good conduct; (Army. Brit.) Sleeve-badge denoting lance-corporal. 'One stripe.'
4623	V	*Rom.* (Cap.) Sanserif form of V. 'V-sign', symbol of victory. (Winston Churchill, 1939–1945 war.)
4624	V	*Elec.* Volt or volts.

417

4624·1		*Mag.* Magnetic potential; energy distribution.
4624·2		*Phys.* Thermal parameter. (Nuclear) V-particle.
4624·3		*Rom.* (Cap.) 22nd letter of the a. Cardinal number 5.
4625	$\bigvee$	*Arab. Num.* Seven, eq. 4670.
4626	$\bigvee$	*Mus.* (Stringed instruments.) Up-bow.
4627	$\bigvee$	*Elec.* 3-phase winding, vee-connected.
4627·1		*Log.* Eq. 4631.
4627·2		*Meteor.* (USA.) Soft rime.
4627·3		*Print.* (Proof correction. USA.) Insert in superior position.
4628	$\bigvee$	*Meteor.* (USA.) Hard rime.
4629	V	*Elec.* Volt or volts.
4629·1		*Phon.* Voiced labio-dental fricative consonant, v as in van.
4629·2		*Rom.* (l.c.) 22nd letter of the a. (*ITA*) v as in van.
4630	V	*Mus.* Eq. 4631·1.
4631	$\bigvee$	*Log.* Or, expressing an alternative. (Latin, *vel.*)
4631·1		*Mus.* Stress mark, sforzando.

4631·2		*Rlwy.* (Attached to symbol for well. USA.) Abandoned.
4632	V	*Sh., Pitman's.* Diphthong, the long *i.*
4633†	V	*Acc.* (Cz.) Diacritical mark modifying pron. of e to ye, c to ch, n to ny, r to rzh, s to sh and z to zh.
4633·1		*Phon.* Fall/rise in tone or pitch.
4634†	V	*Phon.* Voice.
4635	V̲	*Geom.* Equiangular.

TABLE 334

4640	—⌐—	*Elec.* (USA.) Double-throw switch.
4641	⟋	*Engn.* (USA.) Bevel weld.
4642	*V*	*Astron.* Radial velocity. (With negative sign) potential energy of a unit mass in the gravitational field of the galaxy.
4642·1		*Elec.* Volt or volts; electromotive force; potential, potential difference; electric tension.
4642·2		*Engn.* Vertical component of force.
4642·3		*It.* (Cap.) Eq. Rom. V.

4642·4		*Mech.* Potential energy.
4642·5		*Nav. Arch.* Speed of vessel in knots. (Obs.) speed in feet per second.
4642·6		*Opt.* Reciprocal dispersive power; constringence.
4643	Λ	*Elec.* Eq. 4578·1.
4643·1		*Gk.* (Cap.) Eq. 4578·2.
4643·2		*Phys.* (Nuclear.) Eq. 4578·3.
4644		*Egy. Num.* (Hier.) eq. Arab. 10,000.
4645		*Heb.* Eq. 4119.
4646		*Run.* Eq. Rom. L.
4647		*Ger.* (l.c.) 12th letter of the a., eq. Rom. l.
4648†		*Acc.* (It.) Eq. 4587.

TABLE 335

4654	$\checkmark$	*G/use.* Eq. 4138.
4655	$\checkmark$	*Math.* (Obs.) Square root. (Christoph Rudolff, 1525.) See 4753.
4655·1		*Print.* (Proof correction. USA.) Space evenly; less space.

420

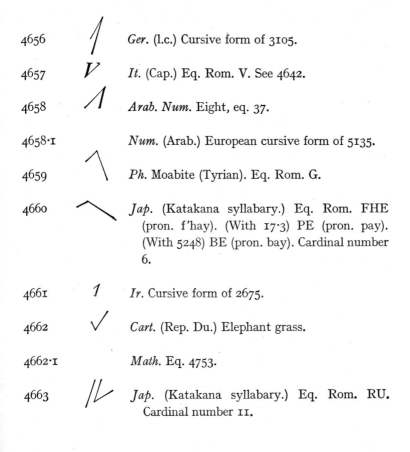

4656	/	*Ger.* (l.c.) Cursive form of 3105.
4657	*V*	*It.* (Cap.) Eq. Rom. V. See 4642.
4658	/1	*Arab. Num.* Eight, eq. 37.
4658·1		*Num.* (Arab.) European cursive form of 5135.
4659	\	*Ph.* Moabite (Tyrian). Eq. Rom. G.
4660	⌒	*Jap.* (Katakana syllabary.) Eq. Rom. FHE (pron. f'hay). (With 17·3) PE (pron. pay). (With 5248) BE (pron. bay). Cardinal number 6.
4661	1	*Ir.* Cursive form of 2675.
4662	√	*Cart.* (Rep. Du.) Elephant grass.
4662·1		*Math.* Eq. 4753.
4663	//⌐	*Jap.* (Katakana syllabary.) Eq. Rom. RU. Cardinal number 11.

TABLE 336

4668	*L*	*Astron.* The sun's geocentric longitude with reference to the ecliptic; planetographic longitude with reference to the north pole of the earth's equator; luminosity of a star.
4668·1		*Elec.* Inductance; self-inductance.

421

4668·2   *Engn.* Span. (Hydraulics) length of weir-crest.

4668·3   *It.* (Cap.) Eq. Rom. L.

4668·4   *Nav. Arch.* Length between perpendiculars; lift.

4668·5   *Phys.* Heat of vaporization at constant pressure; kinetic potential; torque; thermal force in cross-magnetic and non-magnetic materials. (Light) luminance, photometric brightness. (Heat) latent heat.

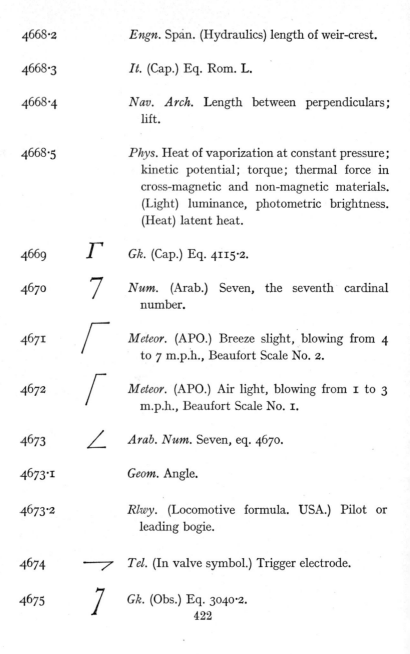

4669 Γ *Gk.* (Cap.) Eq. 4115·2.

4670   7   *Num.* (Arab.) Seven, the seventh cardinal number.

4671   *Meteor.* (APO.) Breeze slight, blowing from 4 to 7 m.p.h., Beaufort Scale No. 2.

4672   *Meteor.* (APO.) Air light, blowing from 1 to 3 m.p.h., Beaufort Scale No. 1.

4673   *Arab. Num.* Seven, eq. 4670.

4673·1   *Geom.* Angle.

4673·2   *Rlwy.* (Locomotive formula. USA.) Pilot or leading bogie.

4674   *Tel.* (In valve symbol.) Trigger electrode.

4675   7   *Gk.* (Obs.) Eq. 3040·2.

TABLE 337

4680	**Y**	*High.* (L. UNS, 1953.) Road forks.
4681		*Elec.* (USA.) Target, X-ray anode.
4682		*Run.* Eq. Rom. Y.
4683		*Run.* Eq. 4693·1.
4684		*Heb.* Zayin, 7th letter of the a., eq. Rom. Z. Cardinal number 7.
4685		*Jap.* (Katakana syllabary.) Eq. Rom. TO (pron. as Eng. toe). (With 5248) DO (pron. doh). Cardinal number 7.
4685·1		*Run.* Eq. Rom. C.
4686		*Jap.* (Katakana syllabary.) Eq. Rom. I (short), as in Fr. si; E, as in Eng. we. Cardinal number 1.

TABLE 338

4690		*Mil.* (L. Army. R.A.F. Sleeve badge. Brit.) Corporal. 'Two stripes.'
4690·1		*Police.* (L. Rep. Sleeve badge. Brit.) Acting sergeant.
4691		*Elec.* U-point for routiner access.

4691·1   *Rom.* (Cap./l.c.) Form of 4814·4 or 2787.

4692   *T*   *Astron.* Observed time of transit; perihelion time; tangential velocity.

4692·1   *It.* (Cap.) Eq. Rom. T.

4692·2   *Mag.* Intensity of magnetization.

4692·3   *Mech.* Kinetic energy; torque.

4692·4   *Nav. Arch.* Thrust; period.

4692·5   *Phys.* Period, esp. of harmonic motion; absolute temperature. (Light) transmission factor for luminous flux.

4692·6   *Therm.* Absolute temperature.

4693   ⟨   *Jap.* (Katakana syllabary.) Rom. Eq. YI (pron. yee).

4693·1   *Run.* Eq. Rom. K.

4694   ⟨   *G/use.* Insert; omission.

4694·1   *Print.* (Proof correction.) Marginal caret, eq. 4588.

4695   ⊿   *Hyd.* Spar buoy. (Inter.) floating beacon.

4696   ⊿   *Hyd.* (Rep. Inter.) Fishing stakes.

TABLE 339

§ 1. *Arrows Vertical or Diagonal*

4700	↑	*Run.* Eq. Rom. T.
4701	↑	*Math.* Tends up to the limit.
4702	↑	*Elec.* Sliding contact.
4703	⋀	*Prop.* Eq. 4725·1.
4704†	↗	*Print.* (Proof correction, esp. in math.) Insert thick space (6 units).
4705†	↑	*Chem.* (In equation.) Evolved as a gas.
4706	⅄	*Meteor. Aero.* Light icing.
4707	↓	*Math.* Tends down to the limit.
4708†	↓	*Bot.* Irregular; zygomorphic.
4708·1		*Chem.* (In equation.) Precipitated.
4709	↗	*Elec.* Variability. (Superimposed on 4398 or 5062) variable.
4710	↘	*Geol.* Inclined strata; (APO) dip.

§ 2. *Arrows Horizontal*

4713	⟶	*Hyd.* (Inter.) Ebb-tide stream.

4713·1		*Meteor.* Cold winds.
4714	$\longrightarrow$	*Elec.* (USA.) Male contact, plug.
4715	$\longrightarrow$	*Alg.* Is replaced by. (Cayley.)
4715·1		*Cal.* Approaches the limit.
4715·2		*Chem.* (In structural formulae) co-ordinate bond. (In equations) yields.
4715·3		*G/use.* (APO.) Pay attention to; direction to be understood.
4715·4		*Log.* The direction in which a relation holds; an asymmetrical relation; transformation or implication.
4715·5		*Math.* Tends towards.
4716†	$\rightarrow$	*Math.* (Over a symbol.) Vector quantity.
4717	$\twoheadleftarrow$	*Math.* (Obs.) Eq. 4598·2.
4718	$\longleftarrow$	*Log.* Eq. 4715·4.
4718·1		*Meteor.* (USA.) Ice crystals.
4719†	$\leftarrow$	*Log.* (Over the letter R.) Relata of a relation.

TABLE 340

4725	⬆	*Cart.* (With horizontal line above.) Eq. 4917.

4725·1   *Prop.* Pheon, broad arrow. The mark of Brit. Government property, said to have replaced the Rose and Crown in the 14th cent.

4726   ↓   *Alch.* Water.

4727   *Mil* Eq. 1339.

TABLE 341

4732   *Engn.* (In pipe symbol. USA.) Check valve.

4733   *Elec.* (USA.) Blow-out coil.

4734   *Mus.* Loud pedal.

4735   *Engn.* Flash weld.

4736   *Run.* Eq. Rom. S.

4737   *Rus.* (Cap./l.c.) Ee, 9th letter of the a., eq. Rom. E (long).

4738   И   *Gk.* (Cap.) Nu, 13th letter of the a., eq. Rom. N.

4738·1   *Phys.* (Nuclear) neutron.

4738·2   *Rom.* (Cap.) 14th letter of the a. (Med. ext. of Rom. num.) cardinal number number 90 or 900.

4739   N   *Phon.* Uvular nasal consonant, n as in Eskimo eɴina.

TABLE 342

4745   *High.* (L. Brit.) Double bend. (Inter.) dangerous bends.

4746   *Elec.* (USA.) Eq. 2075.

4747   *Engn.* (Plumbing. USA.) Vacuum outlet.

4748   *Engn.* (Fire protection.) Eq. 4855.

4749   *Mil.* Gun emplacement or emplacements.

4750   *Chem.* Number of molecules.

4750·1   *It.* (Cap.) Eq. Rom. N.

4750·2   *Mech.* Revolutions per minute; modulus of elasticity, shearing or rigidity.

4750·3   *Phys.* Avogadro number; rate. (Nuclear) nucleon.

4751   *Ger.* (l.c.) Cursive form of 515.

4752   *Run.* Eq. 4736.

4753   *Math.* Radical, root-sign; square-root. (Derived from 4655.) See also 4869.

4754   *Math.* (Between e.g. x and y) the numberobtained by y multiplications of x.

4755   𝄴   *Num.* (Arab. 15th cent. Ital.) Eq. mod. 5.

4756   ↩   *Sh., Pitman's.* Dash.

4757   ∧   *Mus.* Eq. 4850.

TABLE 343

4761   Z   *High.* (L. White chalk.) Foreigners live here: tell ex-army story. (Tramps' 'smogger'.)

4762   ⨼   *Engn.* (In pipe symbol. USA.) Angle valve check.

4763   ⟋   *Engn.* (Shipbuilding. With symbol for fillet weld.) Staggered fillets.

4763·1   *Tel.* Series.

4764   ⟍▭   *Egy.* (Hier.) Eq. Rom. M.

4765   Z   *Am.* (Cherokee syllabary.) Eq. Rom. NO.

4765·1   *Rom.* (Cap./l.c.) Sanserif form of Z.

4766   Z   *Gk.* (Cap.) Zeta, 6th letter of the a., eq. Rom. Z.

4766·1   *Min. Crys.* Vibration direction of largest refractive index.

4766·2   *Rom.* (Cap.) 26th letter of the a. (Med. ext. of Rom. num.) cardinal number 2,000.

429

4767	Ƨ	*ITA.* (Augmented Rom.) 'Reversed-Z'. z or s as s in is.
4768	*Z*	*Chem.* Atomic number.
4768·1		*Elec.* Impedance.
4768·2		*Engn.* (Hydraulics.) Elevation head; normal displacement.
4768·3		*It.* (Cap.) Eq. Rom. Z.
4768·4		*Mag.* Attractive force per unit area; vertical component of earth's magnetic intensity.
4768·5		*Mech.* Modulus of section; relative viscosity.
4769	Z	*Meteor.* Haze.
4769·1		*Phon.* Voiced alveolar fricative consonant, z as in zoo.
4769·2		*Rom.* (l.c.) 26th letter of the a. (*ITA*) z as in zoo.
4770	Z	*Alg.* The third unknown.
4770·1		*Astron.* Zenith distance.
4770·2		*Chem.* Valency of an ion.
4770·3		*Elec.* Impedance.
4770·4		*Engn.* (Hydraulics.) Potential head.

430

4770·5		*Geom.* Cartesian co-ordinate; cylindrical co-ordinate.
4770·6		*It.* (l.c.) Eq. Rom. z.
4770·7		*Log.* Variable individual.
4770·8		*Phys.* Nuclear charge.

TABLE 344

§ I. *One Angle Inside the Other*

4775	$\bigwedge\!\!\bigwedge$	*Meteor.* Heavy squalls during last three hours.
4776†	$\bigwedge\!\!\bigwedge$	*Pros.* Eq. 5648.
4777†	$\bigwedge\!\!\bigwedge$	*Print.* (Proof correction, esp. in math.) Insert en quad (9 units).
4778	$\langle\!\langle$	*Engn.* (Across pipe symbol.) Screwed joint.
4779	$\ll$	*Math.* Is much less than.
4780	$\gg$	*Math.* Is much greater than.
4781	$\langle\!\langle$	*Cart. Mil.* (USA.) Lock; water-gate; dam.
4782	$\ll$	*Math.* Eq. 4779.
4783	$\gg$	*Math.* Eq. 4780.

431

| 4784 | « | *Punc.* (Fr./Continental.) Guillemets; quotation marks introducing quoted matter. |

| 4785 | » | *Punc.* (Fr./Continental.) Guillemets; quotation marks closing quoted matter. |

§ 2. *No Angle Inside Another*

| 4787 | ⚡ | *Arab. Num.* Four, eq. 3527. |

| 4788 | ⟋ | *Elec.* (In symbol for overhead line.) Insulated overlap span. |

| 4789 | ⟨ ⟩ | *Math.* Angular brackets, eq. 4416·2. |

| 4790 | ⇌ | *Chem.* Eq. 4945. |

| 4791 | ∨∧ | *Print.* (Proof correction. USA.) Even space. |

| 4792 | ⋛ | *Math.* Is greater or less than; is not equal to. |

| 4793 | ⋝ | *Math.* Eq. 4794. |

| 4794 | ⋛̳ | *Math.* Is greater than, equal to, or less than. |

TABLE 345

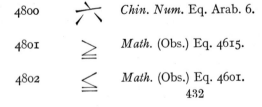

| 4800 | 𣥂 | *Chin. Num.* Eq. Arab. 6. |

| 4801 | ≧ | *Math.* (Obs.) Eq. 4615. |

| 4802 | ≦ | *Math.* (Obs.) Eq. 4601. |

432

4803	$\geqq$	*Math.* (Obs.) Eq. 4615.
4804	$\leqq$	*Math.* (Obs.) Eq. 4601.

TABLE 346

4810	**Y**	*High.* (L. Brit.) 'Y-sign'. Road forks.
4811	⊥	*Elec.* 3-phase 3-wire winding, star connected.
4812	Y	*Tel.* Shunt.
4812·1		*Rom.* (Cap.) Sanserif form of 4814·4.
4813	⋎	*Alch.* Iron.
4814	Y	*Genetics.* (Of chromosomes.) Female.
4814·1		*Gk.* (Cap.) Eq. 2523·1.
4814·2		*Min. Crys.* Vibration direction of intermediate refractive index.
4814·3		*Phys.* (Nuclear.) Hyperon, an elementary particle of greater mass than a proton but less than a deuteron.
4814·4		*Rom.* (Cap.) 25th letter of the a. (Med. ext. of Rom. num.) cardinal number 150.
4815	*Y*	*Elec.* Admittance.

4815·1		*It.* (Cap.) Eq. Rom. Y.
4816	⋀	*Gk.* (Obs.) Digamma, eq. Rom. V or W; some-times eq. 3005.
4817		*Run.* Eq. Rom. A.
4818		*Ph.* Moabite (Tyrian). Eq. Rom. K.
4819	Y	*Phon.* Close front vowel, as ü in Ger. fünf.

TABLE 347

4825	⋀	*High.* (L. White chalk.) Food is sometimes given here. (Tramps' 'smogger'.)
4826		*Rlwy.* Mine tunnel.
4827		*Tel.* Electromagnetic horn.
4828		*Numis.* Mint mark, the letter A.
4829	F	*Astron.* Optical path through the atmosphere.
4829·1		*Elec.* Faraday's constant; flow of magnetic induction.
4829·2		*Engn.* Shearing force. (Hydrology) run-off.
4829·3		*It.* (Cap.) Eq. Rom. F.
4829·4		*Mag.* Magnetomotive force.

434

4829·5	*Mech.* Force; free energy; specific normal force. (USA) gravitational force, weight.
4829·6	*Nav. Arch.* Centre of flotation.
4829·7	*Phys.* Change in thermal conductivity in a cross field. See 4863. (Light) luminous flux.
4829·8	*Therm.* Free energy; Helmholtz function.
4830	*Meteor.* (APO.) Breeze gentle, blowing from 8 to 12 m.p.h., Beaufort Scale No. 3.
4831	*Meteor.* (APO). Breeze moderate, blowing from 13 to 18 m.p.h., Beaufort Scale No. 4.
4832	*Metoer.* Thick altostratus.
4833	*Num.* (Arab.) Continental cursive figure 4.
4834	*Geom.* Projectivity; projective correspondence projective transformation.
4835	*Log.* Is included in. (Of propositions) implies.

TABLE 348

4840   *High.* (L. White chalk.) A strict workhouse; hard work demanded here. (Tramps' 'smogger'.)

4841   *Mil.* (L. R.A.F.) Sleeve badge, senior technician.

435

4842   *Mil.* (L. Army, R.A.F.) Sleeve badge, sergeant.

4842·1   *Police.* (L. Brit.) Sleeve badge, sergeant.

4843   *Gk.* (Cap.) Eq. 4857.

4843·1   *Rom.* (Cap.) Eq. 4857·2.

4844   *Ph.* Moabite (Tyrian). Eq. Rom. SH.

4845   *Am.* (Cherokee syllabary.) Eq. Rom. LA.

4845·1   *Elec.* Watt.

4845·2   *Rom.* (Cap.) 23rd letter of the a.

4846   *Astron.* Spatial velocity relative to the sun; factor of dilution of radiation.

4846·1   *Elec.* Electrical energy; reluctance.

4846·2   *Engn.* Load.

4846·3   *It.* (Cap.) Eq. Rom. W.

4846·4   *Mech.* Weight; work; energy.

4846·5   *Phys.* Angular velocity.

4847   *Geom.* Eq. 4635.

4848   *Meteor.* Dew.

4848·1   *Phon.* Bi-labial semi-vowel, w as in will.

436

4848·2   *Rom.* (l.c.) 23rd letter of the a. (*ITA*) w as in we.

4849   **M**   *Phon.* 'Turned-w', the voiceless fricative w eq. ow and pron. as in why.

4850   **ʌʌ**   *Mus.* Custos, indicating at the end of a page of music the position of the first note on the next page. Another form is given in 4757, and sometimes the upper mordent sign is used. See 4933.

TABLE 349

4855   *Engn.* (Fire protection.) Mansard roof.

4856   *Engn.* Heating or cooling coil.

4857   **M**   *Gk.* (Cap.) Mu, 12th letter of the a., eq. Rom. M.

4857·1   *Rel. Rec.* NN, as in 'N or M' in the Church of England catechism, for 'Name or Names'.

4857·2   *Rom.* (Cap.) 13th letter of the a. Cardinal number 1,000.

4857·3   *Rus.* (Cap./l.c.) Em, 14th letter of the old a., 13th of the mod., eq. Rom. M.

4858   **M**   *Mag.* Intensity of magnetization; horizontal component of earth's magnetic intensity; magnetic polarization; pole strength.

4858·1   *Rom.* (Cap.) Sanserif form of M.

4859	M	*Am.* (Cherokee syllabary.) Eq. Rom. LU.
4859·1		*Rom.* (Cap.) Eq. M, 4857·2.
4859·2		*Run.* Eq. Rom. E.
4860	M'	*Elec.* Peltier effect in longitudinal magnetic and non-magnetic materials.
4861	Σ	*Cal.* Finite sum.
4861·1		*Gk.* (Cap.) Sigma, 18th letter of the a., eq. Rom. S.
4862	M	*Astron.* Mean anomaly; absolute magnitude; mass of a star.
4862·1		*Chem.* Molecular weight.
4862·2		*Elec.* Mutual inductance; Peltier effect in cross magnetic and non-magnetic materials. (As a prefix) meg-, mega-, million.
4862·3		*Engn.* (Structural.) Bending moment.
4862·4		*It.* (Cap.) Eq. Rom. M.
4862·5		*Mech.* Moment; moment of resistance.
4862·6		*Nav. Arch.* Metacentre.
4863	F'	*Phys.* Change in thermal conductivity in a longitudinal field.

4864	Σ	*Gk.* (Cap.) Eq. 4861·1.
4864·1		*Phys.* (Nuclear.) Sigma particle, a hyperon.
4865	_⋀_	*Meteor. Aero.* Light turbulence.
4866	$\overline{\wedge}$	*Geom.* Perspective correspondence.
4867	⋂	*Tel.* (In valve diagrams.) Filament cathode; cathode. (Eq. 4181.)
4868†	⇑	*Print.* (Proof correction, esp. math.) Insert em quad (18 units).
4869	$\sqrt{}$	*Math.* Root. (Without an index) square root. This form of the root sign is a combination of the radical (4753) and the vinculum (5288·1).

TABLE 350

(See also Table 314)

4873	$\times$	*Engn.* (Associated with pipe symbol. USA.) Welded.
4873·1		*G/use.* Eq. 4361.
4874	X	*Alch.* Talc. (*A Compleat Body of Chymistry*, 17th cent.)
4874·1		*Com.* (Of ale.) Single strength, originally denoting that the old ten shilling duty had been paid.

4874·2   *Genetics.* (Of chromosomes.) Male.

4874·3   *Gk.* (Cap.) Chi, 22nd letter of the a., eq. Rom. CH.

4874·4   *Log.* Variable function involving one variable.

4874·5   *Min. Crys.* Vibration direction of smallest refractive index.

4874·6   *Phys.* (Of radiation.) Röntgen (rays).

4874·7   *Rel.* Cross; Christ; Christian/ity.

4874·8   *Rom.* (Cap.) 24th letter of the a. (Obs.) early form of T. Cardinal number 10.

4874·9   *Rus.* (Cap.) Kha, 23rd letter of the old a., 22nd of the mod., eq. Rom. (C)H (slightly guttural).

4875   X   *Rlwy.* (With letters BM. USA.) Bench mark.

4876   X   *Phon.* Voiceless velar fricative consonant, ch as in Scots loch.

4876·1   *Rom.* (l.c.) 24th letter of the a.

4876·2   *Rus.* (l.c.) Eq. 4874·9.

TABLE 351

4880      *High.* (L. White on red. Brit., 1964.) Level crossing without gate or barrier.

440

4881		*Her.* St Andrew's cross.
4882		*Run.* Eq. Rom. N.
4883		*Chin. Num.* Eq. Arab. 10.
4884		*Rom. Num.* (Obs.) 'Lazy-X'. Eq. M, Arab. 1,000.
4885		*Astron.* Ionization potential.
4885·1		*Elec.* Reactance.
4885·2		*It.* (Cap.) Eq. Rom. X.
4885·3		*Mag.* Eq. 3083·1.
4886		*Math.* Does not divide into without remainder.
4887		*Pol.* (l.c.) Eq. 4151.

TABLE 352

4892		*Rlwy.* (USA.) Air pipe reducer or bushing (arrow pointing to smaller pipe.)
4893		*Run.* Eq. 3525.
4894		*Run.* Eq. Rom. M.
4895		*Tel.* Aerial, antenna.

441

4896	V	*Run.* Eq. Rom. F.
4897	H	*Run.* Eq. Rom. H.
4898	N	*Run.* Eq. 4897.
4899		*Ph.* Moabite (Tyrian). Eq. Rom. Z.
4900		*Geol.* Vertical cleavage.
4901	*H*	*Astron.* Hour angle.
4901·1		*Engn.* Horizontal component of force. (Hydraulics) total head.
4901·2		*It.* (Cap.) Eq. Rom. H.
4901·3		*Mag.* Eq. 4373.
4901·4		*Phys.* (Heat.) Total heat; heat per unit mass.
4902	K	*Rom.* (Cap.) Eq. 4168·3.
4903	*K*	*It.* (Cap.) Eq. Rom. K. See 4178.
4904		*Print.* (Proof correction.) Insert hyphen.

TABLE 353

4910	*E*	*Astron.* Equation of time; eccentric anomaly; colour excess. (Of variable stars) number of periods elapsed.

442

4910·1		*Chem.* (Of reaction.) Activation energy.
4910·2		*Elec.* Electric potential; impedance; electric field.
4910·3		*Engn.* (Hydrology.) Evaporation.
4910·4		*It.* (Cap.) Eq. Rom. E.
4910·5		*Mech.* Energy; Young's modulus of elasticity.
4910·6		*Phys.* (Light.) Illumination.
4911	⊢	*Log.* Symbol of assertion; see 4386, 4388 and 4389.
4912	⋁	*Rel.* Versicle.
4913		*Ph.* Moabite (Tyrian). Eq. Rom. TS.
4914		*Ph.* Moabite (Tyrian). Eq. Rom. I.
4915	↑	*Print.* (Proof correction.) Raise.
4916	↓	*Print.* (Proof correction.) Lower.
4917		*Cart.* Bench mark. The horizontal line or 'bench' is at a stated altitude above sea-level, calculated from the mean sea-level at Liverpool in OS maps of Great Britain published before 1929, and thereafter from mean sea-level at Newlyn, Cornwall.

| 4918 | | *Cart.* Inverted bench mark. The horizontal line is at a stated distance below sea-level; see 4917. |

| 4919 | | *Cart.* (Admiralty. Brit.) Eq. 4917. |

TABLE 354

| 4925 | | *Elec.* (USA.) Eq. 4733. |

| 4926 | | *Engn.* Spray. |

| 4927 | | *Math.* Correspondence. |

| 4928 | | *Chem.* Eq. 4945. |

| 4928·1 | | *Log.* Equivalence; double implication; mutually applies; one-to-one correspondence; asymptotically equivalent to. |

| 4928·2 | | *Meteor.* Ice needles. |

| 4929 | | *Gk.* (Cap.) Eq. 5373. |

| 4930 | | *Jap.* Eq. 2849. |

| 4931 | | *Ger.* (l.c.) Cursive form of 2994. |

| 4932 | | *Cart. Hyd.* (Inter.) Battery. |

4933	$\wedge\!\!\wedge$	*Mus.* Upper mordent, pralltriller, signifying the following group of three notes: the principal note, the note above it, the principal note again; to be played in that order as quickly as possible, with the acc. on the third note.
4934	$\wedge\!\!\wedge\!/$	*Math.* (Obs.) 4th root. (Christoph Rudolff, 1525.)

TABLE 355

4940	)(	*High.* (L. UNS, 1953.) Narrow bridge.
4941		*Mil.* (L. R.A.F.) Sleeve badge, drum major.
4942	*NIIN*	*Rom. Num.* (Obs.) Eq. XVIII, Arab. 18.
4943	)(	*Engn.* Mashed stitch weld.
4944	↓↑	*Tel.* Squeeze section.
4945	⇌	*Chem.* Reversible reaction.
4946	⇔	*Meteor.* Frost fog.
4947	)(	*Cart.* (APO.) Bridge.
4947·1		*Meteor.* Waterspouts seen during the last three hours.
4948	$\wedge$	*Meteor. Aero.* Moderate turbulence.

445

TABLE 356

4952	7	*Num.* (Arab.) Continental figure 7.
4953	—✕—	*Elec.* (USA.) Knife switch.
4954	*L*	*Pol.* It. (Cap.) Eq. 4151.
4955		*Meteor.* (APO.) Breeze fresh, blowing from 19 to 24 m.p.h., Beaufort Scale No. 5.
4956		*Meteor.* (APO.) Breeze strong, blowing from 25 to 31 m.p.h., Beaufort Scale No. 6.
4957		*Ph.* Moabite (Tyrian). Eq. Rom. H.
4958		*Jap.* (Katakana syllabary.) Eq. Rom. YA (pron. yah).
4959		*Geol.* (APO.) Open arrow. Dip of cleavage.
4959·1		*Meteor.* Eq. 4272.

TABLE 357

4964		*Engn.* Water element in condenser unit.
4965		*Engn.* Tundish drain.
4966		*Engn.* (Fire protection.) North-light or saw-tooth roof.

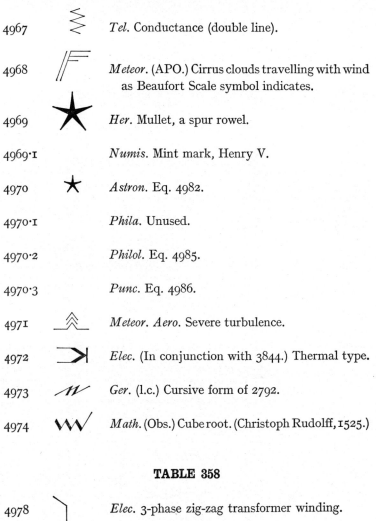

4967　　　*Tel.* Conductance (double line).

4968　　　*Meteor.* (APO.) Cirrus clouds travelling with wind as Beaufort Scale symbol indicates.

4969　　　*Her.* Mullet, a spur rowel.

4969·1　　　*Numis.* Mint mark, Henry V.

4970　　　*Astron.* Eq. 4982.

4970·1　　　*Phila.* Unused.

4970·2　　　*Philol.* Eq. 4985.

4970·3　　　*Punc.* Eq. 4986.

4971　　　*Meteor. Aero.* Severe turbulence.

4972　　　*Elec.* (In conjunction with 3844.) Thermal type.

4973　　　*Ger.* (l.c.) Cursive form of 2792.

4974　　　*Math.* (Obs.) Cube root. (Christoph Rudolff, 1525.)

TABLE 358

4978　　　*Elec.* 3-phase zig-zag transformer winding.

4978·1　　　*Insig.* Eq. 4476. *Cf.* 4312.

4979　　　*Engn.* (Across pipe symbol.) Flanged and bolted joint with flanges screwed on.

447

4980		*Pot.* China mark, Dresden (Meissen).
4981		*Ger.* (l.c.) Cursive form of 3024.
4982		*Astrol/n.* Sextile; fixed star.
4982·1		*Com.* (USA.) Correct quotation.
4982·2		*Meteor.* Snow.
4983†		*Punc.* Eq. 4986.
4984		*Mus.* Breath mark.
4985		*Philol.* Hypothetical or reconstructed form of a word or phrase.
4985·1		*Phon.* (Before a word.) Proper name.
4986†		*Punc.* Asterisk, star, a mark of reference used to indicate a point in a text to which a footnote bearing the same mark refers; a distinguishing mark; a mark of emphasis.

TABLE 359

4990		*Meteor.* Snow and fog.
4991		*Elec.* Rotary spark gap.
4992		*Bot.* Northern hemisphere.
4993		*Bot.* Southern hemisphere.

448

4994	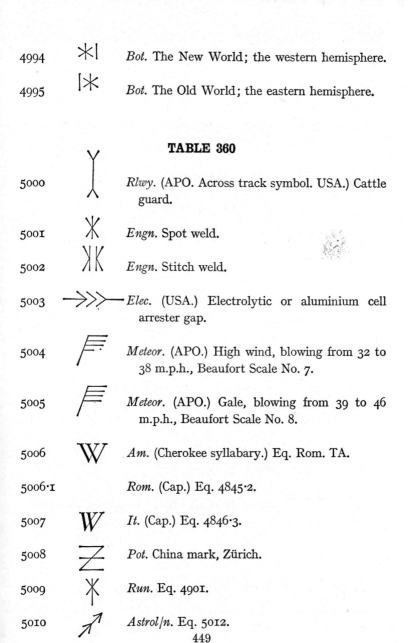	*Bot.* The New World; the western hemisphere.
4995		*Bot.* The Old World; the eastern hemisphere.

TABLE 360

5000		*Rlwy.* (APO. Across track symbol. USA.) Cattle guard.
5001		*Engn.* Spot weld.
5002		*Engn.* Stitch weld.
5003		*Elec.* (USA.) Electrolytic or aluminium cell arrester gap.
5004		*Meteor.* (APO.) High wind, blowing from 32 to 38 m.p.h., Beaufort Scale No. 7.
5005		*Meteor.* (APO.) Gale, blowing from 39 to 46 m.p.h., Beaufort Scale No. 8.
5006		*Am.* (Cherokee syllabary.) Eq. Rom. TA.
5006·1		*Rom.* (Cap.) Eq. 4845·2.
5007		*It.* (Cap.) Eq. 4846·3.
5008		*Pot.* China mark, Zürich.
5009		*Run.* Eq. 4901.
5010		*Astrol/n.* Eq. 5012.

449

5010·1		*Bot.* Eq. 1084.
5011		*Alch.* Iron.
5012		*Astrol/n.* 9th sign of the Zodiac, Sagittarius, the Archer.
5013		*Math.* Converges to.
5014		*Cart.* (Du.) Bamboo bush.
5015		*Insig. Com.* (Brit. Obsnt.) Rail freight.

TABLE 361

5020		*Meteor.* Intermittent heavy snow.
5021		*Meteor.* Continuous moderate snow.
5022		*Punc.* Asterism, a mark of emphasis or to attract attention.
5023		*Punc.* Eq. 5022.
5024†		*Punc.* Mark of ellipsis, indicating an omission.

TABLE 362

5030		*Meteor.* Intermittent moderate snow.
5031		*Meteor.* Continuous slight snow.

450

5032   *Meteor.* Continuous heavy snow.

5033   *Cart.* (APO. '6-inch' map. OS.) Bridge over river or canal.

5034   *Cart.* (APO. '6-inch' map. OS.) Aqueduct.

5035   *Cart.* (APO. Rep.) Water pipes or conduits underground.

5036   *Engn.* (APO. Rep. Heating. USA.) Medium pressure return pipe.

5037   *Engn.* (APO. Rep. Heating. USA.) High-pressure return pipe.

5038   *Rlwy.* (APO. Rep. USA.) Barbed wire fence.

5039   *Geol.* (Rep.) Extrusive igneous rocks.

TABLE 363

5045   *Rlwy.* (L. Rep. Brit.) Sign by trackside to warn engine-driver of water-trough between rails.

5046   *Rlwy.* (USA.) Air-pipe combination cock and union.

5047   *Geol.* (APO.) Synclinal axis.

5048   *Numis.* Mint mark, the sun, Edward IV.

451

5049   *Alch.* Ammoniac salt. (*A Compleat Body of Chymistry*, 17th cent.)

5050   *Chem.* Asymmetrically placed carbon atom.

5051   *Rel.* (RC.) Commencement of response in verses of psalms.

5052   *Astrol/n.* Eq. 4982.

5052·1   *Punc.* Eq. 4986.

5053   *Egy.* (Hier.) Water. Eq. Rom. N.

5054   *Mus.* (Rep.) Shake, trill, the note written and the note above played in (usually) rapid alternations.

5055   *Rlwy.* (APO. Rep. USA.) Rail fence.

5056   *Rlwy.* (APO. Rep. USA.) Gasoline, petrol pipe.

TABLE 364

§ 1. *With No Lines Crossing*

5061   *Engn.* Heat load.

5062   *Elec. Tel.* Resistance, resistor.

5063   *Engn.* (Heating and ventilating. USA.) Capillary tube.

5064   *Tel.* Conductance (single line).

5065   *Meteor.* (APO.) Gale strong, blowing from 47 to 54 m.p.h., Beaufort Scale No. 9.

5066   *Meteor.* (APO.) Whole gale, blowing from 55 to 63 m.p.h., Beaufort Scale No. 10.

5067   *Meteor.* (APO.) Storm, wind blowing from 64 to 73 m.p.h., Beaufort Scale No. 11.

5068   *Meteor.* (APO.) Hurricane, blowing at more than 73 m.p.h., Beaufort Scale No. 12.

5069   *Meteor.* (APO. Obs.) Direction of wind.

5070   *Cart.* (APO. '25-inch' map. OS.) Flow of water, the number of flight-strokes indicating miles per hour.

5071   *Hyd.* (Inter.) Eq. 3159.

5072   *Hyd.* (Inter.) Flood-tide stream.

§ 2. *With Crossed Lines*

5075   *Meteor. Aero.* Severe icing.

5076   *Elec.* 3-phase circuit.

5077   *Math.* Is not congruent or identical with.

453

5078 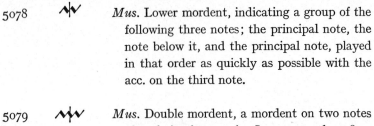 *Mus.* Lower mordent, indicating a group of the following three notes; the principal note, the note below it, and the principal note, played in that order as quickly as possible with the acc. on the third note.

5079 *Mus.* Double mordent, a mordent on two notes played simultaneously. See 4933 and 5078.

5080 *Mus.* Eq. 5079.

5081 *Engn.* (APO. Rep. Heating. USA.) Medium pressure steam pipe.

5082 *Engn.* (APO. Rep. Heating. USA.) High pressure steam pipe.

5083 *Rlwy.* (APO. Rep. USA.) Worm fence.

TABLE 365

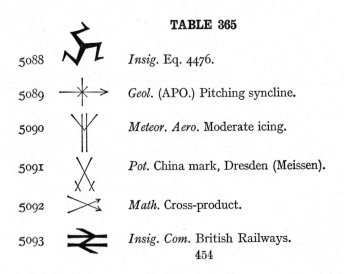

5088 *Insig.* Eq. 4476.

5089 *Geol.* (APO.) Pitching syncline.

5090 *Meteor. Aero.* Moderate icing.

5091 *Pot.* China mark, Dresden (Meissen).

5092 *Math.* Cross-product.

5093 *Insig. Com.* British Railways.

454

5094	$\neq$	*Log.* Other than.
5094·1		*Math.* (Or reversed) Is not equal to.
5095		*Math.* Eq. 4510.
5096		*Math.* Eq. 4510.
5097		*Run.* Eq. 4817.
5098		*Print.* Eq. 4021·1.
5099		*Cart.* (Ant. OS.) Mine; quarry.
5100		*Cart.* (APO. Rep.) Pylons (conventionally spaced).

Cl.II, Ord.I, Fam.III, Gen.I

TABLE 366

5104	**❘**	*Num.* (Arab.) Eq. 5135.
5104·1		*Rom.* (Cap.) Sanserif form of 5125·2.
5105†		*Og.* Eq. Rom. H.
5105·1		*Run.* Eq. Rom. I.
5106		*Og.* Eq. Rom. A.
5107†		*Og.* Eq. Rom. B.

5108 | *Engn.* (Across pipe symbol.) Joint.

5109 | *Tel.* Short circuit (double line).

5110 | *Tel.* (In valve symbol as three-quarters of a diameter.) Internal shield.

5111 | *Arith.* Contains. (Dedekind.)

5111·1 | *Egy. Num.* One, unity, eq. Arab. 1.

5111·2 | *Engn.* (Brit.) Butt weld. (USA.) flash or upset weld.

5111·3 | *Log.* Relative product.

5111·4 | *Meteor.* (USA.) A decrease in intensity in the phenomenon indicated by the preceding symbol; an increase in intensity in the phenomenon indicated by the succeeding symbol.

5111·5 | *Mus.* Bar-line, dividing the stave into bars and usually preceding each strong acc.

5111·6 | *Print.* (Proof correction.) Eq. 5214·5. (USA, at left of copy) set in smaller type.

5112 | *Num.* (Arab.) Eq. 5135.

5113 | *Sh., Pitman's.* (Thin) T.

5114 | *Sh., Pitman's.* (Thick) D.

456

5115   **❚**   *Mus.* Rest four measures.

5116   **❚**   *Rlwy.* (Cutting across symbol for rail. Brit.) Insulating rail joint with track circuit on both sides. (Terminating symbol for rail) buffer stop.

5117†   **∣**   *Phon.* (Before a syllable.) Principal stress. (In Sw.) simple tone.

5118†   *Fr.* Eq. 2711.

      ∣

5118·1   *Phon.* Syllabic consonant. (Before a syllable) secondary stress.

TABLE 367

5125   **I**   *Gk.* (Cap.) Iota, 9th letter of the a., eq. Rom. I.

5125·1   *Nav.* Vessel fit to carry goods for short voyages only.

5125·2   *Rom.* (Cap.) 9th letter of the a. Cardinal number 1, unity. (Used in conjunction with 322) eq. 1975·1.

5125·3   *Rus.* (Cap. Obs.) 'Ee with a dot', the old 10th letter of the a., eq. Rom. e (long).

5126   **{**   *Ass. Num.* Eq. Arab. 10.

5127   **I**   *Phon.* (Obsnt.) Eq. 2354.

TABLE 368

5132	Υ	*Ass. Num.* One, unity, eq. Arab. 1.
5133		*Arab.* Alif, 1st letter of the a., eq. Rom. A. Cardinal number 1.
5134	1	*Phon.* Alveolar lateral non-fricative consonant, l as in lip.
5134·1		*Rom.* (l.c.) 12th letter of the a. (*ITA*) l as in lion.
5134·2		*Trig.* Direction cosine.
5135	1	*Num.* (Arab.) One, unity, the first cardinal number.
5136†	^{1}	*Cal.* (Above and before a number or symbol.) Derivative as to.
5137†	$^{\prime}$	*Mus.* (Over a note.) Very staccato. (Vocal score) breath mark.
5138†		*Mus.* (Under a note.) Very staccato.

TABLE 369

5144		*Mil.* Infantry column of route.
5145	$\mid\ \mid$	*Engn.* (USA.) Square weld.
5146	$\parallel$	*Tel.* Sealing material.

458

| 5147 | | *Tel.* Diaphragm. |

5147   I   *Tel.* Diaphragm.

5148   ‖   *Engn.* (Across pipe symbol.) Flanged and bolted joint. (At end of pipe symbol) blank flange.

5148·1   *Geom.* Is parallel to.

5148·2   *Print.* An indication on copy for compositor to begin a fresh line. (Proof correction) straighten ends of lines, align type.

5148·3   *Pros.* Caesura, cesura, a pause in the metre.

5149†   ‖   *Og.* Eq. Rom. D.

5150   ‖   *Og.* Eq. Rom. O.

5151†   ‖   *Og.* Eq. Rom. L.

5152 | | *Math.* Enclosure for determinants. (Containing positive number) absolute value or modulus.

5153   ‖   *Mus.* Double bar-line, denoting a change of key or tempo; conclusion of a movement or section; end of a line in a hymn/song; termination of a composition.

5154†   ‖   *Print.* Parallels, a mark of reference used to indicate a point in a text to which a footnote bearing the same mark refers.

5155†   ‖   *Pros.* Eq. 5148·3.

5156   ▐   *Elec.* Plug; moving member of contact switch.

TABLE 370

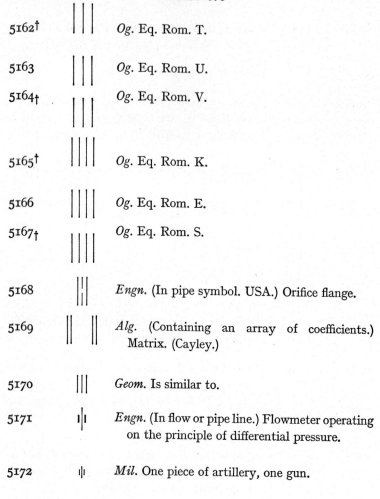

5162† ||| *Og.* Eq. Rom. T.

5163 ||| *Og.* Eq. Rom. U.

5164† ||| *Og.* Eq. Rom. V.

5165† |||| *Og.* Eq. Rom. K.

5166 |||| *Og.* Eq. Rom. E.

5167† |||| *Og.* Eq. Rom. S.

5168 ||| *Engn.* (In pipe symbol. USA.) Orifice flange.

5169 || || *Alg.* (Containing an array of coefficients.) Matrix. (Cayley.)

5170 ||| *Geom.* Is similar to.

5171 |∤| *Engn.* (In flow or pipe line.) Flowmeter operating on the principle of differential pressure.

5172 ∤|ı   *Mil.* One piece of artillery, one gun.

TABLE 371

5178† ||||| *Og.* Eq. Rom. Q.

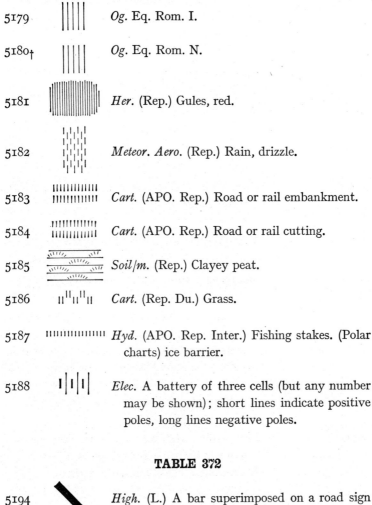

5179		*Og.* Eq. Rom. I.
5180†		*Og.* Eq. Rom. N.
5181		*Her.* (Rep.) Gules, red.
5182		*Meteor. Aero.* (Rep.) Rain, drizzle.
5183		*Cart.* (APO. Rep.) Road or rail embankment.
5184		*Cart.* (APO. Rep.) Road or rail cutting.
5185		*Soil/m.* (Rep.) Clayey peat.
5186		*Cart.* (Rep. Du.) Grass.
5187		*Hyd.* (APO. Rep. Inter.) Fishing stakes. (Polar charts) ice barrier.
5188		*Elec.* A battery of three cells (but any number may be shown); short lines indicate positive poles, long lines negative poles.

TABLE 372

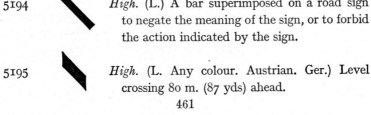

5194		*High.* (L.) A bar superimposed on a road sign to negate the meaning of the sign, or to forbid the action indicated by the sign.
5195		*High.* (L. Any colour. Austrian. Ger.) Level crossing 80 m. (87 yds) ahead.

461

5196   \   *Sh.*, *Pitman's*. (Thick) B. Billion (million million), billionth.

5197   \   *Sh.*, *Pitman's*. (Thin) P.

5198   ⏋   *Sh.*, *Gregg's*. NK.

5199   ⌐   *Sh.*, *Gregg's*. NG.

5200†   \   *Com. Num.* (L. Traditional notation at Portland stone quarries.) One-half.

5201   ▰   *Mus.* (With num. above.) Eq. 4378.

5202   \   *Sh.*, *Gregg's*. *Punc.* Full stop, period.

5203†   \   *Acc.* Grave. (Fr.) Placed over a vowel to broaden the sound, or to distinguish different words with the same spelling. (Gk.) denoting that the pitch of a vowel is not to be raised. (Ital.) placed over a vowel to open it, also used to indicate stress. (Port.) stress. (Sp.) stress.

5203·1   *Pros.* Grave acc. used rarely in Eng. pros. to indicate that an extra syllable is to be made by sounding a vowel normally mute.

5204†   \   *Phon.* High falling tone or pitch. (Preceding a syllable) denotes second element of a compound tone.

5205†   \   *Phon.* Low falling tone or pitch.

462

TABLE 373

5210	/	*Og.* Eq. Rom. M.
5211	/	*Ind. Num.* (3rd cent. B.C.) Unity, eq. Arab. 1.
5212	▬	*Mus.* (With num. above) Eq. 4378. (Attached to ends of notes) replaces the 'hooks' of quavers, semiquavers, etc., serving to link successive notes in a manner depending on both the tempo and the appearance of the script. (Crossing the stem of a note or placed immediately above or below a semibreve) repeat mark, repeat the note at quaver intervals.
5213	*I*	*Astron.* Intensity.
5213·1		*Elec.* Current; ionic strength.
5213·2		*It.* (Cap.) Eq. Rom. I.
5213·3		*Mag.* Intensity of magnetization; magnetic polarization.
5213·4		*Mech.* Moment of inertia; planar/rectangular moment of inertia; second moment.
5213·5		*Nav. Arch.* Transverse moment of inertia of waterplane.
5213·6		*Phys.* Radioactivity. (Light) luminous intensity, candle-power. (Heat) total heat.

5214	/	*Bot.* Grafted on, budded on, the scion being named before the stroke and the stock after it.

5214·1   *Com. Mon.* (Obs.) The solidus, shilling, shillings.

5214·2   *G/use.* (Through a letter, word or group of words.) The stroke or slash, signifying take out, delete, ignore, incorrect. (Between letters, words, etc.) separate, distinguish, begin a new line.

5214·3   *Math.* Divided by, replacing 5301·5 in fractions.

5214·4   *Meteor.* (Drawn parallel with the shaft of a Beaufort Scale symbol.) Cirrus cloud travelling with wind indicated. See 4968.

5214·5   *Print.* (Proof correction.) Finishing stroke, indicating the end of a marginal note. (Through a cap.) replace by l.c.

5214·6   *Punc.* The stroke, separating alternatives or words in apposition, and sometimes conveying both these meanings, thus signifying the word and, or. (Obs.) the virgule, comma; early form of hyphen to indicate the splitting of a word at the end of a line.

5215   /   *Sh., Pitman's.* (Thick) J.

5216   /   *Sh., Gregg's.* J; *Pitman's* (thin) CH.

5217   /   *Sh., Gregg's.* D.

5218   ╱   *Sh., Pitman's.* (Thin) R, terminal sound.

464

5219   /   *Sh.*, *Gregg's*. CH.

5220   ——   *Sh.*, *Pitman's*. (Thin.) Eq. 451.

TABLE 374

5225   /   *Sh.*, *Gregg's*. SH.

5226   /   *Sh.*, *Gregg's*. T.

5227†   /   *Sh.*, *Gregg's*. Diacritical mark lengthening a vowel.

5228†   /   *Cal.* Derivative.

5228·1   *Chem.* Monovalent.

5228·2   *Math.* Dash, used to distinguish an element from others of the same kind denoted by the same letter.

5229†   /   *Acc.* Acute. (Fr.) Placed over a vowel to sharpen the sound, or to indicate that a vowel which is normally mute should be sounded. (Cz.) placed over a vowel to lengthen it. (Gk.) raises the pitch of a vowel; see also under *Gk.* (Ir.) placed over a vowel to lengthen it. (Ital.) placed over a vowel to close it; also indicates stress. (Pol.) see under *Pol.* (Port. Sp.) stress; sometimes used to distinguish different words with the same spelling; see also under *Port.* and *Sp.* (Rus.) placed over a vowel to lengthen it.

465

5229·1		*Astron.* Minutes of arc.
5229·2		*Cal.* Derivative.
5229·3		*Com.* Foot, feet.
5229·4		*Gk.* Diacritical mark to indicate that a cardinal number is less than 1,000.
5229·5		*Math.* Minutes of arc. (Mensuration) foot or feet.
5229·6		*OE. MS.* Diacritical mark to indicate a long vowel.
5229·7		*Pol.* Diacritical mark modifying the pron. of o to u, s to a thin sibilation, z to a soft voiced hissing sound, c to ts and n to a very thin dental consonant.
5229·8		*Port.* Diacritical mark to denote the interrogative use of a word. See also under Acc.
5229·9		*Punc.* Eq. 3422·3.
5229·01		*Sp.* Diacritical mark to denote the interrogative use of a word. See also under Acc.
5230†	╱	*Mus.* (After a note.) Augmented.
5230·1		*Phon.* High rising tone or pitch.
5231†	╱	*Phon.* Low rising tone or pitch.

466

| 5232† | ✓ | *Gk.* Diacritical mark to indicate that the cardinal number following is to be multiplied by 1,000. |
| 5233† | ✓ | *Punc.* (Ger.) Eq. 3423·2. |

TABLE 375

5238		*High.* (L. Any colour. Ger. Austrian.) Level crossing 160 m. (175 yds) ahead.
5239	//	*Og.* Eq. Rom. G.
5240	//	*Ind. Num.* (3rd cent. B.C.) Eq. Arab. 2.
5241		*Mus.* (With a num. above.) Eq. 4378. (Across the stem of a note) repeat mark, repeat at semiquaver intervals.
5242	═	*Sh., Gregg's. Punc.* Dash.
5243	═	*Jap.* (Katakana syllabary.) Eq. Rom. NI (pron. nee). Cardinal number 4.
5244	=	*Sh., Gregg's. Punc.* Hyphen.
5245†	═	*Sh., Pitman's.* Initial capital letter.
5246	⫽	*Punc.* (Ger.) Gothic hyphen, eq. 5332·4.
5247†	//	*Chem.* Bivalent.

467

5247·1		*Math.* Dash-dash, eq. 5228·2.
5248†	\\	*Jap.* (Katakana syllabary.) Diacritical mark indicating a voiced sound.
5249†	//	*Punc.* (Ger.) Inverted commas, a quotation mark closing quoted matter.
5250†	//	*Punc.* (Ger.) Double commas, a quotation mark introducing quoted matter.
5251†	//	*Ger.* Cursive form of 6080·1.
5252†	//	*Astron.* Seconds of arc.
5252·1		*Com.* Inch or inches.
5252·2		*Math.* Seconds of arc. (Mensuration) inch or inches.

TABLE 376

5257		*High.* (L. White on black. Brit.) Hazard ahead.
5258		*High.* (L. Any colour. Ger. Austrian.) Level crossing 240 m. (262 yds) ahead.
5259		*Print.* (Proof correction.) Straighten crooked line or lines.
5260	///	*Og.* Eq. Rom. NG.

468

5261	/////	*Og.* Eq. Rom. Z.
5262	///	*Ind. Num.* (3rd cent. B.C.) Eq. Arab. 3.
5263	≃	*Jap.* (Katakana syllabary.) Eq. Rom. MI (pron. mee).
5264†	///	*Chem.* Trivalent.
5264·1		*Math.* Dash-dash-dash, eq. 5228·2.
5265†	///	*Math.* (Obs. Mensuration.) Line or lines.
5266†	////	*Chem.* Tetravalent.

TABLE 377

5271	/////	*Og.* Eq. Rom. R.
5272		*Her.* (Rep.) Vert, green.
5272·1		*Hyd.* (Rep.) Green.
5272·2		*Mil. Cart.* (Rep.) Built-up area.
5273		*Meteor. Aero.* (Rep.) Eq. 5182.
5274	//////////////	*Mil.* (Rep.) Abatis, abattis, barricade.
5275		*Meteor. Aero.* (Rep.) Eq. 5182.
5276		*Engn.* Nickel.

469

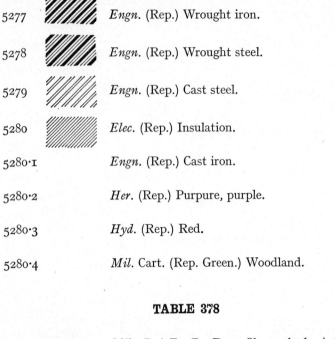

5277   *Engn.* (Rep.) Wrought iron.

5278   *Engn.* (Rep.) Wrought steel.

5279   *Engn.* (Rep.) Cast steel.

5280   *Elec.* (Rep.) Insulation.

5280·1   *Engn.* (Rep.) Cast iron.

5280·2   *Her.* (Rep.) Purpure, purple.

5280·3   *Hyd.* (Rep.) Red.

5280·4   *Mil.* Cart. (Rep. Green.) Woodland.

TABLE 378

5285   *Mil. R.A.F.* (L. Rep. Sleeve badge.) Flying officer.

5286   *Mil. R.A.F.* (L. Rep. Sleeve badge.) Pilot officer.

5287   *Chin.* Yang, the principle of stability, signifying the sun, light, warmth, goodness, male.

5287·1   *Punc.* Mark of ellipsis, indicating an omission.

5288†   *Bot.* (In floral formula.) Inferior position.

5288·1   *Math.* Vinculum, implying that the expression below it is to be treated as if enclosed in brackets.

470

5288·2   *Mus.* (Sol-fa notation.) Higher octave.

5289†   ————   *Bot.* (In floral formula.) Superior position.

5289·1   *G/use.* The underline, used for emphasis.

5289·2   *MS.* Emphasize; set in italics.

5289·3   *Mus.* (Sol-fa notation.) Lower octave.

5289·4   *Print.* (Proof correction.) Set in italics.

5290   ——   *Sh., Gregg's.* M; *Pitman's* (Thin) K.

5291   ————   *Cart.* (APO. Rep.) Rlwy.

5291·1   *Hyd.* (APO. Rep. Thin. Inter.) Road or trail of 3rd degree of importance; (thick) light rlwy., tramway.

5291·2   *Engn.* (APO. Rep. Fire protection.) Fire-resisting wall or partition. (USA. Heating) hot-water heating supply, low-pressure steam pipe. (Plumbing) soil, waste or leader, above grade.

5291·3   *Rlwy. Cart.* (APO. Rep. USA.) Street block or other property boundary line. (Between symbols for rails) ballast of earth. (Red) survey line.

5292   ————   *Cart.* (APO. Rep. Very thin. '1-inch' map. OS.) Contour line. See 100 and 144.

TABLE 379

5297   ————   *Engn.* (USA.) Weld to be flush with surface.

5298   ————   *Elec.* (Arch. plans. USA.) Branch circuit concealed in ceiling or wall.

5299   ————   *Chin. Num.* One, unity, eq. Arab. 1.

5300   ————   *Chem.* (APO. In structural formulae) convalent bond.

5300·1   *Chess.* Moves to.

5300·2   *Fr. Punc.* (At beginning of paragraph.) A quotation mark to introduce or indicate continuation of quoted matter. Also as under *Punc.*

5300·3   *Ind. Num.* (3rd cent. Hindu.) One. unity, eq. Arab. 1.

5300·4   *Mayan. Num.* Eq. Arab. 5.

5300·5   *Mus.* (Sol-fa notation.) Prolongation of note. (Between two letters standing for notes) a whole tone.

5300·6   *Punc.* Dash, inserted to mark a break in the continuity of thought, or in the construction of a sentence; a mark of suspense, omission; a substitute for a name or word it is not desired to print. (In pairs) marks of parenthesis.

5300·7   *Sh., Pitman's.* (Thin) K.

5300·8		*Tel.* (Morse code.) Eq. Rom. T; general answer. (Nav. fog signal) steam vessel under way.
5301	——	*Sh., Gregg's.* N; *Pitman's* (Thick) G.
5302	——	*Astron.* South.
5302·1		*Bot.* Absence of a particular feature.
5302·2		*Elec.* Negative charge; negative ion; negative pole; cathode; electron.
5302·3		*G/use.* Deficiency; absence; less. (In margin) note, pay attention, a mark of emphasis.
5302·4		*Mag.* Diamagnetic.
5302·5		*Math.* Minus, the subtraction sign, less. (First appeared in print, 1489; first used in math. by M. Stifel, 1544.) The line separating the numerator and denominator of fractions.
5302·6		*Meteor.* Barometer falling.
5302·7		*Nav.* South of the equator.
5302·8		*Opt.* Laevorotation.
5303†	——	*Acc.* Macron, indicating a long vowel.
5303·1		*Arab. & Egy.* A macron sometimes used when printing in Rom. characters to indicate that the sound is only approximately represented.

473

5303·2   *Chem.* Radical, radicle. (Obs. Over an atomic symbol) two atoms or their equivalent. (Over the initial letter of an acid) organic, of organic origin. (Berzelius, 1818.)

5303·3   *Crys.* (Over a figure in a Millerian index.) The face of the crystal cuts the axis indicated on its negative side.

5303·4   *Log.* Negation; without.

5303·5   *Math.* The bar, indicating a minus quantity. (Logarithms.) A minus characteristic. (Above a letter in MS.) vector; mean, average. (Above a final figure) approximate. (Higher arith.) conjugate. (Topology) the closure of a set. (Obsnt. Above a contraction, e.g. lim. or bd.) greatest limit, bound, etc.

5303·6   *MS.* Contraction.

5303·7   *Mus.* Moderate stress. (Used to extend the stave) ledger line.

5303·8   *Phar.* (Over the letter A.) Contraction for *alius atque alius*, 'now this, now that', meaning (take) of each.

5303·9   *Phys.* (Nuclear.) The 'bar', placed over the symbol for a particle to indicate its anti-particle.

5303·01   *Pros.* Long foot or syllable, eq. two moræ.

5303·02   *Rom. Num.* Multiplied by 1,000. (In MS., placed over Rom. num. following the letters HS or IIS) an indication that the *sestertium* is referred to, and not the *sestertius*.

5304†   ——   *Hyd.* (Beneath a num. relating to a rock or shoal.) Measured from the mean sea-level or datum on which the chart is based.

5304·1   *Math.* (Obsnt. Below a contraction, e.g., lim. or bd.) Lowest limit, bound, etc.

5304·2   *Mus.* Moderate stress. (Used to extend the stave above or below) ledger line.

TABLE 380

§ 1. *Thick Line of Even Width*

5308   *High.* (L. White. On road surface. Rep. Brit.) Keep to the left of the line, which may not be crossed for any purpose.

5309   *Mil.* (L. Rep. Sleeve badge. RAF.) Air commodore.

5310   *Rlwy. Cart.* (USA.) Ballast of broken stone.

5311   *Mil.* Transport on march.

5312 ━━━━ *Cart.* (APO. Rep. 'ɪ inch'-map. OS.) Double rlwy. track. (Red) ɪst class road. (Yellow) 2nd class road. (Blue) canal. (USA.) Rlwy.; (red) main road.

5312·ɪ *Elec.* (Arch. plans. USA.) Feeder.

5313 ━━ *Elec.* Section insulator, overhead line.

5314 ━ *Chin.* Eq. 5287. (Num.) eq. 5299.

5314·ɪ *Elec.* Direct current.

5315 ━ *Sh., Pitman's.* (Thick) G.

5316 ▬ *Mus.* (Below 4th line.) Semibreve rest, rest one measure. (Above 3rd line) minim rest.

5317 ▬ *Cart.* (Ant. OS.) Rom. burial.

5318 ─ *Sh., Pitman's.* (Thick) Long vowel, a(w), ō or ōō, according to position.

§ 2. *Thick Line of Uneven Width*

5324 *High.* (L. UNS., 1953.) Dip or sharp depression in road surface.

5325 *High.* (L. UNS., 1953.) Bump or sharp rise in road surface.

5326 *High.* (L. UNS., 1952.) Uneven road.

5327 *High.* (L. UNS., 1953.) Rough road.

5328   *Rlwy.* (Brit.) Automatic train control ramp.

5329   *Print.* Swelled rule, an ornamental line used in display sheets such as title-pages, bills, notices, advertisements, etc.

§ 3. *Very Short Lines*

5332   –   *Com.* Zero; none.

5332·1   *Com. Mon.* (On cheques. Brit.) Eq. 5986·1.

5332·2   *Meteor.* (After a stroke.) Height not reported.

5332·3   *Phon.* Retracted variety.

5332·4   *Punc.* The hyphen, used to join words to make compound words or phrases, to separate syllables, or to separate two vowels belonging to different syllables. (At the end of a line) an indication that a word has been broken but is completed in the following line.

5332·5   *Sh., Pitman's.* (Thin) U. (Thick) OH.

5333   –   *Sh., Pitman's.* (Thin) Short vowel, o(n), ŭ or ŏŏ, according to position. (Thick) ōō, long.

5334[†] –   *Sh., Pitman's.* (Thin) ŏ, short. (Thick) see 5318.

5334·1   *Phon.* High level tone or pitch.

5335†   –   *Phon.* Low level tone or pitch.

5335·1   *Phon.* Eq. 5332·3.

477

TABLE 381

5340   ———————— *High.* (L. White chalk.) Will offer shakedown for the night. (Tramps' 'smogger'.)

5341   ▬▬▬ *Mil.* (L. Rep. Sleeve badge. RAF.) Flight-lieutenant.

5342   ═ *Engn.* (Shipbuilding. With symbol for fillet weld.) Chain fillets.

5343   ═ *Engn.* (With pipe symbol running between component lines.) Sleeve joint.

5344   ═ *Chem.* (In structural formulae.) Double bond. (In equations) yields, forms.

5344·1   *Chess.* Is exchanged for, becomes.

5344·2   *Chin. Num.* Eq. Arab. 2.

5344·3   *Engn.* Backing strip weld.

5344·4   *Geom.* Is similar to.

5344·5   *G/use.* Equals; is the same as.

5344·6   *Ind. Num.* (3rd cent. Hindu.) Eq. Arab. 2.

5344·7   *Log.* Is identical with; equals.

5344·8   *Math.* Equals. (First used in math. by Robert Recorde, 1557.)

5344·9   *Mayan Num.* Eq. Arab. 20.

5344·01   *Meteor.* Mist; visibility from 1,100 yds. to 2,200 yds.

5344·02   *Print.* (Proof correction.) Parallel. (USA.) straighten line or lines.

5344·03   *Rlwy.* (USA. Locomotive formula.) Cylinders.

5345†   =   *Log.* Double negation.

5346 ========   *Cart.* (APO. Rep. OS.) 3rd class road. (Blue) canal. (USA.) Rlwy.

5346·1   *Engn.* (APO. Rep.) Pipe, piping.

5346·2   *Hyd.* (Inter.) Road or trail of 1st degree of importance.

5346·3   *Rlwy. Cart.* (APO. Rep. USA.) Ballast of burnt clay.

5347†   *G/use.* (Rep.) The double line, double rule, double underline, denoting strong emphasis.

5347·1   *Print.* (Proof correction.) Set in small caps.

TABLE 382

5351   *Mil.* (L. Rep. Sleeve badge. RAF.) Air vice-marshal.

5352   *Tel.* (In valve symbol.) Intermediate anode.

5353   *Chin. Num.* Eq. Arab. 2.

5354   *Chin.* Ying, the principle of the broken or infirm, signifying darkness, cold, changeableness, evil, female.

5354·1   *Pros.* Spondee.

5354·2   *Tel.* (Morse code) Eq. Rom. M. (Nav. fog signal) vessel under way having no way on.

5355   *Cart.* (APO. Rep. OS.) 1st class road. (USA. Red) dual road, carriage ways metalled and 7·5 m. (8·26 yds.) wide.

5356   *Cart.* (APO.) Rep. OS. 2nd class road.

TABLE 383

5361   *Mil.* (L. Rep. Sleeve badge. RAF.) Wing commander.

5362   *Chin.* The trigram, K'ien, 1st of the Eight Categories of Fate (Pa-kua), attributed to the legendary Emperor Fu Hsi (c. 2850 B.C.) signifying heaven, heavenly force.

5363   *Chem.* Is equivalent to. (In structural formulae) triple bond.

480

5363·1	*Chin. Num.* Eq. Arab. 3.
5363·2	*Geom.* Is congruent with, identical with.
5363·3	*Ind. Num.* (3rd cent. Hindu.) Eq. Arab. 3.
5363·4	*Log.* Is equivalent to; is symmetrical with. (USA.) if, and only if.
5363·5	*Math.* Congruent (Gauss). Is identical with, equivalent to.
5363·6	*Mayan Num.* Eq. Arab. 30.
5363·7	*Meteor.* Fog; visibility less than 1,100 yds.
5363·8	*Print.* (Proof correction.) Straighten crooked line or lines.
5364†	*Print.* (Rep. Proof correction.) Set in caps.

TABLE 384

5370	*Mil.* (L. Rep. Sleeve badge. RAF.) Air marshal.
5371	*Mil.* (L. Rep. Sleeve badge. RAF.) Squadron-leader.
5372	*Chin. Num.* Eq. Arab. 3.
5373	*Gk.* (Cap.) Xi, 14th letter of the a., eq. Rom. X.

5373·1   *Phys.* (Nuclear.) Xi particle, a hyperon.

5374   ≡   *Meteor.* Ground fog.

5375   ⹀   *Meteor.* Low fog.

5376   — — —   *Meteor.* Fractonimbus.

5376·1   *Pros.* Molossus.

5376·2   *Tel.* (Morse code.) Eq. Rom. O.

TABLE 385

§ 1. *Lines in Two Rows Only*

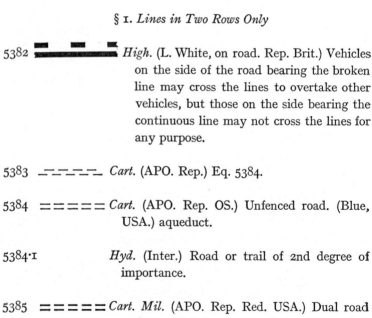

5382   *High.* (L. White, on road. Rep. Brit.) Vehicles on the side of the road bearing the broken line may cross the lines to overtake other vehicles, but those on the side bearing the continuous line may not cross the lines for any purpose.

5383   *Cart.* (APO. Rep.) Eq. 5384.

5384   *Cart.* (APO. Rep. OS.) Unfenced road. (Blue, USA.) aqueduct.

5384·1   *Hyd.* (Inter.) Road or trail of 2nd degree of importance.

5385   *Cart. Mil.* (APO. Rep. Red. USA.) Dual road under construction.

482

5386   ==== *Hyd.* (Inter.) Leader cable.

5387   ‒ ‒ ‒_ _ _ *Rlwy. Cart.* (APO. Rep. USA.) Ballast of granulated slag.

5388   ⁻⁻⁻⁻⁻⁻⁻ *Rlwy. Cart.* (APO. Rep. USA.) Ballast of scrunnings.

§ 2. *Lines in Three Rows Only*

5391   *Chin.* The trigram, Toui, 2nd of the Eight Categories of Fate (Pa-kua), attributed to the legendary Emperor Fu Hsi (*c.* 2850 B.C.) signifying steam, mist.

5392   *Chin.* The trigram, Li, 3rd of the Eight Categories of Fate (Pa-kua), attributed to the legendary Emperor Fu Hsi (*c.* 2850 B.C.), signifying heat.

5393   *Chin.* The trigram, Tchen, 4th of the Eight Categories of Fate (Pa-kua), attributed to the legendary Emperor Fu Hsi (*c.* 2850 B.C.), signifying thunder.

5394   *Chin.* The trigram, Suen, 5th of the Eight Categories of Fate (Pa-kua), attributed to the legendary Emperor Fu Hsi (*c.* 2850 B.C.), signifying wind.

5395   *Chin.* The trigram, Khan, 6th of the Eight Categories of Fate (Pa-kua), attributed to the legendary Emperor Fu Hsi (*c.* 2850 B.C.), signifying water.

483

5396   — — *Chin.* The trigram, Kan, 7th of the Eight Categories of Fate (Pa-kua), attributed to the legendary Emperor Fu Hsi (*c.* 2850 B.C.), signifying mountains.

5397   ≡ ≡ *Chin.* The trigram, K'ouen, 8th of the Eight Categories of Fate (Pa-kua), attributed to the legendary Emperor Fu Hsi (*c.* 2850 B.C.), signifying earth, earthly force.

5398   ≡ *Meteor.* Fog, sky discernible; shallow fog.

5399   ≡ *Meteor.* Wet fog.

§ 3. *All Other Signs*

5401   ▌ ▌ ▌ *High.* (L. White on black or dark road-surfacing, across road. Rep. Brit.) 'Zebra crossing', giving priority over vehicular traffic to pedestrians wishing to cross the road.

5402   *Mil.* (L. Rep. Sleeve badge. RAF.) Marshal of the Royal Air Force.

5403   *Mil.* (L. Rep. Sleeve badge. RAF.) Group captain.

5404   *Mil.* (L. Rep. Sleeve badge. RAF.) Air chief marshal.

5405   *Mus.* (Rep.) The Great Stave, Staff, a set of eleven lines (and ten spaces) on which marks can be made to indicate all the notes through three octaves.

484

5406 *Mus.* (Rep.) Stave, staff, in which five lines (and four spaces) selected from the Great Stave provide for the specific indication of notes within a limited range.

5407 *Her.* (Rep.) Azure, blue.

5407·1 *Hyd.* (Rep. Red.) Blue.

5407·2 *Soil/m. Geol.* (Rep.) Clay.

5408 *Cart.* (Rep.) Eq. 5863.

5408·1 *Geol.* (Rep.) Shale.

5409 *Engn.* (Rep.) Stone.

5410 *Rlwy.* Cart. (Rep. USA.) Tidal flat.

TABLE 386

§ 1. *All Parts of Equal Length*

5415 *High.* (L. White, on road. Rep. Brit.) Keep to the left of the line except for the purpose of overtaking another vehicle.

5416 *Hyd.* (APO. Rep. Fine lines each 12 mm. long. Inter.) Maritime limits in general; co-tidal lines; line of turn of currents; reserved area.

485

5417 ——— ——— ——— *Engn.* (APO. Rep. Heating. USA.) Boiler blow-off pipe.

5418 —— —— —— —— *Engn.* (APO. Rep. Heating. USA.) Hot-water heating return pipe; low pressure return pipe. (Plumbing) soil, waste or leader pipe, below grade.

5419 ——— ——— ——— *Cart.* (APO. Rep. '25-inch' map. OS.) County boundary.

5420 — — — — *Rlwy. Cart.* (APO. Rep. USA.) Township property line not fenced.

5421 — — — — — *Tel.* (Morse code.) Zero, cipher, nought, none. (Obs.) CH.

5422 - - - - - *Cart.* (APO. Rep. '25-inch' map. OS.) Urban district boundary.

5423 - - - - - *Engn.* (Plumbing. USA.) Vent pipe.

5424 — — — — *Cart.* (APO. Rep. Thick. '1-inch' and '6-inch' maps. OS.) County boundary.

5425 - - - - - *Engn.* (APO. Rep. Fire protection.) Combustible wall or partition.

5425·1 *G/use.* The broken or 'pecked' line, incorrectly called a 'deckle', eq. 6167·2.

5426 - - - - - - *Elec.* (APO. Rep. Arch. plans. USA.) Branch circuit exposed.

486

5427   – – – – – –   *Cart.* (APO. Rep.) Footpath, bridle path; eq. 5035.

5427·1   *Hyd.* (APO. Rep. Inter.) Road or trail of 4th degree of importance.

5427·2   *Tel.* Jumper.

5428   – – – – – – – –   *Chem.* (In structural formulae.) Hydrogen bond.

5428·1   *Hyd.* (APO. Rep. Inter.) 5-metre line; (on land) track or footpath.

5429   – – –   – – –   – – –   *Hyd.* (APO. Rep. Inter.) 6-fathom or 15-metre line.

5430   – – – –   *Tel.* (APO. In valve diagrams.) Grid.

§ 2. *Parts of Unequal Length*

5435   ▬ ▬ ▬   *Rlwy.* Cart. (APO. Rep. Thick. USA.) State boundary line.

5436   ▬ – ▬   *Engn.* (APO. Rep. Heating. USA.) Air-relief line.

5436·1   *Rlwy.* Cart. (APO. Rep. Thin. USA.) County boundary line; city or village boundary line.

5437   ——– - ——– -   *Engn.* (APO. Rep. Heating and air conditioning. USA.) Make-up water pipe. (Plumbing) cold-water pipe, drinking-water flow pipe.

5438   —– - —– - —–   *Elec.* (APO. Rep. Arch. plans. USA.) Branch circuit concealed in floor.

487

5438·1   *Engn.* (APO. Rep. Fire protection.) Incombustible but fire susceptible wall or partition.

5439 ————————— *Hyd.* (APO. Rep. Inter.) 50-metre line.

5440 ———— ——— *Rlwy.* Cart. (APO. Rep. USA.) Company property right-of-way line.

5441 ———————— *Engn.* (APO. Rep. Plumbing. USA.) Drinking-water return pipe; hot-water pipe.

5442 ——— ——— —— *Rlwy.* (APO. Rep. USA.) Refrigerant supply pipe line.

5442·1   *Engn.* (APO. Rep. Plumbing. USA.) hot-water return pipe.

5443 ——— ———— —— *Rlwy.* (APO. Rep. USA.) Oil supply pipe line.

Cl.II, Ord.I, Fam.III, Gen.II

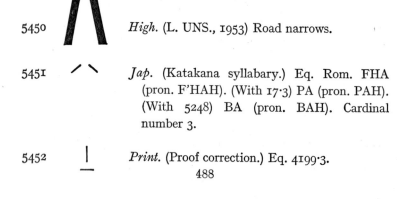

TABLE 387

5450   *High.* (L. UNS., 1953) Road narrows.

5451   *Jap.* (Katakana syllabary.) Eq. Rom. FHA (pron. F'HAH). (With 17·3) PA (pron. PAH). (With 5248) BA (pron. BAH). Cardinal number 3.

5452   *Print.* (Proof correction.) Eq. 4199·3.

5453		*Geom.* Eq. 4278.
5454		*Cart.* (Du.) Rock.
5455		*Rlwy. Cart.* (USA.) Evergreen tree.
5456		*Tel.* (In valve diagrams) Screen grid.
5457		*Tel.* Screen.
5458		*Cart.* Eq. 5469.
5459		*Cart.* (Rep. '6-inch' map. OS.) Osiers.
5460		*Soil/m.* Peat.
5461		*Cart.* (Rep. '6-inch' map. OS.) Furze, gorse.

TABLE 388

5466		*High.* (L. Brit. Obsnt.) Tram pinch.
5467		*Com. Mon.* (Obs.) Shilling or shillings.
5467·1		*Meteor.* Height not reported.
5468		*Tel.* (In valve diagrams.) Screen grid.
5469		*Cart.* (APO. '6-inch' map. OS.) Quarry, clay pit.

489

5470  *Cart.* (APO. Rep.) Hachures, a form of shading used to show the relief of the land, the length, thickness and number of the lines, which are drawn at right-angles to the contours, indicating the gradient.

5471  *Geol.* (Rep.) Intrusive igneous rock.

Cl.II, Ord.II, Fam.I, Gen.I

TABLE 389

5475 *High.* (L. Red triangle. Dan.) Priority ends.

5476 *Afr.* (Cameroons.) Ideograph signifying a fly.

5476·1 *Cart.* (Inter.) Trigonometrical point, station.

5476·2 *Meteor.* (USA.) Frozen raindrops; grains of ice.

5477 *Alch.* Lead.

5478 *Meteor.* Rain showers.

5479 *Mus.* Acciaccatura, short appoggiatura, a grace-note, the 'crushing-note', a quaver of small size placed before a note and 'crushed in' without provision for time, as an introductory flourish.

490

5480		*Meteor.* Showers of sleet.
5481		*Cart.* (Rep. Du.) Rubber plantation.
5482		*Cart.* (Ant. OS.) Rom. bath-house; probable Rom. villa.
5483		*Alch.* Philosopher's sulphur. (*A Compleat Body of Chymistry,* 17th cent.)
5484		*Mil.* Armoured car.

TABLE 390

5490		*High.* (L. White and black, across road. Rep. Obs. Brit.) Proposed 'panda crossing', giving priority to pedestrians wishing to cross the road for a period indicated by an electric signal operated by the pedestrians.
5491		*Engn.* (USA.) Globe valve.
5492		*Elec.* (Arch. plans. USA.) City fire alarms station.
5493		*Engn.* (USA.) Snap-action valve.
5494		*Mil.* Cavalry unit.
5495		*Rlwy.* (L. Brit.) Visual road crossing signal warning board.

491

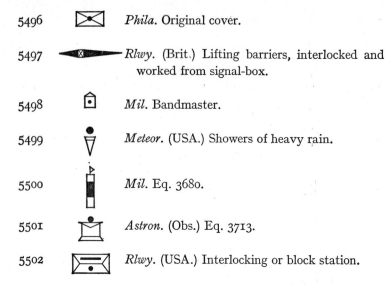

5496   *Phila.* Original cover.

5497   *Rlwy.* (Brit.) Lifting barriers, interlocked and worked from signal-box.

5498   *Mil.* Bandmaster.

5499   *Meteor.* (USA.) Showers of heavy rain.

5500   *Mil.* Eq. 3680.

5501   *Astron.* (Obs.) Eq. 3713.

5502   *Rlwy.* (USA.) Interlocking or block station.

Cl.II, Ord.II, Fam.I, Gen.II

TABLE 391

5507   *Engn.* (Fire protection.) Police headquarters.

5508   *Elec.* (Arch. plans. USA.) Push-button.

5509   *Alch.* Urine. (*A Compleat Body of Chymistry,* 17th cent.)

5509·1   *Meteor.* Ground wet.

5510   *Mil.* Vehicle driver. (Infantry) runner.

5511   *Alch.* Sulphur.

492

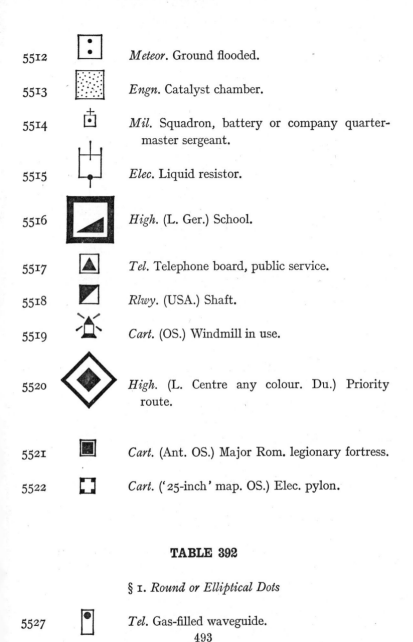

5512   *Meteor*. Ground flooded.

5513   *Engn*. Catalyst chamber.

5514   *Mil*. Squadron, battery or company quarter-master sergeant.

5515   *Elec*. Liquid resistor.

5516   *High*. (L. Ger.) School.

5517   *Tel*. Telephone board, public service.

5518   *Rlwy*. (USA.) Shaft.

5519   *Cart*. (OS.) Windmill in use.

5520   *High*. (L. Centre any colour. Du.) Priority route.

5521   *Cart*. (Ant. OS.) Major Rom. legionary fortress.

5522   *Cart*. ('25-inch' map. OS.) Elec. pylon.

TABLE 392

§ 1. *Round or Elliptical Dots*

5527   *Tel*. Gas-filled waveguide.

493

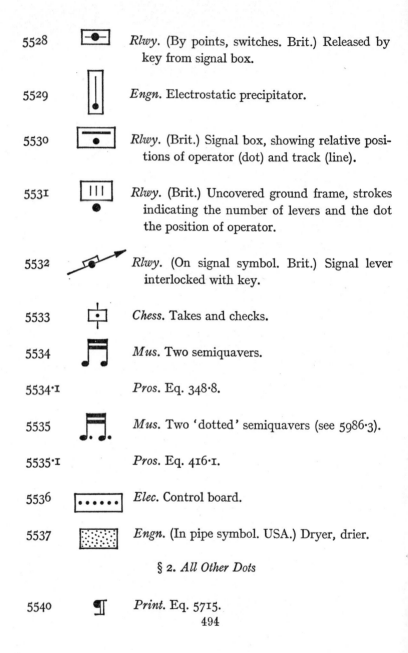

5528   *Rlwy.* (By points, switches. Brit.) Released by key from signal box.

5529   *Engn.* Electrostatic precipitator.

5530   *Rlwy.* (Brit.) Signal box, showing relative positions of operator (dot) and track (line).

5531   *Rlwy.* (Brit.) Uncovered ground frame, strokes indicating the number of levers and the dot the position of operator.

5532   *Rlwy.* (On signal symbol. Brit.) Signal lever interlocked with key.

5533   *Chess.* Takes and checks.

5534   *Mus.* Two semiquavers.

5534·1   *Pros.* Eq. 348·8.

5535   *Mus.* Two 'dotted' semiquavers (see 5986·3).

5535·1   *Pros.* Eq. 416·1.

5536   *Elec.* Control board.

5537   *Engn.* (In pipe symbol. USA.) Dryer, drier.

§ 2. *All Other Dots*

5540   *Print.* Eq. 5715.

494

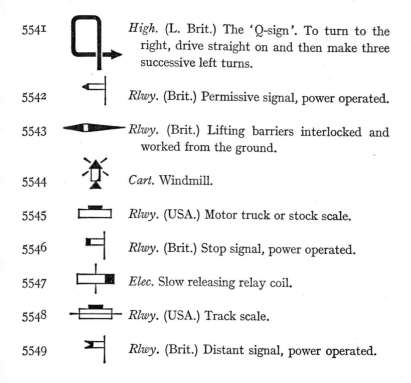

5541		*High*. (L. Brit.) The 'Q-sign'. To turn to the right, drive straight on and then make three successive left turns.
5542		*Rlwy*. (Brit.) Permissive signal, power operated.
5543		*Rlwy*. (Brit.) Lifting barriers interlocked and worked from the ground.
5544		*Cart*. Windmill.
5545		*Rlwy*. (USA.) Motor truck or stock scale.
5546		*Rlwy*. (Brit.) Stop signal, power operated.
5547		*Elec*. Slow releasing relay coil.
5548		*Rlwy*. (USA.) Track scale.
5549		*Rlwy*. (Brit.) Distant signal, power operated.

TABLE 393

§ 1. *Round or Triangular Dots*

5555		*Engn*. Air release valve.
5556		*Engn*. Power-operated valve.
5557		*Elec*. Pantograph collector.
5558		*Rlwy*. (USA.) Drawbridge rail lock.

495

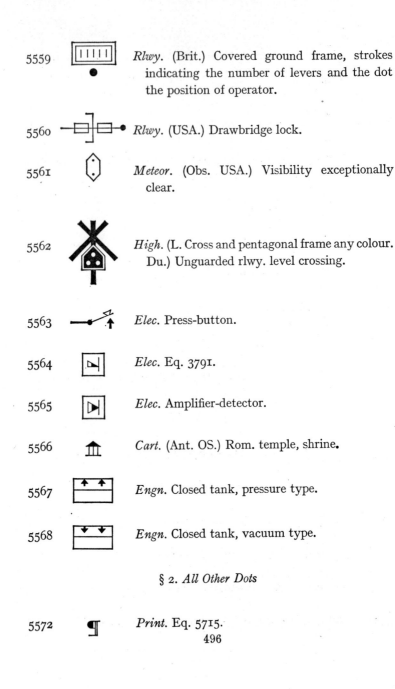

5559   *Rlwy.* (Brit.) Covered ground frame, strokes indicating the number of levers and the dot the position of operator.

5560   *Rlwy.* (USA.) Drawbridge lock.

5561   *Meteor.* (Obs. USA.) Visibility exceptionally clear.

5562   *High.* (L. Cross and pentagonal frame any colour. Du.) Unguarded rlwy. level crossing.

5563   *Elec.* Press-button.

5564   *Elec.* Eq. 3791.

5565   *Elec.* Amplifier-detector.

5566   *Cart.* (Ant. OS.) Rom. temple, shrine.

5567   *Engn.* Closed tank, pressure type.

5568   *Engn.* Closed tank, vacuum type.

§ 2. *All Other Dots*

5572   *Print.* Eq. 5715.

496

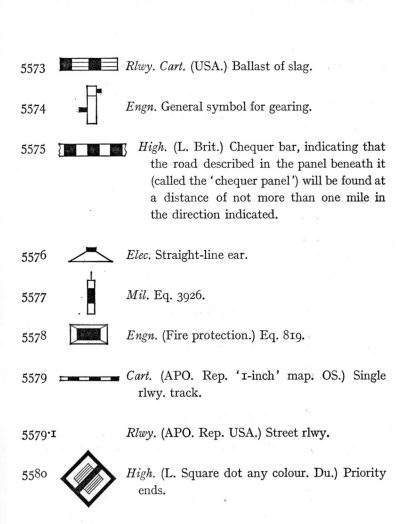

5573   *Rlwy. Cart.* (USA.) Ballast of slag.

5574   *Engn.* General symbol for gearing.

5575   *High.* (L. Brit.) Chequer bar, indicating that the road described in the panel beneath it (called the 'chequer panel') will be found at a distance of not more than one mile in the direction indicated.

5576   *Elec.* Straight-line ear.

5577   *Mil.* Eq. 3926.

5578   *Engn.* (Fire protection.) Eq. 819.

5579   *Cart.* (APO. Rep. '1-inch' map. OS.) Single rlwy. track.

5579·1   *Rlwy.* (APO. Rep. USA.) Street rlwy.

5580   *High.* (L. Square dot any colour. Du.) Priority ends.

5581   *Cart.* (Ant. OS.) Rom. pot.

5582   *High.* (L. Red on white bar and post support. Rep. Brit.) Half-barrier level crossing, forbidding road traffic to cross railway line unless bar is lifted.

497

TABLE 394

5587		*Jap.* Eq. 5263.
5588		*Meteor.* Sleet.
5589		*Cart.* Golf course.
5590		*Rel.* Ind. Eq. 4521·1.

TABLE 395

5595		*Engn.* Open drain.
5596		*Mil.* Trench mortar.
5597		*Elec.* Thermostat.
5598		*Mus.* Quaver. The thick line is termed the 'hook'.
5599		*Mus.* Appoggiatura, a grace-note, the 'leaning note', a quaver of small size placed before a note on which it is said to 'lean', distinguished from the acciaccatura by sharing the time of the principal note.
5600		*Mus.* Eq. 5598.
5601		*Mus.* Eq. 5599.

498

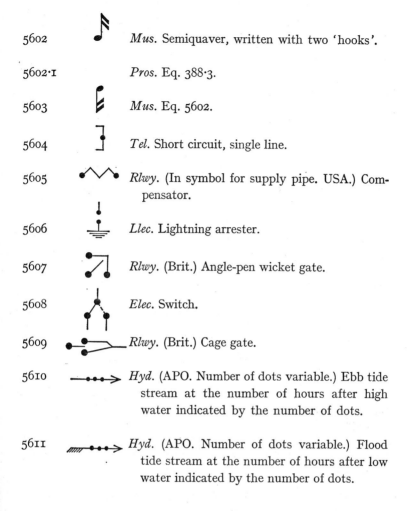

5602		*Mus.* Semiquaver, written with two 'hooks'.
5602·1		*Pros.* Eq. 388·3.
5603		*Mus.* Eq. 5602.
5604		*Tel.* Short circuit, single line.
5605		*Rlwy.* (In symbol for supply pipe. USA.) Compensator.
5606		*Llec.* Lightning arrester.
5607		*Rlwy.* (Brit.) Angle-pen wicket gate.
5608		*Elec.* Switch.
5609		*Rlwy.* (Brit.) Cage gate.
5610		*Hyd.* (APO. Number of dots variable.) Ebb tide stream at the number of hours after high water indicated by the number of dots.
5611		*Hyd.* (APO. Number of dots variable.) Flood tide stream at the number of hours after low water indicated by the number of dots.

TABLE 396

§ 1. *Not More Than Four Lines*

| 5616 | | *Mil.* Commanding officer. |

499

5617	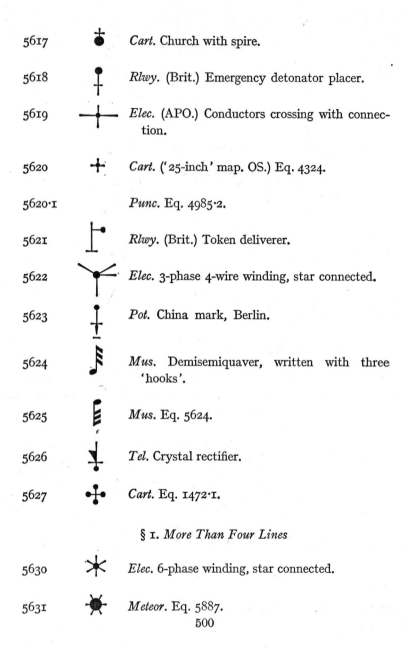	*Cart.* Church with spire.
5618		*Rlwy.* (Brit.) Emergency detonator placer.
5619		*Elec.* (APO.) Conductors crossing with connection.
5620		*Cart.* ('25-inch' map. OS.) Eq. 4324.
5620·1		*Punc.* Eq. 4985·2.
5621		*Rlwy.* (Brit.) Token deliverer.
5622		*Elec.* 3-phase 4-wire winding, star connected.
5623		*Pot.* China mark, Berlin.
5624		*Mus.* Demisemiquaver, written with three 'hooks'.
5625		*Mus.* Eq. 5624.
5626		*Tel.* Crystal rectifier.
5627		*Cart.* Eq. 1472·1.

§ 1. *More Than Four Lines*

| 5630 | | *Elec.* 6-phase winding, star connected. |
| 5631 | | *Meteor.* Eq. 5887. |

5632	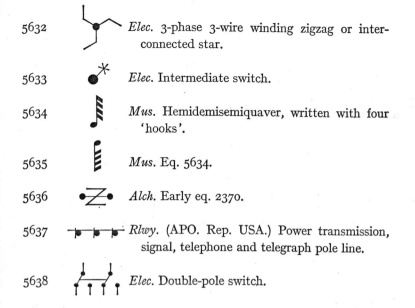	*Elec.* 3-phase 3-wire winding zigzag or inter-connected star.
5633		*Elec.* Intermediate switch.
5634		*Mus.* Hemidemisemiquaver, written with four 'hooks'.
5635		*Mus.* Eq. 5634.
5636		*Alch.* Early eq. 2370.
5637		*Rlwy.* (APO. Rep. USA.) Power transmission, signal, telephone and telegraph pole line.
5638		*Elec.* Double-pole switch.

TABLE 397

5643		*Pot.* China mark, Strasbourg, mark of the Hannong family.
5644	E!	*Log.* The following (adjacent) term exists.
5645		*Ger.* (l.c.) Cursive form of 2641.
5646		*Math.* Direct sum.
5647	ɨ	*Phon.* 'Crossed-i'. Close central vowel, as Rus. yu, 1633.

501

| 5648† | Ȧ | *Pros.* Pause of two moræ. |

| 5649† | ⋏ | *Print.* (Proof correction, esp, in math.) Insert thin space, of 3 units. |

TABLE 398

| 5654 | Ë | *Rus.* (Cap.) Modified yeh, 6th letter of the a., eq. Rom. yō (short). See 4385·6. |

| 5655 | | *Alch.* Distilled vinegar. (*A Compleat Body of Chymistry*, 17th cent.) |

| 5655·1 | | *Hyd.* (Inter.) Rock awash at low tide or mean water level. (Obs.) eq. 4325. |

| 5656 | ※ | *Alch.* Eq. 5655. |

| 5656·1 | | *Mus.* Presa, indicating where a vocal part takes up a theme. |

| 5656·2 | | *Punc.* Eq. 4986. |

| 5657 | | *Hyd.* Eq. 4325, but with limiting danger line. (Inter.) a rock of small area covered by less than 10 metres of water at low tide. |

| 5658 | | *Hyd.* (APO. Inter.) Submerged wreck dangerous to shipping, exact depth unknown. |

| 5659 | | *Engn.* Sand filter. |

502

5660 ⋎⋯⋎⋅ *Cart.* (APO. Rep. '6-inch' map. OS.) Rural district boundary.

5661 ⤬⋯⤬⋅ *Cart.* (APO. Rep. Obs. '6-inch' map. OS.) Poor Law Union boundary.

5662 ⋅⋅+⋅—⋅+⋅ *Cart.* (APO. Rep. OS). National boundary.

5663 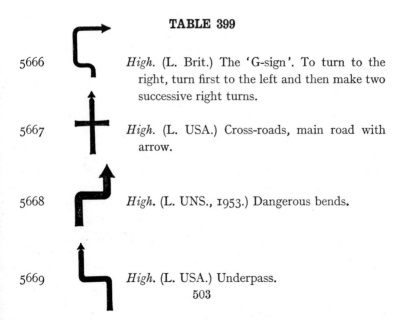 *Soil/m.* (Rep.) Silty sand.

5664 *Soil/m.* (Rep.) Loam.

Cl.II, Ord.II, Fam.II, Gen.II

TABLE 399

5666 *High.* (L. Brit.) The 'G-sign'. To turn to the right, turn first to the left and then make two successive right turns.

5667 *High.* (L. USA.) Cross-roads, main road with arrow.

5668 *High.* (L. UNS., 1953.) Dangerous bends.

5669 *High.* (L. USA.) Underpass.

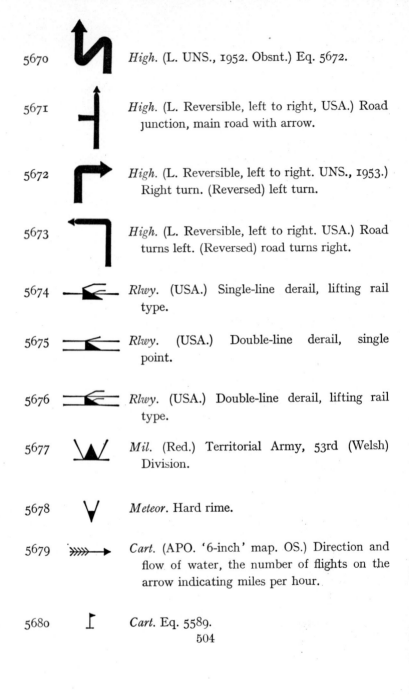

5670 *High.* (L. UNS., 1952. Obsnt.) Eq. 5672.

5671 *High.* (L. Reversible, left to right, USA.) Road junction, main road with arrow.

5672 *High.* (L. Reversible, left to right. UNS., 1953.) Right turn. (Reversed) left turn.

5673 *High.* (L. Reversible, left to right. USA.) Road turns left. (Reversed) road turns right.

5674 *Rlwy.* (USA.) Single-line derail, lifting rail type.

5675 *Rlwy.* (USA.) Double-line derail, single point.

5676 *Rlwy.* (USA.) Double-line derail, lifting rail type.

5677 *Mil.* (Red.) Territorial Army, 53rd (Welsh) Division.

5678 *Meteor.* Hard rime.

5679 *Cart.* (APO. '6-inch' map. OS.) Direction and flow of water, the number of flights on the arrow indicating miles per hour.

5680 *Cart.* Eq. 5589.

504

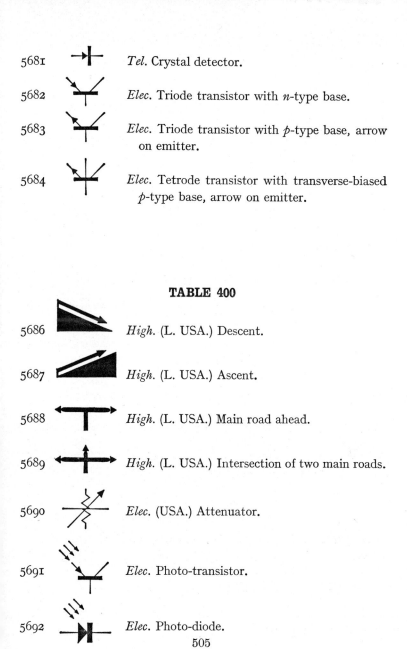

5681   *Tel.* Crystal detector.

5682   *Elec.* Triode transistor with *n*-type base.

5683   *Elec.* Triode transistor with *p*-type base, arrow
        on emitter.

5684   *Elec.* Tetrode transistor with transverse-biased
        p-type base, arrow on emitter.

TABLE 400

5686   *High.* (L. USA.) Descent.

5687   *High.* (L. USA.) Ascent.

5688   *High.* (L. USA.) Main road ahead.

5689   *High.* (L. USA.) Intersection of two main roads.

5690   *Elec.* (USA.) Attenuator.

5691   *Elec.* Photo-transistor.

5692   *Elec.* Photo-diode.

505

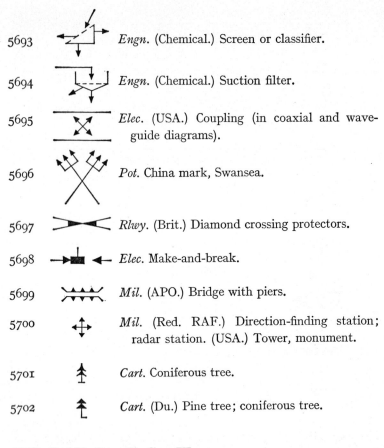

5693 *Engn.* (Chemical.) Screen or classifier.

5694 *Engn.* (Chemical.) Suction filter.

5695 *Elec.* (USA.) Coupling (in coaxial and wave-guide diagrams).

5696 *Pot.* China mark, Swansea.

5697 *Rlwy.* (Brit.) Diamond crossing protectors.

5698 *Elec.* Make-and-break.

5699 *Mil.* (APO.) Bridge with piers.

5700 *Mil.* (Red. RAF.) Direction-finding station; radar station. (USA.) Tower, monument.

5701 *Cart.* Coniferous tree.

5702 *Cart.* (Du.) Pine tree; coniferous tree.

Cl.II, Ord.II, Fam.II, Gen.III

TABLE 401

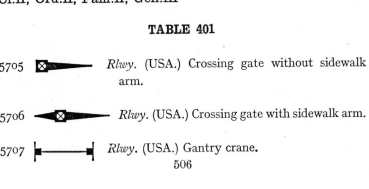

5705 *Rlwy.* (USA.) Crossing gate without sidewalk arm.

5706 *Rlwy.* (USA.) Crossing gate with sidewalk arm.

5707 *Rlwy.* (USA.) Gantry crane.

5708	⸮	*Punc.* (Obs.) Note of interrogation. ('Breeches Bible', 17th cent.)
5709	ꞇ	*Rom.* (l.c.) 'Old English' r.
5710	⛪	*Cart.* Church with tower.
5711	⊢⊤⊤⊤⊤⊤⊤⊤	*Rlwy.* (APO. Rep. USA.) Picket fence.

TABLE 402

5715	¶	*Print.* Pilcrow, blind P, paragraph; a mark of reference. (Proof correction) new paragraph. (In Bible) mark to direct the eye to matters mentioned in the chapter-headings of the Authorized Version, but often reprinted in editions which exclude the chapter-headings.
5716	ℙ	*Print.* Eq. 5715.
5717	⌂	*Cart.* (Ant. OS.) Rom. farm or similar site.
5718	⎍	*Elec.* Bell connected to fire alarm.
5719	⊐	*Jap.* Eq. 4387.
5720	⚒	*Hyd.* (Inter.) Mine, quarry.
5721	⚔	*Elec.* Arc.
5722	⚘	*Alch.* Eq. 3884.

5723	�	*Mus.* Eq. 4364.
5724	✳	*Hyd.* Position of light.
5725	❁	*Punc.* Eq. 4986.
5726	❋	*Mus.* Pedal release mark; release loud pedal.
5727	⚠	*Cart.* (Obs.) Windmill.

Cl.II, Ord.II, Fam.III, Gen.I

TABLE 403

5731	❗	*High.* (L. In red triangle. Brit., 1964.) Unspecified temporary danger ahead.
5732	Y⟩	*Ass. Math.* Sign of subtraction.
5733	Y⟩	*Ass. Num.* Eq. Arab. 100.
5734	!	*Bot.* Mark of authenticity; certainty of descriptive statement.
5734·1		*Chess.* Good move.
5734·2		*Log.* See 5644.
5734·3		*Math.* Factorial.

508

5734·4		*Punc.* Note of exclamation, 'screamer', expressing emotion, esp. surprise or admiration; mark of emphasis; mark of address, used after a name or phrase in the vocative case.
5735	i	*Punc.* (Sp.) Note of exclamation introducing a passage to be closed by 5734·4.
5736	j	*Ger.* (l.c.) 10th letter of the a., eq. Rom. j.
5737	i	*Math.* Eq. 2647·6.
5737·1		*Phon.* Close front vowel, ee as in eel.
5737·2		*Rom.* (l.c.) 9th letter of the a. (*ITA*) i as in ink.
5737·3		*Rus.* (l.c. Obs.) 'Ee with a dot', the old 10th letter of the a., eq. Rom. e (long).

TABLE 404

5742		*Rlwy.* (USA.) Farm gate.
5743		*Punc.* 'Old English', 'Black Letter', semicolon, eq. 3450. *Cf.* 3451·1.
5744		*Jap.* (Katakana syllabary.) Eq. Rom. UN.
5745		*Punc.* It. Eq. 5734·4.
5746		*Punc.* It. (Sp.) Eq. 5735.

| 5747 | i | *Rom.* (l.c.) Sanserif form of 5737·2. |

| 5748 | — • | *Tel.* (Morse code.) Eq. Rom. N. |

| 5749 | • — | *Tel.* (Morse code.) Eq. Rom. A. |

| 5750[†] | | *Hyd.* (Over a num. Inter.) No bottom found at depth indicated. |

| 5751[†] | | *Mus.* (Over a note.) Mezzo-staccato; portamento. |

| 5752† | | *Mus.* (Under a note.) Mezzo-staccato; portamento. |

TABLE 405

| 5756 | | *Ass. Num.* Eq. Arab. 1,000 (*Math.*) sign of division. |

| 5757 | | *Cal.* Approaches the limit. |

| 5758 | —● ● ●— | *Elec.* (USA.) Multigap arrester. |

| 5759 | — • — | *Tel.* (Morse code.) Eq. Rom. K; carry on. (*Num.*) check for O (nought). |

| 5760 | • — — | *Tel.* (Morse code.) Eq. Rom. W; light required. (Nav. fog signal) I require medical assistance. |

| 5761 | — — • | *Tel.* (Morse code.) Eq. Rom. G. |

TABLE 406

5766	☰•	*Meteor.* Rain and fog.
5767	╪	*Punc.* Eq. 4986.
5768	☀	*Punc.* Eq. 4986.
5769	.— — —	*Tel.* (Morse code.) Eq. Rom. J.
5770	— — —.	*Tel.* (Morse code. Obs.) Eq. diphthong Œ.
5771	— —.—	*Tel.* (Morse code.) Eq. Rom. Q; wait a minute.
5772	.— — —	*Tel.* (Morse code.) Eq. Rom. Y.
5773	.— — — —	*Tel. Num.* (Morse code.) Eq. Arab. 1.
5774	— — — —.	*Tel. Num.* (Morse code.) Eq. Arab. 9.

TABLE 407

5778	≡	*Alch.* Iron.
5779	∶/	*Jap.* (Katakana syllabary.) Eq. Rom. SHI (pron. she). (With 5248) ZHI (pron. zhee).
5780	•／•	*Mus.* Repeat as many times as this sign is repeated.
5781	•⸬•	*Mus.* Repeat at quaver intervals, eq. 5212 (more usual).

511

5782	÷	*Math.* The sign of division; divided by. (First used by John Pell *c.* 1630, and by Rahn, 1659.)
5783	•|•	*Bot.* Zygomorphic.
5784	—:	*Math.* (Obs.) difference between; excess over.
5785	:—	*Punc.* Colon-dash; as follows.
5786	•• —	*Tel.* (Morse code.) Eq. Rom. U. (Nav. fog signal) you are standing into danger.
5787	— ••	*Tel.* (Morse code.) Eq. Rom. D. (Nav. fog signal) vessel towing or not under control.
5788	• — •	*Tel.* (Morse code). Eq. Rom. R; message received. (Nav. fog signal) you may feel your way past me.
5789†	˸˴	*Acc.* (Gk.) Diaeresis-grave, a combination of 6080·2 and 5203.
5790†	˸ʹ	*Acc.* (Gk.) Diaeresis-acute, a combination of 6080·2 and 5229.

TABLE 408

5797	≑	*Math.* Eq. 5798.
5798	≒	*Math.* Is approximately equal to.
5799	≓	*Log.* Is equivalent to.

5800	:‖	*Mus.* Eq. 5815.
5801	‖:	*Mus.* Eq. 5816.
5802	— •• —	*Tel.* (Morse code.) Eq. Rom. X.
5803	• — — •	*Tel.* (Morse code.) Eq. Rom. P.
5804	• — • —	*Tel.* (Morse code. Obs.) Eq. diphthong Æ.
5805	— • — •	*Tel.* (Morse code.) Eq. Rom. C; correct.
5806	•• — —	*Tel.* (Morse code, obs.) Eq. Rom. UE.
5807	— — ••	*Tel.* (Morse code.) Eq. Rom. Z.
5808	•• — — —	*Tel. Num.* (Morse code.) Eq. Arab. 2.
5809	— — — ••	*Tel. Num.* (Morse code.) Eq. Arab. 8.

TABLE 409

5812	═:	*Meteor.* (USA.) Wet fog.
5813	∷	*Math.* Geometrical proportion.
5814	:—:	*Math.* Eq. 5813.
5815	:‖	*Mus.* Repeat mark, indicating end of passage to be repeated.
5816	‖:	*Mus.* Repeat mark, indicating beginning of passage to be repeated.

5817   *Her.* (Rep.) Ermine.

5818   ● ● ● —   *Tel.* (Morse code.) Eq. Rom. V; address from. (Nav. fog signal) I require assistance.

5819   ● ● ● — —   *Tel. Num.* (Morse code.) Eq. Arab. 3.

5820   — ● ● ●   *Tel.* (Morse code.) Eq. Rom. B.

5821   — — ● ● ●   *Tel. Num.* (Morse code.) Eq. Arab. 7.

5822   ● ● — ●   *Tel.* (Morse code.) Eq. Rom. F.

5823   ● — ● ●   *Tel.* (Morse code.) Eq. Rom. L.

5824   ● ● ● ● —   *Tel. Num.* (Morse code.) Eq. Arab. 4.

5825   — ● ● ● ●   *Tel. Num.* (Morse code.) Eq. Arab. 6.

TABLE 410

5829   *Elec.* Photo-sensitive mosaic.

5830   — ● ● — ● ●   *Rlwy.* Cart. (APO. Rep. USA.) Land-grant boundary line.

5831   — ● ● — ● ● —   *Hyd.* (APO. Rep. Inter.) 20-fathom or 20-metre line, as indicated on chart. See 5849.

5832   — ● ● ● — ● ● — ● ●   *Hyd.* (APO. Rep. Inter.) 7-metre line.

5833   — ● ● ● — ● ● ● —   *Hyd.* (APO. Rep. Inter.) 8-metre line.

5834   ──·····─····   *Hyd.* (APO. Rep. Inter.) 9-metre line.

5835   ─·········─······   *Hyd.* (APO. Rep. Inter.) 50-fathom line.

5836   *Engn.* (Rep.) Brass or bronze.

5837   *Soil/m.* (Rep.) Sandy clay.

5838   *Rlwy.* Cart. (Rep. USA.) Cultivated land.

TABLE 411

5845   ─ • ─ • ─   *Elec.* Tel. (APO. Rep.) Boundary.

5846   ___.___.   *Rlwy.* Cart. (APO. Rep. USA.) Reservation boundary line.

5847   .___.___.   *Hyd.* (APO. Rep. Inter.) 100-metre line; in some charts a number of hundreds is indicated by the number of dots.

5848   _._._   *Hyd.* (APO. Rep. Inter.) 1,000-metre line; in some charts a number of thousands is indicated by the number of dots.

5849   _._._   *Hyd.* (APO. Rep. Inter.) 10-fathom or 10-metre line, as indicated on chart; in some charts the number of dots indicates the initial figure and (for fathoms) the number of dashes the power of ten, i.e., the number of noughts; for metres, the length of the dash indicates the power of ten, except that a very short dash is used instead of five dots to represent 5.

515

5850   ⸺ᐧ⸺ᐧ⸺   *Cart.* (APO. Rep. OS.) County and parish boundary coinciding. ('1-inch' geol. map.) contour line. (Obs.) English county boundary.

5850·1   *Elec.* (APO. Rep.) Circuit connection.

5850·2   *Hyd.* (APO. Rep.) Inter. boundary.

5851   ⸺ᐧ⸺ᐧ⸺   *Hyd.* (APO. Rep. Inter.) 6-metre line.

5852   ⸺⸺ᐧᐧ⸺⸺ᐧᐧ   *Hyd.* (APO. Rep. Red.) 200-fathom line. See 5849.

5853   *Soil/m.* (Rep.) Sandy peat.

TABLE 412

5858   ⸺ ⸺ᐧ⸺ ⸺   *Rlwy. Cart.* (APO. Rep. USA.) Foreign right-of-way line.

5859   ⸺ ⸺ ⸺ᐧᐧ⸺ ⸺   *Cart.* (APO. Rep. '25-inch' map. OS.) Municipal ward boundary.

5859·1   *Hyd.* (Inter.) 17-metre line.

5860   ⸺ᐧ⸺ᐧ⸺   *Hyd.* (APO. Rep. Inter.) 60-metre line.

5861   ᐧ⸺ᐧ⸺ᐧ⸺ᐧ   *Hyd.* (APO. Rep. Red.) 100-fathom line. See 5849.

5862   ᐧ⸺ ⸺ ᐧ⸺ ⸺   *Hyd.* (APO. Rep. Red.) 1,000-fathom line. See 5848.

5863   *Cart.* (Rep.) Marsh.

TABLE 413

§ 1. *With Vertical Lines*

5868		*Rlwy.* (USA.) Switch stand.
5869		*Elec.* Plug.
5870		*Mil.* Sentry.
5871		*Tel.* Coupling probe.
5872		*Rlwy.* (USA.) Stick marker, normally lighted.
5873		*Rlwy.* (USA.) Dry hole with showing of oil.
5874		*Cart.* ('25-inch' map. OS.) Eq. 4325.
5875		*Mus.* Eq. 5726.
5875·1		*Rlwy.* (USA.) Gas well with showing of oil.
5876		*Elec.* Pull switch.
5877		*Mus.* Eq. 5878. (Obs. USA.) 'shaped' or 'patent' note, signifying sol of the tonic sol-fa. (Esp. in Southern States, mid and late 19th cent.)
5878		*Mus.* Crotchet.
5879		*Mus.* (USA.) Eq. 5906.

5880   *Mus.* (Obs. USA.) 'Shaped' or 'patent' note, signifying re of the tonic sol-fa. (Esp. in the Southern States, mid and late 19th cent.)

§ 2. *All Other Signs*

5885   *Elec.* 1-way switch.

5886   *Rlwy.* (USA.) Small oil well.

5887   *Meteor.* (USA.) Sleet.

5888   *Mil.* Mine.

5889   *Engn.* (Fire protection.) Unprotected column or stanchion with wall above.

5890   *Elec.* Strain insulator.

5891   *Cart.* (OS.) Bus and/or coach station.

5892   *Elec.* Flag or grid indicator contacting alarm.

5893   *Hyd.* Eq. 4334.

TABLE 414

5898   *High.* (L. APO. Brit.) Direction arrow; proceed in the direction indicated.

5899   *High.* (L. Brit.) Advance direction sign.

5900   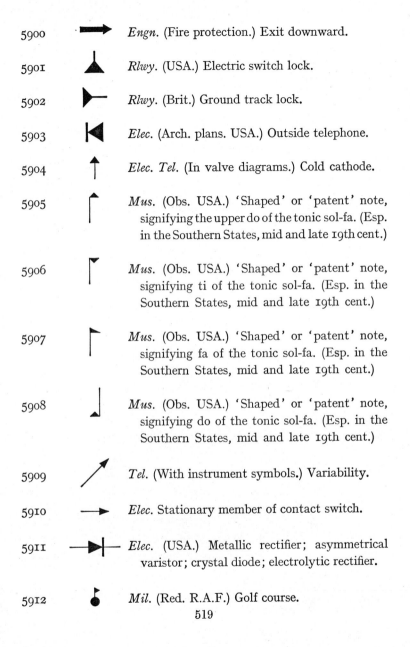   *Engn.* (Fire protection.) Exit downward.

5901   *Rlwy.* (USA.) Electric switch lock.

5902   *Rlwy.* (Brit.) Ground track lock.

5903   *Elec.* (Arch. plans. USA.) Outside telephone.

5904   *Elec. Tel.* (In valve diagrams.) Cold cathode.

5905   *Mus.* (Obs. USA.) 'Shaped' or 'patent' note, signifying the upper do of the tonic sol-fa. (Esp. in the Southern States, mid and late 19th cent.)

5906   *Mus.* (Obs. USA.) 'Shaped' or 'patent' note, signifying ti of the tonic sol-fa. (Esp. in the Southern States, mid and late 19th cent.)

5907   *Mus.* (Obs. USA.) 'Shaped' or 'patent' note, signifying fa of the tonic sol-fa. (Esp. in the Southern States, mid and late 19th cent.)

5908   *Mus.* (Obs. USA.) 'Shaped' or 'patent' note, signifying do of the tonic sol-fa. (Esp. in the Southern States, mid and late 19th cent.)

5909   *Tel.* (With instrument symbols.) Variability.

5910   *Elec.* Stationary member of contact switch.

5911   *Elec.* (USA.) Metallic rectifier; asymmetrical varistor; crystal diode; electrolytic rectifier.

5912   *Mil.* (Red. R.A.F.) Golf course.

TABLE 415

5918		*Meteor.* Thick fog in last hour, but not at time of observation.
5919		*Mus.* (Obs. USA.) 'Shaped' or 'patent' note, signifying la of the tonic sol-fa. (Esp. in the Southern States, mid and late 19th cent.)
5920		*Mus.* (Obs.) Early form of 3862.
5921		*Rlwy.* (USA.) Fire hydrant.
5922		*Mil.* Infantry unit.
5923		*Engn.* Fusible plug.
5924		*Mil.* Tank.
5925		*Mus.* (Obs.) Early form of 1622.
5926		*Mus.* (Stringed instruments.) Harmonic.
5927		*Mus.* (Obs.) Early form of 5878. (USA.) 'shaped' or 'patent' note, signifying mi of the tonic sol-fa. (Esp. in south, mid and late 19th cent.)
5928		*Punc.* 'Old English', 'Black Letter', eq. 3423·2.

520

TABLE 416

5933   *High.* (L. White on black. Brit.) Clearway.

5934   *High.* (L. APO. Brit.) Two-way road.

5935   *Engn.* (Across pipe symbol.) Butt-welded joint.

5936   *Engn.* (Across pipe symbol.) Flanged and bolted joint, seal welded.

5937   *Rlwy.* (Brit.) Spring wicket gate.

5938   *Engn.* (Fire protection.) Arrow on stairs points in upward direction.

5939   *Rlwy.* (On signal symbol. Brit.) Signal lever released by token. (By points or switches) released by token.

5940   *Engn.* (Across pipe symbol.) Flanged and bolted joint with flanges welded on.

5941   *Rlwy.* (USA.) Dragging equipment detector.

5942   *Rlwy.* (Brit.) Derailer.

5943   *Engn.* Valve, closed.

5944   *Elec.* (Arch. Plans. USA.) Home run to panel board.

5945   *Engn.* Angle valve, closed.

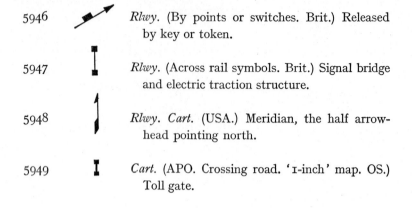

5946   *Rlwy.* (By points or switches. Brit.) Released by key or token.

5947   *Rlwy.* (Across rail symbols. Brit.) Signal bridge and electric traction structure.

5948   *Rlwy. Cart.* (USA.) Meridian, the half arrowhead pointing north.

5949   *Cart.* (APO. Crossing road. '1-inch' map. OS.) Toll gate.

TABLE 417

5955   *Meteor.* (APO. Rep.) Warm front at ground.

5956   *Meteor.* (APO. Rep.) Cold front at ground.

5957   *Meteor.* (APO. Rep.) Occluded front.

5958   *Meteor.* (APO. Rep.) Stationary front.

5959   *Mus.* Eq. 5726.

5960   *Cart. Mil.* (APO. Rep. Red. USA.) Secondary road, metalled and about 4 metres wide.

5961   *Rlwy.* (APO. Rep. USA.) Woven-wire fence.

5962   *Cart.* (APO. Rep. '6-inch' map. OS.) Single rlwy. track.

5963   *Cart.* (APO. Rep. Belgian.) Road with kilometre stones.

5964   *Cart.* (APO. Rep. Ant. OS.) Rom. aqueduct.

5965   *Rlwy.* (APO. Rep. USA.) Board fence.

5966   *Cart.* (APO. Rep. Belgian. Ital.) Rlwy.

5967   *Cart.* (APO. Rep. Fr. Ger.) Road with avenue of trees.

Cl.III, Gen.I

TABLE 418

5970   *High.* (L. Red. Brit.) General sign indicating warning or restrictions.

5971   *Astron.* New moon.

5971·1   *Chem.* Carbon. (John Dalton's elements, 1806–1807.)

5971·2   *Meteor.* (USA.) Sky completely overcast.

5971·3   *Punc.* (In very large scripts.) Eq. 5987·5.

5972   *Cart.* (Ant. OS.) Rom. cantonal capital.

5973   *Cart.* (Ant. OS.) Rom. walled town.

5973·1   *Engn.* (Fire protection.) Section police station.

5974   ●   *Arab. Num.* One, unity, eq. 5135.

5974·1   *Cart.* Town. (On railway) station.

5974·2   *Elec.* Local switch; permanent terminal; connection. (In electron tube and valve diagrams. USA.) gas-filled.

5974·3   *Engn.* (USA.) Field weld.

5974·4   *Hyd.* (Inter.) Eq. 5724.

5974·5   *Mayan Num.* One, unity, eq. Arab. 1.

5974·6   *Meteor.* Eq. 5975·1.

5974·7   *Min.* Eq. 5975·2.

5974·8   *Punc.* (In large scripts.) Eq. 5987·5.

5974·9   *Rlwy.* (USA.) Oil well; non-stick marker, normally lighted.

5975   ●   *Cart.* Eq. 5974·1.

5975·1   *Meteor.* (Standard size of dot 1 mm. in diameter.) Rain.

5975·2   *Min.* Crys. Atom.

5975·3   *Punc.* Eq. 5987·5.

5975·4   *Tel.* (Morse code.) Eq. Rom. E. (Nav. fog signal) I am directing my course to starboard.

TABLE 419

*(Note: In the Braille signs the positional 'H' is
not classified.)*

| 5978 | • | *Cart.* (Ant. OS.) Rom. material found here. |

5978·1   *Sh., Gregg's.* Eq. Rom., H.

5978·2   *Sh., Pitman's.* (Thick.) Long vowel, a(h), a or e, according to position.

5978·3   *Tel.* (Morse code.) See 5975·4.

5979   *Braille a.* (Embossed.) Eq. Rom. A.

5980   *Braille Acc.* (Embossed.) Accent.

5981   *Braille Punc.* (Embossed.) Comma, virgule.

5982   *Braille Punc.* (Embossed.) Apostrophe.

5983   *Braille.* (Embossed.) Cap.

5984†   *Cal.* (Obs.) Derivative; fluxion (Newton).

5984·1   *Chem.* Eq. 4325·1.

5984·2   *Ger.* (Over a cursive letter.) The Umlaut, eq. 6080·1.

5984·3   *Ir.* Diacritical mark indicating that a letter is to be followed by an aspiration and may be represented by its Rom. eq. followed by an h.

5984·4

Math. Point placed over a decimal figure to indicate that it recurs an infinite number of times.

5985†   •

Gk. Punc. The colon, eq. 6066·6, an inverted full stop or 'turned point'.

5985·1

Mus. (Above a note.) Play staccato.

5985·2

OE. MS. Diacritical mark used in some MSS. to distinguish the C and G with front pronunciations.

5985·3

Phon. Palatalization. (Over y) voiceless or breathed.

5985·4

Rom. 'Dot' placed over the l.c. i as a distinguishing characteristic. (First used in the 11th cent. to distinguish ii from u.) Used also as eq. 5988·2.

5986   •

Cart. Eq. 15·1. ('6-inch' map. OS.) pump, guide post, signal post. (Associated with a number) surface level obtained by spirit levelling.

5986·1

Math. (Brit.) Decimal point, separating the whole numbers from the fractions. Because numerals are generally of the size of caps. the decimal point is in fact a 'turned point' (*see* 5985). (First used by Pelazzi of Nice, 1492.) (USA.) eq. 5987·3.

5986·2

ME. MS. Punc. Comma or full stop.

5986·3   *Mus.* (After a note or rest.) The 'dot' which increases the value of the note or rest by half its original value. (Placed after a first dot) increases the value by one-half the increment already conferred by the first dot.

5986·4   *Sh., Pitman's.* (Thin.) Short vowel, a(m), e or i, according to position.

5987   **.**   *Chem.* Combined with; co-ordinate linkage. (Obs.) one equivalent of oxygen.

5987·1   *Com.* (Port.) 1,000 contos, 1,000 million reis.

5987·2   *Log.* And, expressing joint assertion; the termination or commencement of an expression which is to be considered as a whole.

5987·3   *Math.* (Except USA.) Multiplied by; multiplication of scalar quantities. (Secondary Continental usage) a mark inserted in large numbers instead of a comma to separate hundreds from thousands, etc. (USA.) the decimal point, eq. 5986·1.

5987·4   *Mus.* (Sol-fa notation.) Divided beat.

5987·5   *Print.* (*Rep.*) Leader(s), providing a horizontal guide to the eye to align widely separated text.

5987·6   *Punc.* Full stop, full point, period, indicating the end of a sentence; used also to indicate an abbr., esp. if last letter is changed.

5988†	*Sh., Pitman's.* (Thin.) Short i. (Thick.) ee.
5988·1	*Phon.* Esp. close vowel. (Under a consonant) voiceless or breathed.
5988·2	*Rom.* Diacritical mark used in Rom. transliterations of Arab., Heb., Ind., etc., scripts with letters which fail to represent the original sounds exactly.
5988·3	*Sh., Gregg's.* Diacritical mark shortening a vowel.
5988·4	*Mus.* (Below a note.) Play staccato.

TABLE 420

§ 1. *Triangular Dot*

5993		*High.* (L. Brit.) Steep hill.
5994		*High.* (L. UNS., 1938.) Steep hill.
5995		*Rlwy.* (Brit.) Automatic train control ramp.
5996		*Rlwy.* (Brit.) Scotch block. (USA.) lifting block.
5997		*Rlwy.* (USA.) Point or switch set for straight track.
5998		*Rlwy.* (USA.) Point or switch set for turnout.

528

5999	▲	*Elec.* Telephone point, public service.
6000	▲	*Cart.* (Ant. OS.) Rom. villa.
6001	▲	*G/use.* (APO.) Employed as an arrow-head, eq. 4715·3.
6002	▲	*Meteor.* Hail.
6002·1		*Cart.* (OS.) Youth hostel. (Obs.) trigonometrical point.
6003	▼	*Phon.* Half-length vowel.

§ 2. *Square and Rectangular Dots*

6008	■	*Tel.* Metal matching rod.
6009	■	*Min. Crys.* (Etching pit.) Crystal face perpendicular to a tetragonal or di-tetragonal axis.
6009·1		*Punc.* Eq. 5987·5.
6009·2		*Rlwy.* (USA.) Iron monument.
6010	■	*Mus.* (In the third space.) Eq. 6019.
6011	■	*Cart.* (Ant. OS.) Small Rom. fort or 'fortlet'.
6012	■	*Cart.* ('25-inch' map. OS.) Telephone call box.
6013	◆	*Arab. Num.* Nought, zero, eq. 8·4.
6013·1		*Mus.* (Obs.) Early form of 107.

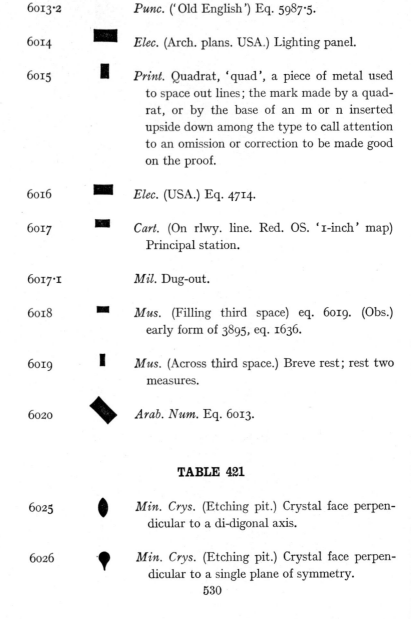

6013·2		*Punc.* ('Old English') Eq. 5987·5.
6014		*Elec.* (Arch. plans. USA.) Lighting panel.
6015		*Print.* Quadrat, 'quad', a piece of metal used to space out lines; the mark made by a quadrat, or by the base of an m or n inserted upside down among the type to call attention to an omission or correction to be made good on the proof.
6016		*Elec.* (USA.) Eq. 4714.
6017		*Cart.* (On rlwy. line. Red. OS. '1-inch' map) Principal station.
6017·1		*Mil.* Dug-out.
6018		*Mus.* (Filling third space) eq. 6019. (Obs.) early form of 3895, eq. 1636.
6019		*Mus.* (Across third space.) Breve rest; rest two measures.
6020		*Arab. Num.* Eq. 6013.

TABLE 421

6025		*Min. Crys.* (Etching pit.) Crystal face perpendicular to a di-digonal axis.
6026		*Min. Crys.* (Etching pit.) Crystal face perpendicular to a single plane of symmetry.

530

6027	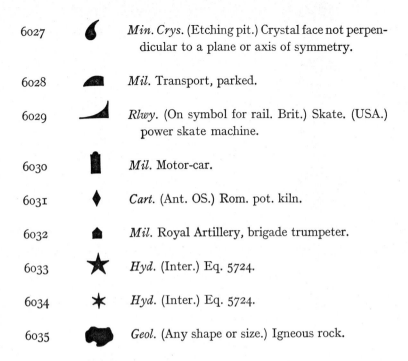	*Min. Crys.* (Etching pit.) Crystal face not perpendicular to a plane or axis of symmetry.
6028		*Mil.* Transport, parked.
6029		*Rlwy.* (On symbol for rail. Brit.) Skate. (USA.) power skate machine.
6030		*Mil.* Motor-car.
6031		*Cart.* (Ant. OS.) Rom. pot. kiln.
6032		*Mil.* Royal Artillery, brigade trumpeter.
6033		*Hyd.* (Inter.) Eq. 5724.
6034		*Hyd.* (Inter.) Eq. 5724.
6035		*Geol.* (Any shape or size.) Igneous rock.

TABLE 422

6038		*High.* (L. Dan.) Roundabout; gyratory traffic moving in direction of arrow.
6039		*High.* (L. White on red. Inter.) One-way street; no entry.
6040		*High.* (L. White on blue. Inter.) Keep to the right.

531

6041   *High.* (L. White on blue. Brit., 1964.) Follow the direction indicated by the arrow.

6042   *High.* (L. White on blue. Inter.) One-way street.

6043   *High.* (L. White on blue. Brit., 1964.) Keep to the left.

6044   *High.* (L. White on blue. Brit., 1964.) Turn left ahead.

6045   *High.* (L. White on blue. Brit., 1964.) Pass on either side.

6046   *Meteor.* (USA.) Sky more than nine-tenths cloud, but not completely covered.

TABLE 423

6049   *High.* (L. White on blue. Inter.) Drive with care.

6050   *High.* (L. Background any colour. Austrian.) Priority ends.

6051   *High.* (L. Arrows white and coloured, background any colour. Du.) Priority continues.

6052	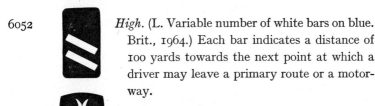	*High.* (L. Variable number of white bars on blue. Brit., 1964.) Each bar indicates a distance of 100 yards towards the next point at which a driver may leave a primary route or a motor-way.
6053		*High.* (L. Brit.) Hospital; St John Ambulance.
6054		*Mil.* (Red on black.) Territorial army, 3rd Infantry Division.
6055		*Cart. Mil.* (USA.) Watermill, windmill, wind-motor.
6056		*Insig.* (Yellow or gold on pale blue, or black and white. Brit.) The Open University.

Cl.III, Gen.II

TABLE 424

(*Note: In the Braille signs the positional* 'H' *is not classified.*)

6058		*Mil.* Vedette, a mounted sentry.
6059		*Meteor.* Intermittent moderate rain.
6060		*Phon.* Full-length vowel.
6061		*Punc.* (Ger./Gothic.) Eq. 6066·6.

6061·1		*Heb. Punc.* Eq. 5987·5.
6061·2		*Rom. Punc.* 'Old English', 'Black Letter', eq. 6066·6.
6062		*Braille a.* (Embossed.) Eq. Rom. B.
6063		*Braille a.* (Embossed.) Eq. Rom. K.
6064		*Braille Punc.* (Embossed.) Semi-colon; opening mark of parenthesis.
6065		*Braille.* (Embossed.) Letter. (Punc.) closing mark of parenthesis.
6066		*Chem.* Double bond.
6066·1		*Com.* (Port.) Conto or contos; 1 million reis; 1,000 escudos. (Brazil) 1,000 milreis.
6066·2		*Log.* A mark used to bracket off an expression.
6066·3		*Math.* Ratio; is to.
6066·4		*Mus.* (Sol-fa notation.) Beat.
6066·5		*Numis.* Abbr.
6066·6		*Punc.* The colon, indicating the expectant pause before an elaboration, an enumeration of details, a list, a quotation, or matter not connected syntactically with the previous sentence but too strongly linked to it in sense to warrant separation by a full stop; abbr.

534

TABLE 425

*(Note: In the Braille signs the positional 'H' is
not classified.)*

| 6071 | • • | *Meteor.* Continuous slight rain. |

6071   • •   *Meteor.* Continuous slight rain.

6072   *Rlwy.* (Brit.) Track circuit interrupter at trap or catchpoints.

6073   *Braille a.* (Embossed.) Eq. Rom. C.

6074   *Braille Punc.* (Embossed.) Colon.

6075   *Braille Punc.* (Embossed.) Hyphen. (Repeated) dash.

6076   *Braille a.* (Embossed.) Eq. Rom. E.

6077   *Braille a.* (Embossed.) Eq. Rom. CH.

6078   *Braille a.* (Embossed.) Eq. Rom. I.

6079   • •   *Tel.* (Morse code.) Eq. Rom. I. (Nav. fog signal) I am directing my course to port.

6080†   •• ˙   *Eng.* Eq. 6080·2.

6080·1   *Ger.* The Umlaut, a diacritical mark modifying the sound of a (ah) to either a (as in air) or e (as in get), o to either eu (as in Fr. peu) or i (as in bird), u to Fr. u (as in lu), and diphthong au to oi (as in loin).

6080·2		*Gk.* Diaeresis, a mark placed over one of two adjacent vowels, esp. like vowels, to indicate that they do not form a diphthong but are to be sounded separately.
6080·3		*Phon.* (Over a vowel.) Central vowel.
6080·4		*Rus.* (Over E, cap. or l.c.) A change in the vowel sound from ĕ to ŏ.
6080·5		*Sw.* Diacritical mark shortening the sound of the vowel a, and modifying o to eu (as in Fr. peu).
6081	··	*Math.* (Obs.) Eq. 5302·5.
6081·1		*Punc.* Tandem colon, indicating a pause or suspense.

TABLE 426

(*Note: In the Braille signs the positional* 'H' *is not classified.*)

6083		*Braille a.* (Embossed.) Eq. Rom. M.
6084		*Braille a.* (Embossed.) Eq. Rom. SH.
6085		*Braille a.* (Embossed.) Eq. Rom. U.
6086		*Braille a.* (Embossed.) Eq. Rom. D.
6087		*Braille a.* (Embossed.) Eq. Rom. F.

6088		*Braille a.* (Embossed.) Eq. Rom. H.
6089		*Braille a.* (Embossed.) Eq. Rom. J.
6090		*Braille Punc.* (Embossed.) Note of exclamation.
6091		*Braille Punc.* (Embossed.) Full stop.
6092		*Braille Punc.* (Embossed.) Question mark; opening quotation mark.
6093		*Braille Punc.* (Embossed.) Closing quotation mark.

TABLE 427

(Note: In the Braille signs the positional 'H' is not classified.)

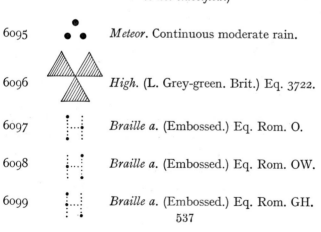

6095		*Meteor.* Continuous moderate rain.
6096		*High.* (L. Grey-green. Brit.) Eq. 3722.
6097		*Braille a.* (Embossed.) Eq. Rom. O.
6098		*Braille a.* (Embossed.) Eq. Rom. OW.
6099		*Braille a.* (Embossed.) Eq. Rom. GH.

| 6100 | | *Braille a.* (Embossed.) Eq. Rom. WH. |

| 6101 | | *Braille a.* (Embossed.) Eq. Rom. S. |

| 6102 | | *Math.* & *G/use.* Therefore. |

| 6103 | | *Math.* Because, since. |

TABLE 428

| 6108 | | *Meteor.* Intermittent heavy rain. |

| 6109 | | *Jap.* Eq. 5263. |

| 6110 | | *Tel.* (Morse code.) Eq. Rom. S. (Nav. fog signal) my engines are going full speed astern. |

| 6111 | | *Braille a.* (Embossed. The positional 'H' is not classified.) Eq. Rom. L. |

| 6112 | | *Chem.* Triple bond. |

6112·1   *Pros.* Anacrusis.

| 6113 | | *Punc.* Ellipsis; marks of omission; *points de suspension*; indicating a space in which missing matter is to be supplied by the imagination; a suspense in the meaning; a mark preceding an interruption; 'leaders', introducing a new paragraph. See 5987·5. |

TABLE 429

(Note: In the Braille signs the positional 'H'
is not classified.)

6118   *Braille a.* (Embossed.) Eq. Rom. P.

6119   *Braille a.* (Embossed.) Eq. Rom. TH.

6120   *Braille a.* (Embossed.) Eq. Rom. R.

6121   *Braille a.* (Embossed.) Eq. Rom. W.

6122   *Braille a.* (Embossed.) Eq. Rom. V.

6123   *Braille.* (Embossed.) Numeral.

6124   • • • •   *Tel.* (Morse code.) Eq. Rom. H.

6125   • · • •   *G/use.* And so on.

6125·1   *Punc.* Eq. 6113.

TABLE 430

6129   *Com.* (L. Red or magenta on yellow ground. Inter.) Caution, radioactive material.

6130   *Com.* (L. Black on yellow ground. Brit.) Caution, radioactive material.

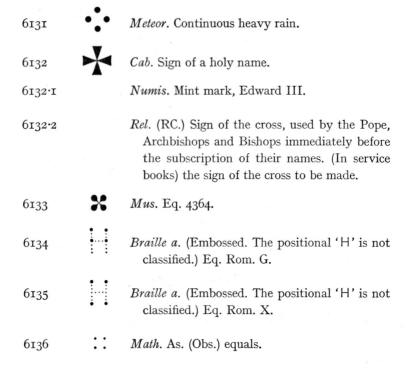

6131   *Meteor.* Continuous heavy rain.

6132   *Cab.* Sign of a holy name.

6132·1   *Numis.* Mint mark, Edward III.

6132·2   *Rel.* (RC.) Sign of the cross, used by the Pope, Archbishops and Bishops immediately before the subscription of their names. (In service books) the sign of the cross to be made.

6133   *Mus.* Eq. 4364.

6134   *Braille a.* (Embossed. The positional 'H' is not classified.) Eq. Rom. G.

6135   *Braille a.* (Embossed. The positional 'H' is not classified.) Eq. Rom. X.

6136   *Math.* As. (Obs.) equals.

TABLE 431
(*Note: In the Braille signs the positional* 'H'
is not classified.)

6141   *Braille a.* (Embossed.) Eq. Rom. N.

6142   *Braille a.* (Embossed.) Eq. Rom. ED.

6143   *Braille a.* (Embossed.) Eq. Rom. OU.

6144	⠞	*Braille a.* (Embossed.) Eq. Rom. T.
6145	⠵	*Braille a.* (Embossed.) Eq. Rom. Z.
6146	⠪	*Braille.* (Embossed.) The.

TABLE 432

(Note: In the Braille signs the positional ' H ' is not classified.)

6151	☆	*Hyd.* Eq. 5724.
6152	• • • • •	*Tel. Num.* (Morse code.) Eq. Arab. 5.
6153	⠟	*Braille a.* (Embossed.) Eq. Rom. Q.
6154	⠯	*Braille.* (Embossed.) And.
6155	⠷	*Braille.* (Embossed.) Of.
6156	⠮	*Braille a.* (Embossed.) Eq. Rom. ER.
6157	⠽	*Braille a.* (Embossed.) Eq. Rom. Y.
6158	⠾	*Braille.* (Embossed.) With.
6159	⠿	*Braille.* (Embossed.) For.

6160 · · · · · *G/use.* (Rep.) Eq. 6125.

6160·1 *Punc.* Eq. 6113.

TABLE 433

6165 ▬ ▬ ▬ *Rlwy.* Cart. (APO. Rep. On boundary line. USA.) Fence.

6166 · · · · *Engn.* (Fire protection.) Open side to building.

6167 ············ *Cart.* (APO. Rep. '6-inch' map. OS.) Sketched contour.

6167·1 *Chem.* (In structural formulae.) Electron bond.

6167·2 *G/use.* (Rep.) Dotted line, used as a guide for handwriting; used to fill a blank space; used to indicate parts in a diagram, etc.

6167·3 *Print.* (Rep. Proof correction, as underline.) Stet, cancel correction.

6168 · · · · · · · *Cart.* (APO. Rep. OS.) Parish boundary.

6168·1 *Hyd.* (Inter.) 1-fathom or 1-metre line. (Enclosing very small area) limits of dangerous area described in legend. (On land) road or trail of 5th (and last) degree of importance. (Obs.) 100-fathom line.

6169 ·· ·· ·· ·· *Hyd.* (APO. Rep. Inter.) 2-fathom or 2-metre line.

6170 ... ... *Hyd.* (APO. Rep. Inter.) 3-fathom or 3-metre line.

6171 .... *Hyd.* (APO. Rep. Inter.) 4-fathom or 4-metre line.

6172 .... *Hyd.* (APO. Rep. Inter.) 5-fathom line.

6173 .... *Hyd.* (APO. Rep. Obs.) Eq. 5429.

TABLE 434

6176 :::::::::::::: *Cart.* (APO. Rep. '6-inch' map. OS.) Unfenced minor road.

6177 ::::::::::: *Cart.* (APO. Rep. '6-inch' map. OS.) Unfenced main road.

6178 *Hyd.* Shoal.

6179 *Hyd.* (Inter.) Fish weir.

6180 *Cart.* (APO. OS.) Sand pit.

6181 *Cart.* (APO. Rep. OS.) Gravel, shingle.

6182 ▲▲▲▲▲▲▲▲ *Mil. Cart.* (APO. Rep. USA.) Masonry revet-
▼▼▼▼▼▼▼ ments; earth dykes.

6183 *Cart.* (Rep. OS.) Rough pasture.

6184 *Cart.* (Rep. OS.) Furze, gorse.

543

6185   *Hyd.* (Rep. Along a shore. Inter.) Breakers.

6186   *Hyd.* (APO. Rep. Red.) Yellow.

6186·1   *Geol.* (APO. Rep. Black.) Eq. 6188·1.

6186·2   *Her.* (APO. Rep. Black.) Or, gold.

6186·3   *Print.* (APO. Rep. Any colour.) 'Dots', 'dotted' tint, used to distinguish parts of a diagram for reference or ornament.

6187   *Cart.* Plantation.

6187·1   *Print.* & *G/use.* (Rep.) Eq. 6186·3.

6188   *Cart.* (APO. Rep.) Sand. (Red.) eq. 6186.

6188·1   *Geol.* (APO. Rep.) Sandstone.

6188·2   *Her.* (APO. Rep.) Eq. 6186·2.

6188·3   *Print.* & *G/use.* (Rep.) Stipple, a shading 'tint' used to distinguish features in a diagram, etc., for reference or ornament, or to indicate shadow in a drawing.

6188·4   *Soil/m.* (APO. Rep.) Sand.

APPENDICES

I. ALPHABETS

ROMAN

*Numbers in italics refer to entries where
letter-symbol meanings are given.*

	Printed				Cursive	
	Caps	*l.c.*	*It. caps*	*It. l.c.*	*Caps*	*l.c.*
A	3626·5 *3627*	310 2153·1	*3664*	218 1600 1765 1769 *1920·5*	1599 1706 2595	1603
B	*2084·2* *2085·2*	1625 1952·2	*2116·2*	*1645·3* 2139	651	1839·1
C	*320·3* 321	*324·4*	*330·3* 331	*334·3*	223	334·6
D	*1975·1* *1976·1* 3100·1	1623 *1951·2*	*2115·3*	*1601·2* 1919	155 312	*135·1* 237 680 1836
E	2265·1 *4384* *4385·5*	877 1677 2220·3	*4910·4*	*207·2* 2222	*246·1*	193 207·7 516·1 1742
F	*4302·2*	2611 2770·1	*4829·3*	*3053·5* 3125	2597	248 2156

545

	Printed				Cursive	
	Caps	*l.c.*	*It. caps*	*It. l.c.*	*Caps*	*l.c.*
G	*2230·1* 2266·1 2267	*43·5* 1922·1	*2251·2*	*123·1* 2117	1855	1582 1923
H	*4373·1* *4374·3*	2397·2	*4901·2*	2282 *3008·1*	1730 2334 2858	1780
I	5104·1 *5125·2*	5737·2 5747	*5213·2*	2647·4 2888	*646·1* 2130	2647·9
J	*2346·1* 2606·1 2673	2640·1	2620 *2676* 3163	*2645·1* 2646	1837	1829·1
K	*4168·3* 4286 4902	4171·1	*4178·3* 4903	1782 1830 1932 2600 2601 2807 3152 *3204·3*	2594	1782
L	*4125·3*	5134·1	*4668·3*	2677·1	212 245·1	198·1 1741·1 2150·1
M	4843·1 4857·2 *4858·1* 4859·1	3016 2537·1	*4862·4*	3017·3	3017·7 3045	3017·7

546

	Printed				Cursive	
	Caps	*l.c.*	*It. caps*	*It. l.c.*	*Caps*	*l.c.*
N	4738·2	2400·1 2735	4750·1	2993·3	3046	2993·01
O	8·8 102·3	11·4	103·1	108	670 140·1	140·1
P	681·1 2005·5 3220	1621 1942·2	2141·2	1646·3 3238	650 681·1	3007
Q	41 66·2 71 1000 1170 1353 1665	1620 1941·2	120 121 134 1591·3 1604 1666	1656·1	63 1657 215 222	1657
R	655·1 2015·1 2032·3 2033 2187·1 2284·1	2613·1	2173·3	2883·3 2916	156·1 649·1 655·1	1748 2921
S	570·3 571·1	574·1 2674 2902·2	579·3	580·3	157 1705	1705 2172
T	3223·1 4191·2	2772·2	4692·1	2774·1	2580 2581 3033	1805 3054
U	2381·2 2395	2736·2	2742	2995·2	2860	2995·5

APPENDICES

	Printed				Cursive	
	Caps	*l.c.*	*It. caps*	*It. l.c.*	*Caps*	*l.c.*
V	4623	4629·2	4642·3	335	213	213
	4624·3		4657	544	2931	546
				2622		2931
				2696·3		
				2920		
				2930		
W	3632	4848·2	3530	217	1729	1729
	4845·2		4846·3	2624·3	2992	2992
	5006·1		5007			
X	684·1	4876·1	4885·2	352·5	2341·1	352·8
	4874·8			526	2857	
				626		
				2873		
Y	2367	2787	2912	2586	1715	1715
	4691·1	4691·1	4815·1	3037·4	2425	
	4812·1			3114		
	4814·4					
Z	4765·1	4769·2	4768·3	634	1788	182·1
	4766·2			3158		1788
				3200		
				3201		
				3205		
				4770·6		

Augmented Rom. (ITA), special characters

Vowels: 169, 148·4, 1611, 1635, 2203, 2299, 2309, 2564.

Consonants: 1933, 1940, 2297, 2308, 2850, 2907, 3020, 3021, 3022, 4767.

GERMAN

*Numbers in italics refer to entries where
letter-symbol meanings are given.*

Rom. eq.	Printed		Cursive	
	Caps	*l.c.*	*Caps*	*l.c.*
A	2582	2128	1607	1614
B	*1897*	2142	263	1839
	3212			
C	*561*	515	179	4751
D	*313·1*	3154	209	1747
	3110			
E	*562·1*	2792	221	4973
	2929			
F	*541·1*	3162	2437	1806
	3430			
G	540	2127	1583	1610
	644			
H	*560*	2824	1864	1838
I	*623*	2641	3111	5645
J	*623*	5736	1716	1829
K	3211	4454	177	2190
L	*622·1*	4647	245	198
				1741
				2150
M	563	3024	261	4981
	2411			
N	2868	2994	176	4931
O	311	2106	140	140
P	*3190·1*	2926	1731	264

APPENDICES

| Rom. | Printed | | Cursive | |
eq.	Caps	l.c.	Caps	l.c.
Q	314	2140	130	1615
R	2212·1	2632	156	402
				419
				527
S	603	565	178	199
	618	2080		4656
		2132		
		3105		
T	636	4431	2598	2755
U	3039	3039	2863	2500
V	638	2135	1594	1609
W	2047	2137	115	1612
X	2880	2316	2341	1728
		2880		
Y	2867	2825	175	181
Z	350	1606	220	182
				428

Ligatures

ch	—	2189	—	1842
ck	—	2197	—	1811
sz	—	1911	—	1809
tz	—	2188	—	1800

GREEK

*Numbers in italics refer to entries where
letter-symbol meanings are given.*

Rom.	Gk.	Caps	l.c.
A	alpha	3626·3	83, *1740·5*, 1751, *1920·4*
B	beta	2084	44, 236, *1697·4*
G	gamma	*4115·2*, 4669	203, 216, 517, 518, 552, 1752, *2727·5*, 2804, 2914, 2915, 2919
D	delta	3519, *3587·1*, *3584·5*	138, *165·5*, 166
E	epsilon	*4385·1*	345, *429·5*, 516, 2467, 2719
Z	zeta	*4766*	545, *553·3*, 576
E	eta	*4374·2*	*2421·4*, 3009
Th	theta	*214·1*, 816·6, 876·3, *892*	*1678·5*, 1679
I	iota	5125	*2680·2*, 2681
K	kappa	*4168·1*	525, 2942, 3005, 3156, *4169·3*
L	lambda	*4578·2*, *4643·1*	2788, *3038·4*
M	mu	4843, 4857	254, *2408·3*, 3010
N	nu	*4738*	519, 2623, *2697·3*
X	xi	4929, *5373*	*406·3*, 407, 567
O	omicron	8·1	11·1
P	pi	*4250·2*	2375, 2542, 2852, 2853, 2997, 3160, *4379·3*

Rom.	Gk.	Caps	l.c.
R	rho	2005·2	142, 1007, *1148·5*, 1943
S	sigma	365, 960, 2747, *4861·1*	139, 613·1, 615, *1186·4*
T	tau	4191·1	2791, *3040·2*, 3098, 4675
U	upsilon	2365, 2523·1, 2882, 3035, 4814·1	614, 386·2
Ph	phi	1354, *1362·2*, 1626, *1669*	1355, *1377·5*, 1670, 1744
Ch	chi	3083, *4874·3*	*3051·1*
Ps	psi	2469, *3089·1*	*2470·3*, 3086, 3090
O	omega	347, *1226·2*, 2245	124, *348·3*, 1435

RUSSIAN

Where lower-case references are missing the forms are the same as for the capitals. All the italic capitals and the italic lower-case letters where references are missing are similar to the Rom. forms but sloped.

Rom.	Rus.	Printed			Cursive	
		Caps	*l.c.*	*It. l.c.*	*Caps*	*l.c.*
A	ah	3626·6	2153·2	1920·9	2595·1	1603·1
B	beh	2009	136	—	648	1590
V	veh	2084·3	—	—	651·1	1839·2
G	geh	4115·6	—	582	3033·1	582
				2908·1		2908·1
D	deh	2108	2108·1	135·2	155·1	135·2
					312·1	1582·1
YĔ	(y)eh⎫	4385·6	2220·4	—	246·2	207·8
YŎ	(y)oh⎭	5654	2224	—	246·2	207·8
ZH	zheh	3188	—	—	2342	—
					3061	
Z	zeh	340	342	—	332	332
						1788·1
Ē	ee	4737	—	2995·6	2860·1	2995·6
E	'ee with a dot'	5125·3	5737·3	2647·01	2581·1	2647·01
Ĕ	ĕe	2314	—	2996	2860·1	2996
K	kah	3203	—	—	2594·1	1804
L	el	2607	—	—	2859	2918
M	em	4857·3	—	—	3045·1	—

Rom.	Rus.	Printed			Cursive	
		Caps	*l.c.*	*It. l.c.*	*Caps*	*l.c.*
N	en	4374·4	—	—	2334·1	2998
					2858·1	
Ŏ	o	8·9	11·5	—	670·1	140·2
P	peh	4250·5	—	2993·02	2861	2993·02
R	er	2005·6	1942·3	1646·8	650·1	3007·1
S	ess	320·4	324·5	—	223·1	334·7
		321·1				
T	teh	4191·3	—	3017·8	2865	3017·8
U	oo	2367·1	3037·8	—	2425·1	1715·1
F	ef	1362·7	1914	1916	119	1915
KH	kha	4874·9	4876·2	352·9	2857·1	352·9
TS	tseh	4396	—	2875	1718	1798
CH	cheh	2398	2399·1	—	550	—
SH	shah	4395	—	3018	2864	3018
SHCH	shchah	4485	—	2876	1719	1799
—	yer	2008	—	1602	645	—
—	yerü	2042	—	—	2862	2338
—	yer'	2006·1	—	—	671	—
(Y)EH	yat'	2043	—	1647	3232	3235
(A)Y	eh	2295	—	—	647	338
Ŭ	yoo	1633	—	—	1589	1613
YA	yah	2031	—	—	1929	—
F	feetah	128·1	—	—	129	—
		875				
		1676·1				
U	ízhütsa	2621	—	—	2809	—

	HEBREW			ARABIC	
Rom.	*Heb.*		*Rom.*	*Arab.*	
A	aleph	3206	—	alif	5133
B	beth	3150	B	ba	3471
G	gimel	2797	T	ta	3492
D	daleth	4118	TH	tha	3493
Ḥ	he	4152	J	jim	2656
W	vau	2707	Ḥ	ḥa	2704
Z	zayin	4684	KH	kha	2655
H	cheth	4251	D	dal	2679
T	teth	2881	DH	dhal	2658
Y	jod	583	R	ra	436
K	caph	2743	Z	za	3472
L	lamed	3155	S	sin	420
M	mem	2513	SH	shin	3494
N	nun	2796	Ṣ	ṣad	1771
S	samek	2126	Ḍ	ḍad	3410
—	ayin	2633	Ṭ	ṭa	1767
P	pe	2871	Ẓ	ẓa	1768
Ṣ	tsadek	3153	—	ayin	343
Q	koph	3101			376
R	resh	4119			427
SH	schin	2635			2505
T	tau	2869	GH	ghain	2516
					3475
			F	fa	3426
			Q	qaf	3457
			K	kaf	2536
			L	lam	2345
			M	mim	2605
			N	nun	3467
			H	ha	189
			W	waw	3420
			Y	ya	3497

MORSE CODE

A	5749	L	5823	W	5760	*Numerals*	
B	5820	M	5354·2	X	5802	1	5773
C	5805	N	5748	Y	5772	2	5808
D	5787	O	5376·2	Z	5807	3	5819
E	5975·4	P	5803			4	5824
F	5822	Q	5771	*Letter*		5	6152
G	5761	R	5788	*Combinations*		6	5825
H	6124	S	6110	Æ	5804	7	5821
I	6079	T	5300·8	CH	5420	8	5809
J	5769	U	5786	Œ	5770	9	5774
K	5759	V	5818	UE	5806	0	5421

BRAILLE

A	5979	Q	6153	OU	6143	Dash	6075
B	6062	R	6120	OW	6098	Exclama-	
C	6073	S	6101	SH	6084	tion	6090
D	6086	T	6144	TH	6119	Full stop	6091
E	6076	U	6085	WH	6100	Hyphen	6075
F	6087	V	6122			Parentheses	6064–5
G	6134	W	6121	*Words*		Query	6092
H	6088	X	6135	AND	6154	Quotes	6092–3
I	6078	Y	6157	FOR	6159	Semi-colon	6064
J	6089	Z	6145	OF	6155		
K	6063			THE	6146	*Other*	
L	6111	*Combinations*		WITH	6158	*characters*	
M	6083	CH	6077			Accent	5980
N	6141	ED	6142	*Punctuation*		Capital	5983
O	6097	ER	6156	Apostrophe	5982	Letter	6065
P	6118	GH	6099	Colon	6074	Numeral	6123
				Comma	5981		

2. SELECTED GRAPHIC SIGNS

Note: The list of *Standard Shading Tints* (page 576) is in part supplementary to the *Cartography, Engineering, Geology* and *Hydrography* lists, and includes also examples from Heraldry and Soil Mechanics.

The several references to ' *USA* ' do not imply that similar signs are not used elsewhere, but that the signs have (in most cases) been approved by the American Standards Association. The other technical signs are those accepted by the British Standards Institution, H.M. Ordnance Survey, foreign national authorities, international convention, or common usage.

Foreign references apply to all the numbers following them up to the next foreign reference or the next entry.

Astronomy

Aquarius, 4563·1
Aries, 500
Asteroid, 710
Cancer, 93, 1547
Capricorn, 1726
Ceres, 2479
Comet, 1235
Conjunction, 1172·1
Distance, mean, 2283, 3237
Earth, 816·1
Gemini, 3886
Juno, 1107, 4463
Jupiter, 2370·2
Leo, 45, 600
Libra, 2493
Light-year, 4268
Longitude, moon's, 285, 286
—, sun's, 3363·2
Mars, 1122·2
Mercury, 966·2
Moon, first quarter, 284·1, 383, 3415
—, full, 10·1
—, last quarter, 280·2, 364, 3414
—, lower limb, 1892
—, new, 5971

Moon, upper limb, 1893
Moon's longitude, 285, 286
Neptune, 2328, 2412, 2482·1
Node, ascending, 97, 605, 617
—, descending, 96, 604, 616
North, 4323·1
Nutation, 3584
Opposition, 36, 1518
Pallas, 4007
Pisces, 2936, 2953
Planet, 15
Pluto, 65, 2007, 2017
Quadrature, 3931
Quintile, 281, 282, 3363·2
Sagittarius, 5010, 5012
Saturn, 3095·2
Sextile, 4970, 4982
Solar mass, 851
South, 5302
Star, fixed, 4970, 4982, 5052
Station mark, 3567·1
Sun, 3363·2
—, lower limb, 1403
—, upper limb, 1401
Sun's centre, 1386·1
— longitude, 3363·2
Taurus, 73·1
Uranus, 1114

Venus, 1101·1
Vesta, 2575, 3713
Virgo, 2599, 2982

Botany

Absence of feature, 5302·1
Actinomorphic, 816·2, 1273
Annual, 10·2, 710·1, 3363·3
Authenticity, mark of, 5734
Biennial, 284·2, 695·1, 1122·4, 3396
Bract (floral diagram), 380
Budded on, 5214
Certainty, mark of, 5734
Chimaera, 4323·3
Climbing plant, 484
Clone, 2310
Cotyledons, accumbent, 1209
—, conduplicate, 1084, 5010·1
—, folded, 1207, 1208
—, incumbent, 1206
Crossed with, 4363·1
Diclinous, 1480
Dioecious, 1482
Evergreen, 3582·2
Female, 10·2, 1101·2
Graft-chimaera, 4323·3
Grafted on, 5214
Hybrid, 4363·1
— graft, 4323·3
Indefinite number, 104, 239
Inferior (floral formula), 5288
Irregular, 4708
Joining of parts (floral formula), 490, 635
Male, 1122·3, 3746·1
Monocarpous, 10·2, 3363·3
Monoclinous, 966·4
Monoecious, 1458, 1481
Naturalized, 273
New World, 4994
Northern hemisphere, 4992
Old World, 4995
Ornamental, 4354

Perennial, 2370·3
Petal (floral diagram), 283
Plant, useful, 4512
Polygamous, 1443, 1484
Regular, 816·2, 1273
Sepal (floral diagram), 315
Shrub, 2330, 3145
—, large, 2250
—, small, 2311
Southern hemisphere, 4993
Stamen (floral diagram), 302, 303
Suffructicose plant, 2311
Superior (floral formula), 5289
Symmetrical bilaterally, 4354
Tree, 2287, 2813, 3145
—, small, 2250
Uncertainty, mark of, 2510
Undershrub, 2311
Variety, 273
Winding to left, 437
— to right, 440
Woody-stemmed plant, 3095·3
Zygomorphic, 4354, 4708, 5783

Cartography

Antiquity (unspecified), 1472·1
Bamboo bush, (Du.) 5014
Barrow, 4325, 4336
Battery, 4932
Battle, 2088
Beacon, 3636
Bench mark, 4917 ff.
—, probably stable, 837
Boundary, county, 5419, 5424, 5850
— limit, 1517
—, municipal ward, 5859
—, national, 5662
—, parish, 5850, 6168
—, Poor Law Union, 5661
—, ridings, 4539
—, rural district, 5660
—, urban district, 5422

Bridge, 4947, 5033
Bridle path, 5427
Bus or coach station, 5891
Bush, 3356
Canal, 5312
Celtic fields, 145
Church, (*Fr.*) 15·1, 3366
— with spire, 1100·3, 5617
— with tower, 5710
— without spire or tower, 4325, 5874
Cinchona, quinine, tree, (*Du.*) 1081
Clay pit, 5469
Coconut palm, 2695, (*Du.*) 4162
Coffee plantation, (*Du.*) 3366
Conduit, 5035
Contour line, 100, 144, 5292
—, sketched, 6167
Corn, (*USA*) 2917
Cutting, 5184
Dam, (*USA*) 4781
Electricity transmission line, 3920
Elephant grass, (*Du.*) 4662
Embankment, 5183
Flow, *see* Water
Footpath, 5427
Forest, (*Du.*) 1193
Golf course, 5589, 5680
Gradient, 4141, 4142, 4262
Jungle, secondary, (*Du.*) 1200
Level, 4324, 5986
Lock, 4104, 4261, (*USA*) 4781
Marsh, 5863
Mausoleum, 4325, 4336
Mine, 5099
Mosque, 2515, 3474
Orchard, 2560
Palm, coconut, 2695, (*Du.*) 4162
—, sago, (*Du.*) 4155
—, sugar, (*Du.*) 4161
—, swamp, (*Du.*) 3063, 4317
Plantation, 15·1, 5986
—, coffee, (*Du.*) 3366
—, rubber, (*Du.*) 5481

Post, 5986
Property, identity link, 2903, 3055
Pump, 5986
Pylon, 5100, 5522
Quarry, 5099, 5469
Radio mast, 2111
Railway, 5291, (*Belgian, Ital.*) 5966, (*USA*) 5312, 5346
— cutting, 5184
—, double track, 3988, 5312
—, electric, (*USA*) 3988
— embankment, 5183
—, light, 4571
—, mineral, 4538
—, narrow gauge, 4571
—, single track, 5579, 5962
— station, 5974·1
— —, principal, 3765, 6017
Station, bus or coach, 5891
—, railway, 3765, 5974·1, 6017
—, trigonometrical, 5476·1, (*Du.*) 1090, (*Fr.*) 3366
Road, dual, (*USA*) 5355
—, first class, 5312, 5355
—, second class, 5312, 5356
—, third class, 5346
—, unfenced, 5383, 5384
—, —, main, 6177
—, —, minor, 6176
— with kilometre stones, (*Belgian*) 5963
— with trees, (*Fr., Ger.*) 5967
Rock, (*Du.*) 5454
Roman aqueduct, 4569, 5964
— bath-house, 5482
— building (unspecified), 3585
— burial, 5317
— camp, temporary, 3765
— —, training, 3553
— canal, 4567
— capital, cantonal, 5972
— colony, 3371
— farm, 2036, 5717
— fort, 3747
— —, small, 6011
— fortress, legionary, 3752

Number, No., 4020
Per, 1865, 2081
Per cent, 1499, 1530
Per thousand, 1531
Peso(s), 2053
Portland quarry numerals, 4352, 4429, 4430, 4509, 5200
Pound(s) sterling, 211, 262, 1717, 1796, 1856, 4557
Pound(s) weight, 1639, 1963, 4020
Radioactive material, 3399, 6129, 6130
Reis, 3130, 5987·1, 6066·1
Sherry, Amontillado, 994
—, Dos cortados, 2838
—, Dos palmas, 2909
—, Fino, 2670, 2765, 2766, 2838, 2909, 2910, 2911
—, Oloroso, 1598, 2766
—, Palma, 2670
—, Palma cortado, 2765
—, Palo cortado, 2766
—, Pata de galena, 3047
—, Pedro Ximenez, 1099
—, Quatro palmas, 2911
—, Raya, 2671
—, second grade, 2671
—, Tres palmas, 2910
Shilling(s), 5214·1, 5467
Yard(s), 4366
Yen, 4294, 4500

Electronics and Telecommunications

Aerial, 3835, 4480, 4895, (USA) 3548, 3858, 3877, 4477
—, dipole, (USA) 4260
Alternating current, 587, 628, 639
Amplifier, 2546, 3672, 3674, (USA) 3621, 3648
Anode, 4323·5, (valve diagrams) 1085, 4209
—, intermediate, 1106, 5352

Antenna, see Aerial
Arc, 5721
Arrester, lightning, 5606
—, multigap, 5758
Attenuator, 4417, (USA) 5690
Barretter, 2074
Battery, central, 26
—, local, 10·5
Bell, 1990
Buzzer, 1991, 1992, (USA) 3829
Capacitance, 4398
Capacitor, see Condenser
Cathode, cold (valve diagrams), 1085, 1160, 1227, 5904, (USA) 1191
—, filament, 4867, (USA) 4135
—, hot (valve diagrams), 4181
—, indirectly heated, (USA) 4254
—, ionically heated, (USA) 1130, 1131
Cell, battery or accumulator, 4400
—, photo-electric, 1440, (USA) 1256
—, photo-voltaic, 2430
—, selenium, (USA) 1255
Choke, 2258
—, coupling, 4418
Circuit breaker, 3822
—, oil, 3848
Clock, impulse, 802
—, master, 744
—, synchronous, 776
Coaxial cable, 1265, 1394
Coil, operating, (USA) 2075, 4746
Condenser, capacitor, 4398, 4478, 4479, (USA) 2842
—, electrolytic, 3890
—, feed-through, (USA) 1438
—, fixed, 4527
—, shielded, 4498
—, shunt, 2854
—, split-stator, (USA) 2890
—, variable, 2855
Conductance, 4967, 5064

Relay coil, slow, 3571, 5547
Relay-set, 3817
Repeater, one-way, (*USA*) 3673
Resistor, 2074, 3712, 4564, 5062
—, liquid, 5515
—, non-linear voltage, 3535, 3565
Resonator, 955, 2257
—, cavity, 4, 3452, 3490
Screen, 5457
—, internal (valve diagrams), 2964
Selector, two-motion, 3915
Selenium cell, (*USA*) 1255
Series, 4763·1
Shield, internal (valve diagrams), 5110
Shim, 4524
Short circuit, 5109, 5604
Shunt, 4812
— capacitor, 2854
— inductor, (*USA*) 2561
— winding, 1845
Socket, 2040, 2462, 3372, 3765·1, 4180
Spark-gap, 2089, 4468
Squeeze section, 4944
Standing wave indicator, 3165, 3181
Susceptance, 1843, 1859, 1862, 1863
—, capacitive, 4399
—, inductive, 249·1
Switch, 1212, 1551, 5608, (*USA*) 1452, 1453, 1528, 1529
—, change-over, 3507
—, double-pole, 5638
—, gas, 3486
—, knife, 4953
—, main, 3940
—, press-button, 5563
—, sector, (*USA*) 3537
Switch-hook, gravity, 1006
Telephone, 4215
— bell, (*USA*) 1031
— board, 5517

Telephone dial, 3393
— exchange, automatic, 2812
— handset, (*USA*) 921
— point, internal, 3583·3
— —, public service, 5999
— receiver, 3844, (*USA*) 1436
— —, thermal type, 4972
— set, subscriber's, 2484
— transmitter, 1091, 1536
Tetrode, transistor, 5684
— valve, 1283
Thermoelement, 4183
Thermostat, 5597
Transducer, photoconductive, (*USA*) 1255, 1264
—, photovoltaic, (*USA*) 1256
—, thermomechanical, (*USA*) 2319
Transformer, 1808, 1871 ff.
—, auto-, 965, 1868, 1869
— winding, 32
Transistor, 1287
—, photo-, 5691
—, tetrode, 5684
—, triode, 5682, 5683
Trigatron, 2082
Triode, transistor, 5682, 5683
— valve, 1282, 1284
Tube, *see* Valve
Turnbuckle, 1457
Valve, diode, 1280, 1281
—, pentode, 1286
—, screen grid, 1285
—, tetrode, 1283
—, triode, 1282, 1284
Varistor, (*USA*) 5911
Wave-guide, circular, 6·5
—, dielectric-filled, 3821
—, gas-filled, 5527
—, rectangular, 3768
—, tapering, 4609
—, twisted, 3149

Flow indicator, 3805
— restrictor, 4077
Flowmeter, 5171
Furnace, 1888, 3814, 3819
Gauge, 1415
Heat exchanger, 3874, 3985
Heat load, 5061
Heater, oil, 3969
—, unit, (*USA*) 3779
—, water, 3960, 3968
Hopper, 4093
Hydrant, 4491
Injector, 3870
Joint, butt-welded, 5935
—, expansion, (*USA*) 3808
—, flanged and bolted, 4979, 5148, 5936, 5940
—, flexible, 2950
—, sleeve, 4089, 5343
—, soldered, 10·6
—, spigot and socket, 1974
—, wiped, 10·6
Kiln, 2976
Mill, ball or tube, 22
Mixer, 2000
Montejus, 1995
Oil cooler, heater, 3969
Pipe, piping, 5346·1
—, heating, (*USA*) 5036, 5037, 5418, 5442·1
—, steam (heating, *USA*) 5081, 5082
—, terminating downward, (*USA*) 889
—, — upward, (*USA*) 3362
—, vent, (*USA*) 5423
—, water, (*USA*) 5437, 5441
—, welded, (*USA*) 4873
Plate column, 3823
Plug, (*USA*) 2051, 2475
Precipitator, electrostatic, 5529
Pre-heater, air, 3967
Pump, 1416, (*USA*) 4499
—, centrifugal, 1329
—, reciprocating, 3872
—, rotary, 1330
Receiver, (*USA*) 1993, 3941

Receiver, steam, 1228
Reducer, concentric, (*USA*) 2094, 3655
—, eccentric, (*USA*) 2095, 3523, 3536
Re-heater, steam, 3966
Scale trap, (*USA*) 1994
—, thermostatic, 3551
Screen, 4160, 4291
Seal, liquid, 3930, 4280
Separator, 1366
—, centrifugal, 1250, 3903
—, grease, (*USA*) 3570
—, liquid, 3956
—, magnetic, 2157
—, oil, (*USA*) 1024
—, steam, 1365
Settling tank, 4060
Shower, (*USA*) 847, 1269, 1985
Silo, 4093
Spray, 4926
— drier, 4071
—, pond, (*USA*) 2098
Sprinkler system, (*USA*) 1567
Stack, smoke, 3875
Steam pipe, (heating, *USA*) 5081, 5082
— receiver, 1228
— re-heater, 3966
Stirrer, 1835
Strainer, 3798, 3946, (*USA*) 2078
Sump, roof, (*USA*) 1460
Superheater, 3935
Switch, pressure, (*USA*) 3780, 3781
Tank, *see* Vessel
Thickener, 4445
Tower, 3766, 3977
—, cooling, 4050, (*USA*) 3820
Trap, boiler return, (*USA*) 2011
—, drain, 3837
—, float, (*USA*) 3764·2
—, float and, (*USA*) 3551
—, scale, (*USA*) 1994, 3551
—, thermostatic, (*USA*) 742, 817·2

Strata, contorted, 3157
—, horizontal, 4323·6
—, inclined, 4710
—, — gently, 4438
—, — steeply, 4437
—, overturned, 2368
—, undulating, 625, 3142
—, vertical, 4349
Strike, 2368
—, contorted, 3192
—, undulating, 3128
Syncline, 5047
—, pitching, 5089
Tin ore, (*Min.*) 2370·5
Zinc ore, (*Min.*) 4426
Zone symbol, enclosure for,
    (*Min., Cryst.*) 4416·3

Hydrography

Air port, limit of, 3071
Anchorage, 980, 987, 990
Battery, 4932
Beacon, 16·1, 1019, 1033, 1045,
    1137, 1230, 2872, 3366·1,
    4283, 4288, 4289, 4297, 4497
—, floating, 1132, 3836, 4456,
    4695
—, light, 1139
Boundary, customs, 4540
—, international, 4539·1, 5850·2
—, territorial waters, 4541
Buoy, bell, *see* gong
—, can, black, 1199
— —, white, 1071
—, conical, black, 1202
—, —, white, 928
—, gong or bell, middle ground,
    927
—, —, pass to port, 1074
—, —, pass to starboard, 929
—, light, 1342
—, —, middle ground, 935
—, —, pass to port, 1072
—, —, pass to starboard, 936

Buoy, mooring, 1573 ff.
—, pillar, 1056
—, spar, 1075, 4695
—, spherical, black, 1201
—, —, black and white, 952
—, —, white, 926
— with topmark, 949, 950,
    1053, 1057, 1502
Cable, leader, 5386
—, submarine, 597
Chimney, 15·4
Church or chapel, 4335
Co-tidal line, 5416
Current, 3159, 5071
—, line of turn of, 5416
Datum, reference to, 5304
Depth, fathoms, 5429, 5831,
    5835, 5849, 5852, 5861, 5862,
    6168·1 ff.
—, metres, 5428·1, 5429, 5439,
    5832 ff., 5847 ff., 5851, 5859·1,
    5860, 6168·1 ff.
— unknown, 5750
Ebb-tide stream, 4713, 5610
Eddy, 662, 675
Ferry, 2110
Fish weir, 6179
Fishing stakes, 4201, 4568,
    4696, 5187
— zone, limit of, 1882
Flood-tide stream, 5072, 5611
Footpath, 5428·1
Ice barrier, 5187
Life-saving station, 4334
Light, position of, 3346, 5724,
    5974·4, 6033, 6034, 6151
Light vessel or float, 939, 940
Limits, fishing zone, 1882
—, maritime, 5416
Marabout, 1030
Minaret, 2504
Mine, 5720
Moslem tomb, 1030, 1261
Mosque, 937, 1261
Nipa palm, 3064
Observation spot, 818·1
Overfalls, 641

Pagoda, 3727
Quarry, 5720
Radio station, 15·4, 3380
Reserved area, 5416
Road, 1st degree, 5346·2
—, 2nd degree, 5384·1
—, 4th degree, 5427·1
Rock awash, 4325, 5655·1, 5657
Sea-level, reference to, 5304
Semaphore station, 3365·1
Shoal, 6178
Shrine, Shinto, (Du.) 3727
Signal, submarine sound, 98
Signal station, 3365·1
Telegraph station, 3365·1
Temple, 3727
—, Buddhist, 3963
Tide rips, 641
— stream, 4713, 5072
Tower, 15·4, 1054
Trail, 1st degree, 5346·2
—, 4th degree, 5427·1
Watermill, 2052
Weir, fish, 6179
Windmill, 1340
Wire drag used, 4244
Wreck, submerged, 4536, 5658
—, visible at low water, 1094, 1240

Meteorology

Air, clear, 270·1
—, light, 4672
— masses, changing, (USA) 4096
— —, mixed, (USA) 4086
—, smoky, (USA) 1546
Altocumulus, 416, 418, 2087
— in bands, 2554
— castellatus, 2490
—, confused, 2940
—, isolated, 2452
Altostratus, 2087

Altostratus, thick, 4832
—, thin, 4599
Atmosphere, see Air
Aurora, 1989
Barometer falling, 5302·6
— fell in last 3 hours but now rising, 4143
— rising, 4323·02
— steady, 6·3
— unsteady, (USA) 584
Beaufort scale, 4671, 4672, 4830, 4831, 4955, 4956, 5004, 5005, 5065 ff.
Breeze, fresh, 4955
—, gentle, 4830
—, moderate, 4831
—, slight, 4671
—, strong, 4956
Calm, 6·3, 25·1, 747
Cirrocumulus, 2529
Cirrostratus, 2353
—, advancing, (USA) 2355
— covering sky, 2552
—, fibrous, 2453
— in part of sky, 2455
Cirrus, abundant, 2366
—, advancing, (USA) 2355
—, anvil form, 2353
—, with 'hooks', 2351
—, isolated wisps, 2352
—, thundery type, 3113
—, travelling, 5214·4
Cloud, trace of only, 890
Corona, lunar, 2466
—, solar, 857·4
Cumulo-nimbus, 1980, (Aero.) 1895
Cumulus, 418
—, large, 1894
—, small, 1970·2
Dew, 2029
Drizzle, 3421, (Aero.) 5182, 5273, 5275
—, continuous moderate, 3456
—, — slight, 3441
—, — thick, 3458
— with fog, 2625

569

Drizzle, frozen, (*USA*) 3685·1
—, intermittent moderate, 3440
—, — thick, 3455
Dull, 43·2
Dust devil, 249
— storm, (*USA*) 3175
Fog, 2625, 5363·7
—, ground, 5374
—, low, 5375
—, shallow, 5398
—, thick in last hour, 5918
—, wet, 5399, 5812
— with frost, 4946
— with rain, 2625, 5766
— with snow, 4990
Fractonimbus, 5376
Front, cold above ground, 2114, 3726
—, — at ground, 5956
—, instability, 4566
—, occluded, 5957
—, stationary, 5958
—, warm above ground, 2090
—, — at ground, 5955
Frost, with fog, 4946
—, glazed, 586
—, hoar, 4243·1
Gale, 5005
—, strong, 5065
—, whole, 5066
Graupel, 3583·6
Ground, flooded, 5512
— frozen hard, 3778
— wet, 5509·1
— with hail lying, 4163
— — snow drifting, 4441
— — snow lying, 3796, 4163
Hail, 6002
— on ground, 4163
—, soft, 3583·6, 3645
—, —, showers, 3706
Halo, lunar, 1972
—, solar, 816·8
Haze, 239·2
Height not reported, 5332·2, 5467·1

Hurricane, 5068, (*USA*) 70
Ice, crystals, (*USA*) 4718·1
—, grains, (*USA*) 5476·2
—, needles, 4928·2
Icing, light, (*Aero.*) 4706
—, moderate, 5090
—, severe, 5075
Intensity, (*USA*) 5111·4
Light air, 4672
Lightning, 4182
— occurred in past hour, 4231·1
Mirage, 278
Mist, 5344·01
Observation within sight of station, 490·6
Precipitation within sight, 3476, 3477
Rain, 5975·1, (*Aero.*) 5182, 5273, 5275, (*USA*) 914
—, continuous heavy, 6131
—, — moderate, 6095
—, — slight, 6071
— with fog, 2625, 5766
—, intermittent heavy, 6108
—, — moderate, 6059
— showers, 5478
— —, heavy, (*USA*) 5499
Rainbow, 391·2
Raindrops, frozen, (*USA*) 5476·2
Rime, hard, 5678, (*USA*) 4628
Sandstorm, (*USA*) 3175
Showers, 3601
—, hail, 3706
—, rain, 5478
—, —, heavy, (*USA*) 5499
—, sleet, 5480
—, snow, 3654, (*USA*) 3689
Sky clear, 6·3
— clouded, 1 tenth, 800, (*USA*) 857·4
— —, less than 1 tenth, (*USA*) 868·1, 3377
— —, 2–3 tenths, 867·1, (*USA*) 3341
— —, 4–6 tenths, 897, (*USA*) 3350

Sky clouded, 7–8 tenths, 899, (USA) 3342
— —, 9 tenths, 808, (USA) 3351
— —, more than 9 tenths, 803
— —, completely, 901
— obscured by fog, dust, etc., 908, (USA) 817·7
— overcast, 11·2, 747, (USA) 5971·2
— —, nearly, (USA) 6046
— threatening, 3547
Sleet, 5588, (USA) 5887
—, showers, 5480
Smoke, (USA) 3099
Snow, 4982·2
— and fog, 4990
—, continuous heavy, 5032
—, — moderate, 5021
—, — slight, 5031
— drifting on ground, 4441
— — at height, 4440
—, granular, (USA) 3685·1
— on ground, 3796, 4163
—, intermittent heavy, 5020
—, — moderate, 5030
— showers, 3654, (USA) 3689
Snowstorm, 4464
—, heavy drifting, 4069
Squalls, 4582·3
—, heavy, 4775
Storm, 5067
Stratocumulus, 2491, 2557
—, high, 416
Stratus, 2491
Sunshine, 3363·8
Swell in open sea, 531
Thunderstorm, 4315, (Aero.) 3539
—, heavy, (USA) 4475
—, moderate, (USA) 4427
—, slight, (USA) 4315
Tornado, (USA) 70
Turbulence, light, (Aero.) 4865
—, moderate, 4948
—, severe, 4971

Visibility exceptional, 270·1
— 1,100–2,200 yards, 5344·01
— less than 1,100 yards, 5363·7
— reduced by smoke, (USA) 274·1
Waterspout, 4947·1
Wind, cold, 4713·1
—, direction of, 5069
—, high, 5004
, warm, 2991, 4273, 4959·1, 4273

Military Records and Plans

Abattis, 5274
Adjutant, 1352
Aerodrome, 3373
— with radar, 1406
Aircraft depot, 2974
— park, 77
Airship, 2068
Anti-aircraft guns, headquarters, 784, 787, 789, 791
—, plotting station, 846
—, section, 900
Armoured car, 5484
— column, 3680, 5500
— unit, 3678
Army co-operation, squadron (R.A.F.), 2970
Army corps, 3841, 3928
Balloon, 1627
Bandmaster, 5498
Barbed wire entanglements, 252, 4542
Barricade, 5274
Battalion, 3929
Battery, 3927
— commander, 1313
— quartermaster sergeant, 5514
— second in command, 1399
— sergeant-major, 3959
Bombing squadron, 3453
Boundary, international, 2889

Seaplane station, 3381
Searchlight, 746, 1210
Section commander (R.A.),
  1100·4
— leader (R.E.), 1100·4
Sentry, 5870, 6058
Sergeant-major, 3958, 3959
Signalling station, 3864
Squadron, 3927
—, Army co-operation
  (R.A.F.), 2970
— commander, 1313
—, fighter (R.A.F.), 3065
— quartermaster sergeant,
  5514
— second in command, 1399
— sergeant-major, 3959
Tank, 5924
— column, 3926, 5577
— trap, 3753
— unit, 3925
Telegraph station, 816·9
Territorial Army, 722, 4523,
  5677, 6054
Tower, 5700
Transport, horse, 1516, 1520
— on march, 5311
—, motor, 1456·1, 1485
—, parked, 6028
Tree, 1685
Trench mortar, 5596
Troop, 3839
— leader, 1100·4
— section sergeant, 3883
Troops (unspecified), 3550
Trumpeter, 3675, 6032
Unit, armoured car, 3678
—, cavalry, 5494
—, infantry, 5922
—, second in command, 1459
—, tank, 3925
Vedette, 6058
Windmill, 4068
Wire entanglements, 252, 4542
Wood, 1685
Woodland, 5280·4

Philately

Block, four or more stamps,
  3783·1
—, more than four stamps,
  2097, 3790
Cover, original, 5496
Obsolete, 4354·1
Unused, 4087, 4970·1
Used, 8·6
— stamp on complete cover,
  3724
— — on piece, 3583·8

Pottery (China Marks)

Berlin, 5623
Bow, 967, 1112, 1325, 1902,
  2329
Bristol, 4323·08
Burslem (Rogers), 1122·6
Chelsea, 947, 1092, 3602
Copenhagen, 532
Delft, 4293
Derby, Crown, 721
— (Joseph Hills), 3602
Dresden, see Meissen
Limbach, 230
Longport (Rogers), 1124
Longton (Turner), 1688
Lonhuda (Ohio), 1044
McLaughlin (Ohio), 2841
Meissen, 3067, 3910, 4980, 5091
Moscow, 3538
New Milford (Connecticut), 1638
Nottingham, 1121, 2840, 2963
Paris (Theodore Deck), 1998
Plymouth, 920, 1121, 2371
Rookwood (Ohio), 1595
Sèvres, 260
Strasbourg (Hannong), 5643
Swansea, 4483, 5696
Volkstedt (Germany), 2574
Worcester, 292, 3573, 4108
Zürich, 5008

Stick marker, (*USA*) 1360, 5872
Switch, (*USA*) 5997, 5998
—, block, 1418, 1420
—, line, (*USA*) 3944
—, lock, 923, 1999, (*USA*) 5901
—, power, (*USA*) 1040, 1043
—, stand, (*USA*) 5868
Token exchanger, 2361
— instruments, 1997, 5621
— receiver, 2360
—, release by, 5939, 5946
Track, circuit interrupter, 6072
— indicator, 923
— instrument, (*USA*) 1411
— pan, (*USA*) 2091
— sanded, 3947
— scale, (*USA*) 5548
Treadle, 1158, 1356, 1357, 1521, 1522
Train control inductor, 3586·1
— stop, 4449
— —, inductive, (*USA*) 805, 857·5, 876·6
— —, trip, (*USA*) 1060, 1299, 1300, 1301, 1327, 1343 ff.
Turntable, 1273·3, 1393, (*USA*) 907
Water column, 1082
— trough, warning, 5045
Wheel, *see* Locomotive formulae
Wig-wag, (*USA*) 1087

Standard Shading Tints

Aluminium alloys, (*Engn.*) 3996
Blue, azure, (*Her.*) 5407, (*Hyd.*) 5407·1
Boulder clay, (*Soil/m.*) 1552
Brass, (*Engn.*) 5836
Breakers, (*Hyd.*) 6185
Breccia, (*Geol.*) 3734
Bronze, (*Engn.*) 5836
Built-up area, (*Cart., Mil.*) 5272·2

Calcareous clay, (*Soil/m.*) 3032
— matter, uncemented, (*Soil/m.*) 496
Chalk, Lower, (*Geol.*) 3993
—, Middle, (*Geol.*) 3992
—, Upper, (*Geol.*) 3991
Clay, (*Soil/m.*) 5407·1
—, boulder, (*Soil/m.*) 1552
—, calcareous, (*Soil/m.*) 3032
—, fissured, (*Soil/m.*) 3737
—, sandy, (*Soil/m.*) 5837
—, silty, (*Soil/m.*) 4545
—, weathered, (*Soil/m.*) 3208
Concrete, (*Engn.*) 3404
Conglomerate, (*Geol.*) 38, 3734
Copper, (*Engn.*) 3995
Cross-hatching, (*G/use*) 3979·1, 3980·1, 4031
Cultivated land, (*Cart., Du.*) 3978, (*USA*) 5838
'Dotted' tint, (*G/use, Print.*) 6186·3, 6187·1, 6188·3
Ermine, (*Her.*) 5817
Furze, (*Cart.*) 5461, 6184
Glasshouses, (*Cart.*) 3978
Gold, or, (*Her.*) 6186·2, 6188·2
Gorse, *see* Furze
Grass, (*Cart., Du.*) 5186
Gravel, (*Cart.*) 6181, (*Soil/m.*) 38
—, sandy, (*Soil/m.*) 3404·2
Green, vert, (*Her.*) 5272, (*Hyd.*) 5272·1
Hachures, (*Cart.*) 5470
Hatching, *see* Cross-hatching
Hoggin, (*Soil/m.*) 1553
Igneous rocks, (*Geol.*) 4544, 6035
—, extrusive, (*Geol.*) 5039
—, intrusive, (*Geol.*) 5471
Insulation, (*Elec.*) 5280
Iron, cast, (*Engn.*) 5280·1
—, wrought. (*Engn.*) 5277
Lead, (*Engn.*) 3980
Limestone, (*Geol.*) 3990
Loam, (*Soil/m.*) 5664
Made ground, (*Soil/m.*) 3978·1

Marl, (*Soil/m.*) 3032
Marsh, (*Cart.*) 5408, 5863
Mechanical tint, (*Print.*) 3979·3, 3980·3, 4031·1
Metamorphic rocks, (*Geol.*) 640
Nickel, (*Engn.*) 5276
Obstruction, (*Mil.*) 3980·2
Osiers, (*Cart.*) 5459
Pasture, rough, (*Cart.*) 6183
Peat, (*Soil/m.*) 5460
—, clayey, (*Soil/m.*) 5185
—, sandy, (*Soil/m.*) 5853
—, silty, (*Soil/m.*) 4546
Pebble-bed, (*Geol.*) 38
—, with sand, (*Geol.*) 3404·1
Plantation, (*Cart.*) 6187
Purple, purpure, (*Her.*) 5280·2
Rain, drizzle, (*Meteor.*, *Aero.*) 5182, 5273, 5275
Red, gules, (*Her.*) 5181, (*Hyd.*) 5280·3

Ricefield, (*Cart.*, *Du.*) 3994
Rocks, igneous, (*Geol.*) 4544, 5039, 5471, 6035
— metamorphic, (*Geol.*) 640
Sable, black, (*Her.*) 3979·2
Sand, (*Cart.*) 6188, (*Soil/m.*) 6188·4
—, silty, (*Soil/m.*) 5663
Sandstone, (*Geol.*) 6186·1, 6188·1
Shale, (*Geol.*) 5408·1
Shells, (*Soil/m.*) 496
Shingle, (*Cart.*) 6181
Silt, (*Soil/m.*) 4544·1
Steel, cast, (*Engn.*) 5279
—, wrought, (*Engn.*) 5278
Stone, (*Engn.*) 5409
Tidal flat, (*Cart.*, *USA*) 5410
Woodland, (*Cart.*, *Mil.*) 5280·4
Yellow, (*Hyd.*) 6186
Zinc, (*Engn.*) 3979

3. PROOF CORRECTIONS

bold/cap — ⬚ The Man from Porlock — Centre

s.c. — In the summer of 1897 Coleridge, being — 7

\# — in ill health, retired to a lonely farmhouse — ⊂

on the borders of Somerset and Devon

(/) — between ~~Porlock and~~ Linton. He records — stet

that he was reading Purchas's Pilgrimage — ital

when he fell asleep in his chair at some

such sentence as/ 'Here the khan Kubla — cap.

take back — la commanded a palace to be built, and a

eq.# — stately garden thereunto; and thus ten

miles of fertile ground were enclosed with — i

a wall. He slept for about three hours, — l.c.

during which time he was confident that

em — he had composed without effort two or — em

three hundred lines of verse. On waking, — N/P

X — he at once took pen, ink and paper and, — H

the — without hesitation, wrote first fifty four

U/ital/U — lines of "Kubla Khan". At that point he

was unfortunately called out by a person

w.f — on business from Porlock, and detained

U — by him for above an hour On returning to

his room he found, to his surprise and

trs. — mortification, the that remainder of the

rom. — poem had 'passed away like the images

on the surface of a stream into which a — trs.

U — stone had been cast.

578

The corrected page would appear thus:

The Man From Porlock

IN THE SUMMER of 1797 Coleridge, being in ill health, retired to a lonely farmhouse on the borders of Somerset and Devon (between Porlock and Linton). He records that he was reading *Purchas's Pilgrimage* when he fell asleep in his chair at some such sentence as: 'Here the Khan Kubla commanded a palace to be built, and a stately garden thereunto; and thus ten miles of fertile ground were inclosed with a wall.' He slept for about three hours, during which time he was confident that he had composed—without effort—two or three hundred lines of verse.

On waking, he at once took pen, ink and paper and, without hesitation, wrote the first fifty-four lines of *Kubla Khan*. At that point he was unfortunately called out by a person on business from Porlock, and detained by him above an hour. On returning to his room he found, to his surprise and mortification, that the remainder of the poem had 'passed away like the images on the surface of a stream into which a stone had been cast.'

579

4. TYPEFACES AND FLOWERS

These typefaces show something of the range of variations on the basic Roman alphabet used for display purposes and decoration.

XYZABCDEFGHIJKLMN

ULTRA Bodoni n19

qrstuvwxyz.!

rstuvwxyz

ABCDEFGHIJKLM

ABCDEFGHIJK

ABCDEF

ABCDEFG

ABCDEFGHIJK

CDEFGHI

CARLTON CA

ROCKWELL HEAVY CONDE

ABCDEFGHIJKLMNO

Monotype Script Series 351

Grosvenor Script   A B C D E F G H

ABCDEFGHIJK

581

Printers' 'flowers' are unit ornaments which can be used alone or assembled to make borders and other decorative designs, as in the following examples.

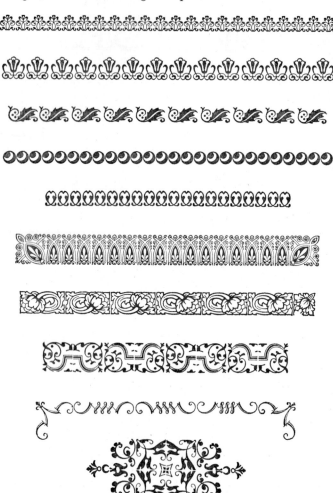

BIBLIOGRAPHY

A LIST of all the books, documents and museum exhibits consulted in the compilation of this glossary to determine which of the many forms of old-established signs are most characteristic, or best preserve their remoter origins, would be of little use to the reader. In many such cases there must remain a certain latitude of opinion in which dispute is of little profit and less interest. The position is quite otherwise with modern signs, whether invented for the dissemination of technical information or for the communication of ideas between people of different races and languages. For such purposes conventions have been called at various times to establish national and international standards, and these have often been published by bodies of official or semi-official status. A sample selection of publications of this nature is given below, and it is felt that this may have some guidance value, although it is impossible to keep pace with the continual issue of revisions and additions that progress demands. Revision, however, does not make established signs invalid; generally it merely involves the simplification or combination of existing signs for special purposes.

It should be pointed out that an international standard sign is not necessarily an obligatory sign (though some may legally become so), but is usually no more than the result of a general agreement between advisory committees or learned societies. Such a sign may never be used except by a few meticulous specialists, but if it does fall into common use this is, in most cases, no more than the result of voluntary adoption spreading from individual to individual or from group to group. This freedom from 'law' is an excellent thing, for it means that only the really inspired signs finally survive.

On the other hand, some international systems of signs (such as certain traffic and road signs, and those used on weather maps) are employed rigorously and compulsorily for all official purposes by the governments of the countries concerned, and communication then soon becomes difficult for those who do not fall into line. Nevertheless an international standard sign is seldom the only 'correct' sign that may be used; it is simply the most expedient sign to employ in the modern world and is therefore generally to be preferred to any purely national convention.

The following representative titles have been arranged as far as possible so that their subjects come in alphabetical order. Included among them are a few on standard technical abbreviations which may be of some use to the reader, although mere abbreviations are not included in the body of this work. Where dates are not given, this is either because no dates are printed on the publications or because new editions or reprints are frequently issued. It should not, however, be assumed that the dates which are quoted are necessarily of the latest or final editions. The publications of the British and American Standards authorities, for example, are revised or enlarged as new occasions arise, though it is very rare for any basic alteration to be proposed. Information on signs used in the more specialized subjects should be sought in appropriate textbooks, but it would be impracticable to include such in this list. The history of ancient symbols and obsolescent forms may be found in large encyclopaedias, the appendices to *Webster's Dictionary* and other such publications, and in the manuscript departments of museums and libraries. A few treatises on such subjects are included in the following list.

BIBLIOGRAPHY

Abbreviations

Am., American   Inst., Institute
Assoc., Association   Instn, Institution
Brit., British   Inter., International
Dept, Department   Mech., Mechanical
Elec., Electrical   OS, Ordnance Survey
Engn., Engineers   Soc., Society
Engng, Engineering   Stand(s), Standard(s)
HMSO, Her Majesty's   UNO, United Nations
  Stationery Office   Organization

Abbreviations for Use on Drawings. Am. Stand Z 32.13. Am.
Stands Assoc., New York, 1950.
Aeronautical Sciences, Letter Symbols for. Am. Stands Assoc.
Y 10.7. The Am. Soc. of Mech. Engn., New York, 1954.
Alchemists, The. F. Sherwood Taylor, M.A., B.Sc., Ph.D.
William Heinemann, London, 1951.
Alchemy. E. J. Holmyard. Penguin Books (Pelican), Har-
mondsworth, 1957.
Alphabet, The. David Diringer, D.Litt., M.A. Hutchinson
Scientific and Technical, London, 1953.
Alphabet, The A B C of Our. T. Thompson. The Studio Publica-
tions, London and New York, 1942.
Astronomical Union, International. Commission 3 (Notations).
Transactions of the Inter. Astronomical Union, Vol. VI,
London, 1939.

*Charts and Nautical Documents, Repertory of the Technical
Resolutions Adopted by the International Hydrographical
Conferences, 1919–1947*. Inter. Hydrographic Bureau,
Monaco, 1948.
*Chemical and Petroleum Plant, Symbols for Use on Flow
Diagrams of*. Brit. Stand 974. Brit. Stands Instn, London,
1953.

Chemical Engineering, Letter Symbols for. Am. Stands Assoc. Z 10.12. The Am. Soc. of Mech. Engn., New York, 1946.

Chemistry, Historical Studies in the Language of, M.P. Crosland. Heinemann, London, 1962.

Compressing Plant, Graphical Symbols for. Brit. Stand 1553, Part 3. Brit. Stands Instn, London 1950.

Electrical Diagrams, Graphical Symbols for. Am. Stand Y 32.2. Am. Stands Assoc., New York, 1954.

Electrical Purposes, Graphical Symbols for General. Brit. Stand 108. Brit. Stands Instn, London, 1951.

Electrical Quantities, Letter Symbols for. Am. Stands Assoc. Z 10.5. Am. Inst. of Elec. Engn., New York, 1949.

Electrical Symbols for Architectural Plans, Graphical. Am. Stands Assoc. Y 32.9. Am. Inst. of Elec. Engn., New York, 1943.

Engineering Symbols and Abbreviations. Brit. Stand 560. Brit. Stands Instn, London, 1934.

Fire Protection Drawings, Graphical Symbols for. Brit. Stand 1635. Brit. Stands Instn, London 1950.

Gas Quantities in Reciprocating Internal Combustion Engines, Symbols, Terms and Definitions for. Brit. Stand 1798. Brit. Stands Instn, London, 1951.

Heat and Thermodynamics Including Heat Flow, Letter Symbols for. Am. Stands Assoc. Z 10.4. The Am. Soc. of Mech. Engn., New York, 1943.

Heating, Ventilating and Air Conditioning, Graphic Symbols for. Am. Stands Assoc. Z 32.2.4. The Am. Soc. of Mech. Engn., New York, 1949.

Highway Code, The. The Ministry of Transport and Civil Aviation. HMSO, London.

Hull and Propeller Resistance and Propulsion, Strength and

Vibration, Standard Nomenclature and Symbols. The Brit. Shipbuilding Research Assoc., London, 1949.

Hydraulics, Letter Symbols for. Am. Stands Assoc. Z 10.2. The Am. Soc. of Mech. Engn., New York, 1942.

Illuminating Engineering, Nomenclature and Photometric Standards. Am. Stands Assoc. Z 7.1. Illuminating Engng Soc., New York, 1942.

Instrumentation, Graphical Symbols for. Brit. Stand 1646. Brit. Stands Instn, London, 1950.

Language, The Loom of. Frederick Bodmer. George Allen & Unwin, London, 1944.

Letter Symbols, Signs and Abbreviations: Part 1, General. Brit. Stand 1991. Brit. Stands Instn, London, 1954.

Map Characteristics. (Separate sheets issued for the '1-inch', '6-inch' and '25-inch' maps of the OS.) HMSO, London.

Map Reading, Notes on. The War Office. HMSO, London.

Maps: Roman Britain, Monastic Britain, etc. OS. HMSO, London.

Maps of the Ordnance Survey, Conventional Signs and Writing Used on the. OS. HMSO, London.

Mathematical Papers, Notes on the Preparation of. The London Mathematical Soc. C. F. Hodgson & Son, London.

Mathematical Sorts, 'Monotype'. The Monotype Corporation Ltd, London.

Mathematical Symbols. Am. Stands Assoc. Z 10f. Am. Inst. of Elec. Engn., New York, 1928.

Mathematics, 4-line. The Monotype Corporation Ltd., London, 1958.

Mathematics, The Treasury of. 2 vols. Henrietta Midonick. Philosophical Library, New York, 1965. Penguin Books (Pelican), Harmondsworth, 1968.

Mechanics of Solid Bodies, Letter Symbols for. Am. Stands Assoc. Z 10.3. The Am. Soc. of Mech. Engn., New York, 1948.

Meteorological Glossary, The. The Air Ministry. HMSO, London, 1943.

Meteorology, Letter Symbols for. Am. Stands Assoc. Y 10.10. The Am. Soc. of Mech. Engn., New York, 1953.

Metric System, Changing to the. Conversion factors, symbols and definitions. National Physical Laboratory, Ministry of Technology. HMSO, London, 1967.

Music, Introducing. Ottó Károlyi. Penguin Books (Pelican), Harmondsworth, 1965.

Music, Rudiments of. C. H. Kitson. Oxford Univ. Press, 1937.

Number, Man and. Donald Smeltzer, B.Sc. Adam & Charles Black, London, 1953.

Phonetic Association, The Principles of the International. Inter. Phonetic Assoc., London, 1949.

Phonetic Principles, An English Pronouncing Dictionary on Strictly. 10th ed. Daniel Jones. J. M. Dent & Sons Ltd, London, 1949.

Phonetics, English. Walter Ripman. J. M. Dent & Sons Ltd, London, 1947.

Physics, Letter Symbols for. Am. Stands Assoc. Z 10.6. The Am. Soc. of Mech. Engn., New York, 1948.

Physics and Chemistry Dictionary and Handbook, The New. Robert W. Marks. Bantam Books, New York, 1967.

Pipe Fittings, Valves and Piping, Graphical Symbols for. Am. Stands Assoc. Z 32.2.3. The Am. Soc. of Mech. Engn., New York, 1949.

Pipes and Valves, Graphical Symbols for. Brit. Stand 1553, Part 1. Brit. Stands Instn, London, 1949.

Plumbing, Graphical Symbols for. Am. Stands Assoc. Z 32.2.2. The Am. Soc. of Mech. Engn., New York, 1949.

Power Generating Plant, Graphical Symbols for. Brit. Stand 1553, Part 2. Brit. Stands Instn, London, 1950.
Printer's Terms, The. (In five langaages.) Rudolf Hostettler *et al.* Alvin Redman, London, 1959.
Proof Corrections, Printers' and Authors'. Brit. Stand 1219. Brit. Stands Instn, London, 1945.
Prosody. *A Dictionary of Modern English Usage.* 'Technical terms'. H. W. Fowler. Oxford Univ. Press, 1940.

Railroad Use, Graphical Symbols for. Am. Stands Assoc. Z 32.2.5. The Am. Soc. of Mech. Engn., New York, 1950.
Railway Signalling Symbols: Part 1, Schematic Symbols. Brit. Stand 376. Brit. Stands Instn, London, 1951.

Scientific and Engineering Terms, Abbreviations for. Am. Stands Assoc. Z 10.1. The Am. Soc. of Mech. Engn., New York, 1941.
Signs and Abbreviations. The Admiralty, Hydrographic Dept, London.
Star Atlas, Norton's. A. P. Norton, B.A., and J. Gall Inglis, F.R.A.S. Gall & Inglis, Edinburgh, 1959.
Structural Analysis, Letter Symbols for. Am. Stands Assoc. Z 10.8. The Am. Soc. of Mech. Engn., New York, 1949.
Symbols, Signs and Abbreviations Recommended for British Scientific Publications. Report of the Symbols Committee representing The Royal Soc., The Chemical Soc., The Faraday Soc. and The Physical Soc. The Royal Soc., London, 1951.
Symbols, Standard Nomenclature and. The Brit. Shipbuilding Research Assoc., London.

Telecommunications, Graphical Symbols for. Brit. Stand 530. Supplements Nos. 2 and 3. Brit. Stands Instn, London, 1953.
Telecommunications, Symbols Common to. Post Office Engng Dept, London.

Traffic Signs, Regulations and General Directions, 1964, The. HMSO, London, 1964,

Traffic Signs, Report of the Departmental Committee on. Ministry of Transport. HMSO, London, 1946.

Traffic Signs for Motorways, Final Report of Advisory Committee. HMSO, London, 1962.

Transport and Communications Review, Vols. V and VII. UNO, New York, 1952-3.

Weather Atlas, Cloud and. Hugh Duncan Grant, F.R.Met.Soc. Coward-McCann, New York, and G. Harrap, London, 1944.

Weather Maps with Tables of the Specifications and Symbols, Instructions for the Preparation of. Meteorological Office, Form 2459. Air Ministry. HMSO, London, 1946.

Webster's New International Dictionary of the English Language. 2nd ed., Appendices. G. and C. Merriam Co., Springfield, Mass., 1934. G. Bell and Sons, London, 1937.

Welding, Graphical Symbols for. Am. Stands Assoc. Z 32.2.1. The Am. Soc. of Mech. Engn., New York, 1949.

Welding, Scheme of Symbols for. Brit. Stand 499, Section 7. Brit. Stands Instn, London, 1952.

Welding Symbols for Shipyard Drawings. Brit. Stand 1303. Brit. Stands Instn, London, 1946.

INDEX
OF SIGNS WITH NAMES

For common class-names, such as China mark,
Monogram, Numeral, etc., references to typical
examples only are given. For letters of alphabets
see Appendices.

591

Brace, 620·1, 620·3, 2925,
2989·2, 3034
Bracket(s), angular, 4789
'curly', 635·2
inclined open, 4028
open, 3896
round, 490·5
square, 4416·5
Breath mark, 3422·1, 4138·2,
4582·4, 4584, 4984, 5137
Breve, 1636, 3765·3, 3895,
6018. *See also* Accent
rest, 6010, 6018, 6019
Broad arrow, 4725·1
Broken line, 5425·1
Büchse, 3761·1

Caesura, cesura, 5148·3, 5155
Cancer, 93, 1547
Cap, 2380·1, 3466
Capricornus, 1726
Caret, 4588, 4694·1
Cartouche, 2061
Cedilla, 2711, 2712
Character. *See* Hieroglyph,
Letter, Numeral, etc.
Chequer bar, 5575
China mark. *Examples:* 532,
1092, 1998, 2841, 3602, 4353
Cipher, *See* Zero
Circumflex. *See* Accent
Clef, C, 2332, 3048, 3207, 4023,
4024
F, 3432, 3433, 3434
G, 224, 1711, 3413; *for tenor
voice,* 1712, 1732, 1857
Cleft stick, 2463
Colon, 5985, 6061, 6061·2,
6066·6, 6074
tandem, 6081·1
Colon-dash, 5785
Comma(s), virgule, 3423·2,
5214·6, 5928, 5981, 5986·2
double, 3444, 5250
inverted, 3424·1, 3442, 5249
Contour, contour line, 100, 101,
144, 679, 5292, 5850

Corona, 3466·1, 3468·1
Cross, 4361, 4873·1, 4874·7;
Tables 311 to 314
Celtic, 1274
crosslet, 4534
Greek, 4323·7
handled, hafted, 1819
Jerusalem, 4554·1
Lorraine, 4507, 4508
Maltese, 4332
open, 4415
Papal, 4533
pierced, 1047
potent, 4554·1
Red, 4331
Restoration, 1047
St Andrew, 4881
St Cross, 4554·1
St George, 4348
St John, 4332
saltire, 4362·2
sign of the, 6132·2, 4323·09
triple-beam, 4522
voided, 533
Crossed-C, 2304
-c, 2305
-D, 1986
-d, 958, 1104·1, 1111, 1820
-E, 2336, 2410
-g, 1931
-h, 2409, 3011
-i, 5647
-L, 211, 1717, 4151, 4557, 4954
-l, 2775, 3085, 4887
-lb, 1963
-M, 3566, 4105
-O, 1375
-o, 1376
-P, 2053
-p, 1962
-R, 2055
-S, 3075, 3076, 3077, 3088,
3129, 3130
-u, 2196
-Y, 4294, 4500
-7, 1807, 2768, 4952
Crossed swords, 2088

Nabla, nabula, 3599·1
Natural, 4009
Note, crushing, 5479
  early forms of, 3765·3, 3862,
    3863, 3895, 4006, 5920,
    5925, 5927, 6013·1, 6018
  grace, 5479, 5599, 5601
  leaning, 5599, 5601
  patent/shaped, 5877, 5879,
    5880, 5905, 5906, 5907,
    5908, 5919, 5927
  See Crotchet, Quaver, etc.
  See Exclamation, Interroga-
    tion, etc.
Nought. *See* Zero
Numeral. *Examples:* 103·3, 512,
  601, 2303, 2705, 3400, 4429,
  4579, 4755, 4800

Obelus, obelisk, 4354·2
  double, 4512·1
Oloroso symbol, 1598
Omega, tilde, 1900
Omission, marks of, 192, 4588,
  4694, 5287·1, 5300·6, 6113,
  6125·1, 6160·1
Open bracket, 3896, 4028
  cross, 4415
Ornament. *See* Grace-note,
  Mordent, Shake, Trill, Turn

Palma, the, 2670
Palma cortado, 2765
Palo cortado symbol, 2766
Panda crossing, 5490
Paragraph, 2016, 4613·1, 5715,
  5716
Parallels, 5154
Parenthesis, marks of, 490·8,
  2999, 5300·6, 6064, 6065
Pata de galena symbol, 3047
Pedal release, 1239, 5726, 5959
Pentacle, pentagram, 3729
  inverted, 3731
Period. *See* Full stop
Pheon, 4725·1

Pictograph. *Examples:* 280, 782,
  939, 1205, 1750, 1882, 2740
Pilcrow, 5540, 5572, 5715, 5716
Pisces, 2936, 2953
Plimsoll mark, 1389, 4562
Plus, 4323·01, 4452, 4453, 4492,
  4493·2
Point, decimal. *See* Decimal
  point
  full. *See* Full stop
  turned. *See* Inverted full stop
Points de suspension, 6113,
  6125·1, 6160
Pomega, 1900·1
'Pothook', 581, 2520
Pralltriller, 4933
Presa, 5656·1
P-X symbol, 1099

Q-sign, 5541
Quadrat, 'quad', 6015
Quatro palmas, 2911
Quaver, 3106, 5598, 5600
  rest, 2708
Question mark, 'query'. *See*
  Interrogation, mark of
Quotation marks, 'quotes',
  6092, 6093
  double, 3442, 3443, 3445,
    4784, 4785, 5249, 5250,
    5300·2
  single, 3422·3, 3423·2, 3424·1

Radical, root-sign, 4655, 4753
Raya, the, 2671
Red Cross. *See* Cross
Reference, marks of, 273·1,
  4354·2, 4512·1, 4970, 4983,
  4986, 5052·1, 5154, 5715,
  5716. *See also* Tint
Repeat marks, 1273·2, 1640,
  5212, 5241, 5780, 5781,
  5800, 5801, 5815, 5816
  See also 'Ditto' marks
Rest, 5115
  bar, 4378, 5201, 5212, 5241
  breve, 6010, 6018, 6019